"*The Cygnus Mystery* is an intellectual ac
influence of the Cygnus constellation on t
Collins takes readers into deepest, darkest
making a compelling case for Palaeolithi
subtle astronomical events is necess ... human prehistory."

Jeremy Narby, anthropologist and author of *The Cosmic Serpent*

"Even for those of us who have long admired Andrew Collins' work, *The Cygnus Mystery* is a revelation – a breathtaking quest for the origins of human spirituality that takes us from the dawn of mankind to the cutting edge of modern science. An extraordinary depth of research covers ancient myths and symbols from across the globe, the mysteries of shamanic consciousness and the realms of quantum physics and astronomy – and more. His argument and conclusions are compelling; Andrew is certainly on to something very important."

Lynn Picknett and Clive Prince, authors of *The Templar Revelation*, the confirmed inspiration behind Dan Brown's *The Da Vinci Code*

"Andrew Collins's stunning speculations and writing have served as an inspiration for a new generation of thinkers. When I began reading *The Cygnus Mystery*, I had hoped he could duplicate the brilliance of his earlier book *From the Ashes of Angels*. He didn't. He exceeded it. *The Cygnus Mystery* clearly explains seemingly impenetrable mysteries of the origins of humanity, life, genetic evolution, and ancient rituals performed the world over."

Dr. Greg Little, psychologist (USA), prehistorian and author of *Grand Illusions*

"The book investigates the interest for the human mind in the stars of Cygnus, an interest which is probably as old as the time in which this constellation was hosting the north celestial pole, around 15,000 years ago. Although some of the author's views might be difficult to share for the sceptical mind, the book has an easy to follow analysis which helps the reader to understand the deep relationship of our ancestors with the sky."

Dr Giulio Magli, astrophysicist and archaeoastronomer, author of *Misteri e Scoperte dell'archeoastronomia*

"This book takes us on a journey of profound and often terrifying revelation. Can it be true that life began on Earth because of cosmic radiation? And what does this mean for the future? Andrew Collins yet again will stun the reading public with a theory that makes *The Da Vinci Code* look like *Mary Poppins*."

Philip Gardiner, author of *Gnosis: The Secret of Solomon's Temple Revealed*, *Secrets of the Serpents* and co-author of *The Serpent Grail* and *The Shining Ones*

Andrew Collins is a popular writer of history, archaeology and science. For over 30 years he has explored the relationship between archaic religious beliefs and the cosmos, examining the origins of human civilization, the development of technology and the inspirations behind magic and religion. His discoveries have led to several thought-provoking books that challenge the way we think about the past. Andrew is also the organizer of the Questing Conference, Britain's premier event on revisionist history, forbidden archaeology and ancient wisdom. Born in 1957, he lives with his wife Sue in Essex.

www.andrewcollins.com

Also by Andrew Collins

Beneath the Pyramids
From the Ashes of Angels
Gods of Eden
Gateway to Atlantis
Tutankhamun: The Exodus Conspiracy (with Chris Ogilvie-Herald)

THE CYGNUS MYSTERY

Unlocking the Ancient Secret of Life's Origins in the Cosmos

ANDREW COLLINS

WATKINS PUBLISHING
LONDON

First published in the UK in 2006 by
Watkins Publishing, Sixth Floor, Castle House,
75–76Wells Street, LondonW1T 3QH

This edition published in 2011

Designed and typeset by Jerry Goldie Graphic Design

Printed and bound in the United Kingdom

British Library Cataloguing-in-Publication data available

ISBN: 978-1-78028-099-8

www.watkinspublishing.co.uk

CONTENTS

LIST OF ILLUSTRATIONS

LIST OF PLATES

PICTURE CREDITS

The author wishes to thank the following for permission to use their images in this book:

Illustrations: 4, 39, 43, Yuri Leitch; 7, Bildarchiv Preussischer Kulturbesitz, Berlin; 9, Greg Little; 13, E J Lindgren-Utsi; 14, Herbert Kuhn; 22, Alan Sorrell/Richard Sorrell; 29, John Dewer/RCAHMS; 35, Éric Aubourg; 36, British Museum; 44, 45, Jean-Dominique Lajoux; 47, Harald Hauptmann; 48 a & b, German Archaeological Institute (DAI); 50, NASA.

Plates: 4, 5, 6, 11, 23, German Archaeological Institute (DAI); 12, British Museum; 13, Roz Harrendence/Sue Woodward; : 16, Rodney Hale/Melford Designs; 22, Regis Madec; 24, Yuri Leitch; 25, Robert Nicholls/Palaeocreations.com; 27, Dr Sergio Ripoll; 28, NASA/CXC/SAO; 29, Dana Berry (CfA/NASA); 30, J A Biretta et al/NASA/Hubble Hertitage Team (STScI/AURA); 32, Anthony Murphy/Mythicalireland.com.

Acknowledgments

Thanks go out to these people without whom *The Cygnus Mystery* could not have been written: Sue Collins, my wife, the pillar of stability in my life, whose philosophical insights and editorial suggestions have made this a much better book; Richard Ward, for instigating this quest in the first place, and for his additional research; David Southwell, whose inspirational insights have swelled my knowledge of Cygnus in religions worldwide; and Rodney Hale, for his technical support, and for keeping the whole thing on the straight and narrow.

In addition to this, I would like to thank Greg and Lora Little, for their continued friendship and support, and for inspiring the America section; Michael Mann, for having faith in me; and Osman Baydemir, the Mayor of Diyarbakir, for getting me to write this book.

Thanks go out also to Aden and Marjorie Meinel; Adriano Forgione; Alan Alford; Ann Smith; Anthony Murphy and Richard Moore; Arif and Necla Akkaya; Buster and Abbie; Carl and Lynn; Caroline Wise and Mick Staley; Catherine and Joan Hale; Chris Ogilvie-Herald; Chris Tedder; Clive and Deb Harper; Clive Prince; Colin Wilson; Crichton Miller; Denis Montgomery; Duncan Roads; Eileen Buchanan; Filip Coppens; Gary Osborn; Geoff Stray; Gerry and Bali Beskin at Atlantis Bookshop; Gillian Holmes; Giulio Magli; Graham and Santha Hancock; Halil Baynan; Heather Hobden; Ian Lawton and Liz Swanson; J James; Jeremy Narby; Jim Kaler; John 'Mushroomer' Allen; John Billingsley; John Day; John and Doris Van Auken; Johnny Merron; Jonathan Hesketh, of the Creswell Crags Visitors Centre; Jonathan Harris; Josep Martí Ribas; Juan Antonio Belmonte; Leigh Library, all staff there particularly Keith and Mavis; Lynn Picknett; Marcus Allen; Marion Popenoe Hatch; Martin Gray of SacredSites.com; Martin J Powell; Matt Kyd and Renny Djunaedi; Michael A Rappenglück; Michael Carmichael; Nigel Foster; Nigel Skinner Simpson; Noam Soker; Paul Pettitt; Paul Weston; Penny Stopa and all editorial staff at Watkins Publishing; Peter Bently; Philip Gardiner; Robert Guendl; Romano Corradi; Serena Love; Sheer Faith; Steven Gawtry; Storm Constantine and Jim Hibbert; Tim Glover; You-Hua Chu; Yuri Leitch; and Fields of the Nephilim's 'Mourning Sun', forever the soundtrack to this book.

This book is dedicated to the swan worldwide,
With particular concern for those under the care of
The Swan Sanctuary, Shepperton, Middlesex, England.
www.swanuk.org.uk.

And also to Rodney Hale, the original Q.

‘LAM is the Tibetan word for Way or Path, and Lama is He who Goeth …
Its numerical value is 71, the number of this book.’

Ou Mh, 1919.

Introduction

When did humanity's fascination with the stars begin? As we shall see, Palaeolithic cave art in Western Europe dating back as far as 17,000 years ago shows key stars and star groups in highly abstract form. These images must once have figured prominently in the religious experiences of those who made the paintings deep underground, which would have included communication with perceived otherworldly intelligences, very likely through the aid of hallucinogenic substances and other shamanic-based practices. Such supernatural entities – depicted as anthropomorphs (human-like forms), chimeras (animal hybrids) and therianthropes (human-animal hybrids) – were unquestionably seen as inhabiting starry realms we can only dream of today.

It was a connection made and never forgotten, as is evidenced from the recent discovery of the world's earliest stone temple in southeast Turkey, built around 11,500 years ago by an unknown race at the end of the last Ice Age (*see Chapters One and Two*). The temple was aligned to the same stars that their Palaeolithic ancestors in Western Europe had recognized as important thousands of years earlier. This emphasis on the importance of the stars continued right down to the construction, some 6,000 years later, of some of the wonders of the ancient world such as Egypt's Great Pyramid and Britain's Avebury monument. Both reflect specific stellar influences, unquestionably incorporated into their original designs.

It did not end there, either, for the passage of notable stars is marked by key temples in India, China, Mexico and Peru. It is a theme found also among the gigantic prehistoric earthen mounds and structures built by the native peoples of North America. All were designed to reflect the influence of the stars, which feature again and again in their archaic cosmologies and creation myths. These record that our first ancestors came from the sky at the beginning of time or during some bygone epoch, and that it is to the sky that the souls of the righteous would return in death.

Universally, indigenous peoples and ancient civilizations have seen the Milky Way as the 'road' or 'river' to the sky-world, where life of all kinds prospers away from the Earth. Indeed, such ideas might have been more openly accepted among civilized societies had it not been for the rational thinking of the Greek philosopher Aristotle (384–322 BC). He reasoned that the generation of life on Earth was spontaneous, in that it simply appeared out of nowhere. Even though his views were finally disproved by the great French chemist Louis Pasteur (1822–1895), it would take many more years for science to come around to the idea that life on Earth might have originated elsewhere.

Indigenous peoples worldwide have continued to believe in our cosmic origins. As we shall see (*Chapter Nineteen and Appendix*), from the island peoples of the Indonesian archipelago to the tribal nations of North America, and from the earliest kings of China to the Dogon tribe of Mali, there is everywhere a widespread belief that life on Earth was seeded from elsewhere. Even the pharaohs of ancient Egypt believed that in death they would journey by boat to a paradisial realm located among the stars of the northern heavens, inhabited by the gods and goddesses responsible for the creation of the universe and the bringing forth of life on Earth. Indeed, the fundamental belief in returning to the source of creation is found also in monotheistic religions such as Judaism, Christianity and Islam, which all teach that heaven, or paradise, the ultimate destination of the soul, exists above the clouds.

Such ideologies have always been considered belief-orientated at best. Yet now, finally, science is catching up. Evidence for panspermia, the theory of 'life everywhere', is mounting all the time. High-powered space telescopes have detected the existence across the galaxy of organic compounds called PAHs (polycyclic aromatic hydrocarbons), which are the building-blocks of life. What is more, new planets, some of which might support life, are being recorded at a fast rate, and the recent discovery of a carbon-rich substance in the tiny cracks of a Mars rock that fell as a meteorite on Egypt in 1911[1] dramatically increases the chances that the Red Planet not only supported life billions of years ago, but might even have spread it to Earth.

The idea that micro-organisms were able to hitch a ride either inside meteors or comets is now pretty much accepted by science, an opinion that has recently led to some serious papers in peer-reviewed journals. In fact, as I write these words, the British magazine *New Scientist* has a cover story with the headline 'Alien Rain'. It refers to renewed speculation that up to 50 tonnes of micro-organisms fell as red rain during heavy storms in Kerala, southwest India, during 2001, reaching Earth on a meteor or comet.[2] Even if these cell-like structures, which have been found to contain DNA, do not turn out to be extra-terrestrial in origin, the sheer fact that a respected magazine such as *New Scientist* – or indeed *Astrophysics and Space Science*, the journal where the evidence is to be presented in full[3] – displays a genuine openness towards this once taboo subject and is important in itself.

So our distant ancestors might well have been right after all. Life probably does come from deep space, and if this is the case, then how did these obviously very enlightened individuals gain such a profound insight into life's origins? As we shall see, hallucinogenic substances used by Palaeolithic shamans in ritualistic practices might well have played an important role in revealing this inspired information (*see Chapters Eighteen and Nineteen*). Yet it is a process that would seem to have been assisted by their choice of deep caves to acquire 'divine knowledge' and inspiration through otherworldly communications. Why?

In *The Cygnus Mystery* I shall propose that these ancestors of human civilization came to recognize the influence on their lives of cosmic rays emanating from a point source in the night sky – a binary star system in the constellation of Cygnus, the Swan, known as Cygnus X-3. The following account of how this connection came about, and the scientific battle it has already started, are set to alter everything we know about the influence of the stars on our lives, and indeed on human evolution itself. How a previously unrecognized event some 17,000 years ago came to affect the emergence of everything from sacred sites and religious architecture, through to cosmology, astronomy and religion worldwide, is the subject of the rest of this ground-breaking book.

Andrew Collins
March 2006.

PART ONE

MYSTERY OF THE NORTH

CHAPTER ONE

The Oldest Temple in the World

It is around 11,000 years ago, and we are among the Early Neolithic population of southeast Turkey. It is the middle of the night, and stretching away into the darkness is a labyrinth of subsurface rooms, supported by a series of T-shaped pillars that hold up simple roofs. Inside, torches flicker, illuminating features carved in high relief on the stone's smooth surfaces.

The people have come to this sacred place to pay homage to a priestly elite of immense power and cunning. Tonight these cave-like structures seem eerily still as a deathly chant emanates from beyond the hill ridge, causing fear and anxiety to rise inside.

As the strange sound grows stronger, and the summit is reached, several tall figures come into view, clothed from head to feet in cloaks of vulture feathers. Standing in a circle, their eyes seem fixed on a spectacular sight low in the northern sky. It is a pattern of stars in the distinctive shape of a cross that glisten in the cool night air. For these strange individuals, it is a symbol of cosmic life and death.

All of a sudden, the chanting increases and this mesmeric sight is lost from view, only to be replaced with another of equal mystery. Under the cover of darkness, illuminated only by torches, a funeral procession takes place on boggy land in what is today Denmark. The date is *c.*4800 BC, and the body of a teenage woman is being lowered into a freshly dug grave. The feeble remains of a young child are gently placed down next to her on a soft bed made from an enormous swan's wing, freshly cut from the sacred bird slaughtered for the purpose.

This vision, too, is lost as another takes its place. Below are stone rows and a mammoth stone circle, enclosed by an enormous ditch and bank of earth. The date is now *c.*2500 BC, and we are in the megalithic complex of Avebury in England. Once more, night has fallen. A large crowd of individuals, under the control of a priest-magician, waits patiently as the same bright cross of stars moves ever closer towards the northwestern horizon. Soon the veils between this world and the next will part to allow the dead to communicate with the living and the shamans to walk between the worlds.

Again the scene changes, and we see the foundation ceremony of the Great Pyramid on the Giza plateau, viewed from the position of a strange rocky knoll that conceals a profound secret. As night gradually falls, the cross-like group of stars climb into the sky, their presence expressed in terms of a falcon-headed god of death and resurrection.

What follows is the unexpected sight of countless Hindu pilgrims, devotees of the creator god Brahma, who make their way towards the god's shrine in the heart of a massive temple complex at Pushkar in the Indian state of Rajasthan. In the semi-darkness celebrants chant the divine mantra, AUM, and offer up gifts to Brahma's four-faced stone effigy. Above him, over the entrance arch, is the carved form of *kalahamsa*, the Swan-Goose of Eternity, who brought the universe into being by emitting the sound of cosmic creation.

These images fade, and are replaced with the sight of another huge circular earthwork, identical in size and appearance to Avebury. It is the Newark Great Circle, an impressive complex built around the time of Christ by those who would come to be called the Hopewell culture of the Mississippi and Ohio valleys.

Priest-shamans adorned with feathers stand on a bird-foot-like earthwork, known as Eagle Mound, watching the gradual rotation of the celestial highway – the Milky Way – in anticipation of the moment when the newly dead can embark on the 'ghost road' to the sky-world.

Millennia pass, until suddenly we find ourselves in the year 1953. Francis Crick, a microbiologist at the University of Cambridge's Cavendish Laboratory, opens his eyes and snaps out of an altered state of consciousness caused by the ingestion of the psychedelic drug LSD. Going around his head is a powerful revelation – one that will ultimately unlock the secret of life itself.

For some while, Crick and his friend and colleague James D. Watson have been attempting to understand the structure of DNA, the self-replicating molecule of heredity present in all carbon-based life forms. He knows it has to be heliacal in nature, with a sugar-phosphate backbone, yet somehow everything now makes sense.

Crick will stop at nothing until he has confirmed what he knows to be true. He and Watson go on to determine the structure of DNA by building a three-dimensional model of its conceived double-helix pattern and identifying the four base pairs of molecules necessary to hold together the all-important sugar-phosphate chain, which form the building-blocks of life.

Finally, Swiss-born anthropologist Jeremy Narby sits in a humid jungle clearing in the depths of the Peruvian Amazon, waiting anxiously to see what might happen next. It is 1985, and in order to better understand the nature and language of the local shamans – particularly their claim to have received the tribe's immense pharmaceutical knowledge from the spirits of the plants themselves – he has decided to do as they do, and ingest the powerful hallucinogenic cocktail known as *ayahuasca*.

Minutes later, the real world is lost as the jungle disintegrates into a miasma of geometric forms and vibrant colours that seem to flow through his very soul. What follows is a sense of communion with perceived supernatural entities that will convey to him something profound, something that will alter forever our perceptions of the origins of life on Earth.

Never could I have imagined that all these disparate incidents in the history of humanity would come together to change the entire way we perceive who we are, where we come from, and what we believe happens to the soul after death. For none of this information was known to me, when in May 2004 I found myself trudging expectantly across a hot mountainous terrain in southeast Turkey on my way to explore the oldest temple in the world.[1]

Situated close to what is today the borders of Syria and Iraq, the site is known as Göbekli Tepe, meaning 'hill of the navel'. It was built by faceless individuals known to archaeologists by the unimpressive title of PPNA, the 'Pre-Pottery Neolithic A'. This refers to a period (*c.*9500–7300 BC) of the Neolithic Age (late Stone Age) when fired pottery had not yet been invented, and when most of the Northern Hemisphere was still in the grip of the last Ice Age. Whoever they were, these people were responsible for building some of the earliest transitory settlements to spring up anywhere in the world.

Those behind Göbekli Tepe not only constructed three square-planned cult buildings eight to 20 metres (26 to 66 feet) in size, one behind the other, close to the summit of a south-facing hill, but also decorated them with lines and rings of unique T-shaped stone pillars, generally around three metres (ten feet) in height. Almost all of them have smooth surfaces on which appear sculpted high reliefs. Foxes, cranes, waterfowl, spiders, boars, lizards, crocodiles, serpents, birds described as raptors, and a large feline are clearly visible. In the case of the big cat, its elongated form is carved to flow with the curved shape of the megalith ('great stone') chosen for the purpose. Other pillars are shaped to appear as anthropomorphs, human forms. Every one of the dozens of carved stones demonstrates the enormous level of technological expertise behind the construction of this ritual complex, which goes beyond anything ever discovered from this epoch of human history.

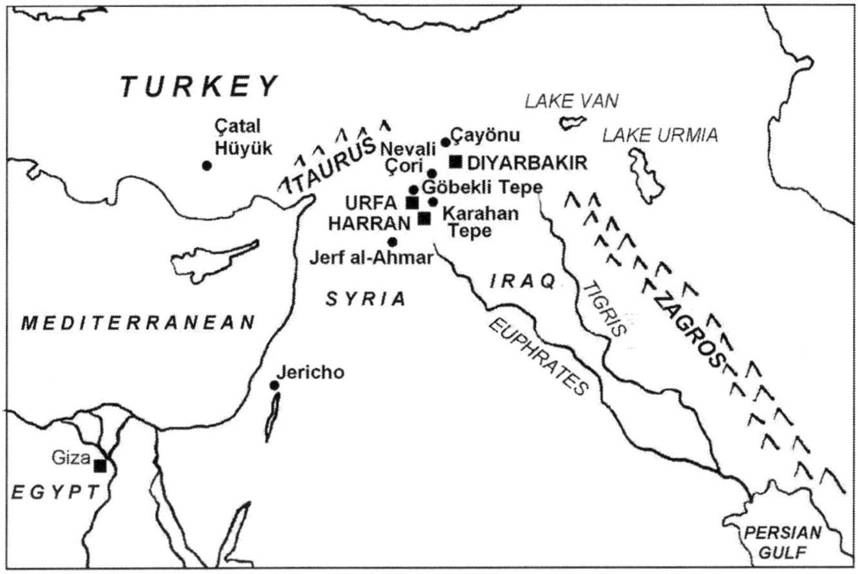

Fig.1. Egypt and the Near East, showing principal Neolithic sites and key places mentioned in this book.

Older than Everything

Perhaps it is important to put Göbekli Tepe into some kind of real time perspective. Carbon-14 tests on organic materials taken from the site confirm a construction date as early as 9500 BC (and arguably earlier – *see Chapter Two*).[2] Therefore this complex, which occupies an area comparable in size to around three tennis courts, existed some 1,500 years before the first city of Jericho, with its unprecedented 'defensive' walls and tower, and 4,000 years before Çatal Hüyük in south-central Turkey, the oldest 'city' in the world. Even more incredible is that Göbekli Tepe pre-dates Stonehenge, the most famous of all megalithic structures, by a full 6,500 years. It also stood proud an amazing 7,000 years before the construction of the Great Pyramid, thought to have been built soon after 2600 BC.

Even more curious is that although the multitude of T-shaped pillars at Göbekli Tepe weigh only a few tonnes apiece, one remaining in a quarry a few hundred metres away is nine metres (29.5 feet) in length and weighs an estimated *fifty* tonnes![3]

On top of all this is the stark realization that the archaeologists involved in the excavations, Klaus Schmidt and Harald Hauptmann of the German Archaeological Institute (DAI) in Istanbul, both renowned experts in southeast Turkey's Neolithic past, have so far found no evidence of any habitation at Göbekli Tepe. This has led them to speculate that the location was a religious centre, with the assorted animals carved on the stone pillars being 'clan' totems. More tentatively, Schmidt favours the veneration here of a divinity, a 'non-terrestrial being', the identity of which remains obscure.[4]

Perhaps it was for these reasons that the site gained the name *Göbekli* ('navel'), or its pre-Turkish equivalent, because it was the centre of activity for several Neolithic communities locally. Although I accepted this solution as meaningful in the evaluation of Göbekli Tepe's role during its suggested period of activity, *c.*9500–7300 BC, for me Schmidt's arguments did not fully explain the great awe an evocative place like this held for those who built it. Nor did such ideas invoke the sheer control that must surely have been exerted on the local population by those responsible for the site's maintenance – arguably, a priestly elite of immense sophistication.

After the end of the last Ice Age there was a sudden flowering of technology following the emergence of agricultural-based societies. This so-called 'Neolithic revolution' is known to have begun in Upper Mesopotamia, a region referred to anciently as the land of Eden, embracing present-day eastern Turkey, northern Syria, northern Iraq and northwest Iran. In my book *From the Ashes of Angels,*[5] published in 1996, I proposed that those responsible for the foundation of the Neolithic revolution were a powerful group of priest-shamans, who seem to be recalled in Judeo-Christian tradition as the 'Watchers' and 'Nephilim', beings of tall stature and pale complexions who trafficked with humanity in some bygone epoch. It is a story told in the *Book of Enoch*, fragments of which were found among the corpus of literature we know today as the Dead Sea Scrolls.

This Neolithic priestly elite were also, I suspect, the founders of the later Sumerian and Akkadian civilizations of Lower Mesopotamia, roughly modern day Iraq. Here, inscribed clay tablets unearthed by archaeologists recount how the gods, known as the Anunnaki, helped mortalkind build the first cities, such as Eridu on the mouth of the Euphrates River, sometime *c.*5500 BC.[6]

This had been my vision of the Early Neolithic in Upper Mesopotamia, expressed again in a second book entitled *Gods of Eden*, published in 1998. It was also how I came to be here at Göbekli Tepe, somewhere I had wanted to visit ever since reading about its discovery in a German magazine in 2000.[7]

Just one week beforehand, I had been contacted by my Turkish literary agent and asked whether I could attend the Third International Festival of Culture at Diyarbakir, the administrative centre of Kurdish-speaking southeast Turkey. Having agreed to make the long journey at such short notice, I asked that my wife Sue and I should be allowed to visit those sites that feature in my books, as well as any new sites, such as Göbekli Tepe, excavated in more recent years. The organizers, including the mayor of Diyarbakir, Osman Baydemir, with whom I had been granted an audience the previous afternoon, agreed to the request, providing me with a driver and translator, who were kindly made available for the entire duration of our visit.

So here I was, about to witness the oldest temple in the world, spread out before our eyes like some forgotten alien outpost exposed to the elements for the first time since it was apparently deliberately buried at the end of its useful life some 9,500 years ago.[8] What I would discover here and at other Early Neolithic sites in the region is set to change entirely our views on the emergence of modern humans from the Ice Age caves of the Upper Palaeolithic epoch. In addition to this it will show, among many other things, that astronomy dates back 17,000 years to when Deneb, the brightest star of Cygnus, occupied the position of Pole Star.

CHAPTER TWO

In the Garden of Eden

Describing Göbekli Tepe as the oldest 'temple' in the world is not entirely accurate, for it is simply a series of subsurface structures once accessed either via square-framed stone portals inserted in the roofs, or south-facing doorways. To go inside them must have been like entering a dark cave cut purposely into the hillside. They are orientated roughly north-south, with the highest structure terminating at the hill's summit, marked today by a lone tree visible for miles around.

During my visit with my wife Sue and our guide Halil, I found the highest and lowest 'cult buildings', as they are known to archaeologists, roofed over with corrugated iron in order to protect them from the elements. This meant that I had to slide down inside the stone-walled structures to take a closer look at the assortment of carved stones which originally acted as internal roof supports.

Most noticeable, however, was the central cult building, which remains open to the sky. It has a full ring of slim pillars creating a circle around six metres (20 feet) in diameter. Yet unlike the megalithic structures of Western Europe, such as Stonehenge and Avebury, where the menhirs (standing stones) delineate the site's circumference, these stones were set on edge, like the spokes of a wheel.

A Chance Discovery

It was at this moment that my thoughts were interrupted by the sight of a group of individuals, including an elderly man with a toothless smile, moustache and black and white head scarf. From their approach across a ploughed field, it was obvious that they were farming folk, taking a break from their daily duties. With handshakes and smiles all round, our guide Halil informed me and Sue that it was this elderly gentleman who had first reported the existence of the site to the museum in the nearby city of Sanliurfa. While tilling the land he had noticed a broken pillar bearing traces of carving. Other pieces then began to emerge that were placed on a boundary wall for safekeeping.

Finally, the German archaeologist Klaus Schmidt came here and recognized the site's potential as an early Neolithic complex, similar to another at nearby Nevali Çori in the Hilvan province, between Diyarbakir and Sanliurfa. This had been excavated by Schmidt's colleague Harald Hauptmann in the late 1980s to early 1990s, before it was submerged following the construction of the Atatürk dam on the Euphrates river. Indeed, from the style of the carvings, it was quite clear that the same culture was responsible for both sites, although the oldest recorded level of Nevali Çori was found to be only *c.*8400 BC.

Excavations began at Göbekli Tepe in 1995, when I was still writing *From the Ashes of Angels*, and they have continued each summer season since. At the time of our visit, Schmidt had not yet reached the lowest occupational levels, meaning that the site could be hundreds of years earlier than the existing proposed foundation date of *c.*9500 BC. Indeed, in his book *Sie bauten die ersten Tempel* ('They Built the First Temples'), published in 2006, he proposes that Göbekli Tepe was begun 12,000 years ago, a statement that seems almost impossible to comprehend.

All too soon, I felt that we were about to overstay our welcome, and with little chance of seeing anything further, we started the return journey back to the car, parked in a field just beyond a distant ridge. The long walk allowed me to ponder on what might have motivated the Pre-Pottery Neolithic peoples of southeast Turkey to site what was arguably one of their most important religious centres on the side of a 300–metre ridge with a commanding view of the southern horizon. Had there been defensive considerations here, as at Jericho, when its well-known fortifications and massive stone tower were constructed *c.*8000 BC? Did the controllers of Göbekli Tepe fear the advance of some unrecorded enemy, who lived on the plains that stretch away towards what are today Syria and Iraq? Unlikely, since no compelling evidence of any kind of ancient battles, or defensive structures, have been discerned in the Neolithic layers uncovered by archaeologists in southeast Turkey.

My own opinion swayed towards an astronomical solution to the location of this enigmatic megalithic complex. Everywhere in the world there exists overwhelming evidence that such monuments were constructed to target significant events on the celestial horizon. Most usually these concern the sun's yearly cycle, particularly at the time of the solstices and equinoxes. If not the sun, then it was the moon that the ancients tracked and marked using megalithic monuments. Every 18.61 years the moon completes one entire cycle, something that was seen as significant by our earliest ancestors, many of whom relied on a lunar calendar to regulate their lives. More controversial is the belief that ancient and sacred architecture might be aligned to the movement of specific planets, or indeed the brightest stars in the night sky, although whether any such alignments existed at Göbekli Tepe was impossible to tell in the short time we spent there.

Tower of Silence

From Göbekli Tepe we journeyed just 44 kilometres (27.5 miles) to the ancient and legendary city of Harran, somewhere I had wanted to visit for many years. As we came to the edge of an unimpressive modern village dominated by prefabricated concrete buildings, we looked around for the entrance to the lost city, and saw before us a great wall within which was a monumental stone arch known as the Aleppo Gate. Local children crowded around eager to help, and quickly one of them offered to act as our guide. He and his friends accompanied us past the impressive gateway, beyond which was another world – a vast desert plain with low mounds and ruins stretching away as far as the eye could see.

Only one structure dominated the view, and this was a tall, rectangular stone tower that came closer to heaven than any other monument we had seen that day. It stood on its own, amid low ruins identified as the Great Mosque, built on the site of a famous temple to the ancient moon god, Sin. The tower had been utilized in Islamic times to call the faithful to prayer in the mosque, but our young friend called it the 'Astronomical Tower', since it had once been used as an astronomical observatory by a people called the Sabians, pagan worshippers of the celestial bodies, who thrived in this city for thousands of years.

The building's fractured summit seemed almost mesmeric. Even though I knew a little about the history of Harran, I had never before heard mention of this compelling monument, some 40 to 50 metres (131 to 164 feet) in height. It seemed almost ethereal in the ambience of the late afternoon sun, and reminded me of the dark tower featured on the Moon and Tower cards of the Tarot pack. It was also like one of the Towers of Silence used by the Zoroastrians of Iran to dispose of their dead through the process of excarnation, a memory most assuredly of the Neolithic death rites so prevalent across Western Asia. I wanted to go across to it immediately, almost as if nothing else mattered here in this city of the Sabians.

Harran (the Latin *Carrhae*), from as early as *c.*2000 BC, had been a centre of trade and commerce linking East with West. Abraham, the greatest of all the Old Testament patriarchs, was said to have been a pagan of Harran before departing for

Canaan, while his brother Haran was one of the 'chiefs' of the Harranians, 'deeply imbued with their religion' and its 'most tenacious adherent'.[1] The city is mentioned in the Old Testament's Book of Ezekiel alongside Eden and Assyria as a trafficker of spice, gold and precious stones.[2] Its temple dedicated to the moon god was famed throughout the ancient world. The kings of Babylon and Assyria saw Harran as the primary sanctuary of the god, and would come here to pay homage to him. In addition to worshipping Sin, the inhabitants of Harran practised their own unique form of sky-religion, and even with the spread of Christianity – which turned nearby Edessa (or Urfa, modern Sanliurfa) into one of Christendom's greatest centres of pilgrimage – the Harranians remained staunchly pagan, keeping themselves to themselves.

People of the Book

In AD 830, presented by the Caliph Ma'mun with a choice between converting to Islam or death, the inhabitants of Harran said that they were 'Sabians', who are mentioned in the Qur'an as a 'People of the Book'. This is an expression used to denote those to whom God has revealed, via a prophet, a holy book; under Islamic law, such peoples have protected (*dhimmi*) status. According to the story, by this time no one knew who the Sabians truly were, including the Caliph's authorities, and so the Harranians wily claim enabled them to continue practising their unique religion under the protection of Islam. Many Harranians did eventually pay lip-service to Islam, although it is clear that they remained loyal to the old faith. This centred around the supernatural influence of the seven planets of antiquity – the sun, moon, Mercury, Venus, Mars, Jupiter and Saturn – as well as the stars to which they made offerings.[3]

Astronomy was the key to understanding the Sabian religion (indeed, their name might derive from the Arabic word *saba*, which expresses a star rising[4]), and in medieval times a number of famous astronomers attached to the court of the Caliph in Baghdad were originally from Harran.[5] These individuals wrote on topics of a celestial nature, and translated ancient texts that had accumulated in Harran as one of the ancient world's most important centres of learning. Among them were many written originally in Egypt during Graeco-Roman times, *c.*330 BC to AD 500. They spoke of matters such as alchemy, magic, and, most important of all, the wisdom of the Egyptians. Attributed apocryphally to Hermes Trismegistus, this corpus of literature became known as the *Hermetica*. Its translation from Arabic into Latin during the Middle Ages would inspire the instigators of the Italian

Renaissance to promote these remarkable works as the key to religion's great mysteries – leading, of course, to the revival in all things Egyptian, a process that has continued to this day.

Thus Harran is seen as the birthplace of the Hermetic tradition, even though there was very little to show for its great achievements on our arrival there in May 2004. The inhabitants had vanished in the mid-thirteenth century when the entire city was razed to the ground by the Mongol hordes under the command of Ghengis Khan. Yet mercifully, by this time the Harranians had managed to pass on at least some of their religious doctrine to other faiths that thrived in the original Garden of Eden.

A Book of Clues

Even though we did eventually visit Harran's castle ruins, and marvel at its ancient village of beehive-shaped mud huts, it was the Astronomical Tower that continued to hold our gaze. As we stood beneath its enormous blocked-up doorway, with the children still hanging around, I craned my neck to watch as crows circled its summit, before settling back down again. It was a tranquil sight that remained fixed in my memory.

Our young guide then miraculously produced a glossy booklet which he seemed eager to sell. Entitled *Harran: The Crossroad of Civilizations*, it was written by two Turkish archaeologists, Cihat Kürkçüoglu and Zuhal Karahan Kara, both of nearby Harran University, the controlling body for archaeological excavations in the region of Sanliurfa.[6] Amazingly, the booklet referred to the discovery in 1997 of a previously unknown Pre-Pottery Neolithic site, located somewhere in the Tektek Mountains northeast of Sogmatar, on the other side of the Harran plain. Known as Karahan Tepe, it was being investigated by Bahattin Çelik of the Turkish Historical Society and the Department of Archaeology and Art History at Hacettepe University.

The site was thought to date back to *c.*9500–9000 BC, since a number of T-shaped pillars similar to those found at Göbekli Tepe had been recorded, including one pictured in the booklet which instantly drew my attention. Carved in high relief on its slim inside edge was a winding snake with a sperm-like head. Similar carvings of serpents on standing stones had already been recorded at both Göbekli Tepe and Nevali Çori, but this example seemed particularly striking.

The discovery of Karahan Tepe was so recent that, to date, only one article had been written on the site, and this had appeared in an academic journal published in Berlin.[7] According to the account, Karahan Tepe covered an area of 325,000 square metres (80 acres). Buried stone pillars, spaced 1.5 to 2 metres (roughly 5 to 7 feet) apart, could be seen protruding some 50 to 60 centimetres (2 feet) above ground level. Other carved stones had already been traced on the surface, including a battered torso of a naked man, and a polished rock that bore scratched animal forms identified as goats, gazelles and rabbits.

The opportunity to visit Karahan Tepe arose just three days later when we inspected the remains of the seven temples of the Sabians at Sogmatar, close to the border with Syria. Each temple is thought to have been dedicated to a particular planet, although this explanation is by no means certain.

Here, the local guardian recognized the name Karahan Tepe, although the somewhat vague directions he offered came to nothing. So after driving around in circles for an hour or more, we found ourselves lost and devoid of any suitable local maps. With sunset fast approaching, and as we were all about to concede defeat, one final point of a finger from a Bedouin on a tractor sent us off in a new direction. We found ourselves on a dirt track that climbed slowly until, in the middle of a great valley basin, we slowed to a halt outside a remote farmhouse.

Karahan Tepe

A small boy appeared and pointed towards a hillside some 500 metres away, and we began the gradual climb on foot through a series of ploughed fields. We saw no sign of any excavations in progress, but as we got nearer to the summit I began to find evidence of Neolithic man's presence here. At first it was just the odd retouched flint, but then, just as at Göbekli Tepe, I started to notice more and more worked tools, until finally they were everywhere.

Engrossed in field walking, I heard Halil calling from much further on as Sue, even closer to the summit, began shouting that she had found something. It then became apparent what all the fuss was about. On the northern and eastern slopes the tips of standing stones were just visible around our feet. Some stood in pairs, while others were clearly in rows aligned north-south. Although many of the menhirs were unfashioned, some resembled the T-shaped pillars observed at Göbekli Tepe, complete with well-worn, almost indistinguishable carvings. Almost all of them were still *in situ*, while others were now just broken fragments, scattered about. The fallen stone with the snake carving was nowhere to be seen, so presumably it had been removed to Harran University for safekeeping.

Further along the hill's eastern flank, we found more stones with their sockets exposed through preliminary excavation. Arif, our driver, attempted to remove some rubble from beneath one, which leant at a more or less horizontal angle. I helped him, and just as I stood up, he leapt back and began pointing excitedly towards the ground in front of the exposed hollow. At first, I could not understand his concern, but then, as my eyes focused, I saw on the sandy earth a large grey scorpion that had crawled out from beneath the pillar, where my hand had been only seconds beforehand.

The exact function of this amazing prehistoric site – bigger even than Göbekli Tepe – remains a complete mystery, although the location was clearly chosen for its commanding views of the surrounding hills both to the north and northeast. Indeed, the orientations of the stone rows and standing pillars seemed to accentuate an interest in the surrounding landscape. Somehow I felt that this extremely ancient site would one day prove to be even more important than Göbekli Tepe.

My musings were then interrupted by the approach of a tall, thin Bedouin shepherd. Even though I spoke no Turkish or Arabic (the inhabitants of the region generally use both), I sensed from his greeting to Halil and Arif that he was annoyed by our presence. But, as is the way there, Arif offered him a cigarette, and as they crouched down an intense discussion got under way. Several minutes passed before Halil looked across and said that everything was okay, although our Bedouin friend still looked uneasy. It later emerged that this man, the owner of the farmhouse in the valley basin, had been told by Harran University not to allow anyone on the site.

The Need for Answers

The atmosphere had changed, and I felt it was time to leave, especially as the following day we were due to fly back to London. I walked away, but then noticed on the ground a finely worked flint, which I picked up and examined. It had the likeness of a bird's head, complete with hooked beak and sunken eye, giving it the appearance of a raptor or scavenger.

As the lines of stones caused the dying sun to cast long shadows within the orange glow that now bathed the site, I gazed northwards and thought about the almost alien mindset of those responsible for the construction some 11,500 years ago of Karahan Tepe, and other similarly aged monuments in this original Garden of Eden. Who were these people, and how did their brains function? What did they believe in, and why did they build such sophisticated megalithic complexes? Were they aligned to the stars, or were other factors at play here? I knew now that my mind would not rest until I had some answers.

CHAPTER THREE

The Direction of Heaven

The view of Harran's Astronomical Tower haunted my thoughts upon our return from southeast Turkey. Unable to sleep one night, I imagined a large key being used by a white clad male figure, a Sabian perhaps, to open its great entrance door, and once inside I climbed the stone staircase towards its dizzy heights. Somehow, I managed to reach the exposed summit, where the minaret must once have been, and attempted to understand why this place felt so important to me.

It got me thinking about the Sabians of Harran, whose fabled city was located so close to the region's Early Neolithic cult buildings. Did the Harranians inherit religious practices that thrived at places such as Nevali Çori, Göbekli Tepe and Karahan Tepe some 11,500 years ago? With a multitude of inspired thoughts now buzzing around my mind, I got up and for the next three hours scribbled down page after page of notes. As the night gradually gave way to the first light of dawn, I felt at last that I might be close to understanding what had gone on, and the key was the keen interest that the Sabians and the Early Neolithic priestly elite shared in the north.

At Karahan Tepe, for instance, many of the T-shaped pillars faced east-north-east, where the sun rose at midsummer, yet the site's primary orientation was north-south, defined by the orientation of the hill and the site's series of stone rows. Göbekli Tepe's own three main cult buildings were likewise orientated roughly north-south, with the highest one close to the top of the hill (*see Chapter One*).

Further north-south orientations are recorded in association with three Neolithic cult buildings uncovered at Çayönü Tepesi, seven kilometres (4.4 miles) south of the town of Ergani in the province of Diyarbakir. This site is slightly later than Göbekli Tepe, dating to what archaeologists refer to as the 'Pre-Pottery Neolithic B' (PPNB) and later Aceramic Period (*c.*7300–5900 BC).[1] Although there was very little to see when we visited Çayönü Tepesi in the company of the mayor of

Ergani and his people one afternoon in May 2004, one structure, known as the 'Skull Building', was found when excavated to have northerly-placed cellars filled with skulls and other human bones, beyond which was a circular apse like those of Norman churches in England. As one archaeologist put it, this place 'served some death cult'.[2] Within the northeastern corner of the nearby 'Terrazzo Building' was a well-like depression that appeared to be the central focus of the structure.[3]

At nearby Nevali Çori, its cult building, which dates back to *c.*8400–*c.*8000 BC, was orientated southwest to northeast, with a niche at the centre of the northwestern wall in which archaeologists discovered a life-sized egg-like head with crude ears and a carved ponytail (*see Chapter Eighteen*).

Mystery of the North

This general focus on the north among the Early Neolithic settlements of southeast Turkey was, I now felt sure, reflected in the religious practices of the Sabians. In addition to being great astronomers who venerated the seven planets and the twelve signs of the zodiac,[4] they conducted regular religious festivals in honour of something they referred to as the 'Mystery of the North', a deity seen as the Primal Cause – the manifestation of God himself. From him emanated 'the Cosmic existencies',[5] which split like rays to become divine principles. These are named as Intelligence (*al-Aql*), the source of spiritual existence, wherein dwelt the lesser deities and human spirits; Soul (*al-Nafs*), the creative force; and, finally, animated passive Matter, which causes the four elements to come into being.[6] Another source spoke of these dynamic forces as Mind, Soul, World Order, Form and Necessity.[7]

For the Sabians, the north, as 'the greatest god',[8] was the source of light and power, as well as the direction of the abode of the dead.[9] It was also their *kiblah*, or direction of prayer, where they were able to fix their attentions on the 'North Star', or Pole Star,[10] which marks the position of the so-called northern celestial pole around which all stars are seen to revolve.

The Mandaeans

Such knowledge derives from those who witnessed the rites of the Sabians, but after they vanished from the pages of history, others inherited their fascination for the Mystery of the North. In the nineteenth century a London newspaper recorded that the 'Sabians' still performed an age-old ritual whereby a priest entered a rectangular tabernacle from the south (recalling the Early Neolithic cult buildings) and paid 'homage to a certain star to the north'. A sheep and dove were then sacrificed, after which a dove was released. This, like a soul freed from the bonds of life, was expected to fly towards the north, the direction of 'the paradise of the elect and the abode of the pious hereafter'.[11] The 'Sabians' mentioned here are actually the Mandaeans, a minority religious group of Lower Iraq and parts of Iran (there are also modern communities in the US and elsewhere).

The Mandaeans, known also as the Nazoreans, Subbi or 'St John's Christians' – due to their reverence for John the Baptist (Yahya bin Zekaria), who is revered as the last and greatest of their prophets, and whose baptismal rites they follow – were first encountered by Western travellers to Iraq and Iran during the Middle Ages. In addition to venerating a supreme being under the name of 'Alaha', they echo the Sabians in recognizing the seven planets as celestial intelligences, applying to them names which are clearly Babylonian in origin.

Even though southern Iraq, along with parts of western Iran, has been their homeland for at least a thousand years, Mandaean sacred texts speak of their ancestors having migrated from a place in the north called 'Inner Harran', thought to be a reference to the city of Harran. Indeed, one of their holy books speaks of the 'interior of the Haran [i.e. Harran]' admitting them.[12] It makes sense, for there is little question that the Mandaeans are descendants of the Harranians, and even accepted the name 'Sabian' as a means of identifying themselves. It comes as no surprise then to learn that the Mandaeans venerated the north as their *kiblah* (direction of prayer), and saw it also as 'the source of light, instruction, and healing: in prayer, as in death, the Mandaean faces the Pole Star. If he wishes to think deeply, he faces north, and sleeps with his head south, so as to rise in the right direction.'[13]

Mandaean tradition speaks of no less than 360 *melki*, or divine beings. Among them is Abathur-Muzania (or Awather-Muzania), whose 'throne' is located 'behind the North star', known as the 'House of Abathur'.[14] It is he 'who judges the souls of men after they have passed through Purgatory, seeing whether they are purged enough to pass on into Paradise'.[15] If deemed pure enough, the soul then makes its onward journey by boat over a celestial 'river', arguably the Milky Way, to one of the countless 'worlds of light', inhabited by their dead kinsmen.[16] In these unimaginable realms, governed by 'great spirits of light', they meet other purified souls as well as their own '*dmutha* or over-soul'.[17]

Denuding the Dead

Did the builders of the Early Neolithic cult buildings, including Göbekli Tepe, the 'oldest temple in the world', likewise see the north as significant to their 'death cult', which seems to have been focused around the act of excarnation? This is the process whereby human remains are denuded by scavenger birds, vultures in particular, before the remaining bones are gathered up and deposited in a disarticulated state within what is known as a secondary burial. This was a regular practice in Neolithic times, and has also been carried out in recent times by various indigenous peoples. For example, such burials form part of the funerary practices of various American tribes, and to this day Tibetans still practise 'sky burial', as they call it. Indeed, like their cousins the Zoroastrians of Iran, the Mandaeans also once practised excarnation, linking them directly with the Neolithic cult of the dead.[18]

Excarnation is also clearly shown in a mural found on a wall of one of the subsurface cult buildings in the Neolithic city of Çatal Hüyük in south-central Turkey, which dates to *c.*6500–*c.*5500 BC. Here we see two wooden towers with steps leading to their upper levels (*see fig. 2*). The one on the right shows two vultures fighting over a headless stick-man representing a human carcass, while on the left a pair of vultures are seen taking a human head under their wing. Since the human soul was

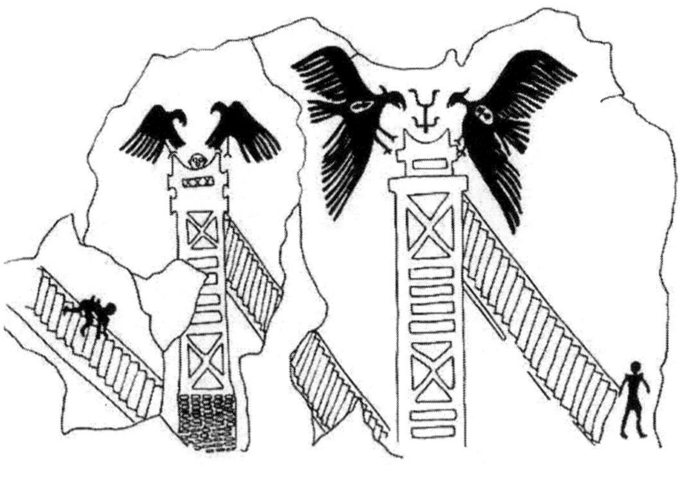

Fig.2 . Neolithic excarnation tower, from a mural found at Çatal Hüyük, southern-central Turkey, and dating to *c.*6500–*c.*5600 BC.

widely thought by ancient cultures to occupy the skull, the birds seem ready to accompany the soul into the afterlife. In effect, each acts as a 'psychopomp', from a Greek word meaning the 'soul-guide' or 'soul-carrier'. In the Neolithic cult of the dead, the skull was generally separated from the body and decorated in order that it might be used for oracular purposes – hence their proliferation at Çayönü Tepesi (*see above, page 15*).

Vulture Shamans

Elsewhere at Çatal Hüyük, actual vulture skulls covered in mortar protrude from walls to give them the appearance of human breasts, showing that the bird was additionally seen as a source of nourishment and new life in the next world. Other murals show vultures as human-bird hybrids with articulated legs, signifying vulture shamans that have adopted this guise so that they might achieve magical flight in order to gain otherworldly knowledge and wisdom of benefit to themselves and the communities over which they held sway.

Vulture shamanism lay at the core of the Early Neolithic cult of the dead, and was present even in the very earliest settlements built in Upper Mesopotamia. Artistic representations of vultures have been found at Nevali Çori, Göbekli Tepe and also at Jerf el-Ahmar, another Pre-Pottery Neolithic site, dating to *c.*9000–*c.*7300 BC, located just over the Turkish border in northern Syria.[19] Cruder bird-men found at Göbekli Tepe and nearby Nevali Çori very likely show vulture shamans, confirming still further the importance of this cult during a very early stage of development in the Neolithic period.

This supposition is also supported by the discovery at a communal cave site named Shanidar, in the Upper Zagros mountains of northern Iraq, of a whole series of severed birds' wings. They came from several species of raptors and scavengers, in particular the bearded vulture and griffon vulture. The context in which these wings were found strongly indicates that they were deliberately buried, following some sort of ceremonial usage.[20] Carbon-14 testing on the remains, which were covered with red ochre – used also on Neolithic human burials and perhaps symbolizing the blood of life – provided dates in the region of 8870 BC.[21] How exactly the wings might have been utilized is open to speculation, although presumably they were fastened to an individual's body in order that they might journey in an altered state of consciousness to otherworldly domains.

Celestial Heaven

I have written extensively on the Early Neolithic cult of the dead and its accompanying vulture shamanism. Yet never had I contemplated the idea that the celestial destination of the Neolithic afterlife, where the priest shamans travelled to obtain divine knowledge and wisdom, might have had a specific direction, or better still *an actual location in the night sky*. I had always seen heaven as purely conceptual, a metaphor for the afterlife. Now I was beginning to think that it was to be found somewhere in 'the north', making sense of the fact that to many ancient and prehistoric peoples this was the direction of divine creation as well as the final destination of the soul. This belief was widespread: both the Babylonians and the early Jews prayed towards the north, while the Shi'ite Muslims of Iraq and Iran also consider the north to be the direction of Paradise.[22]

Yet did such archaic beliefs concerning the role of the north as the direction of the celestial abode and the afterlife really go back to Neolithic times? In the twenty-eight subsurface shrines examined at Çatal Hüyük by British archaeologist James Mellaart during the 1960s, the subject of death and the afterlife was unanimously associated with two directions alone – the east and north.[23] If murals drawn on east-facing walls reflected the direction of both the rising sun, seen as a symbol of new life, and an active volcano venerated by the peoples of Çatal Hüyük, this left the north, the region of darkness, devoid of sunlight, as associated specifically with death and mortality. Combine all this with the north–south orientations of many Early Neolithic cult buildings in southeast Turkey, and there was enough to convince me that I was on to something. However, a lot more research would need to be done before any real conclusions could be drawn. For the moment, I concentrated on attempting to establish further links between the religion of the Sabians and their Neolithic forebears.

The Peacock Angel

The closest descendants of the Sabians of Harran are the Yezidi, followers of an obscure religion binding together various Kurdish tribes that live today mostly in remote regions of northern Syria and northern Iraq (there are also modern communities in Armenia and Europe).[24] Founded some 800 years ago by a Syrian prophet, poet and author of Islamic mystical (i.e. Sufi) works named Sheikh Adi ibn Musafir el-Hakkari (other accounts say a prophet named Yezid), these people preserve indigenous religious customs and beliefs that long antedate the rise of the Yezidi faith. Over the centuries they have been persecuted by the Muslims, who see them as pagan idolaters, apostates and renegades, something not helped by their acceptance of Shaitan (Satan) as a deity who takes his place alongside the Almighty. It is for this reason that European scholars have often viewed them as 'devil worshippers', an appellation they do not merit.

In addition to Shaitan, two other aspects of Khuda, the Kurdish name for God, exist. One is Sheikh Adi (sometimes Yezid), a holy incarnation and avatar, and the other is Malak Ta'us, the Peacock Angel, also known as Azazil. He is Khuda in the form of a bird, who governs over the seven celestial intelligences, or angels.[25] Like the Sabians and Mandaeans, the Yezidi pray towards the north, and in particular the Pole Star (even though they also greet the rising sun each morning).[26] Moreover, it is reported that a decorated wooden casket in which the Yezidi sacred texts were once kept bore symbols signifying the sun, moon and the four elements, as well as Malak Ta'us, the Peacock Angel, in the form of a bird, above which was a star, almost certainly the North Star.[27]

As the direction of Khuda, the north is associated with a Yezidi creation myth that records the coming into being of the universe. Preserved in a thirteenth-century work entitled *Kitab el-Aswad* (*Mas'haf Rish*), known simply as the Black Book,[28] it was first brought to the attention of Western scholars when still kept inside the above mentioned decorated casket. Its curious text tells the story of how Khuda made 'the White Pearl out of His most precious essence'. He brought into existence a bird called Anfar (or ANQR), on the back of which was placed the Pearl (representing the pre-existent universe), wherein he dwelt for forty thousand years.[29] He then created the angels, along with the sun, moon, and human race, which were kept in his mantle. Following this, he 'cried out at the Pearl with a loud cry', and the Pearl then 'fell asunder into four pieces', causing water to gush forth and form the primeval 'sea'.

Next Khuda made a ship in which he dwelt for a further thirty thousand years, before finally he took up residence at Lalish, the most holy shrine of the Yezidi in northern Iraq (presumably in the form of Sheikh Adi, to whom the shrine is dedicated). The great god then created the angel Gabriel as a bird, and commanded him to take two pieces of the pearl and put one beneath the Earth, and the other in the Gate of Heaven. Khuda then placed in them the sun and the moon, and produced the stars from the remaining fragments, which were suspended 'in heaven for an ornament'.

The Sanjak

The Yezidi worship Malak Ta'us, or the Anfar, in the form of a crude metal bird that sits atop a free-standing pole affixed to a circular tray that supports it. Known as a *sanjak,* which just means 'stand', these bird totems, sometimes described as 'cocks',[30] are highly regarded among the Yezidi communities. They are carried secretly from village to village by special *qauwal*-priests, and set up for worship in carefully selected house shrines. They are never shown to outsiders, and very few illustrations exist (*see figs.3a and 3b*) – I know of no authenticated photos.

When put on display, the *sanjak* is said to come 'alive'. The *qauwal*-priest falls into a trance, causing Malak Ta'us to enter the *sanjak,* in which he becomes a divine oracle.[31] Anfar, the name given to Khuda as the bird, is equated with the mythical Anqa of Arabic legend, known as the 'god of heaven',[32] as well as the 'eagle of the Arabians', once venerated by Arab nomads at Harran. It is in fact the fabled Roc, or Rukh, a gigantic eagle popularized in the tales of Sindbad the Sailor.[33]

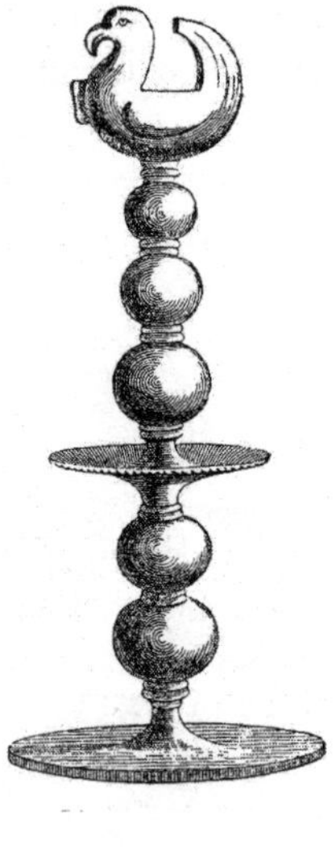

Figs. 3a and 3b. Two examples of the Yezidi sanjak. Left: as seen by Mrs Badger in Bashika, Mesopotamia (Iraq), in 1850. Right: as seen by Sir Austen Henry Layard in 1849. They represent the celestial bird atop the cosmic axis.

Despite these connections, the only modern-day description of the Anfar of the Yezidi is that it bears the likeness of a 'white dove',[34] making little sense of the religion's *sanjak* bird totems. On the other hand, the connection brings to mind the Mandaean ritual in which a dove was released in order that it might climb towards heaven. Not only were doves sacred in Mandaean religion, but they also bore this same honour among the Harranians, who were forbidden to eat or sacrifice either birds with talons or pigeons, a rule that would have extended to doves as well.[35]

Satanic Verses

Interestingly, there is strong evidence to suggest that the Islamic holy shrine of the Kaaba at Mecca in Saudi Arabia was once a Sabian place of worship. This information comes from the great Arabic historian Athar-ul-Bakiya of Albiruni, who *c.*AD 1000 vowed that 'its images originally belonged to them, and that the worshippers of those images belonged to them, and that the worshippers of those images belonged to their community, and that Allah was called Zuhal [Saturn] and Al'uzza [an Arabian love goddess], Alzuhara [Venus].'[36] This is curious since the nineteenth-century English traveller Sir Richard Burton (1821–1890) recorded that the original pagan idol of Mecca was a 'pigeon carved in wood, and above it another, which Ali [Muhammad's cousin and son-in-law], mounting upon the Prophet's shoulder, pulled down.'[37]

The dove is sacred in Islamic tradition, since it is said to have sat on Muhammad's shoulder and whispered in his ear. Most probably, it was a form of Gabriel, through whom Allah is said to have transmitted to the Prophet the entire Qur'an. At Muhammad's birthplace of Mecca, doves and pigeons are treated with the utmost respect. They are allowed to perch on the Kaaba's holy buildings, and it is forbidden to eat pigeons anywhere in the city.[38]

Who or what the two 'pigeon' idols once found at Mecca actually represented is unclear. One was probably a pre-Islamic form of Allah or Gabriel, who was seen as a demiurge – a guardian of earthly creation – while the other was most likely a totemic animal of Allat or al-Uzza, Arabian love goddesses. Both are named in the controversial so-called 'Satanic Verses', verses which, some early sources claim, Muhammad spoke but subsequently rejected as part of the Qur'an on the grounds that they derived not from Allah, but from Satan – hence the term 'Satanic Verses'. They were notoriously made public in 1989 by the Indian-born Muslim author Salman Rushdie in his book of the same name. Sura 53:19–20 of the Qur'an reads:

> Have ye thought upon al-Lat and al-Uzza And Manat, the third, the other?

Initially, these lines are said to have been followed by:

> These are the swans exalted,
> Whose intercession is to be hoped for.[39]

The 'swans' whose intercession should be sought were the three goddesses al-Lat, al-Uzza and Manat (or Anat), called *banat Allah*, the 'daughters of Allah', or 'daughters of the god'.[40] Each one had important shrines at locations close to Mecca.[41] Muhammad, it is said, struck out the offending lines, which apparently acknowledge the existence of other deities, after Allah revealed that Satan had intervened to make the Prophet write them in the first place.

A Direct Survival

Mehrdad Izady, Professor of Near Eastern History at the University of New York, made a study of Yezidi bird totems and concluded that the bronze idols resemble not so much a dove or peacock but the great bustard, a bird that bears some similarity to the turkey. Indeed, he sees the shamanistic practices responsible for the deliberate burial, *c.*8870 BC in the Shanidar cave of northern Iraq, of wings belonging to the great bustard, found alongside those of the vulture as well as other raptors, as 'an indigenous precursor to modern Yezidi practice'.[42] In other words, he proposes a direct survival among the Yezidi of Early Neolithic ritual involving birds.

Fig. 4. Early Neolithic stone totem pole topped by a vulture found at Nevali Çori, after Harald Hauptmann. Like the Yezidi sanjak, it represents the cosmic axis.

I might also add that the remains of a limestone 'totem-pole' displaying human heads topped by a bird were found during excavations at the cult building of Nevali Çori.[43] With regards to this discovery, the excavator, Harald Hauptmann, observed: 'The bird perched upon a human head may have represented the soul of a human or a connection between this world and the beyond.' According to him, the fragment of a 'vulture-like bird' found at the same time might have formed part of a similar 'composite piece'.[44]

Worshippers of the Truth

Even more elusive than the Yezidi are the followers of another tribal religion of Kurdish origin known as *Ahl-i Haqq*, 'Worshippers of the Truth', also called the Yaresan. They live mostly in the mountains of northwest Iran, although some survive in small pockets in northern Iraq, southeast Turkey and Azerbaijan. Very little is known about their faith, which scholars often see as merely a variation of Islamic Sufism.

Similarly to Yezidi cosmology, the Yaresan holy books record how the Divine Essence, known as Ya, took the form of a bird with golden wings, and created the Pearl which then became his residence.[45] Realizing that he was alone, Ya then created Jebra'il (Gabriel), the first angel, who came to learn his art. At his request, Ya created six more angels, who together with Jebra'il were known as the *haftan*. Ya then stepped out of the Pearl, left foot first, and took the name Khavankar. Other creations then emerged from the Pearl, which began to burn and boil, separating matter from spirit.

Clear parallels exist between the Yezidi creation myth and that of the Yaresan. However, in the case of the latter, the bird form of God appears to be a predator, since Khavankar was known as the Eternal Royal Falcon.[46]

Brethren of Purity

Finally, we come to the radical Shi'ite sect known as the Isma'ili Brethren of Purity (*Ikhwan al-Safa'*), who borrowed greatly from the Sabian mysteries.[47] Their *Epistles* speak of a Harranian initiatory ritual that would take place in a windowless temple with its altar located in the north, recalling the subsurface cult buildings of the Early Neolithic era. Following a night vigil, the candidate's guarantor would step forward to offer up a rooster as a substitute for the initiate's own life to Jurjas, a deity associated with the Sabian supreme being, the Mystery of the North (*see above, page 16*). This being accepted, he or she was then marked on the thumb with an iron ring, before being touched ninety-nine times with a tamarisk bough (recalling the ninety-nine names of Allah).

During Sabian festivals celebrating the Mystery of the North, whosoever is bound by a vow made to 'the Lord of Fortune' (*Rab al-Baht*) should attach a firebrand to the wing of a cock or young chicken, and send it forth to the god, i.e. the north. Should the bird be consumed in the flames, then it meant that the offering had been accepted, but if the flames extinguished then it meant that the sacrifice had been refused.[48] The connections between the firebrand ceremonies of the Sabians, the rooster offered up to Jurgas by the Brethren of Purity, and the release of a white dove to honour 'a certain star to the north' by the Mandaeans are self-evident. Clearly, there was a profound relationship between such 'soul' birds and the Mystery of the North, something that I strongly suspected went back to Neolithic times.

Bird of Life and Death

In the knowledge that the north was the most prominent orientation of the earliest Neolithic cult buildings and stone rows in southeast Turkey, I suspected this was the direction of the destination of the soul in death, the place of the afterlife, as early as 9500 BC. If so then there had to be every possibility that the location of 'heaven' was seen in terms of the Pole Star, around which the stars revolved on a daily basis. Originally, the soul bird or psychopomp (soul-carrier) was the vulture, and I suspected that this North Star, as it is known, formed part of a constellation, or asterism, in the northern night sky, personified in the past as either a vulture, or at least a bird of life and death. This in turn would be equated with the bird of creation venerated by the Mandaeans, Yezidi, Yaresan, Brethren of Purity, and the pre-Islamic Arabs, who often made Harran their temporary home – all of these peoples almost certainly derived aspects of their religion from the Sabians, the direct descendants of the earliest Neolithic communities of Upper Mesopotamia.

Turning Back Time

In order to explore this possibility further, certain astronomical factors needed to be taken into consideration. The heavens today are not as they appeared to the observer say, *c.*9500 BC, the age of the earliest Neolithic monuments in southeast Turkey. Due to a wobble in its polar axis, the Earth slowly sways like a spinning-top. This effect causes the relative position of the stars to appear to shift contrary to their daily motion, or yearly rotation, at a rate of approximately one degree every seventy-two years, with one complete cycle taking an estimated 25,770 years, although usually this figure is rounded up to 26,000 years. As a consequence, the twelve zodiacal constellations, and indeed all the stars in the night sky, are seen to alter their positions relative to the ecliptic – the path of the sun through the heavens (*see Chapter Four*).

In addition to causing the so-called 'precession of the equinoxes', the Earth's axial wobble moves the position of the northern celestial pole, the point around which the heavens turn as viewed from the Earth. Over the 26,000–year-cycle the celestial pole follows a circular course that embraces several major and minor stars that will very slowly spiral in and out of pole position. Today the Pole Star is Polaris, the brightest star in Ursa Minor, the Little Bear; but *c.*2800 BC, just before Egypt's Pyramid Age, it was Thuban, a star in the constellation of Draco, the celestial dragon.

In order to take into account the effects of precession, therefore, and see how the night sky might have looked to our Early Neolithic ancestors, I asked my colleague, the technical engineer Rodney Hale, to enter the required coordinates into the Skyglobe 3.6 computer program. This enables the viewer to see the heavens as they might have appeared anywhere in the world over the last 30,000 years.

Through this process, we were able to determine that in 9500 BC no star was close enough to the northern celestial pole to act as Pole Star, even though the pole was to be found in the vicinity of the constellation known as Hercules. In fact, you would need to precess the skies back to 11,000 BC in order to find the previous Pole Star, and this was Vega, the brightest star in the constellation of Lyra. It was a role it played for a period of approximately two thousand years, beginning *c.*13,000 BC, when most of the Northern Hemisphere was still in the grip of the last Ice Age, and the peoples of the Late Palaeolithic (Old Stone Age) epoch lived as nomadic hunter-gatherers.

To discover that there was no Pole Star when the earliest known building phases of Göbekli Tepe and Karahan Tepe were under construction was initially puzzling, leading me to consider that I might be on the wrong track. However, I wondered whether the significance of Lyra as the constellation that included the Pole Star might not have been recognized by Late Palaeolithic peoples, and then passed on by them to the builders of the Early Neolithic complexes in southeast Turkey – even though there exists no direct evidence of Late Palaeolithic activity in the region of Sanliurfa.[49]

In Greek mythology Lyra was the fabled lyre, or harp, that the god Hermes fashioned from a tortoise shell and gave to his half-brother Apollo. He in turn passed it on to his son Orpheus, the musician of the Argonauts. Not only did its enchanting music mesmerize all who heard it, but its charm was able to gain the freedom of Orpheus' wife Eurydice, who had been abducted into the underworld. Following Orpheus's brutal death at the hands of the Maenads, frenzied female followers of the god Dionysos, the lyre was transformed into the constellation that bears its name.

The story of Orpheus's lyre is curious, but I failed to see how it related to the Sabians' belief in the Mystery of the North, or the Early Neolithic monuments of southeast Turkey. Then I turned to the astronomy of ancient Babylon. Here the constellation of Lyra was known in the Sumerian/Akkadian language as *Raditartakhu*, (Babylonian/Assyrian *Karib-Barkhati*), one of a group of three birds (*khu*) that attack the god Marduk (the constellation of Hercules) in the night sky.[50] That Lyra was identified as a bird in ancient astronomy is further borne out in the knowledge that this asterism was sometimes known by the Latin name *Aquilaris*, and was shown as an eagle clutching the fabled lyre in its talons.[51] Yet more pertinent is the knowledge that Lyra, and Vega in particular, was once associated with the 'eagle of the Arabians'.[52]

But even more significant is that Lyra also once bore the name *Vultur cadens*, the 'Falling Grype', or Vulture.[53] Thus in the knowledge that the vulture was a symbol of the transmigration of the soul in Early Neolithic tradition, and featured also in its cult of the dead, did this mean that Lyra gained its avian attributes even before the Neolithic Age? Did Vega once mark the gateway to the celestial abode, seen in terms of the place of the afterlife?

Rodney Hale and I were unable to establish any firm astronomical connections between this star group and either Göbekli Tepe or Karahan Tepe. It just did not fit the evidence at hand. So we returned to Skyglobe and now searched to see what zodiacal constellation rose heliacally (i.e. as the sun was rising) in southeast Turkey around the time of the summer solstice in 9500 BC, towards which many of the pillars at Karahan Tepe seemed to face. We quickly established that it was Libra, the Balance, or Scales. Although identified since ancient times with the scales of justice, the stars of Libra were once simply the 'claws' of Scorpio,[54] a constellation known on the Euphrates by at least 2000 BC. Despite its more obvious association with the scorpion, this star group was seen as a celestial serpent, or dragon, by several ancient cultures.[55] These included the ancient Hebrews, who called it *Akrab*, and identified its serpentine form with the Israelite tribe of Dan, whose emblem was the serpent.[56]

At that moment I recalled the T-shaped pillar with the vertical snake carving found at Karahan Tepe (*see above, page 11*), which arguably once stood facing the east-northeast and thus towards the midsummer sunrise. Others like it were found at Göbekli Tepe.[57] For some reason, I was reminded also of the grey scorpion that had climbed out from beneath a carved stone at Karahan Tepe: was this some kind of strange omen? Would the stars of Scorpio help explain why these age-old stone monuments were turned towards the 'gates of paradise' in the northern night sky? Could this information now lead me to identify the Pole Star and the constellation that truly expressed the Early Neolithic belief in a cosmic bird of life and death?

It was with such thoughts that I at last turned my attentions to Cygnus, the celestial Swan of heaven.

CHAPTER FOUR

The Circle of Cygnus

As we have seen, in 9500 BC there was no Pole Star, just a dark void where it should have been. The only reminder of its proximity were the circumpolar stars that revolve around the northern celestial pole and are never seen to set. Among them was Deneb, the brightest star in the constellation of Cygnus, the celestial swan, known also as the Northern Cross. It took our instant attention, for at a latitude corresponding to southeast Turkey in that distant epoch, it revolved around the celestial pole, virtually kissing the northern horizon on its lower transit, or passage, of the north-south meridian – the imaginary line seen by astronomers to bisect the heavens.

Had this northern star been important to our Neolithic forebears in southeast Turkey, when the first religious buildings anywhere in the world were under construction? If so, then its unusual motion through the sky 11,500 years ago might not have been the only reason for an interest in Deneb, for we find that the stars of Cygnus are located in the middle of the Milky Way, where they mark the start of what is known as the Great Rift, a lane of interstellar dust clouds in which new stars form. This nebulous region stretches down to where the stars of Sagittarius and Scorpio mark the point that the sun crosses the Milky Way on the so-called line of the ecliptic. Here the Great Rift opens out like the mouth of a river estuary. Similar dark areas occur in other sections of the Milky Way, although the Great Rift is by far the most prominent and significant.

Over and beyond this was the fact that before dawn on the summer solstice in 9500 BC, the claws of Scorpio, viewed in many ancient cultures as a serpent or dragon, would be seen above the horizon, marking the base of the Milky Way, which was positioned in a more or less horizontal position, stretching in an anticlockwise direction to where the stars of Cygnus sat low on the northern horizon. I am certain that it was towards the meridian line, which Deneb crossed just above the horizon on its lower transit during this early epoch, that the stone rows at Karahan Tepe and

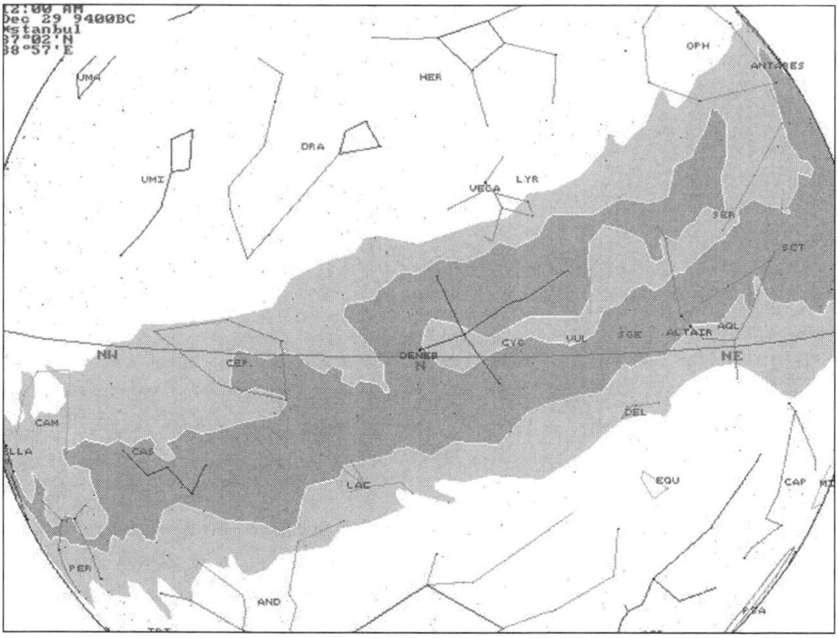

Fig. 5. The northern sky as viewed from southeast Turkey, *c.*9400 BC, with Deneb, the brightest star in Cygnus, making its lower meridian transit (Note that all place names cited on Skyglobe images are merely region indicators: all latitudes and longitudes are correct for the particular locations under discussion).

the cult buildings at Göbekli Tepe were orientated towards (even though some of the stone pillars show an orientation north-northwest – approximately 17.5 degrees west of north – towards where Deneb set. *c.*9025 BC). Even after Deneb stopped being circumpolar in southeast Turkey, *c.*9300 BC, and nightly set in the north-northwest and rose in the north-northeast, cult buildings constructed at other Pre-Pottery Neolithic sites in southeast Turkey, such as Nevali Çori and Çayönü Tepesi, were still aligned towards the north, honouring the direction of a northerly placed heaven, marked by Deneb and the stars of Cygnus. If all this is correct, then it can be no coincidence that thousands of years later this same direction was seen as the place of the Primal Cause among the Sabians and their descendants – the Mandaeans, Yezidi and Brethren of Purity (*see Chapter Three*).

Even if I accepted that the Early Neolithic peoples of southeast Turkey took an interest in Deneb and the stars of Cygnus, had their unique view of the cosmos really remained strong across the millennia, and if so why? As curious as it was to note that the more-or-less horizontally positioned Milky Way linked the claws of Scorpio with the stars of Cygnus before dawn on the longest day of the year in 9500 BC, something was still missing. I did not understand why Deneb would have taken on such a significance, especially as it was only the eighteenth brightest star in the night sky.

In Europe, ever since classical times, the stars of Cygnus have been seen as the celestial swan, flying along the Milky Way, but surely this would have meant nothing to the Neolithic priestly elite of 9500 BC. How would they have interpreted this prominent star cluster?

Legends of the Sky Bird

By 2000 BC, and conceivably much earlier, the stars of Cygnus were seen on the Euphrates river of Upper and Lower Iraq as a celestial bird. In the Sumerian/Akkadian language its name was *Khu-Zaba* (Babylonian/Assyrian *Itstsur-qisti*), meaning 'the Bird-of-the-Forest',[1] identified as the kite, a fierce bird that 'habitually builds in forest trees'.[2] It was one of the three storm birds – along with the constellations Lyra and Altair, the eagle – that 'attacked' the Babylonian supreme god Marduk, represented by the constellation of Hercules. As we shall see, there is a clear mythological connection between Cygnus, Lyra and Aquila, all of which are seen in star-lore as celestial birds. Moreover, their brightest stars, respectively Deneb, Vega and Altair, form a visible relationship in the night sky known to astronomers as the Summer Triangle.

In Arabic star-lore Cygnus was identified not as a swan, but as the 'original' Roc, or Rukh, the mythical bird known also as the Anqa.[3] In addition to this, Cygnus bore various names in the Arab world, all of them relating to a bird of some sort. For example, it was *al-Ta'ir al Arduf* (or *Altayr*), the Flying Eagle, as well as *al-Dajajah*, the Hen, and *al-Katat*, which has connotations of a game bird, such as the mottled partridge or sand-grouse, the *Rijl al-Katai* of Yezidi tradition, represented by them as the bird-foot symbol (see fig. 6). *Al-Katat* can also mean a pigeon,[4] recalling the wooden idols at the Kaaba in Mecca, which, as we saw in the last chapter, was originally a sacred shrine of the Sabians. It recalled also the Anfar bird of the Yezidi, described as a 'white dove', and the dove released to

Fig. 6. The Yezidi symbol representing rijl al-qatai, the sand-grouse foot, the Arabic al-katat, a game bird identified in Arabian star-lore with the stars of Cygnus.

heaven by the Mandaeans during one of their rituals. Were all these birds a memory of the former significance of the Cygnus constellation?

As we saw in the previous chapter, the pre-Islamic goddesses al-Lat, al-Uzza and Manat (or Anat) were referred to in the so-called 'Satanic Verses' as 'swans', and this was not simply a metaphor. Like Aphrodite, Venus and other love goddesses across the Near East and Asia, the three Arabian goddesses would have been associated with a bird, most generally a dove, goose or swan, which were all interchangeable symbols of love, purity and devotion. Since we know that Cygnus was governed by Venus in Classical star lore,[5] there is no reason not to link the three *banat Allah*, or 'daughters of Allah', with the Cygnus constellation. Allah himself is likely to have been represented in pre-Islamic times by one of the 'pigeon' idols at Mecca, which, in the knowledge that the Kaaba is likely once to have been a Sabian shrine, suggests that Allah was originally synonymous with the Primal Cause, celebrated by the Sabians during the Mystery of the North.

There is no literary evidence to show that the dove of the Holy Spirit in Judeo-Christian tradition was ever seen as Cygnus, although as a bird it does share its origin with other celestial birds that were, as we can see, linked with this constellation. As the expression of the *ruach*, the 'breath' or 'spirit of God' (Greek *pneuma*), that 'moved' over the primordial waters in the first chapter of Genesis,[6] the dove takes it place as another Near Eastern bird of creation, like the Anfar of the Yezidi, or the vehicle of Ya in the theology of the Yaresan. Moving on to the star Deneb (known to astronomers as *alpha* Cygni), we find that it derived its name from the Arabic *al-Dhanab al-Dajajah*, the Hen's Tail,[7] whilst in Latin it was *Os rosae*, the 'face of the rose', invoking thoughts, once more, of love and fealty. The Sabians' celebration of the Mystery of the North included a special ceremony known as 'smelling the rose',[8] conjuring images of the mystical symbol of the 'rosy cross', the rose upon the cross. Was this born from some half-forgotten memory of Deneb's former significance in the mysteries of religion?

The Celestial Cross of Christ

Cygnus is commonly known as the Northern Cross because of the unique way it resembles the Cross of Crucifixion as it slides down towards the western horizon each night. Yet its connections with Christianity go back to antiquity, for it was identified specifically as the 'Cross of Calvary', as well as *Christi Crux* ('Christ's Cross') and *Crux cum St. Helena* ('Cross of St Helena'),[9] this last name being a reference to the rediscovery of the True Cross by the Empress Helena, the mother of the Roman emperor Constantine the Great, during her famous pilgrimage to Jerusalem in AD 327. In illustrated planispheres from the seventeenth century onwards, Cygnus is shown sometimes as Christ on the Cross, with six of the asterism's most prominent stars corresponding perhaps to the approximate positions of the Crown of Thorns, the three nails in Jesus's hands and feet, the wound in his thigh made by the lance, and, finally, his Sacred Heart.

In fact, the identification of Cygnus with the Cross of Calvary, a symbol of death and redemption for Christians worldwide, goes back at least to AD 592. In this year St Gregory of Tours (544–595), a French bishop and historian, wrote a tract entitled *De cursu stellarum* ('On The Course of The Stars'). It was intended to instruct monks on how to keep the hours of the day using star constellations (an idea borrowed from Egyptian monasticism) and makes reference to the *crucem maiorem*, 'Greater Cross'.[10] Not only is it clearly stated that this is the stars of Cygnus, but we find that to its left is a Greek letter 'alpha' (A) composed of stars from Delphinus, the celestial dolphin, and to its right an 'omega' (W) seen in the stars of Lyra.[11] 'I am the Alpha and the Omega, the beginning and the end', are words attributed in Revelation to the resurrected Christ,[12] confirming that Cygnus was understood to be the Cross of Salvation. How much older the Christian concept of the Greater Cross might have been is unknown, although it has been suggested that it could date back to the age of Constantine the Great, responsible for instituting Christianity as the state religion of the empire.[13]

Orpheus and the Cross of Redemption

Early Church Fathers spoke out against the use of the wooden crucifix as a symbol of the faith, denouncing it as a pagan idol.[14] Yet since the first letter of 'Christ' in its Greek form is C (*chi* = *kh*), Christians quickly began using the cross for signing, generally on the forehead, and also pictorially as a means of common recognition. Despite this, no evidence has emerged to show that early Christians ever depicted the Crucifixion in religious art, since it was simply too barbaric and shameful a form of execution, being reserved for slaves and the lowest social classes. It was not abolished until the reign of the emperor Constantine I in the early fourth century, which is why, prior to the fifth century, only a handful of crucifixion images exist. One example takes the form of suspected anti-Christian graffiti on a pillar in Rome, dating to between AD 193 and 235. It shows an ass-headed figure being crucified, alongside which are the words 'Alexmenos worships his god', a reference it is thought to Jesus Christ.[15]

Fig. 7. Graeco-Roman magical gem from the mid-third century AD showing the crucified pagan god Orpheus.

The only other notable example of a crucifixion scene from this period is found on a Graeco-Roman magical gem of the mid-third century, kept in a museum in Berlin until, apparently, it went missing during the Second World War. It shows a figure, knees together and bent to one side, on a typical crucifixion cross (see fig. 7) like that so familiar to Christian art. In fact, it might easily have been mistaken for a representation of Christ were it not for its Greek inscription, which reads: *Orpheus Bakkikos* ('Bacchic Orpheus'),[16] a reference to Orpheus, the poet, musician and god of the underworld, who was the founder of the Orphic mysteries of Greece.

The connection here with Orpheus is highly significant, for Greek and Roman frescoes and mosaics showing the god beguiling wild animals with the sweet sound of his lyre bear a striking resemblance to early pictorial representations of Jesus as the Good Shepherd (after John 10:14-5: 'I am the good shepherd.'), the most common manner in which he was portrayed by early Christians, famously in the catacombs of Rome. It is accepted, for instance, that statues and frescoes showing a clean-shaven (in the Roman style) Christ wearing a short tunic, either with a lamb around his neck or holding a flute or lyre, are closely modelled on depictions of Orpheus. Clearly there existed a relationship between the iconography of Jesus and that of the pagan god Orpheus, explained occasionally with the claim that the pagan god's ability to tame wild animals, his journey to the underworld and his violent death reminded Christians of Jesus.

Before the Crucifixion became the greatest Christian symbol of death and redemption, it was clearly not Jesus but Orpheus who was depicted on the cross. Before now, this startling revelation has remained a somewhat embarrassing fact to scholars, for aside from Orpheus's association with the death and resurrection of pagan vegetation gods, such as Dionysus, the Roman Bacchus, which might be seen as precursors of Jesus's own death and resurrection,[17] no other explanation has been forthcoming. However, the knowledge that the Greeks equated the stars of Cygnus with Orpheus, enables us to approach the matter from an entirely new perspective.

Orpheus in the Underworld

Primarily, Cygnus was identified in the Hellenic world as *Ornis*, the Bird, an appellation most probably derived from the fact that its stars were seen as one of the Stymphalian Birds, dangerous man-eating creatures said to have infested the woods around Lake Stymphalus in Arcadia, and linked perhaps with the three storm birds in Mesopotamian myth. To kill the Stymphalian birds was the third of Hercules' twelve labours.

Beyond this, however, Cygnus was the underworld god Orpheus elevated into the night sky as a swan after his brutal death at the hands of the Maenads, so that he might be near to his cherished lyre in the neighbouring constellation of Lyra. It was said that Orpheus's severed head carried on singing even after it was tossed into the Hebrus River, and did so all the way to Lesbos, where it was retrieved by the island's priestesses, who set it up as an oracle in a cave. Here it continued to pronounce the future, even after a serpent had endeavoured to lacerate it, being stopped only when Apollo turned it to stone.[18]

There is a link here I feel to the use of skulls for very similar oracular purposes in the Neolithic death cult, suggesting that Orpheus's demise preserves some memory of these archaic practices. It is therefore interesting to note that Orpheus held a special place among the upper classes of Christian Edessa,[19] modern Sanliurfa, while links existed between the Sabians of Harran and the Greek Orphic mysteries, whose principal symbol was the serpent wrapped around the cosmic egg.[20] More significantly, the Sabians are known for having used 'talking' heads to divine the future.[21] This can be seen as still further confirmation that the Sabians inherited elements of their religious practices from the Neolithic world that had occupied the same region thousands of years beforehand.

To find that Orpheus was additionally associated with the crucifix, and might even have been equated with Jesus Christ during the early centuries of the Christian era is also important. The existence of the aforementioned magical gem with its inscription 'Orpheus Bakkikos' strongly suggests that his archaic cult was associated with the symbol of the cross, and that this might well have derived from Cygnus's role as *crucem maiorem*, the 'Greater Cross' of early Christian tradition. It is strongly possible, therefore, that the familiar image of the crucifix, having been adopted in the fifth century by Latin Christians, in fact derives from the cruciform appearance of Cygnus, venerated originally by the pagan followers of Orpheus.

Navel of the World

All this was essential background information, but it was not enough to confirm the connection between Cygnus and the Early Neolithic stone temples of southeast Turkey. Then I read that Cygnus, similarly to Lyra (*see above, p.27*), was sometimes called *Vultur cadens*, the Falling Grype, or Vulture.[22] In the knowledge that the central motif of the Early Neolithic cult of the dead in Upper Mesopotamia and at Çatal Hüyük in south-central Turkey was the vulture, I realized that its original celestial counterpart was not Lyra, but Cygnus. Had this been seen all that time ago as the original North Star, the destination both of the soul in death and of the astral journeys of the feather-clad vulture shamans, the priestly elite who presided over the Early Neolithic cult centres of Upper Mesopotamia?

Supporting this conclusion are the connections between Cygnus and the mythical Roc, or Rukh (*see above, page 31*), for this made the star group another possible candidate, together with Lyra, for the title 'eagle of the Arabians',[23] venerated by the Bedouin of southeast Turkey – especially given that Cygnus bore the Arabic name *al-Ta'ir al-Arduf* (or *Altayr*), the Flying Eagle.

Cygnus's identity as the Arabian Roc also linked it directly with the Anfar, the cosmic bird of the Yezidi, related most assuredly with the religion's *sanjak* bird totems. If this was so, then the *sanjak*'s pole-like appearance (*see fig. 3*) made it a representation of what is known to cosmologists as the cosmic axis, universally seen by cultures of the past as linking the *axis mundi*, the 'world axis', the point around which the Earth and cosmos revolve, with the northern celestial pole as the pivot point of the heavens.

Each culture had its own *axis mundi*, usually located at what was also regarded as the centre (the 'dead' centre) of the culture's homeland. The axis was generally marked by an egg-like stone, known in Greek as an *omphalos*, meaning 'navel'. This was a reference to the fact that the cosmic axis could be seen as an umbilical cord, with the Earth drawing its life blood from the source of cosmic creation. We are reminded of Göbekli Tepe, which is Turkish for 'hill of the navel', a title that embraces the idea of an *omphalos*, a sacred centre, linked directly with the northern celestial pole.[24]

Climbing the Tree

In ancient cosmologies worldwide, the cosmic axis – which could either relate to the north-south meridian line or the Milky Way[25] – was envisaged as the so-called 'World Tree', such as Yggdrasil in Norse mythology. Although standing in this world with its roots in the underworld, its branches touched the sky-world, called also the 'upper world', 'sky-land' or 'star-land'.

Often a great serpent guarded, or encircled, the base of the World Tree. For example, in Norse tradition the serpent Niðhögg coils around the roots of the Yggdrasil on which perches an eagle, while in ancient Mesopotamian mythology a similar eagle that sits atop the World Tree devours the young of the serpent guarding it. Then in Greek myth there is the multiheaded serpent named Ladon, which guards the tree of golden apples in the garden of the Hesperides, and the king cobra Muchalinda that inhabits the tree of the serpent king, under which the Buddha meditates. Turning to Hindu myth, we find that images and statues of Krishna dancing on the seven-headed serpent symbolize the inverted World Tree, with its outstretched hoods representing the roots. In fact, the concept is universal and includes also the serpent of temptation which in Judaeo-Christian tradition guards the tree of life and death and beguiles Eve, the first woman – whose Hebrew name, spelt variously *hawwa/hevia/chava* – has connotations of both 'life' and 'serpent'.[26]

Finding the Tree Bird

Whilst the serpent guarded the base of the World Tree, a bird often perched in its upper branches, which touched heaven itself. Aside from the examples cited above, there is the macaw that balances on the World Tree in Mayan myth (*see Chapter Six*), or the story preserved in Celtic myth of the god Lleu assuming the form of a bird and doing the same. The anthropologist Mircea Eliade (1907–86), who was one of the world's foremost authorities on shamanism, said that the idea of birds perched in the World Tree often embraced the magico-religious belief that human souls waited in the tree in the form of birds before incarnating on Earth:

> The Goldi, the Dolgan, and the Tungus say that, before birth, the souls of children perch like little birds on the branches of the Cosmic Tree and the shamans go there to find them. This mythical motif is not confined to Central and North Asia; it is attested, for example, in Africa and Indonesia.[27]

If the World Tree (cosmic axis) signified the Milky Way,[28] then there had to be a good chance that the 'bird' at the top of the Tree was a celestial phenomenon located where the Tree met the northern celestial pole in the extreme north of the sky. This made cosmological sense, although there is a problem – the last time that the northern celestial pole made contact with the Milky Way was *c.*13,200 BC, before even Vega became Pole Star. Prior to this time the celestial pole had for thousands of years been slowly crossing the Milky Way, reaching a maximum depth within it *c.*15,500 BC.

On realizing this, I knew that we were getting closer to understanding the greater significance of the Cygnus constellation in the ancient mindset. I say this, for it quickly became clear that between *c.*16,000–*c.*15,000 BC Deneb was the closest star to the celestial pole,[29] effectively making it Pole Star, even though it would not have been fixed but would have travelled in a tiny circle in the night sky. After it moved too far away to be classed as Pole Star, sometime *c.*15,000 BC, its place was taken by a second star in Cygnus, *delta* Cygni, which can be found in the left 'wing' of the celestial swan. This star held on to the role through until *c.*13,000 BC,[30] when it bowed out gracefully in favour of Vega in Lyra, which then remained as Pole Star through until *c.*11,000 BC.[31]

Fig. 8. The precession of the poles, showing the various previous pole stars. Note the proximity to the circle of Vega, Deneb and *delta* Cygni.

In the knowledge that the stars of Lyra are nowhere near the Milky Way, and that the only constellation crossed by the northern celestial pole when passing through the Milky Way is Cygnus, could I go on to identify this asterism as Mircea's Eliade's 'tree bird'? If so, then did this solution now go some way to explaining why the Early Neolithic priestly elite might have been interested in this constellation, orientating their stone temples and avenues towards the meridian line, where Cygnus, centrally placed in the Milky Way, swept low over the northern horizon each night, or where after 9300 BC it ceased to be circumpolar and set on the north-northwestern horizon? I could see no other more logical explanation.

Back to the Age of Scorpio

If so, then what about the serpent at the base of the World Tree? Could we go on to identify this as well? Had it too formed part of the cosmological world-view of the Early Neolithic age? Today, we stand at the threshold of the astrological age of Aquarius, in which the stars of this constellation will soon rise heliacally at the vernal, or spring, equinox, as they will do for the next 2,160 years, or one-twelfth of a precessional cycle of 25,920 years. As this happens, we leave behind the age of Pisces, which has prevailed since the time of Christ. Before that, humanity experienced an age of Aries, preceded in turn, counting backwards, by ages of Taurus, Gemini, Cancer and Leo (which ended *c.*9220 BC and marked the transition between the Late Palaeolithic hunter-gatherer lifestyle and the onset of the agricultural age).

But I wanted to reach back further in time, to the age of Scorpio, between *c.*16,500–*c.*14,300 BC. This was precisely the time-frame when initially Deneb and then *delta* Cygni acted as Pole Star – a fact which then created an incredible possibility. During this distant age, before dawn on the spring equinox, the stars of Scorpio would have been seen low on the eastern horizon, where just an hour later the new sun would have risen into the sky. The Milky Way would have flowed upwards from Scorpio to where Cygnus, the cosmic bird, occupied pole position. Bearing in mind that Scorpio was identified as a celestial serpent in various parts of the world, might its stars have been the original 'snake' that coiled itself around the base of the World Tree (the Milky Way)?

If all of this is correct, then it means that the concept of the World Tree is astronomical in nature and originated when the stars of Cygnus occupied pole position in the night sky, *c.*15,000 BC. This presented another enigma – at this period large parts of the Northern Hemisphere were in the grip of the last Ice Age.

More pressing, however, was what all of this new information might now tell us about prehistoric cult centres such as Karahan Tepe in southeast Turkey. It seemed to be orientated north towards both Deneb and the meridian line, and east-northeast towards the summer solstice sunrise, where the claws of Scorpio marked the rising point of the Milky Way before dawn in 9500 BC. Was it possible that even after Deneb and *delta* Cygni had successively ceased to be Pole Star, *c.* 13,000 BC, the stars of Cygnus, as the 'bird' of the 'World Tree', retained their former mythological significance – with Deneb even going on to be seen as the 'ultimate' North Star?

Did Cygnus become a symbol of the cosmic axis, like the bird atop the Yezidi *sanjak*, or the two stone totem poles found in pieces by Harald Hauptman at Nevali Çori (*see figs. 3 and 4*)? Remember, they were made up of human heads, from the uppermost part of which emerged a bird, positively identified in one instance as a vulture. Were the stars of the celestial bird seen to act as the gateway to heaven, the place of the afterlife? And was this the real reason why the Sabians and their kin venerated the Mystery of the North, because they were echoing extremely ancient beliefs in the potency of Cygnus as the Primal Cause – quite literally the source point of God himself?

As incredible as these concepts might seem, they imply that somewhere on the Eurasian continent,[32] the peoples of the Upper Palaeolithic world created a complete cosmological system that survived intact through to modern times, still forming part of the magico-religious practices of traditional shamanic-based cultures, most obviously in various parts of Asia. Moreover, this same belief system also inspired the Early Neolithic cult of the dead, which saw the vulture, equated as a celestial bird with the stars of Cygnus, as the vehicle for the transmigration of the soul – a concept the Early Neolithic peoples merely inherited from their Palaeolithic forebears.

Yet were these cosmological ideas *truly* Palaeolithic in origin? Had they really survived through until Neolithic times? Were Deneb and the stars of Cygnus universally seen in terms of the gateway to the sky-world, connected with not only the transmigration of the soul, but also cosmic life and death? There was only one way to find out, and this was to examine the magico-religious traditions practised among the indigenous peoples of the American continent, to see if they reflected these same profound ideas of the cosmos.

Discovery of the Americas

Orthodox theories regarding the first peoples to inhabit the American landmass suggest that they travelled across a temporary land bridge, known today as Beringia, which opened up between Siberia and Alaska during the last Ice Age. These migrations from North Asia occurred, according to the traditional academic view, shortly before a sudden change of climate caused the ice fields rapidly to disappear and the resulting meltwaters to submerge the Alaskan gateway *c.*9500–*c.*8000 BC. The golden opportunity afforded by the Beringia land bridge enabled large groups of Asian hunter-gatherers to move into new lands, and in so doing to create the Native American cultures that thrived, supposedly in isolation, until the time of Columbus.

Most forward-thinking scholars of American anthropology now dismiss these widely-held notions regarding the origins of the Native American peoples, saying that they cannot explain the gradual emergence of human settlements all over the American continent around the end of the last Ice Age. There had to be other migrational routes, most probably by sea and including, according to some, from southeast Asia and even Australia. What is more, there is now evidence to suggest that some of the continent's oldest inhabitants arrived by boat from Western Europe at the initial turning point of the Ice Age, *c.*15,000 BC.

For a very long time it was believed that the earliest peoples of the Americas were the 'Clovis' culture, who emerged *c.*11,600 years ago. They take their name from the site from which evidence of their existence was first determined in Clovis, New Mexico, and are defined by their unique stone technology. This included an easily recognizable form of bifaced blade with distinctive fluting called the 'Clovis point'.

Despite repeated evidence of even earlier levels of occupation from many sites in North America, most prehistorians have refused to accept such a possibility. However, when the theory regarding the migration of the first American peoples across the Beringia land bridge was put to the test, no evidence of a stone technology equal to that of Clovis was discovered in Siberia, the culture's assumed original homeland. Dr Bruce Bradley, an expert on prehistoric flint-knapping techniques at the Smithsonian Institution, Washington, became intrigued by the similarity between Clovis points and the seemingly identical stone technology of the Solutrean peoples of southwest France and neighbouring Spain and Portugal, who thrived *c.*20,000–*c.*17,000 years ago. He visited museums in France containing thousands of Solutrean stone tools, and became convinced that not only did they match the unique style of the Clovis stone industry, but that they were fashioned using exactly the same flint-knapping techniques.

This was an incredible discovery, indeed too incredible for most prehistorians. They wanted considerably more evidence before accepting that Europeans were the earliest ancestors of the Native American peoples. However, further evidence of the Solutrean-Clovis link came with the discovery at Cactus Hill, Virginia, of a Clovis-style bifaced point which predated the Clovis horizon of *c.*11,600 BC by at least 4,000–6,000 years. This was even closer in style to the Solutrean tools, produced until *c.*15,000 BC. Indeed, it appeared to represent an intermediary stage between the Solutrean and Clovis stone technologies, adding further weight to the theory.

Based on the similarities between the Solutrean, Clovis and Cactus Hill points, Bruce Bradley and his colleague Dennis Stanford, also of the Smithsonian, went on to propose that West Europeans at the turning point of the last Ice Age, *c.*15,000 BC, used a basic seafaring technology, similar to that of the indigenous Inuit of Alaska, to navigate the melting ice floe and glaciers in versatile skin-covered skiffs to reach the American continent.[33]

Regardless of whether these extraordinary discoveries prove to be correct or not, and they are not accepted by mainstream prehistorians,[34] I strongly suspect that the magico-religious mindset of the first Native American peoples was heavily influenced by shamanic ideologies that originated in the Eurasian continent. Once the Beringia land bridge became submerged, and there was no opportunity to return to Asia, any cosmological ideas transferred to the American continent via this line of transmission would thereafter have evolved in isolation, meaning that if they still matched those present among the shamanic-based cultures of the ancient world, then the two almost certainly had a common origin that dated back to Palaeolithic times.

If I was to discover a previously unrecognized veneration of Cygnus, the cosmic axis and the Milky Way among the original inhabitants of the Americas, then this would greatly increase the chances that my theories regarding the cosmological origins of the Neolithic cult of the dead were correct. As we shall see in the next section of the book, this line of enquiry would provide me with the first major clues to better understanding the minds of those who established the earliest known stone temples in southeast Turkey some 11,500 years ago.

PART TWO

AMERICA

CHAPTER FIVE

On the Wolf Trail

An age-old legend told by each generation of the Blackfoot tribe, whose territories include the Rocky Mountains in the northwest United States, goes as follows: When the Earth was young, and the Spomi-tapi-ksi (sky-beings) who lived in sky-land still visited, mortal humans wandered the forests and trails unable to hunt wild animals or survive the long winters. So the first of the Ksahkomi-tapi-ksi (Earth-beings) to take pity on them were Makoiyi, the wolves. They noticed a youth and his family starving, and so came before them as young men, delivering meat which they took back to their tipi. After this, the wolves allowed the family to run with them, so that they might learn how to cooperate with one another when it came to hunting the buffalo and other such beasts. It was the wolves who said that they were to eat only those animals which have hoofs and horns, while those with paws and claws should be left alone.

When spring came, it was time for the wolves to leave. With sadness they took their original form and departed for good. Yet they are still visible in the night sky as stars which remind us of how we can live together. What is more, in honour of their great compassion towards humankind, the path to sky-land is called the Wolf Trail, although to those who are not of the Blackfoot lineage it is known as the Milky Way.

The Wolf Trail has always been a sacred path that permits the spirits of the dead to enter the next world, where they can lead harmonious lives at one with the wolf. Indeed, there is no question that the wolf is a Blackfoot totem with shamanic overtones, since they believe that the animal's eyes are one and the same as their own: in other words they can see with them to hunt or go on astral journeys. The wolf has always been revered by the Blackfoot, and both man and beast observed a truce not to kill each other – a pact that remained in place until the arrival of the white man.

Blackfoot Battle Shield

A representation of the Wolf Trail was once to be found on the Blackfoot's battle shield.[1] This shows a longitudinal white bar amid a darker region, in the middle of which is a stretched line with an equal-armed cross at the centre (*see fig. 9*). At each end of the white line are circles enclosing large crosses, their arms terminating in T-shaped devices (Tau-crosses) found universally in celestial symbolism.

Almost certainly, the design's longitudinal white line represents the Milky Way, the Wolf Trail, arching from one horizon to the other, meaning that the circles containing the Tau crosses symbolize the Earth, divided into four quarters (each circle also has a double set of twenty V-shaped 'teeth', twenty being a sacred number associated in Native American mythology with the human race, since we have ten fingers and ten toes). The crosses no doubt symbolize a fourfold reflection of the cosmic axis, with the horizontal bar representing the Blackfoot concept of the sky-land. This left only the elongated cross design at the centre of the Wolf Trail, and in my opinion this signifies the stars of Cygnus, or the Northern Cross as it is more usually known in the United States.

If the Blackfoot shield does show the Northern Cross at the centre of the Milky Way, then there is every chance that this arcane knowledge was passed down through countless generations, having been carried into the American continent by settlers from the Eurasian continent sometime prior to the submergence of the Beringia land bridge, *c.*9500–*c.*8000 BC. The manner in which the Wolf Trail myth incorporated a scenario that spoke of the earliest human beings having been taught how to hunt, survive and cooperate, both with each other and the animal kingdom, has a ring of authenticity about it, suggesting that it could well have originated among the hunter-gatherers of the Upper Palaeolithic age.

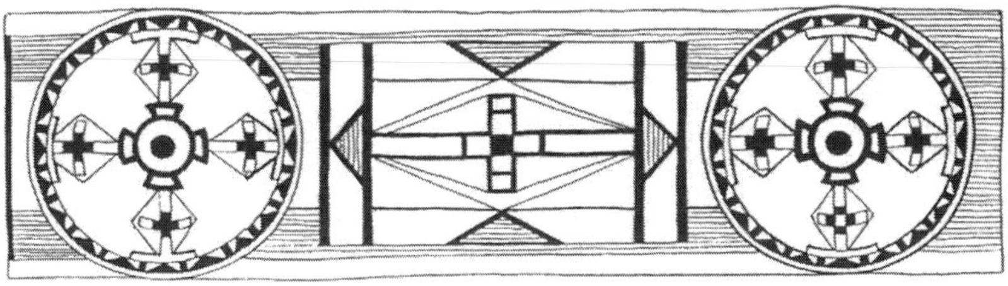

Fig. 9. The Blackfoot concept of the Wolf Trail, with the long white bar symbolising the Milky Way and the central cross most probably representing Cygnus as the 'Cross Star'.

Spider Man and the Giant Turnip

The Blackfoot, like so many other Native American tribes, preserve stories concerning the cosmic axis that joins Earth to heaven via the Pole Star. For them it is accessed through a hole at the base of the sky-world, plugged from above by a giant turnip. On one occasion a mortal named Feather Woman, who was abducted to skyland by a divine being called Morning Star and taken as his wife, defies what she has been told and decides to remove the turnip to see what lies beneath it. Unable to do so, she enlists the aid of two passing cranes.[2] One of them chants the Medicine Song to each of the four directions and the turnip comes free. Looking through the hole, Feather Woman sees the Earth, and her people going about their daily business, making her feel homesick. This indiscretion results in her being sent home, and so with the help of another entity named Spider Man, she and her baby, Star Boy, are let down on a thread.[3]

Whether or not she uses the Wolf Trail on her return journey is not recorded, although later in the same story a being called Poïa, a son of the Sun and Moon, and the divine messenger to the Blackfoot, uses the Wolf Trail as 'the short path to the Earth'.[4]

The characters and places featured in this traditional Blackfoot account are almost certainly stars and other celestial bodies. For instance, Spider Man is the constellation we know today as Hercules, while his lodge is the nearby star group known as the Northern Crown.[5] Hercules was on the path of the celestial pole *c.*9500 BC, suggesting that the two cranes were likewise constellations in the same vicinity, and it was my hunch that they signified stars. Images of cranes, generally in fourfold form, feature prominently on several engraved shell pendants found in Ohio grave mounds of the prehistoric Hopewell culture. These surround an equal-armed 'solar' cross, which is more likely to represent the cosmic axis than the sun, as most scholars seem to believe. If so, then there is every chance that they represent the Northern Cross, which, we find, was known to the Tipai tribe of California as, collectively, the 'Cross Star'.[6] The link between the Pole Star and crosses, swastikas and serpents in Native American art is confirmed by the findings of archaeoastronomer Thaddeus M. Cowan, whose work in this field we shall come to shortly.[7]

The Hopewell Legacy

I felt the need to examine the rich legacy left to us by the Ohio mound-building culture known as the Hopewell, who emerged onto the scene sometime during the first millennium BC. They constructed thousands of gigantic earthworks in all shapes and configurations, the exact purpose of which is unknown. Yet frustratingly, the Hopewell left behind very little trace of their beliefs and practices before passing on the baton of mound-building to their successors – the Fort Ancient culture, who rose to prominence *c.* AD 1000 and who were still present when the first Europeans arrived here in the sixteenth century.

To learn more about the silent world of the Hopewell, Sue and I joined our friends Greg and Lora Little, both of whom have authored books in this field of study.[8] They offered to show us a selection of Native American sites in the states of Ohio, Kentucky and Tennessee,[9] the first of which we reached shortly before sunset one evening in July 2004.

Located in a state park in a suburban area of Newark, Ohio, it consists of a gigantic tree-covered earthwork, ring-like in appearance, with a single opening that leads the visitor into a massive grass and tree-covered recreational area. Known locally as Great Circle, or the Fairgrounds, due to its communal usage by settlers in the nineteenth century, this scenic monument is actually a raised circular henge around 366 metres (1,200 feet) in diameter and three metres (10 feet) in height, with an internal ditch of equal depth filled today with dense undergrowth. Archaeologists have established that it was constructed sometime *c.*100 BC by the Hopewell, although why exactly is the greater enigma.

At the centre of the enormous circular plateau is a curious earthwork known locally as Eagle Mound (*see fig. 10*). Formed out of four conjoined elliptical mounds, it is seen by archaeologists as an 'effigy' mound, in that it has the general appearance of a bird with 'head', 'body' and 'wings'. Its specific positioning at the centre of the henge allows the observer to see the sun rise within the gap formed by the site's only opening at the time of the summer solstice. Exactly when it was constructed is unclear, although probably it originally functioned either as a ceremonial platform or as a communal burial mound, perhaps both.

My first impressions of Newark's Great Circle was that it greatly resembled Avebury, England's largest and second most popular megalithic complex after Stonehenge. At 427 metres (1,396 feet) in diameter, it is similar in size and height to its counterpart in Ohio. Moreover, both monuments have a deep ditch positioned *inside* the circular earthwork, implying that they were constructed for ceremonial, and not defensive, purposes. The only major difference between the two henges is that, unlike Avebury (featured in Chapter Eight), Great Circle has no rings of standing stones – earth alone being seen as sufficient for the needs of the Hopewell people.

For me, it was Eagle Mound that kept drawing my attention, leading Greg to

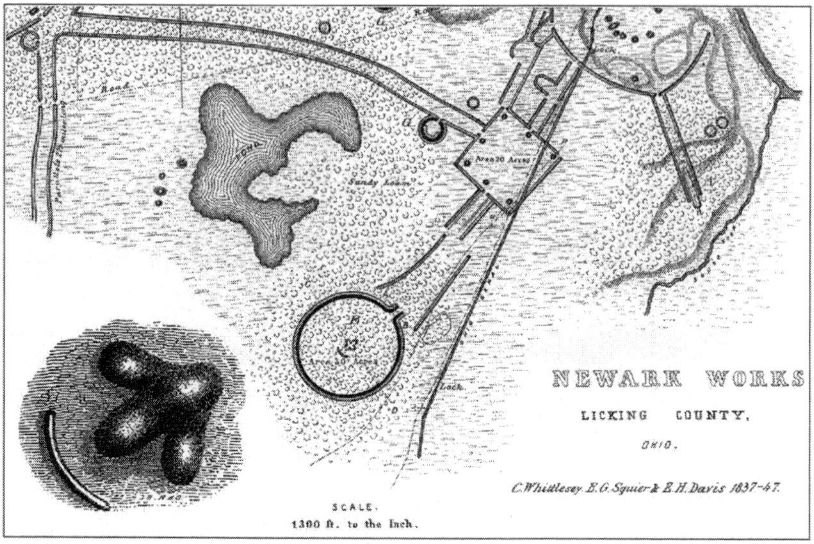

Fig. 10. Great Circle enclosing Eagle Mound, from Squier and Davis, 1837–47, with Eagle Mound both at its centre and enlarged (bottom left).

ask me what I felt about the place. After due consideration, I offered the opinion that the mound's bird-like character was most probably deliberate. If not simply a clan totem, then Eagle Mound's apparent orientation towards the site's only entrance/exit hinted at it signifying some form of avian psychopomp, a 'soul-carrier', the role played by vultures in the Early Neolithic world of southeast Turkey.

I suggested that it was even possible that the bodies of those about to journey beyond death to the sky-world might have been subjected to the process of excarnation, known to have been practised by a number of Native American tribes. I imagined also that for some hours prior to the solstice sunrise a ritual would have been performed on the mound itself. If so, then I wondered whether the henge's opening additionally marked the direction of a constellation that might have risen heliacally, that is immediately prior to the sun on the same day. It might even have been that the Milky Way was seen to rise up into the sky from this position.

Many Native American tribes saw the Milky Way as the 'ghost path' to the land of the dead, accessed via the local horizon. For instance, the Chumash of South California saw the Milky Way as the ghost road to Shimilaqsha, the Land of the Dead, which they located in the west.[10] Similarly, the Cheyenne – American Plains Indians who until the nineteenth century inhabited the regions adjacent to the

Platte and Arkansas rivers – identified the Milky Way as the Hanging Road, along which the spirits journey to enter the afterlife.[11] It was much the same story among the Iroquois, Delaware, Ojibway, Menominee, Cree, Thompson, Northern and Southern Paiute, Ute, and Karok peoples, to mention just a few.[12] All saw the Milky Way as a celestial highway used by the dead to reach the next world, suggesting that this concept might well have had its roots among much earlier cultures, such as the Hopewell, the builders of Newark's Great Circle.

Having voiced my first impressions of the site, Greg told me that archaeological excavations had indeed revealed that excarnation took place here. Moreover, the bones of no fewer than eighteen individuals were recovered from Eagle Mound. As a consequence of this information, I questioned whether this earthwork even represented an eagle, since it might just as easily have been a scavenger, such as a crow or vulture. This said, I respected the fact that both the eagle and the mysterious eagle-like Thunderbird were revered as symbols of the Great Spirit among many Native American tribes, and that often these birds were carved at the apex of totem poles, which, once again, were clear representations of a celestial bird atop the cosmic axis (*see above, page 37*).

It became clear from the many Hopewell sites we were to visit in the days ahead that this faceless people expressed an extremely ancient magico-religious view of the cosmos, reflected in their incredible fine art and also in the complexity of their monuments, which hint at communal activities on an incredible scale. Their festivals and processions must have been something to behold, and whether they were solar, lunar or stellar based, I can imagine that they reflected the ebbs and flows of the Earth's very essence – and yet in the end the Hopewell simply disappeared without trace. Who they were and what happened to them is a complete mystery that simply adds to their lingering mystique, echoed in the silence of earthworks such as the octagons, circles, squares and mounds that remained intact until many were destroyed by European settlers, who did not understand their grace and beauty.

Going Down to Nashville

With a sense of irritation at what was once, but is no more, we reached Greg and Lora's home city of Memphis, Tennessee. Here the investigations continued with a trip out to Nashville's Vanderbilt University, where an afternoon was spent in the Heard Library researching Native American star lore.

By now, I was certain that the Milky Way, as a ghost path to the spirit world, played a significant role in the funerary practices performed by the Hopewell at Newark's Great Circle, an assumption that proved to be stunningly accurate. Back in the United Kingdom, Rodney Hale was able to ascertain that before dawn on the summer solstice *c.*2,100 years ago, an observer standing on Eagle Mound would have been able to watch the Milky Way rising vertically into a more or less overhead position between Great Circle's only opening, where the sun itself would have risen exactly two hours later.[13]

I sensed strongly that the souls of the dead were seen to exit Great Circle and then climb the ghost path either in the form of a bird, or under the protection of an avian psychopomp. Their journey took them to the upper heights of the Milky Way, where they gained access to the sky-world via a 'hole', corresponding to the position of the celestial bird. This 'hole', I felt sure, was not Polaris, the current Pole Star, but Deneb, the brightest star of Cygnus, which would have been seen almost directly overhead in the middle of the Milky Way (*see fig.11*).

The Bird's Foot

Adding weight to this bold assertion is the work of archaeoastronomer Thaddeus M. Cowan of the Department of Psychology, Kansas State University.[14] He has proposed that many effigy mounds are terrestrial representations of constellations since they face the sky; are difficult to identify from the ground; and are extremely large – one 3,500-year-old bird effigy mound at Poverty Point, Louisiana, being 195 metres (640 feet) from wing tip to wing tip.[15] More importantly, he has concluded, for reasons outlined in Chapter Six, that many bird effigy mounds, including Newark's Eagle Mound, *represent the stars of Cygnus.*[16]

Taking the matter one step further is writer Jim Brandon in his compelling book *The Rebirth of Pan* (1983),[17] about American mysteries old and new. Here he suggests that Eagle Mound is not so much an eagle, but the representation of a bird's foot. This seems to have been an extraordinary insight, for research undertaken at Nashville's Heard Library revealed that the Skidi Pawnee (or 'Wolf' Pawnee) recognized a constellation known as Rikutski/Rikucki (the Bird's Foot) or Kit-u-rau-us-u (the Turkey's Foot). Furthermore, there is powerful evidence to suggest that they identified it with the principal stars of Cygnus.[18]

The bird's foot was a device painted as a mark of office on the forehead of warriors during certain rituals, since we read:

> He takes red ointment and with his fingers makes two straight marks down the right side of his face and two down the left side ... then he makes a picture of the bird's foot upon his forehead. That bird's foot

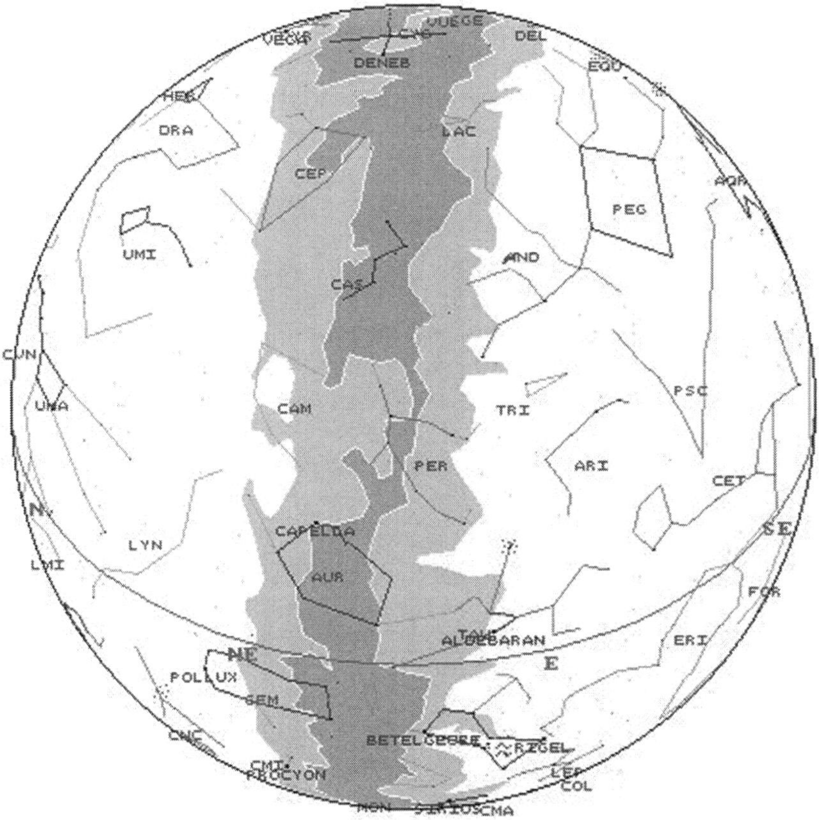

Fig. 11. The Milky Way rising up into the sky to reach the Cygnus constellation as viewed from Great Circle, Newark, two hours before sunrise at midsummer in 100 BC.

is not intended for a real bird's foot; it is the bird's claw picture in the Milky Way in the heavens.[19] (At the same time a ball of down feathers would be placed on the head and an eagle feather attached to the scalp-lock.)[20]

Directly related to the Bird's Foot constellation was 'a star at the north end of the Milky Way which guarded the pathway, [and] received the spirits of the dead' as they entered the upper world.[21] The identity of this star 'in the Milky Way' has caused much debate, with Von Del Chamberlain, a noted expert on Skidi Pawnee star lore concluding initially that it might have been any star between Cygnus and Perseus. Then he proposed it was *delta* Cephei, a faint star in the constellation of Cepheus, connected in classical myth with a crowned king. However, this identification makes no sense, since *delta* Cephei is not even on the Milky Way. Chamberlain went on to suggest Deneb as a possible candidate,[22] a better choice by far, not just because it is located on the Milky Way, but also because it was known to the Skidi Pawnee under the mysterious name of the Second Black Star, its description suggesting that it might have links with death and the afterlife.[23] More peculiar is that the 'star at the north end of the Milky Way', which I feel has to be Deneb, was confused by the Skidi Pawnee with the true Pole Star, Polaris. This implied that the Skidi Pawnee saw Deneb as more important than the current Pole Star, a fact which Chamberlain was unable to explain.[24]

The Bird's Foot constellation was linked in Skidi Pawnee tradition with the Morning Star, seen by Chamberlain as Mars, the protector of warriors.[25] Its 'mark' – three straight lines converging to a single point to form a V shape – was worn when one of their number was dispatched to seek and capture a maiden for sacrifice in the name of the planet. During this archaic practice, the unfortunate girl would wear a hawk on her head as she ascended the scaffold, since the hawk and eagle were both symbols of the Morning Star (the Bird's Foot constellation is occasionally named as 'eagle claw'[26]).[27]

The Skidi Pawnee's ritual sacrifice of the maiden brought to mind the Blackfoot story recounted earlier of how Morning Star abducted Feather Woman to sky-land and took her as his wife (*see above, p.46*). The fact that it was she who removed the giant turnip covering the hole in the celestial pole with the aid of two passing cranes hints strongly at the fact that she was a female personification of the Pole Star, and arguably even an asterism formed from the stars of Cygnus.

The Bird's Foot constellation was familiar also to the Tewa/Tano nation of Arizona, who are related to the Hopi. For them, it was the foot of a celestial turkey, a bird prized among the Pueblo farmers of the Four Corners region. Ethnologist John P. Harrington wrote in 1916 that it is 'an easily learned constellation of the exact form of a turkey's foot',[28] although frustratingly he did not identify it. Ethnoastronomers accept that it was most probably formed, like the Bird's Foot constellation of the Skidi Pawnee, by the principal stars of Cygnus.[29] This makes complete sense, because the Bird's Foot 'mark' can easily be drawn using Deneb (*alpha* Cygni), Gienah (*epsilon* Cygni), Sadr (*gamma* Cygni), and the formally

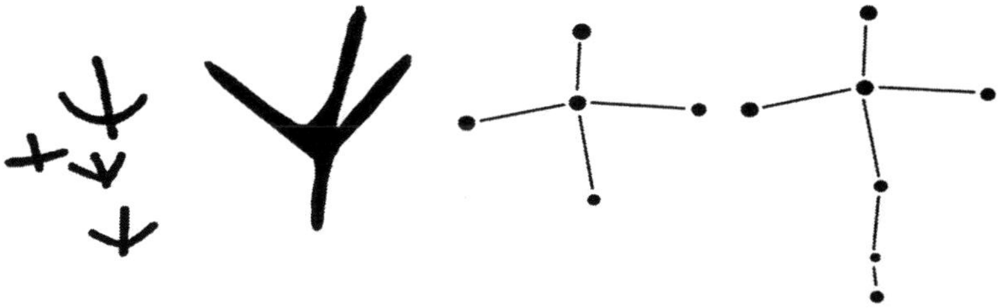

Fig. 12. Petroglyphs of the Bird's Foot, from a site along the Rio Grande (left), and the stars of Cygnus used to form the same symbol, after Miller.

nameless *delta* Cygni (*see fig. 12*). Indeed, in Western astronomy these four stars are sometimes called 'the Triangles', due to their easily recognizable formation.

All this implies that Newark's Eagle Mound might not in fact be an abstract raptor, but simply, as Jim Brandon proposes, the bird's foot symbol. If so, then the fact that this effigy mound would seem to represent the Cygnus constellation, implies that the Hopewell, like the later Skidi Pawnee and the Tewa/Tano, recognized this asterism in terms of the Bird's Foot, or Turkey's Foot. What is more, the fact that Great Circle seems to have been orientated towards the Milky Way on the shortest night of the year, tells us that the Hopewell also saw the Bird Foot's constellation, that is Cygnus, as the destination of the soul in death.

Moving on to the Luiseño tribe of southern California, we find that they envisaged a celestial buzzard composed of the three stars that make up what astronomers call the 'Summer Triangle' – Deneb in Cygnus, Vega in Lyra and Altair in Aquila. This shows, once again, the universal identification of these three stars, as well as this particular area of the heavens, with a celestial bird of one sort or another.[30] Did this avian connection derive originally from the Eurasian continent, as I was beginning to conclude?

The Swan-Mother

The Oneida tribe of New York state preserve a creation myth which tells how Sky Woman descended from the upper world via a hole, or 'pit', i.e. the cosmic axis, created when an apple tree was uprooted by her father, Great Spirit. Her fall into the lower world was cushioned by a flock of swans, which let her down gently onto the back of a giant turtle that emerged from the primeval waters to create the first land. It is for this reason that the Oneida honour the swan in ritual.

Fig. 13. Wooden swans on sky-poles erected next to altars by the Reindeer Tungus shamans of Manchuria, northeast Asia.

We have here yet another link between the Pole Star and a celestial bird, in this instance a swan, a mythological form of the Cygnus constellation. It is a relationship found also among the Reindeer Tungus tribes of northwest Manchuria and Siberia, who erected sky-poles signifying the cosmic axis, on top of which they would affix a carved wooden swan in flight (*see fig. 13*).[31] These bird totems were placed in association with outdoor altars, as this was the manner in which the shaman was able to reach the sky world during ecstatic trance states known as 'soul flights'.[32]

The same process is displayed in rock art found at Perinos on the southern cape of Lake Onega in Russia. Here among a plethora of figures and waterfowl, mostly swans, is the image of a swan atop a sky-pole, which is actually being climbed at right angles by a small walking figure, most obviously a shaman.[33]

It is a magico-religious practice echoed also by the Lapp shamans of Finland, who were said to have been carried on the back of a swan called *Saivo-lodde*, the bird from a magical place called *Saivo*, 'to that realm of mystery where he learned what is hidden to ordinary mortals.'[34]

Linked with the Oneida foundation legend is another told by the ancient Ainu, the original non-Mongoloid inhabitants of Japan. They speak of how their race was created by the union of a goddess who came down from paradise and adopted the mantle of a swan in order to raise and eventually marry a lone child, the last Ainu left alive following an almighty battle with a mortal enemy.[35]

The Buriat shamans of Siberia say that their tribe is descended from an eagle and a swan, and, like the Ainu of Japan, honour an ancestral swan-mother in migration ceremonies during the spring and autumn.[36] They believe that if anyone harms a swan, or even mishandles swan feathers, it will bring about illness and even death, while if a man harms a woman, then he must suffer the wrath of the swans.

Finally, in Central Asia, the Altaian Turks preserve a cosmological myth in which before even the creation of heaven and Earth the highest god Tengere Kaira Khan and his companion, the first man, are depicted as black geese,[37] while the shamans of the Altaian Lebed Tatar tribes say that creation occurred after God ordered a white swan to dive into the primordial ocean and fetch silt that became the first land.[38] This form of myth involving a diving bird (although not always a swan) which creates the first land, is common among the tribal peoples of Central and Northern Asia, and often features a cosmic egg that emerges from the primordial waters to form the physical universe.[39]

Fig. 14. Rock engravings from Perinos, southern cape of Lake Onega, Russia, showing various swans including the ascent of a shaman upon a swan-capped sky-pole.

Such stories provide firm evidence of an age-old cult which saw the swan as sacred on both the American and Eurasian continents, and whose shamans or priests used mantles of swan feathers in order to undertake otherworldly journeys using the sky-pole. Cygnus's strong association with a celestial bird – a buzzard, turkey, crane, eagle, swan or goose in the examples cited in this chapter – all confirm that this star group, with its bright star Deneb, was seen as both the ultimate celestial bird and the cosmic axis of space. This was marked by a hole, like the one featured in the legends of the Blackfoot and Oneida, which enabled the souls of shamans and the dead to enter the sky-world.

In all likelihood, the Oneida's own belief in an original Sky Woman, who descended with the help of swans from the upper world via the sky-pole in order to bring life to the lower world, derives from a similar source to those cited here from Eastern and Northern Asia, and was carried into the American continent during Late Palaeolithic times.

This initial excursion into Native American star lore convinced me that Cygnus played a crucial role in North America's ethnoastronomy going back beyond the age of the Hopewell mound builders to the epoch of the very earliest peoples to arrive from the Eurasian continent. Like so many cultures of the ancient world, the Native Americans would seem to have identified Deneb as the ultimate North Star, and the gateway to the sky-world (even though Polaris, the current Pole Star, became confusingly entangled with this age-old stellar mythos).

As well as the place of the afterlife, the sky-world was thought to have been inhabited by sky-beings, such as the Spomi-tapi-ksi of the Blackfoot, who although personified as constellations, were viewed as sentient beings able to travel to Earth via either the sky-pole, equated with the north-south meridian line, or the Milky Way itself. It was these same routes that shamans on both continents used to communicate with the sky-beings in order that they might either call on their assistance on behalf of the tribe, or learn otherworldly knowledge and wisdom.

There was much more I needed to review in order to understand better the extent to which Native American peoples viewed the stars of Cygnus. Yet for the moment I wanted to transfer my attentions to the ethnoastronomy found in other parts of the American continent. I needed to see whether the same patterns in native star lore and cosmology existed there too, and very quickly it became clear that a profound knowledge of Cygnus, and its relationship to both the northern celestial pole and the Milky Way, was present among many ancient peoples of the Americas. What is more, its stars were almost always seen in association with cosmic life and death and the transmigration of the soul.

CHAPTER SIX

Maya Cosmogenesis

The mysterious origins of the Olmec civilization of central Mexico remain obscure, their lingering legacy being only the series of city complexes they have left behind, generally on the coastal plain of the Gulf of Mexico, south of Vera Cruz and Tabasco. Among the most enigmatic of these is La Venta, built *c.* 1200 BC on an island positioned in a coastal swamp within sight of what was then the Río Palma river.

Before the southern end of the site was partially demolished to make way for a petroleum refinery, making access impossible today, La Venta's central plaza consisted of a group of elliptical mounds positioned either side of a ball court, with a unique 'Great Pyramid' built on a square base at the southern end. Constructed from an estimated 99,109 cubic metres (3.5 million cubic feet) of earth, it was found to be fluted to create the image of a ten-sided pyramid. However, this distinctive effect is now thought by archaeologists to be the result of nearly three thousand years of erosion, and that it was originally a four-sided structure like all other pyramids in Mexico.

Although never excavated, the pyramid most probably contains the tomb of a very important ruler, whose appearance might be gleaned from any of the massive stone heads found at sites like La Venta. Each one sports American-style football helmets, most probably of the type used in the bloody games that we know took place in the ball courts that seem to dominate the various ceremonial centres. These basalt heads, the largest of which are 2.75 metres (9 feet, 4 inches) in height and weigh up to several tonnes, have long been argued to possess African facial features, although the fact that they also have East Asian-like eyefolds suggests that the true answer to the ethnological origins of the Olmec is more complicated than people imagine.

The site's central axis is aligned just west of true north, with another, much smaller, stepped pyramid at its point of termination (*see fig. 16*). The mounds between them were found to contain piles of offerings and other items including jade celts and iron mirrors, as well as a series of buried pavements. Four of these, the most impressive of all, were found to be 4.6 metres by 6 metres (15 feet by 20 feet) in size and made from exactly 485 blocks of serpentine. Before being deliberately covered with thick layers of clay and adobe, they had been beautifully fashioned into abstract jaguar masks, the jaguar being associated with the Olmec understanding of the night sky.

The stone carvings and movable artefacts retrieved from La Venta – many of which are now on display in a local museum park – have increased our knowledge of the Olmec, although in many ways they have also made them even more enigmatic than before. All we know for certain is that prior to their demise *c.*400 BC, the Olmec passed on the baton of civilization in the region to what was then just a fledgling culture, known to us today as the Maya. While the exact relationship between the two cultures remains uncertain, the Maya adopted elements of the Olmec's written language and calendrical system, and saw themselves as their material and spiritual successors.

Eight Degrees West of North

It was the orientation of the La Venta site, precisely eight degrees west of true north, that first intrigued archaeologist Marion Popenoe Hatch at the beginning of the 1970s. She became determined to grasp the site's greater purpose, including the function of its ten-sided pyramid. A colleague suggested that La Venta might have had an astronomical function, since, like various other Olmec sites, it seemed to be targeting something in the northern sky. Starting with the premise that Olmec astronomy took a full thousand years of observations to blossom, Hatch began with a start date of 2000 BC (*see fig. 15*).

Working together with an academic astronomer, the first thing Hatch realized was that no Pole Star existed at that time. This meant that if La Venta's pyramid and mound complex were, as she felt, 'built for the purpose of making astronomical observations and calendrical computations',[1] then she would need to look for a star that might set in alignment with the site's north-northwesterly axis line.[2]

One constellation attracted her immediate attention, and this was Ursa Major, the Great Bear or Big Dipper. This had long been used as an astronomical 'star clock', since its 'bowl', a trapezoid made up of four bright stars, is easily recognizable in the night sky. Furthermore, the constellation is usually circumpolar at this latitude and remains visible (clouds permitting) throughout the year. So after consulting various

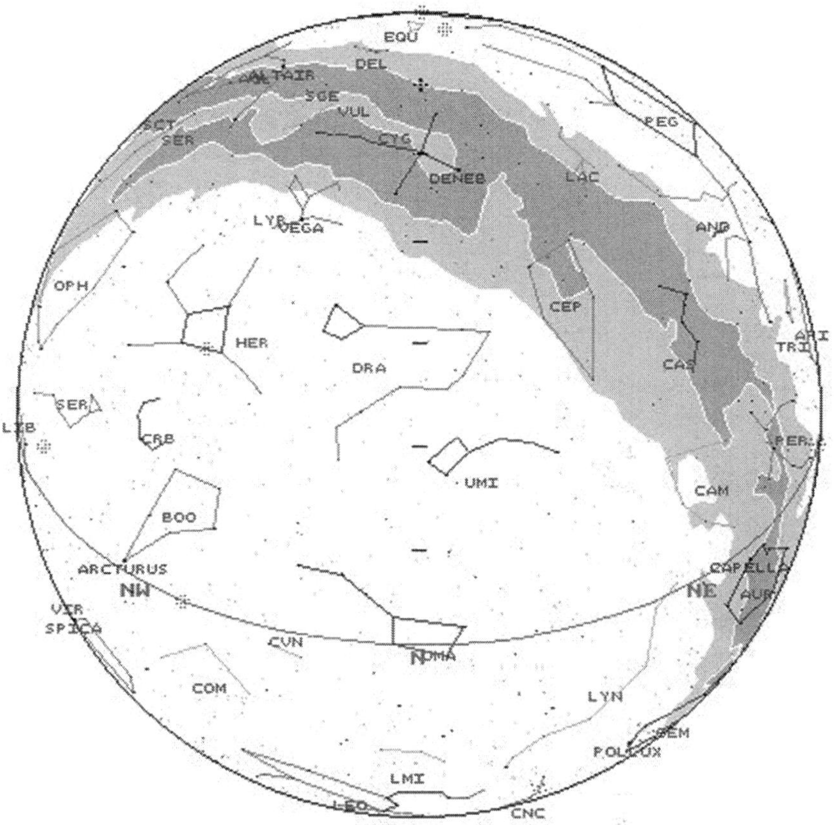

Fig. 15. The northern sky as viewed from Mexico at midnight on midsummer's night 2000 BC, showing Cygnus on its upper meridian transit and Ursa Major on its lower meridian transit.

star charts, Hatch realized that at midnight on 21 June, the summer solstice, the centre point of the Big Dipper's bowl crossed the meridian at its *lowest* point. Indeed, its bottom stars seemed almost to graze the northern horizon. This intrigued her, and so looking closer at the night sky she noticed that at the very same time, Sadr (*gamma* Cygni), the star at the very centre of Cygnus's cruciform pattern, crossed the meridian at its *highest* point.

The sight of the two constellations passing the meridian in opposite directions, one above the other with the celestial pole in the centre, would, so Hatch believed, have appealed to the mindset of whomsoever witnessed this celestial phenomenon. Since it was also the day that signalled the commencement of the rainy season, when the vegetation began to bud, the whole event might well have been seen as a moment of transition, marking the new year, the beginning and end of a calendrical cycle. As Hatch herself commented: 'Such an event would have been rather spectacular when occurring halfway through the night of the same day that the sun rose and set at its northernmost station of the year.'[3]

The Fourfold Calendar of the Olmec

Beyond all this celestial sparring at midnight on 21 June 2000 BC was the sheer fact that as Sadr crossed the meridian, the sun would have been precisely 180 degrees, or twelve hours away, close to the constellation Leo, the celestial lion (actually between Leo and neighbouring Cancer). That this asterism would have made its own midnight meridian transit exactly six months later on 21 December, the time of the winter solstice, placed Cygnus in direct opposition to it.[4]

Furthermore, if an observer were to glance due east at midnight on 21 June 2000 BC, he or she would have seen the Pleiades star cluster just rising. Turning then to face due west the observer would have seen the constellation of Scorpio about to set on the horizon, meaning that the Milky Way would have trailed down from the meridian, where Cygnus was at its zenith, to the position of Scorpio in the west.[5]

This fixed relationship between Cygnus, Leo, the Pleiades and Scorpio provided the Olmec's antecedents with a perfect fourfold division of the solar calendar. For in addition to Leo's midnight meridian transit on 21 December 2000 BC, we find that on 22 September, the autumn equinox, the Pleiades made its own midnight meridian transit, while on 21 March, the spring equinox, Scorpio did the same.[6]

Cygnus, the Pleiades, Leo and Scorpio. Each reached its zenith on the meridian at midnight in 2000 BC on either a solstice or an equinox – the four great turning points of the year. Did these constitute the most important star groups of the night sky during this distant epoch? Such a supposition seemed difficult to deny.

The Purpose of La Venta

The same basic phenomenon of Sadr and the centre point of the bowl of Ursa Major aligning on the meridian at midnight on 21 June would have continued virtually unaltered in the night sky for the next 800–1,000 years, bringing us to the age of the Olmec culture, and the building of La Venta. The slow process of precession would have changed the time that the stars crossed the meridian only slightly. In 1000 BC certain of the stars making up the bowl of Ursa Major would set below the horizon each night just as Sadr reached its highest point. However, at around half past midnight Dubhe (*alpha* Ursae Majoris), the Big Dipper's brightest star, would have crossed the meridian going eastwards as Sadr crossed overhead going westwards.

Due to precession, the centre point of the bowl was now slightly askew of north, and would have been seen to disappear below the horizon at an azimuth of eight degrees west of north – exactly the same orientation as La Venta.

Furthermore, a small mound positioned northwest of La Venta's main pyramid was found to be orientated precisely towards where Sadr set on the horizon in 1000 BC.[7] Thus a gradual accumulation of hard fact finally convinced Marion Popenoe Hatch that the Olmec had been using astronomical calculations that were already 1,000 years old when La Venta was built, and that Cygnus moving in conjunction with Ursa Major heralded the apparent new year from 2000 BC through until the age of the Olmec civilization.

Hatch envisaged La Venta's astronomical observations each midsummer being accompanied by magico-religious rites that would have begun before midnight and culminated sometime after sunrise. In support of this idea, she cited the fact that

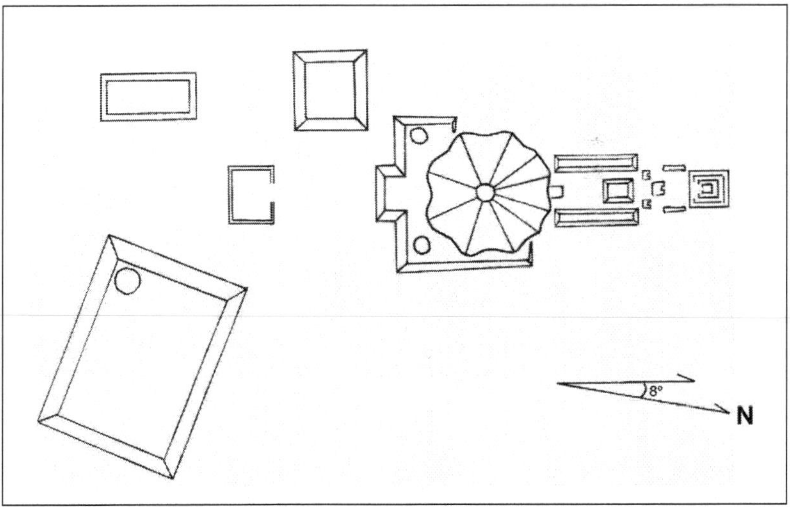

Fig. 16. Plan of the Olmec city of La Venta, showing its central axis eight degrees west of north, which targets the centre point of Ursa Major's bowl on its lower transit in 1000 BC.

among the Maidu tribe of California, it was the role of the priest-shaman to calculate accurately the countdown to midsummer dawn celebrations by observing the stars of the Big Dipper.[8]

All this brought to mind my opinions regarding the solstitial festivities which I imagined having accompanied the appearance of the Milky Way on the horizon at Newark's Great Circle in the hours prior to the appearance of the midsummer sun *c.*100 BC (*see above, page 48*). I felt sure that this event had involved ceremonial practices that continued through to sunrise, when the solar disc appeared on the horizon between the only break in the henge's huge earthen bank.

Marching Bears and Bird Effigies

I thought also about Newark's Eagle Mound, its alignment towards this very same opening, and the role Cygnus would seem to have played in the cosmological world of the Hopewell culture. Archaeoastronomer Thaddeus M. Cowan, who has identified certain Native American bird effigy mounds with Cygnus, noted that they are very often close to *bear* effigy mounds.[9] He sees these as terrestrial representations of the Big Dipper as the Great Bear (Ursa Major) – an Old World attribution that almost certainly goes back to Palaeolithic times.

A set of mounds known as the 'Marching Bear Group' in the Effigy Mounds National Park at McGregor, Iowa, are placed in the immediate vicinity of three bird effigy mounds. These, Cowan suspects, represent the movement of Cygnus in relation to Ursa Major's own shifting position around the celestial pole. In August and September some 2,000 years ago, the Great Bear reached the bottom of its 'summer swing' in the northern sky, i.e. the *lowest* point in its midnight meridian transit. At the same time, as Marion Popenoe Hatch had quite independently worked out in connection with La Venta, the stars of Cygnus cross the meridian directly above those of Ursa Major. This harmonious relationship between the two constellations matches very well the manner in which the bear and bird effigy mounds are laid out on the ground, leading Cowan to conclude that they signify the revolving motion of Ursa Major and Cygnus around the celestial pole in the late summer months.[10]

Not only does this new information strengthen the findings of Hatch concerning the Olmec's use of these two constellations, it also confirms that the Hopewell and their successors represented Cygnus in bird effigy mounds and saw this star group as a celestial time marker. What is more, if Cowan is correct and the Hopewell did identify the stars of Ursa Major with a cosmic bear, then there has to be a chance that this association really does date back to Palaeolithic times and was imported into the Americas from the Eurasian continent prior to *c.* 9500–*c.* 8000 BC, when the Beringia land bridge finally submerged.

The Were-Jaguar

In proposing that the Olmec saw the stars of Ursa Major and Cygnus as important nocturnal timekeepers, Hatch offered several examples of Olmec art to further emphasize this hypothesis (*see fig. 17*). Stone statues and jade figurines of what is called the 'were-jaguar' – a feline-human hybrid – often bear abstract symbols that seem to represent these two constellations. Their heads are flat with a cleft in the middle, while their upper lips are square-shaped and downturned in the exact manner of the 'bowl' of Ursa Major.[11] Sometimes the lip is represented with a carved or incised line that connects four drill holes that likewise resemble the distinctive arrangement of these four stars.

Similar abstract features are found also on Olmec altars and stelae (inscribed standing stones) which might have an open arch, or niche, suggestive of the squared-off jaguar jaws. In addition to this, the 'crossed bands' symbol, familiar to Mayan astronomy and identified by Hatch as Cygnus, will appear either in the eyes, on the forehead, or on the chest of were-jaguar figurines and carvings.[12]

Hatch further points out that the sign used to denote astronomical observations in the art of the Maya was often a pair of crossed sticks in the doorway of a temple, or the head of a man looking through crossed sticks, or even an eye in a notch. All of these signs might well have resulted from the use of the stars of Cygnus to determine time-related events in the solar calendar as well as the exact position of true north, important for the orientation of building structures *(see Chapter Twelve in connection with ancient Egypt)*.[13] Arguably, the were-jaguar, which is thought to show a shaman transformed into a feline creature, represents the celestial intelligence responsible for the movement of these constellations as the keeper of cosmic time.

Interestingly, in at least one Olmec relief the 'crossed bands' symbol appears as the visible eye of a human-headed serpent (*see fig. 18*).[14] Its existence suggests that at one time the stars of Cygnus might have formed part of a superconstellation, arguably a feathered serpent, or serpent-bird, that included the stars of Draco, which Marion Popenoe Hatch found was intimately bound together in Mayan timekeeping, just as Ursa Major and Cygnus had been in Olmec times.

This conclusion followed a careful examination of a Mayan text known as the

Fig. 17. Olmec votive axe from Mexico City in the form of the were-jaguar, symbol of the night sky. Note its down-turned lips, representing the upturned bowl of Ursa Major, along with the faint 'crossed bands' symbol (just visible on his chest, above his hands) representing Cygnus.

Fig. 18. Olmec image of a serpent with the crossed bands symbol as an eye, after Xu. Does it suggest a superconstellation featuring the stars of Draco and Cygnus?

Madrid Codex. Through studying the appearance of crossed bands glyphs in relation to the position of a serpent pictured at different angles on consecutive pages, Hatch determined that this signified the working relationship between Sadr in Cygnus and the stars of Draco.[15] Once again, it was their midnight meridian transit that marked transition points in the Mayan solar calendar, which was broken into three equal seasons – two of 122 days and one of 121 days, with an extra day every leap year. This led her finally to conclude:

> It seems to me that the consistency of the fit of the crossed bands glyph with the path of Cygnus goes beyond coincidence. If the relationship has been correctly analyzed, it becomes apparent that the Maya, for whatever reason, were profoundly interested in this particular constellation (or star).[16]

Thus Sadr, or Cygnus, was seen as a major timekeeper in Mayan cosmology, which goes some way to explain its connection with the celestial bird that we find at the top of the Maya World Tree, known as *Wakah-Chan*, or 'Raised-Up Sky' (see *fig. 19*).

As in similar cosmological myths worldwide, the World Tree of the Maya represents the cosmic axis, the turning point of the night sky. It has its roots in *Xibalba*, the Mayan underworld, its trunk emerging from the middle of the Earth, and its upper branches in heaven. Today the tree remains an important symbol in Mayan religious customs and beliefs, where it is often portrayed as a cross that closely resembles the Christian Cross of Calvary. It can still be seen displayed above traditional altars found throughout Mexico's Yucatan peninsula, where it is known as Yax Che', the First (or Green) Tree.[17]

Maya Cosmos

In their scholarly work, *Maya Cosmos: Three Thousand Years on the Shaman's Path*, published in 1993, American academics David Freidel, Linda Schele and Joy Parker paint a remarkable picture of Maya cosmology. They argue that, as in cultures worldwide, the World Tree of the Maya was seen to penetrate the 'heart of the sky' via the celestial pole, which they describe as the dark region 'near Polaris, the North Star'.[18] Add to this the fact that various pictures of the World Tree in Mayan art show a scorpion at its base (see below), and it becomes clear that the World Tree is a representation of the Milky Way. As Linda Schele wrote in the wake of this momentous discovery:

> I drew in Scorpius and the North Star and then looked at the result. My heart jumped into my mouth. There it was. The Milky Way stretched south to north from Scorpius past the North Star. The *Wakah-Chan* ["raised up sky"] was the Milky Way', known also as *Sak Be* ('The White Road') and *Xibalba Bih* ('Road of Awe').[19]

Should this be so, then it means that the World Tree's cross bar, which combines to give it the distinctive appearance of the Christian Cross, signifies the ecliptic – the point occupied by the stars of Scorpio and Sagittarius. Often this horizontal bar on the Mayan World Tree is capped with the heads of serpents, linking the stars of Scorpio once more with this mythical creature, even though Scorpio seems to have been separately identified as a Mayan asterism called *sinaan*, 'scorpion', which is shown at the base of the cosmic tree symbolizing the Milky Way. If this constellation is the same as our Scorpio, the scorpion, then this is a strange parallel, for it cannot be coincidence that both the Maya and the Babylonians originally conceived of the same set of stars in the night sky as a scorpion. There has to be a common root far back in time, although exactly when is open to debate.

The Mayan concept of heaven, known as the 'heart of the sky', is located where it is in every other tradition examined so far – beyond the point where the World Tree penetrates the northern celestial pole. Perching on top of it is *Itzam-ye*, the Serpent Bird or Celestial Bird, whose name means the 'Way of Itzamna', a Mayan serpent god. Itzam-ye has a direct counterpart among the Yucatec Maya in *K'inich K'ak'mo*, 'Sun-Eyed Fire-Macaw',[20] as well as an ancestor in the form of a winged monster known to scholars as the 'Principal Bird Deity'.[21] He would appear to have been the extremely colourful king vulture (*Sarcoramphus papa*), often shown in Mayan art with a snake in its beak. Macaw, vulture and snake come together in Central America among the beliefs of the Cakchiquel, a Guatemalan mountain tribe related to the Maya. They venerate *Xib'alb'ay Kaqix*, 'Underworld Macaw', described as 'a bird like a vulture that eats snakes'.[22]

The Fall of Seven Macaw

In the *Popol Vuh,* the creation myth of the Quiché Maya of Guatemala, Itzam-ye becomes the fabulous bird *Vucub-Caquix*, 'Seven Macaw'. Aeons ago, when everything was in darkness, Seven Macaw lit up the world with its beauty. But the bird became proud enough to think it was the sun and moon, the lord over all. Then along came *Hunahpu* ('One Blowpiper'), one of the mythological duo known as the Hero Twins, who decided to put Seven Macaw in its place. As it took flight, Hunahpu used his blowpipe to shoot out its face and teeth, taking away the bird's cockiness. This act destroyed Seven Macaw's pride and it eventually died.

Clearly this bird, like the were-jaguar in Olmec tradition, played a role as the keeper of cosmic time, whose haughty rule was cut short when the primordial age came to an end. It thus made sense to look for Itzam-ye/Seven Macaw's true identity among the stars. However, I was puzzled to find that the authors of *Maya Cosmos* equated the cosmic bird with the stars of Ursa Major, the Big Dipper. This identification perhaps derives from the commentary that accompanies a translation of the *Popol Vuh* by Professor Dennis Tedlock of the State University of New York, first published in 1985. Here he states that Seven Macaw's ethnoastronomical role is indicated 'by the fact that some present-day speakers of Quiché [a Mayan language] use his name as a term for the seven stars of the Big Dipper'.[23] No other evidence is

Fig. 19. The Mayan cosmic bird Seven Macaw, or a variation, seated at the top of Wakah Chan, the World Tree, representing the Milky Way from Scorpio to its northern extreme in the vicinity of Cygnus.

provided to support the bird's association with Ursa Major, and I have been unable to verify it elsewhere.

To me something did not add up. To start with, if Itzam-ye sits among the branches of the World Tree, an expression of the Milky Way, then this is where any search to find him should begin. Moreover, the fact that the tree's upper branches penetrate the celestial pole suggests that we should look in the proximity of the pole's ever-shifting path for the identity of the celestial bird.

Only one star group placed on the Milky Way occupies the path of the celestial pole and this, as we know, is Cygnus. In contrast, Ursa Major falls nowhere near the celestial pole, and is some considerable distance away from the Milky Way. Confronted by this information, there seemed no way that Itzam-ye/Seven Macaw could originally have been the Big Dipper – this appellation was quite clearly a modern invention. Much more likely is that Seven Macaw and his variations were all personifications of Cygnus as the celestial bird at the top of the cosmic axis.[24]

Placing Itzam-ye/Seven Macaw actually on the Milky Way makes perfect sense of the story found in the *Popol Vuh*, which features the exploits and adventures of the Hero Twins. After causing the bird's death, they come up against the evil lords of Xibalba, reached along what is known as the Road Xibalba. This can easily be identified as the Milky Way's Great Rift, which begins in the vicinity of Cygnus and ends below the line of the ecliptic, in the 'underworld', Xibalba. Here the Hero Twins are charged with completing a series of impossible tasks and trials set for them by the lords of Xibalba, whom they finally defeat by trickery and cunning. After recovering and resuscitating the remains of their father and uncle, killed earlier by the dark lords, the Hero Twins then rise to heaven. As the *Popol Vuh* recounts with regards to this victory:

> And then the two boys ascended this way, here into the middle of the light, and they ascended straight on into the sky, and the sun belongs to one and the moon to the other.[25]

The Long Count

The precise relationship between the end of a former age, or 'sun', in Mayan cosmology and the beginning of the current one was reckoned by a complex calendrical system known as the 'Long Count'. Implemented by Maya timekeepers sometime *c.*355 BC, it relates to a cycle that lasts exactly thirteen *baktun*s, which corresponds to a period of just over 5,125 solar years. Curiously, the Long Count was designed to commence not when it was first introduced but in the year 3114 BC, a date that almost certainly synchronizes with an earlier Olmec Long Count system.[26] Why such a date should have been chosen for this purpose remains unclear, although quite probably it relates to astronomical calculations of some kind. Whether it has anything to do with the phenomenon of precession is impossible now to tell, although it should be noted that 5,125 years is approximately one fifth of a precessional cycle.

All that can be added with any certainty is that – like the Phoenix in Graeco-Egyptian legend that returns to Heliopolis and is consumed in its own pyre at the end of each world age – Itzam-ye/Seven Macaw came to signify the culmination of one sun, and the commencement of another. As such, it is my belief that cosmological myths of this nature, involving a celestial bird, the World Tree, and the use of stars and constellations to monitor cosmic time, have a universal origin that reaches back to Palaeolithic times. However, I could not leave the matter here, for in recent years a whole new phenomenon has grown up around the end of the current thirteen-*baktun* cycle, scheduled to occur on 21 December 2012.

Cosmogenesis 2012

In 1975 the psychedelic author, explorer and philosopher Terence McKenna, in a book entitled *The Invisible Landscape* (1975) co-authored with his brother Dennis, used a process they called 'Timewave Zero' (*see Chapter Twenty-One*) to calculate the key moments of 'novelty', pinpointing rapid evolution in human development since the start of the species. This highlighted various periods of advancement in technology, civilization, religion and culture. The McKennas then used this same formula to provide a 'Zero Point' when the current cycle would terminate. This turned out to be close to the end of 2012, which only afterwards did they realize corresponded with the completion of the Mayan thirteen-*baktun* cycle at dawn on 21 December 2012.[27]

At the same time as this event is scheduled to occur, the sun on the horizon will align not only with the Milky Way's Great Rift in the vicinity of the stars of Sagittarius, but also with the point in the sky that is the visual centre of our galaxy, the astronomical centre of which lies around 26,000 light years away. In other words, at the moment the solar orb appears, it will seem as if it has come from the dark nebulous heart of our own galaxy.

It is the opinion of a number of well-informed writers, including John Major Jenkins, author of the highly recommended *Cosmogenesis 2012*, that the upcoming galactic alignment is something that the Maya not only planned for 2,300 years ago, but also described in the *Popol Vuh* story of the Hero Twins heralding the birth of the new sun. Jenkins' understanding of Maya cosmology is second to none, and he builds on this in order to strengthen his case. For him, the Milky Way's Great Rift, the 'Road to Xibalba', can be seen as a kind of 'cosmic birth canal', out of which the all-important sun will emerge on 21 December 2012.

Although the eschatological implications of the 2012 alignment are immense for many in the New Age movement, I was surprised that Jenkins' compelling book, which contains a number of illustrations of the Great Rift, fails to note that it emerges in the vicinity of the Cygnus constellation. Indeed, if one were to extend the analogy of the birth canal further, and see the divided branches of the Milky Way on each side of the Great Rift as female 'legs', then Deneb and Sadr fall precisely in the vicinity of the 'uterus'. So if the Maya really were aware of this galactic alignment, then perhaps they might have visualized the completion of the current solar cycle on 21 December 2012 in slightly different terms.

Emergence of the Sun-Egg

Mexican legends of Pre-Columbian origin liken the emergence of the sun to the birth of a 'cosmic egg'. One source speaks of the World Mountain, another universal expression of the *axis mundi*, splitting asunder to bring forth the 'sun-egg', as if emerging from a deep cave, analogous with the Road to Xibalba.[28] Another folktale, recorded by the American writer John L. Stephens during his first expedition to the

Yucatan in 1839, seems to throw even further light on the subject. This is despite the fact that its mundane purpose was to help explain the miraculous foundation of the Temple of the Dwarf, an enigmatic pyramid-like building in the Mayan city of Uxmal, 77 kilometres (50 miles) from the town of Merida in the Yucatan peninsula.

The folktale told to Stephens speaks of an old woman who lives alone in her hut. She is unable to bear children, so accepts an egg into her care. When it hatches a radiant young boy comes forth, who reaches out his arms to her. Thus blessed with a child, she rears him as her own, and for the first year he grows rapidly, but then stops growing completely and thereafter remains a 'dwarf'.

When he comes of age she pits him against the *gobernador,* the local mayor or governor, in a series of trials of strength. Neither gets the better of the other, causing the now anguished *gobernador* to tell the dwarf that unless he can build a city loftier than his own, he will be killed. The dwarf relays the threat to the old woman, who tells him not to despair. The next morning they awake to find themselves inside a great palace unequalled in beauty and magnificence (that is, the Temple of the Dwarf). On seeing this, the *gobernador* sends immediately for the dwarf. He tells him that he should collect two bundles of cogoiol (a kind of hardwood). With one of them the *gobernador* will strike the dwarf. In return, the *gobernador* agrees to be hit by the second bundle. The dwarf goes back to the old woman and cries, yet she simply places a tortilla on his head, and sends him back to the palace.

The ensuing ordeal commences with the *gobernador*'s subjects watching in anticipation. First, he strikes the dwarf to no effect. He uses up all his logs, but never harms his opponent. Realizing now that he will be beaten, the *gobernador* seeks to annul the agreement, but knows this is impossible since it has been witnessed by his chiefs and officials. The dwarf then strikes him on the head, and on the second blow smashes his skull to pulp. The people rejoice, and henceforth the dwarf becomes the new *gobernador*. At the same time, the old woman mysteriously vanishes.

The sequel to the story is that in the village of Mani an old woman sits by the banks of a river inside a deep well that leads to a subterranean passage extending to the town of Merida. She is shaded by a great tree, and by her side is a serpent. From her can be bought small quantities of water, although she will accept no money, since her price is human babies, which are fed to the serpent. It is said that this old woman is the dwarf's mother.[29]

The story is a parable that can be broken down into mythological components. The old woman is the Mexican earth-mother, associated with the fertilizing power of water. The snake is her symbol, as in the Nahua maize goddess Chicomecohuatl ('Seven Serpent'), and the tree that shades her is, of course, the World Tree. The cave is the Road to Xibalba, with the *gobernador* the old sun that rules by divine providence, but who is then challenged and successfully outwitted by the strength and cunning of a new sun, the dwarf. As the radiant child born of the cosmic egg, he goes on to become the rightful ruler of the next world age.

Might all this suggest that the Maya saw the new sun as emerging from a cosmic egg dropped down the Milky Way's Great Rift by a celestial bird (i.e. Cygnus), acting as a keeper of cosmic time?

None of these musings undermine the work of New Age cosmologists such as John Major Jenkins. What they do highlight is an apparent blind spot when it comes to considering the significance played by Cygnus in Olmec and Mayan cosmology, something that was first realized by Marion Popenoe Hatch. She seems philosophical that very few scholars exploring the cosmological world of these two important civilizations have ever really acknowledged her dedicated work in this field of study. I am convinced that Cygnus acted not just as an astronomical timekeeper for both the Olmec and Maya, but also as the herald and progenitor of the sun-egg, the (as yet unrecognized) role it plays in the cosmic events of 2012.

We must now leave behind Central America, and journey on to South America, where Cygnus's role as cosmic creator is never more apparent than at Cuzco, once the capital city of the Inca empire.

CHAPTER SEVEN

Pathway to the Gods

It was with fewer than two hundred armed men that in 1532 the Spanish general Francisco Pizarro (1471–1541) brought about the destruction of one of the greatest civilizations on Earth. The Inca empire of South America extended more than 6,400 kilometres (4,000 miles) along the Andes and embraced mountains, coastal valleys, deserts and tropical lowlands. It included the present-day countries of Peru, Ecuador, Bolivia, and parts of Chile and Argentina, a landmass that exceeded the size of medieval Europe and even that of the Roman empire. It was to take 250 years of war and strife to create, and would last less than one hundred years before its strangely fatalistic demise. In the end, it was the Spaniards' greed for gold that prevented them from ever knowing the secrets of a people who welcomed these bearded white men as gods and brothers, but whose civility and courtesy was betrayed almost beyond belief.

Navel of the World

The royal capital of the Inca was Cuzco, situated at an altitude of 3,246 metres (11,200 feet) amid the Andes mountain range that forms the backbone of Peru. According to tradition, the city was built in the thirteenth century AD by a king named Manco Capac, who styled himself 'son of the sun'. However, archaeologists believe that it had earlier been a stronghold of the Wari, a nation that thrived for several hundred years before the rise of the Inca empire.

Cuzco's original name in the local Quechua language was *Qosqo*, meaning 'navel' or 'centre', reminding us of Göbekli Tepe in distant Turkey (*see above, page 5*) and other *axis mundi* sites around the world. It reflected the fact that Cuzco was the centre of the empire, which was known as *Tawantinsuyu*, meaning 'Four Quarters of the Earth', the beating heart of which was the city's fabulous temple complex known as the Coricancha ('Corral of Gold'), dedicated to Wiraqocha, the creator, and Inti, the sun god.

In addition to the worship that took place in its many temples, the Coricancha was also a splendid astronomical observatory and calendrical device, used for calculating both the movement of the celestial bodies and the position of stars. It was said that emerging from the centre of Cuzco were forty (or forty-two) *seques* (also written *ceques*), or rays, that spread out into the surrounding landscape and continued uninterrupted, sometimes for tens of kilometres, across plains and over mountains. Seen on the ground as trodden paths, they marked the position of no less than 328 *wakas* (or *huacas*), a term discussed below which in this context can be rendered as 'shrines' or 'sacred places'. The most important *seques* are said to have been aligned to points on the horizon where the sun rose and set at the time of the equinoxes and solstices, while others possibly were aligned to the rising of stars. Each one was tended by a priest from a different part of the empire, whose responsibility it was to maintain the *wakas* on his chosen *seque*.

When the first Spaniards entered Cuzco, they witnessed seemingly never-ending festivals at the Coricancha, where the walls and ceilings were quite literally covered in gold. Even after the temple complex was stripped of its riches and replaced by the great church of San Domingo, the ceremonies continued, although now, nominally at least, in the name of Christ, Mary and the saints. Today the Festival of the Sun, or *Ind Raymi*, which takes place every 24 June, the winter solstice, remains a colourful and wonderful spectacle. It provides spiritual meaning not only for the thousands of foreign tourists who descend on the ancient city each year, but also the local Quechua-speaking people who still revere the site.

In the middle of the Coricancha's central courtyard is a curious eight-sided stone box, called *Cuzco Cara Urumi*, the 'Uncovered Navel Stone'. Once lined with 55 kilograms of gold, it is taken to mark the middle of Tawantinsuyu, although how it originally came to be here, and what its function might have been remains obscure. However, evidence is now emerging to better explain Cuzco's former significance as the Inca nation's *axis mundi*, and it will surprise no one to learn that the solution is patently cosmological in nature.

The Celestial River

The Inca – a term which translates as 'Children of the Sun' – possessed a concept they referred to as *waka* (*huaca*), which can be rendered in various ways depending on the context. It describes the spirit of a sacred place, such as a burial ground, shrine or temple building, and also any place where such a spirit resides. A *waka* is somewhere beyond the usual presence of nature – somewhere either enhanced by human hands for religious purposes, or where offerings are made on a regular basis. Indeed, it is anywhere with a sense of spirituality.

Waka can also be applied to locations that have the appearance of a living creature, such as prominent hills and rocky outcrops. Such locations, usually regarded simply as amusing simulacra in Western culture, have always been venerated as sacred by indigenous peoples worldwide. From the native races of North America to the San bushmen of southern Africa and the Aborigines of Australia, natural rock formations are seen as personifying supernatural forces that can affect local communities and those who come into contact with them. This phenomenon is nowhere more apparent than in the rocky landscape of the Peruvian Andes. Terrestrial representations of animals, trees and anthropomorphic figures are not only recognized, but also enhanced through landscape sculpture, which includes the construction and placement of towns, fortresses and agricultural terraces.

Such landscape effigies were intimately connected with Andean mythology. What is more, there exists close to Cuzco a deep river valley, over 100 kilometres (63 miles) long, through which runs the Urubamba, a river known also as the Vilcanota, or Willcammayu, meaning 'Sacred River'.[1] Running from the town of Pisac to the mountain-top fortress of Machu Picchu – known to outsiders only since its discovery in 1911 by American archaeologist Hiram Bingham – it contains several natural *waka* formations that embrace and enhance the belief that it is considered to be a mirror reflection of the *Mayu*, or Celestial River, the Andean name for the Milky Way.[2]

Known as the *Valle Sagrado de los Incas* ('Secret Valley of the Inca'), this sacred landscape played host to a number of important religious festivals honouring the supernatural forms that the Andean folk saw as existing amid the light and dark regions of the Milky Way. Among them were the great ceremonial pilgrimages made at the time of the June solstice recorded by Cristóbal de Molina, a priest at Cuzco's hospital for native people, in his *Fábulas y Ritos de los Incas* ('Fables and Rites of the Inca'), written between 1570 and 1584.[3]

Priests would begin in the city, and then travel southeastwards following the path of the Celestial River, until finally they came upon the pass of La Raya, where the Vilcanota begins and in Inca legend the sun was said to have been born.[4] Once offerings had been made and rites completed, the priests would make their way back to Cuzco, before heading out northwestwards to meet up again with the Vilcanota, which flows southeast-northeast. It was in this manner that the Inca were able to synchronize the Celestial River with its terrestrial counterpart.

In addition to these festivals another major ceremony known as *Mayucati* would take place in Cuzco at the time of the autumn equinox, around 21–23 March.

Offerings were made to the Huatanay River, which flows into the Vilcanota, in the belief that they would be carried all the way to the ancient city of Ollantaytambo, and then northwards towards the sea.[5]

Dark Cloud Constellations

In the West we identify constellations by virtue of lines drawn from star to star, but in South America traditional peoples additionally recognize so-called 'dark cloud' constellations amid the nebulous patches found within the Milky Way. The most obvious example is the Great Rift, although there are several other breaks in the Milky Way's white starry trail, especially in the Southern Hemisphere, where it reaches its southerly extreme in the vicinity of the constellation known as Crux, the Southern Cross, which although much smaller mirrors Cygnus, the Northern Cross of the northern skies.[6]

In addition to star-to-star and dark-cloud constellations, Andean ethnoastronomy includes others that are made up of a mixture of both, and terrestrial representations of all of these variants are found as effigies along the Secret Valley. Extraordinarily enough, they include an enormous condor that emerges from the Mountain of the Condor, above the ancient town of Pisac, where the valley begins;[7] a 'Tree of Origins' above the town of Ollantaytambo;[8] a sacred Llama (*Catachillay*), complete with young, sculpted from a mountain named Tamboqhasa, also near Ollantaytambo;[9] and an almighty Flying Caiman (*Amaru Tupac*), that completely overlies Machu Picchu.[10]

The spiritual reality of these landscape effigies is evidenced in a book entitled *The Sacred Valley of the Incas* by E. Elorrieta and Edgar Elorrieta Salazar. They cite accounts from early colonial sources, such as the respected Spanish Jesuit Bernabé Cobo (1582–1657), who in 1653 recorded:

> They say that these first men, having produced descendants, were changed in that same place, some turned into stones, others into falcons and cóndors and into other animals and birds and this is why the temples and Huacas they adore have different shapes and figures.[11]

The significance of such landscape *wakas* cannot be underestimated. As with their heavenly counterparts, the terrestrial effigies were, and indeed are, believed to enhance the fertility and prosperity of a local community – arguably why that community was founded there in the first place.

Cuzco's Terrestrial Puma

The most powerful of all the landscape *wakas* was reserved for Cuzco itself. Local tradition asserts that the ancient city can be viewed as a gigantic terrestrial puma, its form recognizable in both natural and man-made features. Sacsahuaman – Cuzco's hilltop fortress, famous for its foundation walls composed of breathtaking cyclopean masonry – forms the feline's great head, while its jagged, multifaceted blocks, some weighing up to 200 tonnes apiece, become the creature's razor sharp teeth. The town's main plaza of Huacaypata corresponds with the feline's belly and legs, while the Coricancha, replaced by the colonial church of San Domingo, falls in the vicinity of its genitals. Finally, the spine and tail of the puma are represented by the Tullumayu and Huatanay rivers, which flow into the Vilcanota River.

Inca cosmology alludes to the puma as the totem of *kay pacha*, literally 'this world', or the physical world, of which Cuzco was the *axis mundi*. Yet if the landscape effigies of the Sacred Valley, which celebrate the winding course of the Vilcanota, are to be seen as terrestrial representations of constellations that fall within the Milky Way, then was it possible to identify the celestial counterpart to Cuzco's great puma?

Centre of Origin

It was this mystery that Giulio Magli, professor of Mathematical Physics at the Politecnico of Milan, Italy, set about solving in 2003. He observed that dark cloud constellations are only usually identified within the area of the Milky Way in the Southern Hemisphere as seen from Cuzco around the time of the southern autumn equinox (including a dark spot 'serpent' that winds its way around the stars of Scorpio[12]). However, the part of the Milky Way that is prominent in the Northern Hemisphere becomes visible around October, the beginning of the rainy season, and the most characteristic aspect of this section is, as we have seen, the Great Rift, marked at its highest point by the stars of Cygnus.

From the ground it seems as if Mayu, the Celestial River, has split into two branches, a revealing fact since anthropologist Gary Urton – who has made an exhaustive study of Andean ethnoastronomy – records that this is indeed how it was interpreted in past ages. According to his informant:

> The Milky Way ... is actually made up of two rivers, not one. The two Mayus [rivers] originate at a common point in the north, flow in opposite directions from north to south, and collide head-on in the

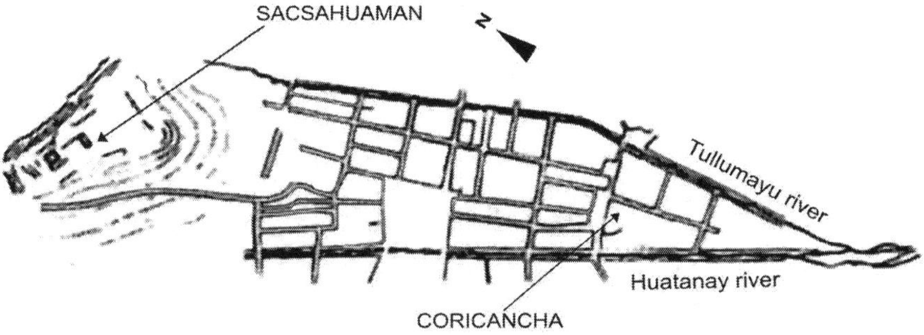

Fig. 20. Cuzco as the City of the Puma, symbol of *kay pacha*, literally 'this world', the *axis mundi*, linked to Cygnus in the Milky Way.

> southern Milky Way... These data indicate that the celestial River has a second center, a 'center of origin,' in the north.[13]

This was an extremely significant discovery. Cuzco lies at a latitude of 13.5 degrees south of the equator, but despite this, north is considered 'up', or 'higher', even though it is the south celestial pole that is visible; its corresponding pole in the north being invisible even one degree south of the equator.[14] Furthermore, it is the southern midwinter (June) solstice that was, and still is, celebrated in the city, and not the southern midsummer solstice (December), which marks the longest day of the year. This is despite the December sun coming within ten degrees of the overhead zenith point – the June solstice being considerably lower. Also, 'Upper Cuzco' is the northern part of the city, while the highest mountain in the empire related to the June solstice and the most northerly part of the empire was marked by a river called 'the highest part of the sky-blue house'.[15]

All of this is pointed out in *The Secret of the Incas* (1996), a work of inestimable significance regarding the Inca cosmological mindset by cultural historian William Sullivan. He states that:

> As the headwaters of the two branches of the celestial river lie in the north, and debouch [empty] in the south, in the vicinity of the

> Southern Cross, the north must be "higher" than south. And, since rivers rise in the mountains, the cosmic mountain must also lie in the northern heavens.[16]

The conclusions from all this are clear. The Inca believed that the celestial centre of what they referred to as *hanaq pacha*, the 'world above', the sky-world, was linked with the 'navel' of *kay pacha*, 'this world', marked by *Cuzco Cara Urumi*, the 'Uncovered Navel Stone' located at the centre of the Coricancha. This celestial 'centre of origin', was to be found at the heart of the Milky Way, and plausibly where the Great Rift broke the Mayu, the Celestial River, into two separate branches.

In this knowledge, Guilio Magli became convinced that the Inca 'centre of origin' in the northern skies was in the proximity of the Cygnus constellation. Using this premise, he went on to identify the celestial form of Cuzco's puma, the equivalent of the sky-jaguar in Mesoamerican mythology, created from the shape of the dark clouds that make up the uppermost section of the Great Rift, where lie the stars of Cygnus. This conclusion is supported by the fact that outside Cuzco, the Tullumayu and Huatanay rivers converge into the Vilcanota, symbolizing the point of divergence of the Milky Way and thus the corresponding terrestrial location of the Inca 'centre of origin' serving *hanaq pacha*, the 'world above'. For Magli, Cuzco's ground-sky relationship thus becomes a perfect example of the Hermetic axiom, 'as above, so below'.

Secrets of the Inca

Not unnaturally, I was staggered to find that Magli had identified Cygnus as the Inca's cosmic 'centre of origin',[17] despite the fact that Cuzco is 13.5 degrees *south* of the equator, and hence in theory the full attention of the empire's astronomer-priests should have been on the southern night sky. Yet this was clearly not the case, as the work of Urton, Sullivan and Magli has shown, and either the explanation is that the ancestors of the Inca came from the north, bringing with them their existing sky-lore, which is strongly possible, or the northern night sky held some special significance to them. If this was the case, then the answer would seem to lie in their intense interest both in Cygnus and the Milky Way, which was both a celestial river and a road for the living and the dead.

So important had the Milky Way been in the pre-Inca mindset that Sullivan proposed that when in AD 650 the Milky Way finally ceased to rise heliacally, i.e. with the sun, at the time of the June solstice, it was seen as a portent of catastrophe.[18] To these people it meant that the pathway to the gods and ancestors was no longer accessible for the living or the dead, and this spelt disaster. Andean myth records that this was the time when the celestial 'bridge' fell into the waters and the creator god Wiraqocha 'left the Earth'. Archaeologists tell us that it was also *c.*AD 650 that violent confrontations began between different warring factions in the Andes, leading to the collapse of law and order, and the emergence of the new militaristic empire of the Wari, who took control of the northern Andean region from their vast and sprawling capital of Huari, northwest of Cuzco. A similar situation occurred *c.*AD 1432, when the other 'branch' of the Milky Way no longer rose with the December solstice, a portentous event that to the son of the first Inca emperor signalled the beginning of the end for the Inca state even as it reached its greatest extent.

Less than a century later, in 1529–30, the empire was struck by a devastating epidemic – probably smallpox, travelling faster through the continent than the Europeans who had brought it – which wiped out as much as eighty per cent of the population in some areas. Many Inca royalty succumbed, including the king and his heir, leading to a massive civil war among rivals to the throne. It was amid this chaos that, in 1532, Pizarro and his men arrived on the shores of Peru.

The World Above

Yet the relationship between humankind and the river or road to *hanaq pacha*, the Inca 'world above', stretches beyond simply that one world reflected the other. According to Andean belief: 'In this world we are exiled from our homeland in the world above.'[19] This is despite the fact that when ordinary people died they went not to heaven, but to *ukhu pacha*, the 'world below'. Sullivan was confused, and asked, 'What did they mean by claiming that their ultimate abode lay "up there," in the sky?'[20]

It would seem that the answer can be found in the fact that only those of noble birth were allowed to enter the 'world above'; everyone else had to make do with the 'world below'. *Yet this did not stop the peasantry from calling* hanaq pacha, *the sky-world, their homeland.* So strong was this native belief that Sullivan felt moved to draw comparisons with tribal beliefs found elsewhere on the American continent. He cited, for instance, the seminomadic Naskapi tribe of Labrador in Canada. Apparently, the Naskapi 'speak of the possibility of contact between worlds along the Milky Way, which they call "ghost trail," or "dead person's path."'[21] Furthermore, for these indigenous peoples, 'the souls of the living originated in the sky, where they "rest in the firmament until they become reincarnated".[22] This recalls the belief among the shamanic societies of Central and North Asia concerning the manner in which the souls of children would perch as little birds in the World Tree, where shamans would go to find them in order that they might incarnate (*see above, page 37*).[23]

Strangely, it turns out that whether an Inca went to the afterlife in the 'world above' or the 'world below', *both* destinations were accessed via the Milky Way. Those going to the former would take the northern 'bridge' of the Milky Way, in the vicinity of Cygnus, whilst those heading for the lower realms would travel south towards the region of Crux, the Southern Cross.[24] It was through the Celestial River's connection with the horizon at the solstices that the Andean peoples found their way to wherever they were going in the afterlife (even though precession eventually meant that the Milky Way no longer rose heliacally at either solstice). I feel that a similar belief system was present among the Hopewell culture of the Ohio Valley (*see above, page 50*), who also saw the Milky Way as the ghost-road to the sky-world, i.e. Cygnus, accessed via the terrestrial horizon at the time of the summer solstice.

If Italian scholar Giulio Magli's findings are correct, then the true 'centre of origin' and gateway to the Andean 'homeland', for everyone exiled on Earth, was in the region of Cygnus. Moreover, it would seem that for the Inca, at least, the earthly access point to this celestial realm at the head of the Great Rift in the Milky Way was Cuzco – the 'navel', or *axis mundi*, of the Inca empire.

The fortuitous field trip to the United States in July 2004 had initiated some extraordinary research which had taken me from the Hopewell culture of the Ohio Valley to the Olmec and Maya of Mexico and the Inca of Peru. Having satisfied myself that the associations between Cygnus, cosmic creation and the transmigration of the soul are to be found throughout the American continent – and so might easily have been imported from the Eurasian continent in Late Palaeolithic times – I now looked closer to home for further clues to what I was now seeing in terms of 'the Cygnus mystery'.

PART THREE

ALBION

CHAPTER EIGHT

The Winged Serpent

In the 1720s, William Stukeley (1687–1765), Freemason, arch-druid and antiquarian *extraordinaire*, could often be seen, cane in hand, strolling through the meadows and orchards of prehistoric Avebury in Wiltshire, England. He would point out memorable features to those in his company and speak passionately on its great mysteries of religion. Never did he tire of his beloved 'Abury' (he wrote it according to the local pronunciation), and as tainted as modern archaeologists perceive Stukeley's views on its divine origins, his extraordinary research into this most enigmatic of monuments becomes the next step in our understanding of the Cygnus mystery.

In order to enter Avebury's vast circular plateau the visitor has first to negotiate its enormous circular bank, which has openings in four directions. At 6.7 metres (22 feet) in height, 427 metres (1,396 feet) in diameter and enclosing 28.5 acres of land, it was constructed from chalk and stone removed from the inner ditch, which originally had a depth of around seven to ten metres (23–33 feet). It surrounds Avebury's Great Circle, a ring with a diameter of 166 metres (544 feet) consisting of approximately 100 standing stones, each regularly three metres in height. Inside its perimeter are two further stone rings, known as North Circle and South Circle. Stukeley estimated each one to have consisted of approximately thirty stones with diameters of 320 feet (98 metres) and 340 feet (104 metres) respectively. A much smaller stone circle was to be found at the centre of North Circle, with another 'circle', now considered to have been a D-shaped monument, in the middle of its southern counterpart.

Stone Avenues

Beyond the Great Circle – which in Stukeley's day embraced the 'town' of Avebury, then made up of thirty cottages and a few coaching inns – were its two fifteen-metre (49 feet) wide avenues of standing stones. One of them headed out of the henge on a winding course southeastwards to form what is known today as the Kennet Avenue, before ascending Overton Hill to terminate 2.5 kilometres (1.5 miles) away from Avebury at an enigmatic megalithic monument called the Sanctuary. Stukeley's hero, the antiquarian and biographer John Aubrey (1626–97) – who wrote about Avebury after stumbling across it whilst out riding in 1648 – described the Sanctuary as two concentric rings of stones, which, unfortunately, even in Stukeley's time were being broken up and used as road infill.

The second avenue started at the northeastern extreme of Avebury's Great Circle and snaked its way west-southwestwards towards the hamlet of Beckhampton before terminating in the proximity of various barrows (circular or oblong mounds), near the village of Cherhill.[1] Midway along its course were three enormous stones grouped together to form a monument known as the Longstone Cove (also called the Devil's Quoits). This lay on the avenue's northern side, with its 'rear' stone forming part of the avenue itself.[2] Originally there were 200 stones in the Beckhampton Avenue,[3] yet today only one remains. Together with the final stone of the Longstone Cove it forms a pair known as Adam and Eve.

The Kneph

Among the illustrations in Stukeley's book *Abury: A Temple of the British Druids*, published in 1743, was a remarkable overhead projection of the local landscape, showing the entire monument with its circles and avenues. This he used to support his contention that Avebury was a terrestrial representation of a gigantic sun disc, with its winding avenues symbolizing a winged serpent.[4] For him, its tail was the end of the Beckhampton Avenue while its head was the Sanctuary monument on Overton Hill. This, he wrote, formed part of a greater hill-ridge known as 'Hakpen' (Hackpen Hill), a place-name he broke into two components – the prefix being, he claimed, a Semitic root meaning 'snake' and the suffix *pen* deriving from the ancient British word for 'head'.[5] Stukeley identified this megalithic serpent as the Kneph, a Graeco-Egyptian form of the Egyptian creator god Khnum.[6] It was a name he decided was formed from the Hebrew *ganaph volare* – 'to fly', 'a wing' or 'winged',[7] expressing the integral relationship between the bird and serpent, a strangely meaningful interpretation as we shall see.

What Was Built When?

Avebury would go through considerable depreciation before finally being restored in the 1930s under the direction of Alexander Keiller (1889–1955), the founder of the Morven Institute of Archaeological Research. Keiller bought up whatever land he could in order to guarantee Avebury's future, and even became lord of Avebury Manor, converting its coach-house into a museum to house the many finds he made during excavations. In the 1960s the entire estate was handed over to the National Trust, which continues to maintain the site today.

Keiller also purchased a local landmark northwest of Avebury called Windmill Hill, on which a fortified Neolithic camp had been constructed in the early fourth millennium BC. Excavations here showed that it was contemporary with a long barrow, located at nearby West Kennet and considered to be the largest of its type in England. It lies due south of the western edge of Avebury's earthen henge, and was built within visual sight of the Sanctuary, positioned to the east-northeast on Overton Hill. Excavations at West Kennet by archaeologists Stuart Piggott and Richard Atkinson in 1955–6 revealed a large quantity of secondary burials, many with their skulls missing, indicating that until its final closure some 1,200 years after its construction *c.*3700 BC, it was likely to have been a ceremonial centre serving the Neolithic cult of the dead.

More bones were found during excavations in 1930 by Maud Cunnington on the site of the Sanctuary, built around the same time as the West Kennet long barrow. Their presence indicated that it functioned originally as a charnel house where excarnation took place. However, it was not until *c.*2600 BC, some 1,100 years later, that Avebury's two inner circles are thought to have been erected. They were followed a century later by Avebury's Great Circle, and then finally by the gigantic ditch and bank, which was covered with earth and grass.

Fitting somewhere into the emerging local picture is the equally enigmatic Silbury Hill, Europe's largest manmade mound, to be seen due south of the western edge of Avebury's henge. Stukeley recorded that it had a base diameter of around 500 feet (152 metres), a summit diameter of 105 feet (32 metres), a height of 170 feet (52 metres) and a volume of 13,558,809 cubic feet (383,943 cubic metres).[8] Silbury is thought to have been constructed *c.*2600 BC, the same time that work began on Avebury's inner circles. However, its ultimate function remains obscure – no burial contemporary with its age has ever been found.

Structural investigations have revealed that Silbury is located on a natural chalk knoll, which was then built up in alternating layers of chalk and earth. A spiral pathway that makes its way to the flat summit was probably part of the original

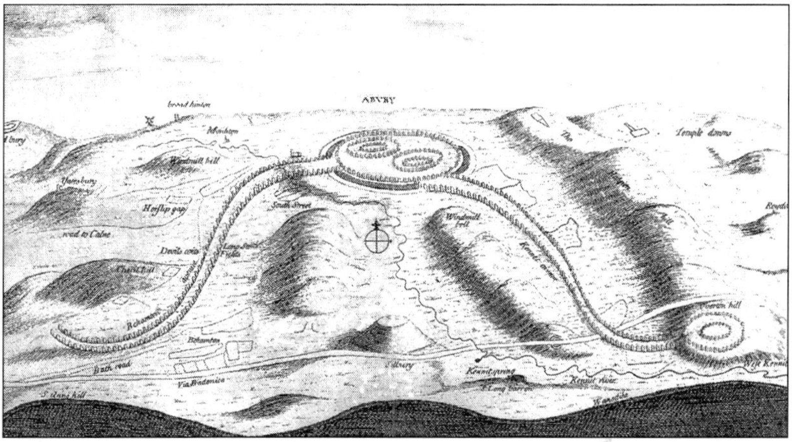

Fig. 21. Avebury monument, complete with its two avenues, as drawn by William Stukeley for his book *Abury*, published in 1743.

design, suggesting that the monument had a purely ceremonial function. The fact that it was deliberately positioned in order that each winter it was surrounded by rainwater tends to suggest that it represents a primeval mound of creation emerging from the waters of chaos, a principle featured in cosmologies worldwide.

Completing Avebury's grand design is the curious fact that the Kennet and Beckhampton avenues are not thought to have been built until *c.*2000 BC, the same time as the second phase of Stonehenge, 32 kilometres (20 miles) away.

Cult of the Dead

The case for Avebury being a centre for the cult of the dead is persuasively argued by Aubrey Burl, one of the foremost authorities on Neolithic funerary practices in Britain. A great number of skulls, in particular, would seem to have been removed from surrounding long barrows, as well as the Sanctuary, and then carried along the avenues into the henge monument, where they were used in rites involving the spirits of the dead.[9] Burl adds that three great stones known, confusingly, as the Cove, which stood in the middle of North Circle (one of the stones having since been destroyed), once pointed towards the moon's northernmost rising. The Longstone Cove on the Beckhampton Avenue, he suspects, was aligned to the midwinter sunrise.

In Burl's final opinion, North Circle with its Cove, entered via the Beckhampton Avenue, was most probably set aside for winter rituals in which the dead 'had offerings brought to them in the "forecourt" of the Cove itself.'[10] He speculates that this structure might have functioned like the dolmen monuments on the island of Ambryn, near Malekula in Melanesia, which he describes as 'settings of stones that symbolized both tomb, the mother's womb and the Cave of the Dead into which a dead man's ghost had to pass on its way to the after-world.'[11] In contrast, Burl concluded that Avebury's South Circle, entered via the Kennet Avenue, was reserved for 'rites of springtime regeneration' and 'the fecundity of the earth'.[12]

A Megalithic Legacy

All this might have been so, but Burl's opinions, although bold, failed to take into consideration other, quite separate findings concerning Avebury's celestial interests made a decade earlier by Alexander Thom, Professor of Engineering at Oxford University. He visited around 450 prehistoric sites in mainland Britain, and surveyed no less than 300 of them. In key books such as *Megalithic Sites in Britain* (1967) he outlined groundbreaking theories proposing stellar alignments for many megalithic monuments and suggested that a geometrical unity was present among them. He also proposed that such structures were built using a standard measure, which he saw as having a value of 2.722 feet (82.967cm), his so-called 'megalithic yard' (MY) (which, incidentally, makes the diameter of Avebury's Great Circle 200 MY and its South Circle exactly 125 MY). He wrote also about the absolute precision of the shape and design of stone circles, which he demonstrated involved the use of Pythagorean or right-angled triangles – this being two millennia before the principle was 'invented' by the Greek mathematician whose name they bear.

Thom and Thom at Avebury

When Alexander Thom and his son Archie turned up at Avebury to survey its stone circles and avenues, they quickly determined what Stukeley had proposed in his own day – that its line of axis was from a massive 'Obelisk' stone, which had once stood at the centre of South Circle, through to the three Cove stones of North Circle, which Burl sees as a symbolic 'womb' and 'Cave of the Dead'.[13] This axis line provided an azimuth of 339.2 degrees,[14] confirmed in the knowledge that a third circle was intended on the same north-northwesterly axis beyond North Circle, while a standing stone with a hole horizontally through it, called by Stukeley 'the ring-stone', had been positioned beyond the south-southeasterly limit of South Circle (today only a stump remains), exactly in alignment with the centre of the two inner circles.[15] Clearly, this stone could have been used to achieve a line of sight, showing that the monument almost certainly faced north-northwestwards, and not the other way around. It was also the stones closest to the Great Circle's north-northwest and south-southeasterly entrances that were the largest in the ring.

Having completed their survey, Thom and Thom checked to see if any stars set on the horizon at an azimuth of 339.2 degrees from the latitude of Avebury around 2000 BC. They concluded that just one fitted the criteria, and this was Deneb, the brightest star in Cygnus. It was a discovery that led them to observe:

> Standing at the obelisk on the line of the centres and looking through the stones at the Cove, one would be looking along the line to the place where Deneb 'set' about 1600 BC.[16]

This was a significant finding as it implied that the dark interior of the Cove might once have functioned as a kind of 'astral launch pad' through to the heavenly domains of Cygnus, the origin point and place of the afterlife in the cosmological beliefs of cultures worldwide. Stukeley recorded that before it fell over and was broken up for use as building material, the Cove's third stone was a full seventeen feet (5 metres) in height, and from its description it is clear that with its partner the pair must have seemed like two bull's horns, directing the eye towards the north-eastern horizon.[17]

The discovery at the base of the Cove of bucrania (ox skulls), deposited when the monument was still in ceremonial use, supports the idea that it was viewed as a symbolic place of death and rebirth. Bucrania, when observed from the front, resemble a woman's uterus, complete with cervix, fallopian tubes and ovaries, a fact that our distant ancestors are unlikely to have missed.[18] Moreover, bull's horns were being used as symbols of life, death and rebirth as early as 6500 BC within the sub-surface cult buildings at Çatal Hüyük in south-central Turkey, as well as at other early sites in both Western Asia and Egypt.

The Deneb Alignment

Avebury was not alone in targeting Deneb, for Thom found several more sites with similar orientations. They included a 100-metre long stone row called the Nine Maidens, originally of nine stones, although now with only six remaining, at St. Columb Major on Cornwall's Bodmin Moor.[19] Faced with such information, the surveyor attempted to rationalize the significance of Deneb in the eyes of megalithic man.

Fig. 22. Avebury, by artist Alan Sorrell. Note the near northwesterly orientation of the inner circles, which target the setting of Deneb in Cygnus.

Thom pointed out that in Scotland, where Deneb was circumpolar during this age, the star's nightly transit of the meridian would have made it a good choice as part of a star-clock that featured also the use of three other stars – Capella, Vega and Arcturus. However, at more southerly latitudes in this same epoch, *c.*2000 BC, Deneb sank beneath the horizon during its daily circuit of the sky, making its lower transit around the time of the winter solstice completely invisible. Yet this meant that exactly six months later, at the time of the summer solstice, it would have made its upper meridian transit, once again marking it out as an important time-keeper. Despite such information, Thom failed fully to comprehend why Deneb featured in the axis of a number of megalithic sites, and why, for instance, its importance was emphasized by 'so many stones as there are in the Nine Maidens' alignment.'[20]

An Unlikely Call

Indeed, the fact that Avebury's central axis might be aligned to the setting of Deneb made little sense at the time, and certainly not to Aubrey Burl, who commented:

> The faintness of Deneb, so dim that it cannot be observed down to the horizon, and the improbability of a date some eight hundred years after the Ring Stone was put up greatly dilutes the probability of this alignment and, in its present state at least, Avebury cannot be regarded as a scientific observatory.'[21]

Burl's harsh words must have seemed like bad news to Alexander Thom, who saw Deneb as forming part of a prominent celestial star-clock that dominated the northern night sky. His greater problem, however, was asserting that Avebury's central axis targeted the star's setting *c.*1600 BC, when archaeologists have firmly established that the two inner circles were erected some 1,000 years beforehand, *c.*2600 BC. Could this clear time discrepancy be explained?

The only solution was to accept that Thom had got the date wrong for the monument's construction, and return to the Skyglobe computer program in order to determine the setting of Deneb for the coordinates of Avebury at the earlier date of 2600 BC. This simple exercise produced some useful results (*see fig. 23*), for it would seem that between *c.*3000–*c.*2500 BC, during which time the inner circles were planned and built, Deneb set into the horizon within half a degree of Thom's original estimate of Avebury's axial orientation.[22] Since no other stars set at this

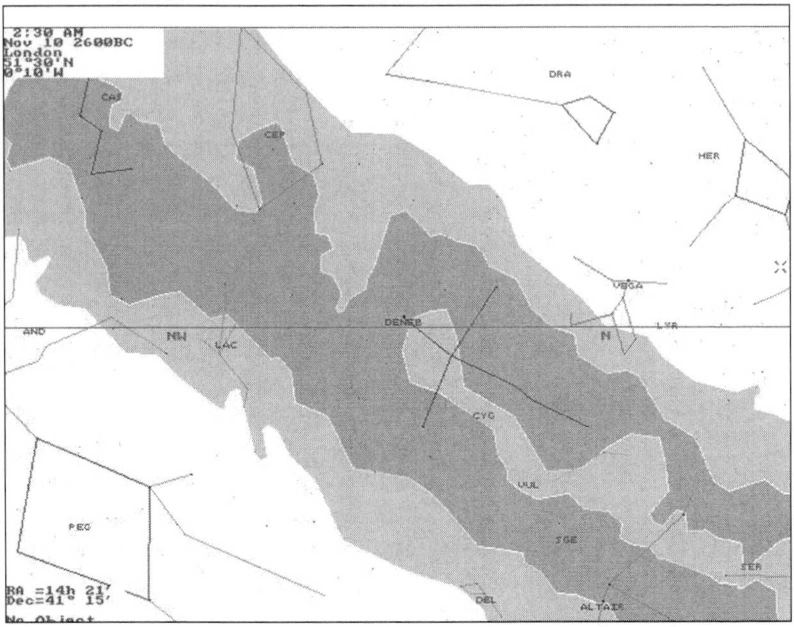

Fig. 23. The northern sky as viewed from Avebury, 2600 BC, showing Deneb about to set in the north-northwest – the exact axis of the Avebury monument.

same azimuth for the epoch in question, then it does suggest that Avebury's central axis did indeed feature Deneb.

Burl, arguably for the right reasons, chose to dismiss Thom's findings concerning Avebury's proposed Deneb alignment. Yet in so doing it demonstrates how little was actually known about archaeoastronomy in the 1970s. Today we can accept that there was once a worldwide proliferation of interest in Cygnus as a symbol of cosmic life and death. What is more, situated at the northern extreme of the Milky Way – universally seen as an astral road or river to the sky-world – it marked the entrance to the realms of light, the abode of the gods and the place of the afterlife, a belief that could well go back to Palaeolithic times.

Such profound knowledge would have been held sacred also by Neolithic priest-shamans who presided over the cult of the dead, which first emerged in the British Isles as early as *c.*4500–*c.*4000 BC. What is more, hard evidence for the existence of this prehistoric religion is surely no better displayed than at Avebury, with its great ceremonial centre, its base for ancestor worship at the West Kennet long barrow and the likelihood of excarnation rites having taken place at the Sanctuary, the head of

Stukeley's megalithic 'serpent'. I was intrigued to see that in his comprehensive work on Avebury and its environs, Stukeley noted that the Kneph might be compared with the story of the hero 'Cycnus', whom he notes was changed by Zeus into a bird, actually a swan, and placed among the stars as the constellation of Cygnus, because of the great compassion he showed to his brother (some say lover) Phaeton.[23] Although Stukeley was merely toying with ideas, and did not linger on the connection, it would now seem that he was closer to the truth than he could ever have imagined.

Such cosmological ideologies were not in the mindset of orthodox archaeologists in Thom's day. Very few scholars would have considered consulting worldwide ethnographical studies in order to determine the prehistoric mindset of the builders of Avebury. It was the opinion of most archaeologists that such sites functioned primarily either as places of ritual celebration and sacrifice, or, more controversially, as solar or lunar observatories, where changes in the agricultural year might be determined by observing the passage of the celestial bodies. To my knowledge, only Burl considered the function of such sites to be shamanic in origin, and related, most probably, to gaining access to the sky-world, the place of the dead, the ultimate heaven. What he should have realized, however, is that Avebury's axial orientation towards the setting of Deneb only strengthens his case.

Avebury Decoded?

One person who should have been better equipped to understand what was going on at Avebury was British-born astronomer Gerald Hawkins (1928–2003), author of international bestsellers *Stonehenge Decoded* (1965) and *Beyond Stonehenge* (1973).[24] It is a little known fact that, having famously used computer calculations to determine that Stonehenge was a Neolithic astronomical observatory designed to predict solar and lunar eclipses, he went on to try his hand at deciphering Avebury's astronomical function.

The matter is discussed by Hawkins in *Mindsteps of the Cosmos* (1983), one of his lesser known works. Here he cites Burl's belief that the Cove faced the most northerly moonrise, an event that would have occurred once every 18.61 years, adding that this was connected in some way 'with death, or maybe rebirth, or dead souls'.[25] So far so good, but then he turned his attentions to Thom's observations at Avebury, without ever crediting him. Hawkins reiterated what Thom noted on the site's axial orientation through the centres of the two inner circles, which provided a bearing of '340 degrees', admitting that 'the star *alpha* Cygni [i.e. Deneb] is on the line'.[26] Yet having said this, he went on to observe:

> I doubt if that was the target because the star is only the 18th-brightest star in the sky, and beyond that are the 5 bright planets and the sun and moon.[27]

Hawkins proposed that if an observer turned 180 degrees to look south-southeast, instead of north-northwest, the rising of Venus might have been witnessed at some point in its cycle. If not that, then perhaps the alignment targeted 'the edge of the band of the zodiac ... or ... it was some long-gone explosive object like a supernova.'[28]

Like Burl before him, Hawkins just could not get his head around the fact that Britain's largest megalithic monument once targeted a little understood star like Deneb, sensing perhaps that there had to be an alternative explanation.

Neolithic Man and the Cosmos

Hawkins might well have changed his opinions on Avebury's astronomical orientation had he digested the contents of Professor John North's monumental work *Stonehenge: Neolithic Man and the Cosmos* (1996), which he must have been aware of before his much-mourned death in 2003. North, formerly of University College London (UCL), surveyed Neolithic funerary and ceremonial monuments throughout ancient Wessex, the territory of Stonehenge and Avebury. He found that a large number of sites bore alignments to, among several other stars, the rising and/or setting of Deneb, which he says 'turns up repeatedly in the analysis of Neolithic monuments'.[29]

Among the sites offered by Professor North as possessing Deneb alignments – which includes the famous long barrow of Wayland Smithy, explored in Chapter Eleven – are some in the vicinity of Avebury. They include the Beckhampton Road and South Street long barrows,[30] and, more crucially, three of the stone-lined chambers belonging to the West Kennet long barrow.[31] Should North's alignments prove to be accurate and meaningful, then there can be no good reason to doubt Avebury's axial alignment towards the setting of Deneb. Moreover, if we now go on to examine Avebury's only recorded examples of rock art, they too will provide us with evidence to link Britain's largest megalithic complex with the cult of Cygnus.

Signs of Cygnus

John Wakefield is the author of a book entitled *Legendary Landscapes: Secrets of Ancient Wiltshire Revealed* (1999), which takes a good look at the geomythic reality of the landscape around Avebury and nearby Alton Barnes, which each summer attracts crop circle enthusiasts from all over the world. In its pages, Wakefield draws attention to the fact that when Keiller and his colleague Stuart Piggott were uncovering and re-erecting buried stones on the south side of the Kennet Avenue in the 1930s, they came across one which they labeled Stone #25S (*see fig. 24*). On examining its underside, which had not been exposed to the elements for many hundreds of years, they saw that it bore two distinct circular carvings which they described as incised 'cup and ring' ornament around a natural hole – a regular feature of megalithic art in other parts of the British Isles.[32] The highest one might just be that – a carved ring, but the lower example is somewhat different. Wakefield sees in it the long neck and head of a swan-serpent hybrid.

The line drawing that appears in Wakefield's book (*see fig. 25*) is without question suggestive of a swan, complete with eye, beak and faint engravings that might even indicate its breast and tail feathers. 'The ouroboros [a serpent biting its own tail] on stone 25S is beaked,' he observes, 'and the tail artistically implies the plumage of a swan's tail, delivering the overall impression of a serpent with the ability to fly – the winged serpent and circle (Cneph).'[33]

What Wakefield does not mention is that at the same time as Keiller and Piggott noticed the carvings on Stone #25S, they came across a highly significant burial at its base. It was positioned at its northeastern corner, complete with a ceremonial beaker. The fact that beneath it were large rocks which had initially held the stone upright after its erection, and above it was the final infill of earth and gravel, means that the remains were interred as all this was taking place, a unique feature in the opinion of the archaeologists involved.[34] Three further burials were found in association with other stones along the avenue. These were likewise positioned at the northeastern corners; however, each was slightly away from the stone hole – *only* the person interred at Stone #25S had been buried in direct relationship to its erection, singling it out as important for some reason.

Taking time out to visit Avebury in order to examine Stone #25S one cold winter's day in early 2005, I quickly became convinced that its circular carvings were indeed artificial. A closer scrutiny easily revealed the presence of chisel marks, while the carvings' outer edges are so smooth that they can only be of prehistoric origin. Unfortunately, having already seen Wakefield's drawing of the lower carving, it is difficult to see it as anything *but* the head and neck of a swan. However, others I showed a picture of the carvings to remarked on how they resembled an overhead view of the monument's two inner circles, which is a very interesting observation. It suggests that the stone might have acted as some kind of abstract map, with the swan's head and neck signifying one of the two circles, arguably South Circle, which is the larger of the two.

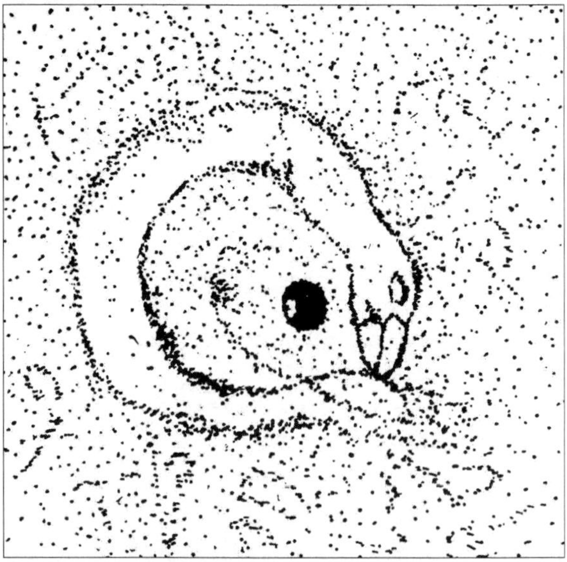

Fig. 24. Avebury stone # 25S showing the two carved images on its western face. The bottom one can clearly be seen to have the head and long neck of a swan-like creature.

Fig. 25. Artist's impression of the lower carving on # 25S at Avebury, after John Wakefield.

Although the resident curator of the National Trust's Alexander Keiller Museum in Avebury was extremely helpful in enabling me to locate Stone #25S along the Kennet Avenue, she disagreed with Keiller and Piggott's conclusions regarding its alleged ornament. She said that the archaeological community no longer deemed the marks artificial, a view I find difficult to share, especially as Keiller and Piggott state that the circles were, in their opinion, made using a 'pocked' technique earlier discerned in connection with megalithic rock art in Ireland.[35]

Place of the Swans

The existence of the swan's neck carving at Avebury is tantalizing evidence of a swan cult here in prehistoric times, which I will attempt in the next two chapters to demonstrate was linked with the constellation of Cygnus. The older folk of the village have told me that until fairly recently colonies of migrating swans would gather each winter in the vicinity of the water-filled moat that encircles Silbury Hill, and also on the nearby Winterbourne and Kennet rivers, which also form part of Avebury's ritual landscape. The birds would remain here through until the early spring, when they would fly north back to their breeding grounds in the Arctic region. If these migrations were taking place in prehistoric times, then they could have formed part of a yearly ritual cycle at Avebury in which festivities reflected the arrival of the swan colonies in November and, more particularly, their departure in the spring. Such simple observations make sense of the fact that in astronomical terms Cygnus is ruled either by Aquarius or Pisces, the period from 21 January to 20 March by our current reckoning. Indeed, one ancient calendar of correspondences I consulted brackets 'Cygnus' in the same column as 'Febrvarivs' and 'Pisces'.[36]

Spring, of course, is the time of renewal in the natural world, and its first stirrings are marked in seasonal terms by the February cross-quarter day celebrated since the advent of Christianity as the feast of Candlemas, which occurs on 2 February. Yet anciently this festival was held on 1 February, the day of a highly significant Celtic goddess known variously as Brighid, Bride, Bridget, Breeshey or Brigantia, the equivalent of a Gaulish goddess whom the Romans equated with their own Minerva.

Was she the primeval goddess of the Neolithic peoples who inhabited Avebury? Was she patron of its cult of the dead, well established by leading prehistorian Aubrey Burl? More importantly, could she provide the key to understanding the development in Britain of the cult of Cygnus in prehistoric times? I shall endeavour to answer these questions in the following chapter.

CHAPTER NINE

Goddess of the Swan

Brighid, Bríd or Bridget of Ireland, Bride of Scotland, and Breeshey of the Isle of Man is an ancient Celtic goddess who has been venerated in different forms for over two and a half thousand years. Her presence was almost certainly felt in the ritual landscape that served the Avebury monument, as sarsen stones found scattered about the downs locally are referred to as Bridestones. Moreover, a potent local water source downhill from the West Kennet long barrow, known as Swallowhead Spring, which feeds the Kennet River, has been proposed as a site of her worship. In the past, heavy surface evaporation in the late summer would cause the spring to dry up, but in early February, around the Celtic feast of Bride, the sacred waters would miraculously gush forth once more signalling nature's return to life at the beginning of spring.[1]

A Saintly Goddess

In ancient Ireland, Bridget was one of three daughters, all of the same name, who presided over, respectively, healing, smithing and poetry, the last of which governed the use of magical charms.[2] She was also patroness of the armies of Leinster,[3] where her main cult centre was in County Kildare. As a Christian saint, St Bridget (or St Bride) was the daughter of a fifth-century Irish chieftain converted by St Patrick. A monastery dedicated to her was built in Kildare, and here nine virgins kept watch over her sacred flame, signifying Bridget's role as 'the ultimate bringer of sunshine, warmth, growth and plenty.'[4]

A separate tradition found mainly in Scotland sees the saint as Jesus's wet-nurse, quite literally a milkmaid at the inn in Bethlehem, as well as 'Mary of the Gael'.[5] Some more outrageous Irish stories even make her the mother of Jesus, perhaps continuing the pagan belief that she was mother of the gods.[6] By virtue of these stories, Jesus was called 'the foster-son of Bride', while the Star of Bethlehem became '*rionnag Brideog*,' the 'star of little Bride'.[7] It was represented in folk art as 'something like a Maltese cross', or a three pronged cross, affixed to corn dollies called *Brideog*, 'little Bride'.[8]

Bride presided also 'over fire, over art and over beauty ... beneath the sky and beneath the sea'.[9] Like Brigantia (meaning 'High One)', the tulelary Great Mother of the ancient British tribe of the Brigantes, who was worshipped from Scotland's Firth of Forth to the Peak District of Staffordshire, Bride-Bridget was also a patroness of sovereignty.[10] Indeed, there can be little doubt that Bride-Bridget, and Brigantia, whose worship and veneration is attested by several Romano-British altar inscriptions, as well as a carved relief from Birrens in Dumfrieshire, in which she appears as a Roman Minerva wearing a mural crown and holding a globe and spear, all evolved from the same female deity. Although unquestionably Celtic in origin, there is every chance that Brigantia and her various forms, right down to the Bride-Bridget of Kildare, replaced a much earlier Bronze Age divinity, whose own origins might easily have stretched back to Neolithic times.

Totems of Bride

Like all previous pagan goddesses, St Bride had zoomorphic totems and symbols. Mention has already been made of her role as milkmaid, while Irish tradition speaks of her being nursed by a white cow with red ears.[11] This connection comes most probably from the fact that her mother, Morrigan, wife of Dagda, was also Boann, the goddess of the Boyne River in County Meath, Ireland, with '*Bóinne*' (*bo fhionn*) meaning 'white cow'.[12]

Scottish poetry – collected among some of the elderly residents of the Western Isles by folklorist Alexander Carmichael for his epic multi-volume work the *Carmina Gadelica* (1899) – speaks of Bride's serpentine form, which is said to 'come from the knoll' on her feast: in other words it awoke from its winter sleep and crept out of its hole.[13] Yet of all the creatures of the animal kingdom it is the bird that most personifies Bride's zoomorphic attributes. The hawk was 'Brigit's bird',[14] the linnet *bigein Bride,* the 'little bird of Bride', the oyster-catcher *gille Bride,* the 'servant of Bride', whilst all cockerel-related activities would generally take place on her feast day,[15] 1 February, which became known as *La Cath Choileach*, the 'Day of Cock-fighting'.[16]

Yet above all it was 'the fairy swan of Bride' that would prove to be the most enigmatic of the saint's avian forms.[17] Aside from Scottish poetry that alludes to her connection with this beautiful creature, a large number of 'Bride', 'Bree', 'Brid',

'Bright' and 'Brig' place-names are found in England and Wales, some with clear swan associations, a point noted by musician-turned-prehistorian Julian Cope in his essential tome *The Modern Antiquarian* (1998). For him, 'Bridgit is everywhere: In our landscape, in our names, in our language. She is Bree – she is Bridgit – she is Britain.'[18]

Cope takes Bride's original name to be the root 'Bree', from her Manx form as Briid, or Breeshey (*bree-sídhi*, the 'fairy Bree').[19] More precisely, most sources give the derivation of Bride as the ancient Celtic root *brig-*, meaning 'high, exalted'. This would be the source of Brigantia and the old Irish Brighid (Bríd is the modern Irish form), as well as the Manx 'Bree' (Manx itself is essentially a form of Irish written in a phonetic orthography based on English and devised only in the 17th century). This etymological root is expressed no better than in the place-name Bredon Hill found in the English county of Worcestershire. The site – associated very likely with a British Iron Age (*c.*700 BC–AD 43) cult of the dead, due to the gruesome discovery here of a whole series of skulls thought to have been placed on spikes over an entrance gateway – takes its name from '-don', from the Old English *dun*, meaning 'hill', while the prefix 'bre-' (Welsh *bre*, hill), is from the same root as Bride and thus arguably relates to the goddess. Around the time of her feast at the beginning of February, an observer standing on the hill's summit looking west will see a swan in flight formed by the inundation of pastures in the vicinity of a U-shaped bend on the River Avon known as the Swan's Neck.[20] As with the return of the sacred waters in spring at Kennet Hill's Swallowhead Spring, such naturalistic phenomena would have been important to the geomythic beliefs of our ancestors.

The Footprint of Bride

The most remarkable tradition featuring Bride's avian form is the annual search for her mark. On St Bride's Eve in Scotland a fire would be kindled, and prayers said in her name. The family would retire to bed, and the next morning the still-warm embers were searched to see if the saint had graced the household with her 'club',[21] or *lorg*, 'footprint'.[22] This we can take to be an unburnt stick or twig resembling a three-pronged fork, like a bird's foot. If found, it was seen as an omen of a good crop and prosperous year. If it was not present, the only way to regain the saint's favour was to go immediately to where three streams met and there bury a cock or pullet as an offering in her name.[23]

Bride's connection with the bird's foot symbol might also relate to the interpretation of her name as 'fiery arrow',[24] which as a simple line drawing resembles a bird's foot. It is tempting to see in the 'club', 'footprint' and even the 'fiery arrow' of Bride the four main stars of Cygnus, made up of Deneb and its three adjacent stars, known to astronomers as 'the Triangles'.[25] This would bring the 'footprint' of Bride in line with the beliefs of Native American peoples who, as we saw in Chapter Five, identified the stars of Cygnus with a star group they referred to as the Bird's Foot, or Turkey's Foot. In Welsh bardic tradition (after the word 'bard', meaning a poet or storyteller) this same symbol (although now reversed) was known as the Awen. It was associated directly with the Gaulish goddess Minerva, the name by which the Romans knew Brigantia or Bride.[26] How old this tradition might have been is unclear, with the earliest references going back only to the fifteenth century.[27]

The Bardic Tradition

The original Celtic bards were said to have worn a *tuigen*, or bird-mantle, which is described in a Gaelic work entitled *Sanas Chormaic* ('*Cormac's Glossary*'), created supposedly by Cormac mac Cuilleanáin (836–908), king-bishop of Munster in Ireland. The work refers to the garment as 'a feathered cloak' made of 'the skins of birds white and many-coloured ... and of mallards' necks and of their crests from the girdle upwards to the neck'.[28] A separate description of a *tuigen* speaks of it as being made 'predominantly of small songbirds' feathers, yet with the collar fashioned from the skin and feathers of the swan ... the swan's neck hanging down behind like the tippet on a modern university gown.'[29]

The almost gruesome nature of the bard's *tuigen* is strangely reminiscent of a shaman's cloak, as well as the wings of the raptors and scavengers found in the Shanidar cave of Northern Iraq. These, we will recall from Chapter Three, were used for shamanic practices by the priestly elite of the earliest Neolithic communities of Upper Mesopotamia. I strongly suspect that the *tuigen* was based on extremely ancient pagan customs and practices relating to the cult of the swan, and possibly even to that of Bridget. The fact that the *Sanas Chormaic* finally received publication in 1868 implies that the revivalist bards of the period adopted similar ideas for their own ritual paraphernalia.

Via Lattea

In addition to these deductions, Bride's role as a lowly milkmaid, nourished by the white cow with red ears, is suggestive of further astronomical implications. According to folk tradition, this connection is related to Olmelg (or Imbolc), the name given to her feast day, 1 February. It translates as 'ewe's milk', signifying the flow of milk that heralds the return of the life-giving forces of spring, causing the animals to bring forth milk.

Yet it might mean more than this, for the Milky Way (*Via Lattea* in Italy and *Voie lactée* in France), connected in the Catholic faith with the Virgin Mary, has for thousands of years been seen as a stream of milk,[30] while in certain English counties it 'marked the path to Heaven'.[31] Since Bride/Bridget is said to have been nourished by a white cow, personified as a sacred river (*Bóinne*, the Boyne), was she associated with the Milky Way on which the celestial swan takes its flight each night? If the answer is yes, then we have in Bride a perfect candidate for the personification of Cygnus as a pagan goddess and Christian saint.

The Swan as Psychopomp

As we have seen, in ancient Anatolia and Western Asia the earliest choice of avian psychopomp ('soul-carrier') was the vulture, due to its involvement in the process of excarnation (*see Chapter Three*). Yet in regions where vultures were not native other species replaced them, and often these were linked with their ability to migrate to and from breeding grounds in the extreme north.

There is little question that in Western Europe the role of 'carrier of souls' fell upon migrating species of waterfowl, the swan in particular. As a result of this relationship, they have over the centuries become entangled with superstitious folklore. In Britain, for instance, it was said that the 'souls of people' were embodied in swans.[32] Moreover, the folk of Corofin in Ireland, near Loch Inchiquin, Co. Clare, believed that if one of the swans on the water were to be killed then a villager would die.[33] In Germany the swan was seen as an omen of death and the underworld.[34] *Es schwanet mir* (literally 'it swans me') was said whenever it was felt that someone had, as we say in Britain, walked over your grave.[35] Lastly, in the village of Kemnitz in Eastern Germany the sight of a swan going into a churchyard at midnight was seen as a portent of death.[36]

A more direct association between swans and the northerly transmigration of the soul comes in the knowledge that in the Scottish Western Isles people saw whooper (or hooper) swans (and also greylag geese) migrating northwards to their breeding grounds in Iceland each spring as carrying the souls of the dead to heaven, which lay 'north beyond the north wind', an expression borrowed from classical mythology. Moreover, should a person be alive when the birds departed, then it was superstitiously believed that the elderly would be inviolate to death until the swans returned in autumn.[37] North, of course, is the direction of Cygnus, the celestial swan, which, being essentially circumpolar in Scotland, would always have been seen in the northern night sky. Is this how the stars of Cygnus became associated with the swan, and why the bird was linked not only with the cosmic axis, but also the journey of the soul into the afterlife – because it was seen to fly towards the celestial pole? If so, then this connection can only have begun when Deneb occupied the position of Pole Star, *c.*15,000 BC.

The Cult of Bride in England

Until now evidence of Bride's veneration in England has been scant, aside from a number of place-names derived from *brig-* and its variations, and the presence of various site dedications in her name, such as the St Bride's wells in the City of London (*see Chapter Ten*) and Glastonbury in Somerset. Recently, however, exciting archaeological evidence has emerged from Cornwall in southwest England of a swan cult that persisted through until the seventeenth century, seemingly in the name of Bride.[38] Excavations since 2003 at a riverside location close to a votive spring outside the village of Saveock, in the north of the county, have uncovered 28 earthen pits lined mostly with swan's feathers.

The contents of some of the feather-lined pits – which are either square or rectangular with a maximum size of 47 centimetres (18.5 inches) in length and a depth of 20 centimetres (8 inches) – had been removed before discovery, although by whom and when is not known. Some contained feathers, flint, swan down and small quartz pebbles. In six instances the contents had not been disturbed. Occasionally pits were found to contain whole birds, either chickens or cockerels, along with the remains of eggs, some containing fully formed chicks. Indeed, so many eggs were found that it seemed like the whole local community had made offerings in this manner. Carbon-14 testing of swan feathers from one pit has indicated a date in the region of AD 1640.

Next to the pits the excavators – under the direction of Marie Jefferis of the Saveock Water Archaeology unit – unearthed a stone-lined water tank serving the votive spring. This was found to contain large quantities of brass pins as well as fragments of textile, human hair, leather strips, and a piece of an iron cauldron, all indicating that the site remained in ritual use through until the seventeenth century.

Jefferis believes that the pits relate in some way to a local cult of Bride, for in her words:

> There seem to be several connections with Brigit linking to the Saveock pits. The swan, whose feathers have been found in the majority of pits, is dedicated to Brigit. So too is the custom of offering eggs to placate her in times of harvest.

Jefferis adds that, 'Brigit is often associated with wells, springs and healing waters,' recalling the Swallowhead Spring just outside of Avebury. Jefferis has also noted that cock-fighting traditionally took place on St Bride's Day, and that those who displeased the saint could regain her favour by burying a cock or pullet at the junction of three streams:

> The Saveock site is situated next to a river which although it is not the junction of three streams, is one of three linked rivers known as Three Waters. All this evidence together seems to indicate the pits having some sort of ritual quality, either as an offering or part of a charm or spell.[39]

I might add that the use of crystals featured in the cult of Bride, and on her feast day girls would fashion a sheaf of corn into the likeness of a woman, and decorate it with:

> ...shining shells, sparkling crystals, primroses, snowdrops and any green they may obtain ... A specially bright shell or crystal is placed over the heart of the figure. This is called *reul-iuil Bride*, the guiding star of Bride, and typifies the star over the stable door at Bethlehem.[40]

The effigy was afterwards paraded around the village by the girls who wore white with their hair unbound as a symbol of purity and youth.[41]

That a secret cult of Bride was present in Saveock, Cornwall, seems indisputable, suggesting that the villagers risked severe punishment and even their lives in order to participate in what was then an outlawed pagan faith that reached back to when the swan was associated with the migration of the soul. Such practices must eventually have died out, but there is firm evidence that even today the cult of Cygnus survives in an archaic royal ceremony that takes place each year on the River Thames. An examination of its suspected origins and development throws yet further light on the seasonal rites of prehistoric Britain, especially those which link the Avebury monument with both the celestial swan and the cult of the dead.

CHAPTER TEN

The Waters of Life

Huge pomp and ceremony still surrounds the sanctity and preservation of the swan in Britain, shown no better than in the quaint summer custom of 'Swan Upping'. This is the annual weighing and counting of all mute swans that live permanently on the River Thames.[1] Since the fifteenth century it has been organized by members of two of London's oldest livery companies – the Vintners and Dyers – who have been granted exclusive rights to keep swans on the river.[2]

The five-day journey, which commences on the third Monday of July,[3] departs from a wharf in the city of London and ends at Abingdon, near the city of Oxford (although originally it went as far as 'Oxford Bridge' in the town itself). The actual process of 'upping' is undertaken by the sovereign's 'Swan Marker', wearing a red jacket with a swan's feather in his cap, who is overseen by a royal 'Swan Warden'. At the lock on the Thames closest to Windsor Castle, the residence of the sovereign, the flotilla of skiffs halts for everyone present to toast His or Her Majesty as 'Seigneur of the Swans', a custom hundreds of years old.[4]

Aside from weighing and counting the birds, young cygnets are allotted, depending on their parentage, to one or other of the companies (any bird with both parents unmarked automatically becomes Crown property). Until the last century, the Vintners' Swan-uppers marked their cygnets with two notches on the lower bill, while those of the Dyers marked theirs with a single notch (today all birds are simply ringed around a leg). In addition to these simple identification marks hundreds more individual swan-marks were used by swan-keepers throughout the land.[5] Perhaps not unnaturally, one of the most prevalent swan-marks was the bird's foot symbol, demonstrating once again its association with the swan,[6] even though all waterfowl do, of course, have webbed feet.

Although the term 'upping' derives from the act of taking 'up' the bird from the water, it also applies to the 'voyage' itself,[7] which has all the hallmarks of an enchanted journey along the Thames to the source of the waters of life. Curiously, the annual Swan Upping ceremony coincides with a yearly meteor shower known as the Alpha Cygnids, which reaches its maxim on 18 July. For a period of around a week, meteors are seen to come from the proximity of Deneb in Cygnus, an astronomical firework display that could not have gone unnoticed.

Before the British calendar changes of the eighteenth century, the Alpha Cygnids would have coincided with the completion of the Swan Upping ceremony, since we know that a swan feast was held on St Swithin's Day, 15 July – as it was also on 11 November, St Martin's Day (*see below*). Although it is unknown whether the founders of Swan Upping were ever aware of this astronomical phenomenon, I would not be the first writer to make the connection.[8]

Official records suggest that Swan Upping took place for the first time in the fifteenth century, although this date relates only to when the Crown granted the Vintners and Dyers rights to own swans on the Thames. There is no reason to conclude that Swan Upping, or some variation of the ceremony, did not exist prior to this time. Indeed, the official Royal Windsor website says that it goes back at least to when the swan was given royal status in the twelfth century.[9] What I wanted to know, however, was whether this arcane practice developed from an even more ancient ceremony once attached to the River Thames.

The Vintners' Company

Originally, Swan Upping included all swans from London Bridge to Oxford Bridge, and would commence from Vintry Wharf, located to the side of Vintners' Hall on Upper Thames Street, which existed as early as the thirteenth century.[10] Just east of here is London Bridge, and between the two was an ancient tavern called the Old Swanne Inn, known to have existed by 1323.[11] Since it was only 200 metres from Vintners' Hall, and formed part of the Vintry Ward,[12] it is unlikely to have been ignored by the local Vintners. The tavern gave its name to Old Swan Wharf, which was located by what is now Swan Pier in Swan Lane, off Upper Thames Street. This is itself circumstantial evidence that Swan Upping is at least as old as this tavern.

The Vintners' Company, who controlled wine imports and regulated the licensing of taverns, is first known from documents dating to the thirteenth century.[13] However, members of the guild, or 'mystery',[14] as it was called, met as early as the twelfth century in the local church of St Martin's Vintry,[15] located just north of the current Vintners' Hall (the church burnt down in the Great Fire of London in 1666 and was not rebuilt). During this time many of London's Lord Mayors were also masters of the Vintners.[16] Indeed, there is a famous legend which records that on

13 November 1363, no fewer than five kings sat down to a feast laid on by one Henry Picard, the Master of the Vintners and Lord Mayor of London. These were the sovereigns of England, France, Scotland, Denmark and Cyprus, and in memory of this occasion even today five cheers are given at Vintners' Company banquets instead of the usual three. The so-called 'Feast of the Five Kings' is legendary in the history of the Vintners' livery company, even though historians strongly doubt that all the named monarchs were present on the day.[17]

Isis of the Thames

In the likelihood that the Vintners' 'mystery' pre-dated the Norman Conquest of 1066, and developed from an existing Saxon guild,[18] I was intrigued to discover that the area around Vintry Wharf had almost certainly been the centre of London's wine trade since Roman times.[19] This led me to another seemingly insignificant line of enquiry that will at first seem irrelevant to this debate. Just 300 metres away from the site of St Martin's Vintry and the old Roman riverside wall, was a temple dedicated to the Egyptian goddess Isis.[20]

The temple's presence in the heart of the city is confirmed by the discovery of a number of related items,[21] including an altar from the third century recording the restoration and rededication of the temple. It was found during excavations within the Roman riverside wall in 1975.[22] Most enigmatic of all was the discovery at the beginning of the 1920s at Southwark, on the south side of the river, of a late first century wine jar.[23] It bears a graffito that reads *Londini ad fanum Isidis* ('London, at the temple of Isis'; *see fig. 26*),[24] which alludes to the existence of a wine merchant in the proximity of the Isis temple, from which the wine jar and its contents originated.

Since the unloading of imported wine from the continent probably took place at a Roman wharf just a few hundred metres south of the temple, and the goddess Isis was seen as the inventor of wine, and even as 'Lady of Wine and Beer', then the existence of the wine container could imply that the temple had jurisdiction over the distribution of wine to taverns in Roman London. If so, then it is possible that the Vintners' Company might have inherited echoes of religious practices and customs associated with the cult of Isis, including its veneration of the swan. More importantly, this information strangely provides a crucial basis for the origins of Swan Upping and its links back to the Neolithic cult of the dead.

As the Roman empire spread, attempts were made to integrate foreign gods and goddesses with existing Roman deities, or *vice versa*, depending on their popularity. Thus we find the cult of Isis being assimilated with that of the Graeco-Roman love

Fig. 26. Wine jug found at Southwark, on the south bank of the Thames at London, bearing the inscription *LONDINI AD FANVM ISIDIS* ('London, at the Temple of Isis'), suggesting the presence of an Isis temple in the city.

goddess Aphrodite/Venus, giving the Egyptian sister-wife of Osiris (the Graeco-Roman Serapis) new attributes and forms. This would have included an association with the swan, a symbol of the love goddess, especially since the goose was already sacred to Isis.[25] I was thus intrigued to find that Vintners' Hall has a 'Swan Room', which can be toured online.[26] It is full of swan imagery, and included until recently a statue of Leda and the Swan (*see Chapter Eighteen*). Yet pride of place on an altar-like table at one end is a stuffed swan.

During an open day in September 2005, I learnt that this bird is ceremoniously paraded around at a great banquet held each year on 11 November, the feast of St Martin (Martinmas). In the past this event – once attended by the ruling sovereign, or his or her representative – included roast swan, although today, because the species is protected, goose is served instead. In fact, it is clear that the aforementioned Feast of the Five Kings was itself a Martinmas banquet, even though historians have pinned it down only to 13 November 1363.[27]

Since both the swan and the goose were symbols associated with the Roman form of Isis, I strongly suspect that these birds were important to her cult in London. Certainly, it is known that colonies of swans nested on this section of the Thames in medieval times,[28] meaning that they are likely to have been present in Roman times. Therefore it is possible that the cultic practices surrounding the worship of Isis might well have included veneration of the swan. I suspect also that her worship included a symbolic journey towards the source of the river, seen as the ever-flowing waters of life.

Day of the Dead

Another clue to the pagan origin of Swan Upping is St. Martin of Tours (*c.*AD 315–97), patron of France, wine and the Vintners' Company. All over Europe geese were eaten in his honour at Martinmas, due to some vague story about his life. Yet the fact that geese and cockerels were also sacrificed on his day argues for a more ancient origin to this tradition.[29] Indeed, we know that Martinmas developed as an extension of the former cross-quarter day of Samhain, the Celtic new year, known also as All Soul's Day, Hallowe'en, or the Day of the Dead. It is around this time that migrating swans (and geese – connected with Cygnus in Welsh star-lore[30]) return from the Arctic, most usually at night under a full moon.[31] Whooper swans in particular make unearthly sounds in flight that must once have been taken as the dead returning to this world, the origin perhaps of the association between Hallowe'en and the skies being alive at this time with witches, fairies and spirits of the dead.

Although these archaic practices are a far cry from Swan Upping, it is likely that the Vintners, many of whom came originally from France, celebrated Martinmas with a goose banquet. However, in London this tradition was amalgamated with pre-existing customs and ceremonies surrounding the swan, which I suspect had lingered on the Thames since Roman times (for instance, there is an ancient church and holy well dedicated to St Bride in nearby Fleet Street, which stands on the site of an earlier Roman structure. Moreover, no fewer than six St Martin's churches stood in the medieval city, the most for any dedicatee other than St Mary, St Michael and All Saints).

As a result of this process swans became the bird of honour at royal banquets, while the Vintners' mystery, or guild, which later evolved into the Vintners' Company, through its powerful royal associations, became – along with the Dyers' Company – guardians of all swans on the Thames. It was a rite celebrated at the time of Swan Upping, which I have no doubt was simply the resurrection of something quite ancient indeed.

Full Circle back to Avebury

As St Martin's Day marked the arrival of migrating swans and geese, St Bride's Day marked the beginning of spring when the birds would depart northwards, carrying the souls of the newly dead towards a northerly placed heaven. It is for this reason that Bride, or Brigit, became associated with swans and the Milky Way, for she is very likely a personification of the Cygnus constellation venerated almost certainly since Neolithic times. This new information now begins to provide a framework for annual rituals at the prehistoric cult centre of Avebury, which becomes Britain's most obvious site for the cult of Cygnus, with its swan associations and axial alignment towards the setting of Deneb.

New life was imagined as arriving with the swans from the sky-world around the time of Samhain, the Celtic new year (Martinmas, etc), while the souls of the dead were seen to depart with the birds in the early spring, following the feast of Olmelg (St Bride's Day), which also coincided with the regeneration of nature, symbolized by the return to life of the Swallowhead spring. During the middle of this four-month period, around midwinter, rites were conducted to ensure the safe passage of the dead into the afterlife, and also the return of the sun following the shortest day of the year.

I agree with Aubrey Burl that Avebury's South Circle, with its accompanying avenue, related to the regeneration of life in the spring, while North Circle, its Cove and the Beckhampton Avenue related more to the darker aspects of Samhain, associated specifically with the cult of the dead. At such times the veils between this world and the next parted to allow two-way communication with the inhabitants of the sky-world via the stars of Cygnus. I find it strangely curious that on a hypothetical journey to the source of the River Thames, if on reaching Reading in Berkshire you were to take the left fork instead of the right one and join the River Kennet instead of the Thames, you would come eventually to its source at the Swallowhead Spring, just south of Avebury.

Swans not Storks

The concept of birds bringing souls back from the land of the dead might well make sense of a powerful legend preserved among the peoples of the Baltic, which speaks of swans bringing newborn babies into this world, a role usually reserved for the stork.[32] It is possible that migrating swans coming into Europe from their northern breeding grounds were originally thought of as bringing new souls to the land of the living, just in the same way that they accompanied them to the sky-world in death. We are reminded here of the skulls of vultures found protruding from the walls of the cult rooms at Çatal Hüyük in south-central Turkey. They were found covered with mortar so that the tips of the beaks formed nipples, conveying the idea of nourishment and new life. Perhaps it was not simply the vulture's role to accompany the dead into the afterlife, but also to bring new souls into the world, a realization that might well provide fresh evidence for a belief among the Neolithic world in the transmigration of the soul.

There are clear indications that in Britain and Europe the swan and goose replaced the vulture of the Near East's Early Neolithic epoch in expressing the profound religious significance of the avian psychopomp, carrying the souls of the dead to *and from* a northerly-placed heaven, linked with Cygnus. Such cultic beliefs and practices arguably continued beyond the Neolithic age, surviving through until Roman times and beyond. Yet can we now go on to find quantifiable evidence that might help prove the apparent relationship between the Neolithic cult of the dead and the Cygnus constellation? The answer is yes, but for this we must leave mainland Britain and journey across the Irish Sea to Ireland's Boyne Valley. Here we will find what is arguably one of the greatest examples of Cygnus's influence on the minds of our Neolithic ancestors.

CHAPTER ELEVEN

Swan Knights and Swan Maidens

The passage grave of Newgrange near Slane in County Meath, around 50 kilometres (31 miles) from Dublin, is a very special monument indeed. Built *c.*3000 BC, it consists of a large mound with an elliptical ground-plan ranging between 79 and 85 metres (260 and 280 feet) in size. It has a curved exterior wall 10.5 to 12 metres (35 to 40 feet) in height, faced with shimmering white quartz, irregularly shaped and interspersed with rounded black nodules of flint. Around its base are enormous kerbstones decorated with abstract Neolithic art such as concentric rings, diamonds, lozenges, zigzags and 'solar' symbols. Surrounding it originally was an enormous ring of ninety-seven megaliths known as the Great Circle, of which only twelve remain. Similarly to Avebury's South Circle *and* the Ring of Brodgar stone circle in the Orkney Isles, it has a diameter of 104 metres (340 feet), precisely 125 of Alexander Thom's megalithic yards (MY), a fact which should raise a few eyebrows.

Beyond this is the knowledge that Newgrange expresses Neolithic man's profound interest in precise alignments with the celestial bodies. Each midwinter's morning, exactly four and a half minutes after sunrise, a shaft of golden sunlight enters a small 'roof box' above the southeasterly-facing entrance. It then penetrates a slim 18–metre (59–feet) stone tube before striking a carved target at the rear of a womb-like chamber, located at the heart of the mound. It is an amazing, and highly symbolic, spectacle that lasts for just over a minute before suddenly the light disappears and the interior walls are once again plunged into darkness.

Angus and the Swan-maiden

As might be expected, Newgrange is surrounded by archaic myth and legend. Known anciently as *Brugh na Bóinne*, 'Palace of the Boyne', this grand monument is said to be the tomb of 'three times fifty sons of kings', belonging to the legendary kingdom of Tara.[1] In more ancient times it was the *brugh* ('palace') or *sídhe* ('mound'), of Angus (or Oenghus) Mac Og, 'Angus the Young Son', a leader of the legendary Tuatha dé Danann, the children of the goddess Danu.[2] Yet even before Angus got his hands on Newgrange, it belonged to his father, Dagda, the 'Good God'. Angus managed to trick him out of it by asking if he could stay there for a night and a day. On being granted this favour, the wily chief claimed it as his own, saying that there would always be a night followed by a day.

In one Irish legend, the *Dream of Angus*, the hero, around whom four birds constantly fluttered as expressions of his kisses,[3] was said to have experienced a dream in which he fell in love with a beautiful maiden.[4] The next day he took no food, and that night she appeared to him once more, this time playing and singing and capturing his heart. Upon rising Angus again took no food, and this cycle continued for one whole year. For a long while he said nothing to those around him, but then finally he revealed the cause of this sickness to his mother, Bóinne, who became worried enough to ask Bodb the Red, the new king of the Dananns of Munster and the brother of Dagda, to go in search of this beautiful maiden. After much searching, he determined that she was Caer Ibormeith ('Yew Berry'), the daughter of Etal Ambuel, a Danann of the *sídhe* of Uaman, in Connacht.

Dagda then dispatched Bodb the Red to persuade Etal Ambuel to allow his daughter to marry Angus. Yet this would be impossible, the Connacht chief told him, for she alternated her form between a maiden and a swan at the end of each year, and on the coming feast of Samhain (1 November) she would join thrice fifty swans on Lough Bel Dragon ('Lake of the Dragon's Mouth'), in which form she would remain for the next twelve months. Etal Ambuel said that Angus's only hope of wooing her was to single Caer out from the other swans and ask her whether she wished to be his wife.

So Angus went to the lake, where he correctly identified her from among the other swans, which were linked as pairs via silver chains fastened around their necks (only Caer had a golden chain), and she agreed to marry him. Through her magic he was then transformed into a swan, and together they flew three times around the lake before flying, side-by-side, to his *brugh* (i.e. Newgrange), where they remained together for the rest of their lives. Apparently, the beautiful singing of the swan-maiden and her husband placed everyone into a trance-like sleep, recalling the manner in which he himself had first come to know her. Another account relates how, during their flight to the *sídhe*, the two swans were 'uttering as they go a music so divine that all hearers are lulled to sleep for three days and nights.'[5]

It is a quaint tale, and what is more, in the Scottish Western Isles, Bride was seen as the wife of Angus, confirming her own role as a swan maiden.[6] Yet it implies that Angus's *brugh* – a word-root that survives in Brow, a local place-name near Newgrange since at least 1541[7] – was the mythical abode of human beings who took the form of swans, and/or communicated with otherworldly beings who appeared as swans or swan-maidens. All this in a country described by one seventeenth-century Irish poet as the 'swan-abounding land'.[8] Should there be any truth in *The Dream of Angus,* then it might just suggest that Newgrange was once a ceremonial centre for the cult of the swan.

Murphy and Moore's Cygnus Enigma

It was with such knowledge that two Irish earth mysteries researchers, Anthony Murphy and Richard Moore, decided to investigate this very possibility. Having watched flocks of migrating swans occupying the waterlogged meadows of the Boyne Valley, they wondered whether there was anything more to Newgrange's Neolithic design and function that might reflect its mythological background. The two men wondered also whether Caer's otherworldly existence might not have had an astral basis – one that linked the *Dream of Angus* and Newgrange with Cygnus, the celestial swan.

Murphy and Moore began their investigations by comparing the shape of Cygnus with the ground-plan of Newgrange's central mound. The monument's interior chambers did bear some relationship with key stars. For instance, Deneb fell in its northern recess, while Sadr (*gamma* Cygni), was positioned at the centre of the stone-lined chamber, penetrated each midwinter's morning by the slim shaft of sunlight. Albireo (*beta* Cygni), the 'beak star' of the swan, was located at the mouth of the entrance passageway, almost as if it was there to receive the sunlight, which, symbolically, would then pass along its gullet to seek out the bird's heart or womb. With such information, Murphy and Moore observed that the monument's interior passage and chambers 'may have been constructed in the shape of Cygnus'.[9]

In spite of this discovery, Newgrange's entrance corridor was not itself aligned to Cygnus, since this targeted the midwinter sunrise. Yet then Murphy and Moore realized something quite extraordinary. If the axial orientation of Newgrange's entrance corridor were to be extended beyond where the sun rises over

Roughgrange Hill, or Red Mountain, an azimuth of 136 degrees, it brings you at a distance of 15 kilometres (nine miles) to another passage grave, or mound, called Fourknocks. Much smaller than Newgrange, Fourknocks has a cruciform chamber with twelve decorated stones, on one of which is a carved relief, thought to be a stylized human face. Clearly, this solstitial relationship between Newgrange and Fourknocks was unlikely to be coincidence, since both monuments form part of the same ceremonial landscape.

The Secret of Fourknocks

Murphy and Moore quickly saw that the angle and elevation of Fourknocks' entrance corridor was too far north ever to have targeted the sun. So they consulted Sky-globe, and waited to see what if any stars might rise over the distant Mourne and Cooley mountains, which appear in the 'window' created by the mound's entrance chamber as viewed from its interior. Assuming a construction date for Fourknocks of 3000 BC, they determined that one star alone fitted the criteria. It was Deneb, which, being circumpolar in Ireland during this age, skimmed the horizon and then rose up slightly to pass right through their proposed 'sky window'.

Thus Newgrange, which Murphy and Moore see as reflecting the likeness of the celestial swan, receives its solar light each midwinter from the direction of Fourknocks, where the starry light of Deneb once entered its inner chamber. On top of this, they were able to determine that:

> On the night of the midwinter solstice, Deneb marks the location of the sun from the time the sun sets until the time the sun rises plus or minus the minutes it takes Deneb to come out into the darkening sky. So observers at either mound could track the position of the sun below the horizon using Deneb as their guide.[10]

The two researchers noted also that during this epoch Deneb crossed the meridian on its lower transit just above sea level; indeed, it is the lowest point it reaches during the whole of the precessional cycle. It was this same phenomenon that occurred at Karahan Tepe in southeast Turkey in 9500 BC, an observation which first alerted me to the significance of Cygnus. For both men, the discoveries they had made in the Boyne Valley signified a moment of cosmic revelation, which Anthony Murphy recalls thus:

> I saw for the first time the system as it was designed to work, I was struck with a breathtaking realization, a revelation of ancient cosmological expertise, and a vision of a crowning achievement of an adept and capable people.[11]

This was powerful new evidence in our hunt to understand the true meaning of Cygnus and the significance of the north to our Neolithic ancestors. A magico-religious belief system that had developed in Upper Mesopotamia *c.*9500 BC as a cult of the dead involving the vulture as a psychopomp and shamanic totem had evolved in Britain and Ireland into something quite different.

The Swan Burial

Beyond these thoughts is tentative evidence that the megalithic builders of Western Europe might well have inherited the connection between the swan and the afterlife from an earlier age known to archaeologists as the Mesolithic era (Middle Stone Age). This was when the inhabitants of Western Europe very gradually went from being nomadic hunter-gatherers to more settled pastoralists and agriculturalists, marking the transition to the Neolithic era, which arrived *c.*4500 BC. To investigate the subject further we must travel to the Danish town of Vedbaek, located about 20 kilometres (12.5 miles) north of Copenhagen.[12] Here, close to an inlet on the coast, archaeologists have discovered a unique Mesolithic cemetery, one of only two of its kind in Scandinavia. A single grave in particular commands special attention, for beneath a small knoll excavators found a double burial composed of a woman of no more than eighteen years of age, and an infant boy, presumably her son.

Lying on her back with hands at her sides, she wore a dress with ringlets of snail-shell beads as well as other small pendants. A folded robe had been used as a pillow beneath her head, and over this her flowing blonde hair could still be seen. On both her face and pelvic region were traces of red ochre powder, a ferrous rock connected since Palaeolithic times with death and the afterlife. In fact, lumps of it were found on the site of the Sanctuary monument on Overton Hill, just outside of Avebury, where excarnation is thought to have taken place.

The most incredible thing about this Mesolithic burial is that the child, who had a flint axe placed next to him for use in the afterlife, was found in the embrace of a swan's encircling wing. What is more, he too had been sprinkled with red ochre, a sure sign that this ritual burial was to enable both the boy and his mother to make a successful transition from this world to the next. Sixteen other burials unearthed in the cemetery, all dated to *c*.4800 BC, showed that, similar to the young woman mentioned here, virtually all of the people interred had been laid out on their backs, with feet together and hands by their sides.[13]

The presence in Grave # 8 of the so-called 'Bogebakken cemetery group' of an enormous swan's wing protecting the body of a small child in its mother's care was not seen as without significance by Steven Mithen, Professor of Early Prehistory and head of the School of Human and Environmental Sciences at the University of Reading. In his book *After the Ice* (2003), he observes:

> Among the nineteenth-century Saami people of northern Europe, swans and wildfowl were the messengers of the gods. Such birds could, after all, walk on the land, swim on the water and fly in the air – adept at moving between different worlds. Perhaps the Mesolithic people had similarly revered their swans and let one fly that poor child away to their afterworld where he could have the life denied to him on earth.[14]

All this is tangible evidence that the peoples of the Mesolithic age, in Scandinavia at least, recognized the swan as a psychopomp, a 'soul-carrier'. In addition to this, there is clear evidence that this swan-related death cult prospered in Northen and Central Europe. Although there seems to be no consensus as to the direction of Valhalla, the realm of the dead in Norse tradition, Jacob Grimm's classic work *Teutonic Mythology* (1888) makes mention of the Norsemen gazing towards the 'door' of the north in prayer (*Norðr horfa dyr*).[15] Moreover, as previously noted, the Germanic and Norse peoples of Western Europe aligned their graves north-south, a tradition suppressed by early Christians who favoured an east-west orientation for burials.

Ride of the Valkyries

In the religion of the Norsemen, swans were seen as Valkyries, shapeshifting female warriors, heroines who gather around the god Odin and his wife Freya in Valhalla, where slain warriors are received into the afterlife. Indeed, Valkyries were the 'conductors of souls to the land of shades'.[16] Belief in their visitations to the physical world were widespread in the Scandinavian countries, where ancient tradition speaks of maidens adorning themselves in 'swan-dresses, swan's plumage ... after the naïve fashion of folk-lore.'[17]

We have already seen how in the *Dream of Angus* (*see above, page 111*), Caer Ibormeith yearly alternated her form between that of a maiden and a swan. In fact, European folklore abounds in stories of fairy-like swan-maidens, who usually appear in groups of three, or seven. Stories handed down across countless generations tell of them arriving at a lake where they remove their swan-shift (or 'wings') and swan-ring (that is, a necklace, like Caer's gold chain), which is left behind in the grass. A peasant then comes along and, on seeing the women, steals their belongings and watches from a safe distance. Once the maidens tire of their play, they approach the man and ask for the return of what is theirs, at which he requests that if one of them becomes his wife, then the others might be allowed to go free. This then occurs, enabling the peasant and swan-maiden to live as man and wife for seven years, until one day he shows her, or she finds, the shift and ring that he has concealed from her all this time. On holding these she immediately makes her escape, causing her husband to die of heartbreak.[18]

All over Europe, and across Asia also, the tale is more or less the same. In one version a farmer finds that on each St John's Day (24 June) his field has been trampled down, and so he asks his two eldest sons to keep watch on this night. For two years running they hear a rustling in the air, before unexpectedly falling into a deep sleep. On the third year the farmer sends his youngest son, who blocks his ears and hides in wait. Suddenly, he beholds three maidens who fly down, lay their wings aside, and trample down the crop with their constant dancing. The young lad then steals their wings and conceals them under a stone, and when the maidens become weary they ask him for their return. In response, he says that two may have their swan-shifts provided that the third becomes his wife.

Then the story takes a different turn, for instead of one of them complying, they simply offer him a drink from a golden pitcher, as fairy folk are wont to do.[19] He thus becomes enchanted by their otherworldly grace, and decides to return their shifts, enabling them to make their escape. Other variations of the story replace swan-maidens with dove-maidens, indicating that the dove simply became a substitute for the swan, quite possibly through Christian influence.[20]

To begin with, this tale shows the strong overlap that once existed between the concept of fairies and swan-maidens. Indeed, in Icelandic and Old Norse the words for swan and fairy are more or less the same,[21] while 'Elbe', the name of the north European river, takes its name from the white swan, even though *elb* is also a name for an elf or fairy.[22] Also of interest here is that in Gaelic, the word for swan, *eala*, *eal*, or *ai*, is the same as for a 'pillared stone', at which a criminal could claim sanctuary. It is also an *elad*, or *ealadh*, a stone 'tomb' or house of the dead, like a dolmen,[23] as well as a cemetery, bringing us back to the swan's association with both mortality and the transmigration of the soul. Indeed, on the Scottish island of Iona, at Port nam Marbh, 'Port of the Dead', where bodies were once taken ashore, there was an *eala* in the shape of an altar. The coffin would be paraded three times clockwise around the stone, before being rested down upon it prior to burial on the holy island.[24]

Mantle of a Swan

Beyond this we come back to the concept of humans shapeshifting into swans. The power of the swan-maiden seems vested in her swan-shift and swan-ring, which symbolize the totemic garments and paraphernalia of the priest-shaman, or female witch. On the removal of these items the power of a swan-maiden diminishes completely, making her as mortal as anyone else. Yet as soon as they are able to get their hands on their swan-shift, the power of flight is restored.

The symbol of the swan-ring is also important, for when seen around the neck of a swan it means that they are of otherworldly origin, since they signify swan-maidens in their totemic form. In certain tales, men throw a shift, ring or chain over a maiden who then instantly becomes a swan.[25]

Similar powers of magical flight and prophecy are also ascribed to swan feathers. For example, in Germany someone who suddenly finds they possess the power of prophecy would say: *Es wachsen mir Schwan-federn* ('Swans' feathers are growing on me').[26] As we saw in Chapter Five in connection with the Buriat shamans of Siberia, swans' feathers were much prized among those shamans who adopted the guise of the bird to go in search of otherworldly communications. We must also not forget the *tuigen* bird-mantle of a Celtic bard, which could include the skin, neck and feathers of a swan (*see above, page 99*).

The Swan Lineage

Still another Norse tale speaks of how a nobleman out hunting in a forest comes upon a beautiful swan-maiden bathing in a river, and removes her golden necklace, rendering the poor thing unable to fly. The nobleman goes on to marry her, and she bears him seven children, all of whom are born with a gold chain around their necks. This gives them the ability, like their mother, to transform at will into swans.[27]

The meaning of this story, and many others like it, is clear. It shows us that the ability to change shape into a swan was possibly seen as hereditary. If so, this explains why across Europe there existed an archaic tradition suggesting that the shamanic process of shapeshifting was passed down usually through a female line, and that the swan was the most powerful totem assumed by these women. This supposition makes sense of European accounts of legendary 'swan knights', such as Lohengrin. He features in various Grail romances written in Germany during the thirteenth century, and became the main character in Richard Wagner's opera *Lohengrin*, first performed in 1850.

In addition to this, certain European royal houses, such as that of Bouillon – from which came the crusader Godfrey of Bouillon (1058–1100), duke of Lower Lorraine and first king of Jerusalem – claimed descent from Helyas, a 'knight of the swan', while chivalric orders dedicated to the name of the swan were created to honour kingship. This included the Order of the Swan, founded in 1440 by the elector Frederick of Brandenburg to honour the Virgin Mary, while at Cleves there was an order of the Knighthood of the Swan.[28] Moreover, it is recorded that when in 1304 the English king Edward I was inducted as a knight, he swore an oath to God on two swans decorated with golden nets.[29] Other instances of kings swearing by swans exist, and I sense this tradition is bound up with the fact that similar oaths were sworn on stone pillars, which, as we have seen, in Gaelic bore the name *eala*, which also means 'swan'.

Somewhere here we may find the true significance of the Swan Upping ceremony on the River Thames, which, the reader will recall, includes a toast to the ruling king or queen as 'Seigneur of the Swans'. Moreover, just a few hundred metres from the site of the former temple of Isis in London is an ancient stone pillar, the final remnant of a *miliarium*, which in Roman times marked the point of convergence of all roads in Britain. Known as the London Stone, it was here that the city's mayors would swear an oath of allegiance to the king upon their investiture. As we have seen, in medieval times the Lord Mayor of London was invariably also the Master of the Vintners' Company, the organizer of the Martinmas swan feast.

Queens also were connected with the swan and goose through their association with the so-called 'goose foot'. As Jacob Grimm observed, the 'spinner' goddess Berhta, or Bertha, the '*goose-footed* queen of German folklore, may fairly suggest swan-maidens', indicating that this was a device associated both with sovereignty and otherworldly birds.[30] In fact, some have seen Bertha's 'big foot' as either that of a goose or a swan.[31] Could she have been a personification of the Cygnus constellation?

As we shall see, similar beliefs concerning swan lineages are to be found in other parts of the world. Yet for the moment we must return to England to determine a more direct link between the concept of shapeshifting swan-maidens and megalithic tomb architecture associated with the stars of Cygnus.

Wayland's Smithy

One of the most interesting megalithic monuments that Professor John North surveyed was Wayland's Smithy, a well-known Neolithic long barrow located just south of the White Horse Hills, near Lambourn in Berkshire. It is about 40 kilometres (25 miles) northeast of Avebury, and was most probably built by the same Wessex culture responsible for the West Kennet long barrow.

Excavations at Wayland's Smithy in 1919 revealed eight skeletons, including a child, while further work done in 1962–3 demonstrated that the monument was built in two stages, firstly *c.*3700 BC and again *c.*3400 BC. During the earliest phase a wooden mortuary chamber was constructed, inside which fourteen articulated and disarticulated bodies were found. Afterwards the burial chamber was blocked by a line of sarsen boulders. These were then hidden beneath a mound of chalk removed from the surrounding ditches, which are no longer visible.

During the second phase of construction a long trapezoid-like mound of chalk was added, measuring 60 metres (196 feet) in length with a width going from six to 15 metres (19 to 50 feet). This was surrounded by kerbstones, as at Newgrange. At one end were six three-metre tall blocking slabs, of which only four remain. They covered an entrance to a central chamber which opened into three further stone-lined cubicles that form a cruciform shape.

North determined that Wayland Smithy displayed a near-northerly alignment to the setting of Deneb in the late fifth millennium BC (a date which might be disputed by orthodox archaeologists). Other alignments here seemed to target the stars of Crux, the Southern Cross, which was at the time visible in southern Britain. This cross-like star group, as we have seen from Peruvian ethnoastronomy (*see above, page 75*), acted as a 'counterbalance' to the Northern Cross at the southern 'end' of the Milky Way. North further noted that:

> When considering Deneb's significance, we hazarded a guess that it was connected with the fact that no brighter star rose and set nearer to the northernmost point on the horizon. In the same way, no brighter star than *alpha* Crucis [i.e. the brightest star in the Southern Cross] rose and set closer to the southernmost point until, that is to say, it finally ceased to rise at Wayland's Smithy at all, in the 28th century BC.[33]

All of this was yet further evidence that key monuments in the landscape of Wessex reflected a basic interest in the brightest star of Cygnus. Even more importantly, the history of Wayland Smithy, like Newgrange in Ireland, is interwoven with folktales that seem only to enhance its association with the celestial swan, for legends speak of it being the abode of Wayland (also spelt Weland, Wieland or Völand), the divine smith in Germanic (including Norse and Anglo-Saxon) tradition. Indeed, it is said that if you leave your horse tethered there overnight, with a silver coin as payment, on returning the next morning it will have been re-shoed.

Völand's Magical Flight

Although this is merely a local folktale, influenced by the fact that Wayland's Smithy is positioned alongside an ancient British trackway called the Ridgeway, in the Icelandic *Poetic Edda*, the figure of Völand plays a quite different role. He spends his youth as a prince and smith making beautiful weapons that no blow can ever break. Then he and his two brothers manage to steal the swan-shifts of three swan-maidens, or Valkyries, whom they come across bathing in a pool. They then convince the maidens to live as their wives, which they do for nine years, before the wives of Völand's brothers take their leave.

However, Völand has been smart, for he possesses a ring given to him by his wife Alwit, meaning that so long as it is in his care she cannot leave. But then the

Fig. 27. Panel from the Franks Casket (*c.*AD 700-750), with Völand on the left-hand side. On the right of the same scene, Æegil catches swans in order to procure wings so that his brother Völand might make his escape.

Fig. 28. Eolhx (or elhaz), the bird's foot rune, seen above Alwit, the Valkyrie swan-maiden and wife of Völand on the Frank's Casket.

evil king Niðuð captures Völand, and steals the ring from him. He cuts the smith's hamstring, making him lame, and forces Völand to work at the royal smithy, located on an island and from which there is no means of escape.

In one version of the *Poetic Edda* found in the *Thithrekssaga*, Völund's brother Ægil shoots three birds and gives him the feathers, which Völand uses to create a feather garment so that he might obtain his freedom.[34] From the panel representing this episode on the Frank's Casket – a decorated whale-bone box of possible Northumbrian origin, dating to *c.*AD 700–50 and housed today in the British Museum – it is clear that the birds caught by Ægil are swans (*see fig. 27*).

In yet other versions of the tale, Völand is aided by his wife Alwit, who transforms the smith into a swan who then makes his escape. She too is depicted on the Völand panel of the Frank's Casket and next to her is a rune symbol known as the *eolhx*, a rigid form of the bird's-foot symbol (*see fig. 28*). It is said to represent a 'plant reed', which signifies a swan-maiden, or Valkyrie, and in particular her other-worldly origin in Valhalla.[35]

Thus Wayland's connection with Wayland's Smithy, built nearly 4,000 years before the arrival of the Anglo-Saxons, exemplifies the relationship between swan-maidens and magical flight, and suggests that the site's focus on Deneb is indicative of shamanic rites performed here during Neolithic times. Accounts of these ritualistic acts might easily have been passed down by word of mouth as abstract stories, until finally in Anglo-Saxon times any notion of priest-shamans achieving shamanic flight in the form of a swan became fused with incoming folktales concerning Wayland's own magical escape in this same guise.

A Priest-King in Mallard Feathers

Before we exit the British Isles in search of a deeper understanding of the Cygnus mystery, there is an additional monument that I feel has to be reviewed, and this is the megalithic stone circle at Callanish. Situated on the Isle of Lewis in the Scottish Outer Hebrides, it is a magnificent sight perched on a raised eminence, immediately south of the small hamlet of Calanais, a drive of around 40 kilometres (25 miles) from Stornoway.

A multi-linear arrangement of tall, slim, jagged stones gives Callanish the appearance of an elongated Celtic cross, something unique in the British Isles. Thirteen stones form a ring 13.1 by 11.3 metres (43 by 37 feet) in diameter, in the middle of which is a striking menhir (standing stone) 4.75 metres (15.5 feet) in height. It supports the western edge of a chambered cairn of a slightly later date, its

Fig. 29. Aerial view of Callanish from the north.

entrance corridor facing east. Heading away from the circle towards the north is a stone avenue, 82.3 metres (precisely 270 feet) in length. It is orientated north-north-east, and terminates in two huge blocking stones. At the southern end of the circle is a north-south aligned stone row 27.4 metres (90 feet) long, with a single stone on its eastern side, indicating that it might once have formed part of an avenue. From the eastern and western sides of the main circle come two further lines of stones, which are either unfinished, or ruined, avenues.

Legend asserts that Callanish is the work of a 'great priest-king' adorned in a coat of 'mallard feathers', recalling the *tuigen* bird-mantles of the Irish bards (*see above, p.99*), which also contained mallard feathers. He arrived in the company of many 'black men', who came in a fleet of ships and used their strength and skills to erect the monument we see today.[36] It is a fascinating story, and one that had drawn my interest long before I embarked on this present book.[37] Yet now I wondered whether the feather-clad 'priest-king' and his seafaring companions might not hold the key to unlocking Callanish's long-assumed role as an astronomical observatory.

Astronomical Observatory

Over the years many have tried to understand this mystery. Druid revivalist and pantheist John Toland (1670–1721) believed that Callanish was intended for the worship of the sun and moon. Astronomer Boyle Somerville, in an article published in 1913, concluded that the monument's north avenue targeted the rising of Capella, the brightest star in the constellation Aurigae, between December and May in the year 1800 BC. In his opinion the west row is aligned to the equinoctial sunset, while the east row marked the rising of the Pleiades in 1750 BC. In addition to this, Somerville deduced that the south row was aligned due south, while single stones located just inside the circle determined a northeast to southwest alignment that marked the lunar maxim every 18.61 years.[38]

Fresh from his success at Stonehenge, Gerald Hawkins also attempted to determine Callanish's celestial plan, which he connected with a date of 1500 BC. He too concluded that the complex was a lunar observatory, pointing out that at its latitude 'the moon at its extreme declination remains hidden just below the southern horizon'. However, he determined that every 18.61 years the lunar orb would only just skim the southern horizon if one were to gaze along its south row.[39]

Alexander Thom likewise arrived in Callanish in order to determine the monument's astronomical significance. He confirmed Somerville's earlier surmise that the south row is aligned precisely north-south (to be precise, it is 180 degrees 1 minute), and thus acted as a meridian marker. He went on to propose that the site's east row was orientated towards the rising of Altair, the brightest star of Aquila, the eagle, in 1760 BC, while the north avenue targeted the star Capella in 1790 BC. Further research indicated that if an observer were to gaze south-southeastwards down the length of the north avenue they would see the moon's maximum setting upon the slope of Mount Clisham, located some 25.5 kilometres (16 miles) away on the Isle of Harris.

Callanish was clearly a multifunctional observatory featuring solar, lunar and stellar alignments. Yet as Aubrey Burl was at pains to point out, the alignments offered by Somerville, Hawkins and Thom reflect a relatively late erection date for the monument, sometime between 1800 and 1500 BC. Thus even if the proposed stellar events *were* once relevant to the monument, they hardly make sense of its construction many hundreds of years beforehand. Indeed, Burl suggested that any future work on astronomical alignments at the site should concentrate on a window between 3250 and 1500 BC.[40]

Despite any vagueness concerning Callanish's date of construction, and Burl's natural hesitance at accepting the offered astronomical alignments, the monument's connection with the moon's 18.61–year standstill cycle has proved more difficult to dismiss. This aside, there are other possibilities regarding Callanish's general astronomical function. For example, it is always assumed that its south row should be understood as a sighting line that looks towards the south, hence the proposed lunar alignments already cited. However, what I do not often see mentioned is that this line of sight is blocked by a rocky knoll some 150 metres (490 feet) south of the circle, obscuring the view of the distant hills almost completely. Not unnaturally, the observer would need to climb this lofty crag in order to see the southern horizon. This implies that the south row more likely functioned as a sighting marker used to observe the meridian transit of stars that revolved around the northern celestial pole.

What else could this site still tell us about its original function during the prehistoric age? Wishing to learn more about Callanish's astronomical functions, my colleague Rodney Hale visited the Isle of Lewis with his wife Joan in August 2005. Aside from making his own observations, which are the basis of my findings here, he learnt that the above-named archaeoastronomers are not the only ones to have conducted surveys here. In the 1980s a team under the charge of C L N Ruggles spent some time at the site, and subsequently drew a remarkable panoramic view of the visible horizon from the perspective of the stone circle.[41] More significantly, it included the lines of declination, which determine the distance in degrees of any star from the celestial pole.

In plain terms, declination can be envisaged as the rings of a hemispherical target, with the 'bullseye' at the summit signifying the northern celestial pole, which is at 90 degrees. Each ring away from the celestial pole signifies a degree, going from 90 down to 0 at the celestial equator. An identical series of rings counting down from -1 degree to -90 degrees make up the angles of declination from the celestial equator to the southern celestial pole. Sticking the two invisible hemispheres together creates what we know as the celestial globe.

Why Cygnus?

One very important point that can be deduced from Ruggles' site plan is that, when not slicing the northern horizon, the stars of Cygnus will very often cross the meridian on their lower transit close to sea level, i.e. at zero-elevation. Indeed, as we have seen, Deneb skimmed the horizon at Karahan Tepe in southeast Turkey in 9500 BC as it did in the Boyne Valley of Ireland in 3000 BC. Yet in the Scottish Outer Hebrides between 3000 and 2000 BC, the approximate date of construction for

Callanish, Deneb was slightly higher, meaning that it could have been used, as Alexander Thom suggested, in conjunction with other stars, as a star-clock, but little else. On the other hand, some of the stars of Cygnus had a lower declination than Deneb. One of them, Sadr (*gamma* Cygni) – the centre point of the cross and also the 'breast' of the celestial swan – is of special interest here.

From *c.*3000 BC through until *c.*2000 BC, the declination of Sadr dropped from 34 degrees to 33.5 degrees, the lowest it comes in the precessional cycle, after which time it very slowly lifts away from the horizon. Such basic astronomical data is important, for it means that during this 1,000–year window Sadr, which is a 2.14 magnitude star, descended at this latitude to within 2–2.5 degrees of sea level on its lower meridian transit. At such a low height it would have fallen below its extinction angle, meaning that, even though it did not set, it will have lost its luminosity due to air haziness, causing it to flicker and then blink out of view as it reached the meridian coming in from the north-northwest. However, it would then have been seen miraculously to regain its luminosity once it had climbed to enough height, arguably around 2.5–3.0 degrees. This would have occurred at an azimuth of 10–11

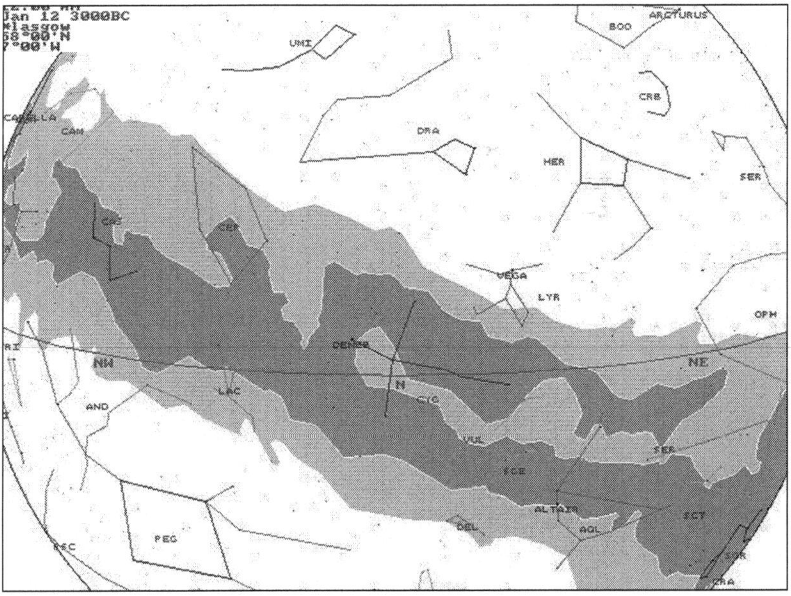

Fig. 30. The northern sky as viewed from Callanish in 3000 BC, showing Sadr (*gamma* Cygni) just above the horizon.

degrees east of north as viewed from Callanish, and just over a degree above an unnamed hill with a height of 140 metres, located about 3.5 kilometres (2.2 miles) to the north-northeast.

The greater significance of this observation is that the azimuth in question, 10–11 degrees east of north, is the precise axial orientation of the monument's north avenue, which clearly targets this very same hill. Such a visual display by the star Sadr would thus have made it seem like it was regaining its light from this unnamed high place, which Rodney Hale and I suspect was reason enough for the builders of Callanish's north avenue to target this extremely subtle astronomical event. It is important here to point out that between *c.*3000–*c.*2000 BC, when Callanish was almost certainly under construction, no other star was at the exact same declination.

One has only to look at an aerial photograph or map of Callanish to see that the rocky knoll to the south represents its chief observation post, since from here a panoramic view of the local landscape can be obtained. Thus the sheer fact that the entire megalithic monument is spread out before you to the north strongly indicates that it was erected as an astronomical instrument to monitor the celestial nuances of the northern night sky. Moreover, the main road on which the hamlet of Calanais is built appears, when looking at it on a map, to be a virtual extension of Callanish's north avenue.

Rodney Hale and I feel that those responsible for Callanish almost certainly saw Sadr as crucially important to their ceremonial activities, even more so than Deneb, Cygnus's brightest star. That the proto-Olmec of Central Mexico might have utilized this same star during roughly the same epoch, *c.*2000 BC, is itself curious, and could lead to discussions concerning a possible cross-fertilization of ideas due to transoceanic contact. Certainly, I had such thoughts in mind when I first wrote about Callanish's feather-clad founder and his black companions back in 2000.[42]

Festival of the Waters

Should the aforementioned 'great priest-king' be a true representation of the ruling elite responsible for creating Callanish, then did they – like their counterparts at Avebury, Newgrange, Wayland's Smithy, and so on – see the stars of Cygnus in terms of an otherworldly abode associated with cosmic life and death? Did the emphasis on the priest-king's feather-coat of 'mallard' feathers, like the *tuigen* of bardic tradition, suggest that Callanish was constructed to reflect shamanic practices concerning the bird as a psychopomp and totem in a manner that arguably went back to Palaeolithic times?

Aubrey Burl, commenting on Callanish's north avenue, notes that it runs slowly downhill towards Tob na Faodhail, the Bay of the Ford. Legends connecting megalithic monuments with water are extremely common, while many more sacred places are deliberately sited close to rivers, lakes and brooks, and this, he suggests, might not simply be for reasons of easy transportation. In his words 'water was intrinsic to the ceremonies',[43] and from Neolithic times down to the Iron Age, water-sources such as springs, wells and rivers were the focus of cultic beliefs and practices, which obviously never died out, as the Swan Upping ceremony on the River Thames and the recent discovery of the Saveock feather pits in Cornwall clearly imply. In this spirit, Burl then suggests that Callanish's north avenue might have, 'linked the circle with a source of water for rites long since forgotten', for he states:

> Early Irish legends tell how the Samhuin feasts on 1 November were observed by lake shores and that it was at this time that water goddesses were metamorphosed into birds with chains of silver or gold.[44]

As we know, those birds were swans, and the Samhain rites (Samhuin is the Scottish Gaelic form) that he refers to concern Caer's transformation in *The Dream of Angus*, which Anthony Murphy and Richard Moore use to demonstrate Newgrange's relationship to the cult of Cygnus. None of this was known to Burl when he went on to write:

> But the mental images of the people of Callanish are lost and one can only visualize ... a procession moving up the avenue from the bay towards the circle. Did its leader wear mallard-feathers?[45]

That the very star which Callanish's north avenue appears to target forms the breast, and arguably even the womb, of the celestial swan is unlikely to be unconnected with this imagined ceremony conjured by Burl. Yes, Cygnus was, or is, a swan, or a goose, but there is no reason that the mallard might not also have stood for this same general influence. Moreover, it is possible that the species of waterfowl associated with the 'great priest-king' became confused over the millennia. Was it perhaps originally a swan or goose, both of which are associated with Cygnus and the northern skies?

Callanish's apparent choice of orientation towards the central star of the Northern Cross does not mean that all stone circles and monuments echo this same interest. The remarkable work of early archaeoastronomers such as Boyle

Somerville, Gerald Hawkins, Alexander Thom and their own great mentor, the British astronomer Sir Norman Lockyer (1836–1920), has demonstrated a wide range of astronomical functions for prehistoric monuments, both in the British Isles and abroad. However, it now seems difficult to deny that some of the most high-profile sites in Britain and Ireland were built and maintained with a specific focus on Cygnus. What is more, there is every reason to believe that this reverence for the celestial swan, and its associations with the afterlife, were inherited from Mesolithic peoples living *c.*8000–*c.*4500 BC, as is shown by the contents of Grave # 8 of the Bogebakken cemetery at Vedbaek in Denmark (*see above, p.114*).

Yet as John North has observed, the evidence he has amassed concerning the orientation of Neolithic funerary monuments points clearly towards the fact that the stellar interests of the Wessex culture were superseded eventually by sites that bore more obvious solar-influenced alignments.[46] This is because, with the exception of Cygnus situated on the edge of the northern circumpolar region, the position of stars in the night sky shift too much due to precession. Only the sun and the moon remain constant in their rising and setting across centuries, something that will have helped single them out as more obvious timekeepers and objects of veneration. Although space could be spent exploring several more sites that John North has determined reflect alignments to Deneb, it is important now that we leave behind the British Isles and journey to Egypt, where we will come even closer to understanding the true origins behind the age-old interest in the stars of Cygnus.

PART FOUR

EGYPT

CHAPTER TWELVE

The Key to Ascension

Two and a half million blocks, ranging from two tonnes to seventy, covering an area of five hectacres and weighing an incredible six million tonnes, all put together with a level of sophistication superior to anything found anywhere on Earth, and there can be no doubting what monument we stand before now. Until the erection of the Eiffel Tower in the late nineteenth century, the Great Pyramid was arguably the tallest artificial structure in the world.[1] Its four sides, each with an average length of 230.36 metres (755.77 feet), are aligned so precisely to the cardinal points, that modern engineers do not even strive to achieve such perfection.[2]

From the flimsiest of evidence, which takes the form of a few lines in the works of the Greek historian Herodotus, *c.*450 BC,[3] along with some workmen's graffiti in one of the relieving chambers within the structure, we learn that the Great Pyramid was built to contain the mortal remains of a pharaoh called Khufu (known to the Greeks as Cheops), who reigned early in the Fourth Dynasty, *c.*2596–*c.*2573 BC.[4] Its two neighbouring pyramids, which are more or less equal in achievement, were constructed on behalf of Khufu's successors Khafre (or Chephren ruled *c.*2550–*c.*2525 BC), and Menkaure (or Mycerinus, ruled *c.*2512–*c.*2484 BC). Respectively, they are known as the Second and Third Pyramids.

Together, these three pharaohs changed the face of ancient Giza. In a matter of three generations it went from being a low-key cemetery at the northern end of a huge necropolis serving the royal city of Memphis into a visual extravaganza that must have been quite spectacular to behold. For example, the reflective glow of the white tura limestone facing-blocks that covered the exterior surfaces of the Great Pyramid – stripped off in the Middle Ages to build the mosques of Cairo – must have made its shimmering form visible for miles around.

The Tomb of Perfection

Despite all the grandiose claims concerning the Great Pyramid, it is quite clear that everything about it – its design, function and ultimate purpose – was the result of just over 500 years of achievement and innovation in funerary architecture. Beginning with Egypt's First Dynasty, *c.*3100 BC, royal burials were placed in rectangular mud-brick structures with sloping sides and stone-lined interiors. Known from their shape as mastabas (from the Arabic for 'bench'), they very gradually developed in size, shape and sophistication, until the first pyramid emerged from this basic design. Constructed at Saqqara, south of Giza, for the Third Dynasty pharaoh Djoser (ruled *c.*2672–*c.*2653 BC), it was essentially a series of square mastabas of decreasing size, placed one on top of the other – creating a structure that was stepped, like the pyramids in other parts of the world.

Subsequent monumental structures built for the pharaoh Snofru (*c.*2620–*c.*2596 BC), the first king of the Fourth Dynasty, at Meidum (another step pyramid), and afterwards at Dahshur, south of Saqqara (the Bent Pyramid and the Red Pyramid, the first 'true' pyramid), were all attempts at perfecting the art of pyramid design. So when Snofru's son Khufu took the throne *c.*2596 BC, there existed a hundred-year-old tradition that climaxed with the Great Pyramid, for thereafter, although numerous such structures were built or started, nothing *ever* came close to eclipsing this great wonder of the ancient world.

Much debate continues over the function of the Great Pyramid and its neighbours on the Giza Plateau. Even though each was used as the perfect tomb, it is likely that, before the burial of the pharaoh, these monuments were the scene of complex magical rites centered around the Egyptian cult of the dead. We first read about them in a series of funerary texts (the so-called 'Pyramid Texts') found inscribed on the interior walls of pyramids built for kings (and some queens) from the end of the Fifth Dynasty, *c.*2400 BC, through until the Eighth Dynasty, *c.*2200 BC.

Gods of the Lower Sky

The Pyramid Texts, along with the 'Coffin Texts' used on coffins from the Eighth Dynasty through until the beginning of the New Kingdom period (thus *c.*2200–*c.*1576 BC), as well as various 'books of the underworld' found inscribed in tombs and on papyri during the New Kingdom (*c.*1575–*c.*1087 BC), and Late Period (*c.*1087–332 BC), were meant to enable the soul (*ba*) of the deceased to achieve ascension in the afterlife, envisaged as a paradisical realm, not too dissimilar to our own Earth, which bore the name Sekhet-Aaru, the 'Fields of Reeds'. This was the

Egyptian Elysian fields which could only be entered after the deceased had become an *akh*, a word meaning 'glorious spirit', at one with the *'Ihmw-šk*, 'Imperishable Stars', or 'Indestructible Stars', equated with the 'Great Ones in the north of the sky'.[5] These were the circumpolar stars, which were seen never to 'die' since they never rose nor set.[6] Yet even by this age there was a certain vagueness about what was actually represented by the term 'Imperishable Stars', with all star groups either north of the ecliptic or north of the Milky Way being included, regardless of whether they were circumpolar or not.[7] However, for the purposes of this book, we will see them in terms of the northern group of constellations, the so-called 'Great Ones', outlined below.

Even more revealing is that at least one Pyramid Text alludes specifically to the deceased pharaoh journeying into the afterlife to become at one with the northern celestial pole:

> ...and you will give satiety to me at the Pole, at that which is the foremost of its flagstaffs.[8]

Such statements make absolute sense of the northerly orientation of the mastabas and pyramids, and demonstrate that originally Sekhet-Aaru, the Egyptian concept of heaven, where the deceased would live in the afterlife, was conceived of as lying in the vicinity of the stars that revolved around the northern celestial pole. Moreover, the soul of the deceased, we find, was seen as a human-headed bird that flew northwards in the manner of a migrating bird,[9] linking Egyptian funerary beliefs with those encountered already in the Near East, North America and much of Europe.

The Tomb of Senmut

The first real clues regarding the nature of Egyptian astronomy come from a quite remarkable tomb, made for Senmut, or Senenmut, chief male adviser to the Eighteenth-Dynasty female pharaoh Hatshepsut, who reigned *c.*1490–*c.*1468 BC. Located at Deir el-Bahri on the west bank of the Nile in the necropolis serving the ancient city of Thebes, Senmut's tomb contains Egypt's earliest known star map. Indeed, its arched roof is covered with mythical figures and circular horoscopes charting everything to be seen in the night sky during this epoch.[10] Why all this profound, and arguably hidden, knowledge of astronomy should have been concealed in Senmut's unfinished tomb (which incidentally was never used, since he apparently fell from grace) is perhaps answered in a boastful statement he made, which reads: 'I had access to all the writings of the prophets – there was nothing from the beginning of time which I did not know'.[11]

The tomb's north-facing ceiling contains a series of astronomical representations, including a lion, ox, crocodile, falcon-headed god and hippopotamus with a crocodile on its back (*see fig. 31*). Most have stars placed over their images, indicating that they are personifications of individual asterisms. Earlier forms of some of these figures, which constitute the northern group of constellations mentioned earlier, do appear in fragmentary form on at least one coffin, that of Heny, who lived in the Eleventh Dynasty, *c.*2134–*c.*1991 BC.[12] However, in Senmut's tomb we see them all together in their full glory for the first time.

Inscriptions accompany the northern star group, which go on to feature in the stombs and cenotaphs of several later kings. For instance, the hippo asterism *Reret* is named as a form of the goddess Isis, the sister/wife of Osiris.[13] It is also associated with the goddess Apet, as well as with Ammit, or Ammut, the composite hippo, lion and crocodile, who devours the souls of those unworthy to enter the afterlife. This striking image is usually identified as the constellation Draco,[14] the dragon, which marks the position of the ecliptic pole, around which the celestial pole makes its circular journey over the 26,000-year precessional cycle. The seven stars are occasionally identified as those of Ursa Minor, the Little Bear, yet this is by no means

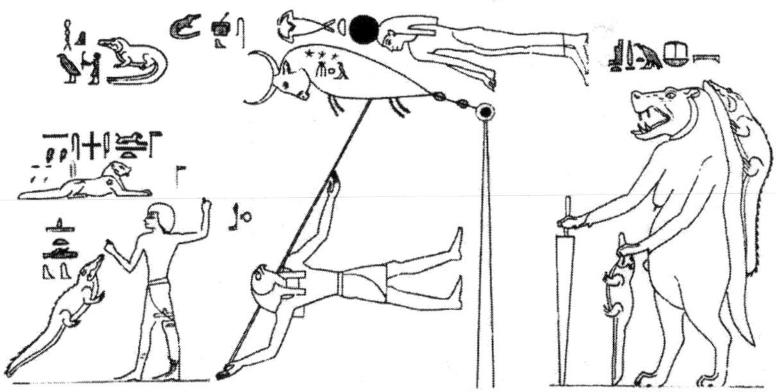

Fig. 31. The northern group of constellations from the ceiling in the tomb of Senmut at Deir el-Bahri, dating from *c.*1490–*c.*1468 BC. Note the falcon-headed god Dwn-'nwy (Cygnus) spearing the 'ox thigh' constellation Mšhtyw (Ursa Major)

certain. As for the crocodile often shown on the hippo's back, this is likely to be another form of Draco, perhaps from a separate tradition.

Left of the hippo is *Mšhtyw*, the Ox or Bull, shown as an oval shape with a bull's head. Yet on other later star maps it is depicted as either an ox thigh, its usual form, or a complete ox. This bovine asterism is without doubt Ursa Major, the Great Bear, or at least its central component, the Plough or Big Dipper. Indeed, simply by turning the constellation upright makes it easy to imagine it as an ox thigh. Moreover, the Bedouin of Egypt's Western Desert have always referred to Ursa Major as 'The Leg'.[15]

Sometimes, the ox in the form of a torso is seen attached to a mast, or pillar, known as the 'Great Mooring Post' (*Mnít*), which in Senmut's tomb is being climbed by the falcon-headed god. It is generally in front of the hippo, and very likely constitutes the cosmic axis, linking the physical world with the northern celestial pole, around which Ursa Major, as the ox thigh, torso or full animal, constantly revolves, unable to break free from its moorings.[16]

The Falcon-Headed God

Most enigmatic of all the figures in the northern group of constellations is the falcon-headed god, who goes by the name of Dwn-'nwy (also *'Nw* or *'N*(*w*)), abbreviated occasionally to An or Anu.[17] As a title Dwn-'nwy can be interpreted as 'he who unfolds two wings',[18] or 'the uplifter of wings or claws'.[19] This figure, with the head of a bird and body of a man, is a very ancient deity indeed. He features in the Pyramid Texts as a proclaimer to the spirits,[20] as well as a form of Osiris,[21] Lord of the Underworld, whose identity is assumed by the deceased in death. The name Dwn-'nwy is also uttered in the same breath as principal deities such as Horus, Set, Thoth and Osiris,[22] showing that even in Old Kingdom times he stood shoulder to shoulder with this important pantheon of gods.

Who exactly Dwn-'nwy might have been was a subject explored by Gerald Avery Wainwright, a British Egyptologist who specialized in the sky-religion of ancient Egypt. In an article entitled 'A Pair of Constellations', published in 1932,[23] he pointed out that the falcon-headed god on the Senmut ceiling is shown with a cord stretched between his two outstretched arms and attached to the bull Mšhtyw, or Ursa Major. Other scenes of this same constellation show the figure holding a spear instead of the rope cord. It points downwards at an angle of around 45 degrees and just about touches the bull in whatever form it takes.[24] Clearly, there was a relationship between these two constellations, which Wainwright noted can be traced back as early as *c.*2100 BC, where they appear together on the aforementioned coffin of Heny.[25]

Wainwright attempted to identify the falcon-headed god by invoking the following criteria. Firstly, the constellation in question had to be positioned in the northern skies, where it is shown in the Senmut astronomical ceiling, and, secondly, it should be in opposition to an upright standing Ursa Major, as the ox thigh. So, after due consideration, he delivered his verdict:

> Guided by these conditions an observer will soon take notice of the four magnificent stars which spread themselves widely across the northern skies in the shape of a double right angle. Actually they form the most noticeable part of the constellation which to-day we call Cygnus.[26]

Cygnus, Wainwright reminds us, is thought of 'as a bird sailing across the sky with wings outstretched'.[27] The four main stars of Cygnus – Deneb (*alpha* Cygni), Sadr (*gamma* Cygni), Gienah (*epsilon* Cygni) and *delta* Cygni – fitted all the criteria, suggesting that they really were the falcon-headed god Dwn-'nwy. Yet since Mšhtyw, the Bull or Ox, was seen by the ancient Egyptians as a personification of Set, god of disorder and chaos (as was the hippo with a crocodile on its back, represented by the stars of Draco), then the falcon-headed god had to represent his mortal enemy, Horus, the son of Osiris (even though the two names appear separately in the Pyramid Texts). Horus the Younger, as he is known to distinguish him from Horus the Elder, the son of Hathor (*see Chapter Fourteen*), avenges his father's brutal death at the hands of Set, who was Osiris's brother. Indeed, one inscription found alongside a depiction of the celestial falcon-headed god reads, 'Horus who fights rebels', an allusion to the near mythical 'Followers of Set'.[28] Thus the old foes were forever seen sparring around the northern celestial pole in a manner captured in both ancient Egyptian art and myth.

Stretching of the Cord

Wainwright goes on to point out that Ursa Major, or Mšhtyw, was fully circumpolar during the Pyramid Age, and that in the absence of a precise Pole Star its movement around the northern celestial pole might well have been used by the ancient Egyptians to determine true north.[29] This was achieved during a ceremony known as *Pedj Shes*, the 'Stretching of the Cord', conducted in the presence of the pharaoh using a *merkhet*, the 'instrument of knowing', which was an ancient plumb bob attached to the end of a horizontal stick with a vertical slit-like sight (recalling very similar instruments utilized by the astronomer-priests of the Maya). Afterwards, the pharaoh, working in conjunction with the goddess Sheshat (no doubt a priestess acting on her behalf), would stretch taut a looped cord between two stakes, or poles. This signified the finding of the north-south meridian line, which would then define the orientation of the planned building or structure. While the ceremony was of great symbolic and spiritual importance (*see below*), and the pharaoh's presence was crucial, his physical involvement was most probably a cosmetic affair, in the same way that a town mayor might lay the foundation stone of a new building.

Various means have been proposed to explain how true north was achieved by the ancient Egyptian priest-astronomers. Measuring the distance between the most northerly rising and setting of the sun at the time of the summer solstice has been suggested, but this would not have been accurate enough to create the precision necessary to align the pyramids, which were often within just a few minutes of a degree off true north.[30] Then there is the theory that a gnomon, a pole stuck into the ground, could have been used – its shortest shadow determining the direction of true north. Yet this idea also lacks the precision necessary to align pyramids.[31] Other methods suggested have included noting the highest and lowest position of a star as it makes its upper and lower transit of the meridian, or simply marking the whereabouts of the Pole Star, or at least the closest star to the pole, yet once again these methods could never have offered the necessary precision.[32]

This left just two other possibilities, both of which involve the observation of stars in the northern night sky. In the first instance, a near circumpolar star would be chosen, and a false horizon created to form a perfectly flat backdrop and to eliminate the fact that a bright star extinguishes (ceases to be visible) around a degree or so above the true horizon. Afterwards, the star's exact point of appearance and disappearance in relation to the false backdrop would be recorded. Dividing the resulting distance into two would reveal the direction of true north.

This theory, first proposed by the late I E S Edwards (1909–96), one of the greatest ever authorities on Egyptian pyramids,[33] is definitely a strong candidate, but one other possible technique exists, and this is the method first proposed by Wainwright in 1932. He suggested observing the movement of a constellation, or indeed the stars of two constellations, around the celestial pole, and then choosing two or more stars that line up vertically to highlight the whereabouts of the meridian line. The *merkhet* could have been used for this purpose, especially in connection with stars making their upper meridian transit.[34] The only problem here is knowing where the meridian is in the first place, suggesting that if this method is valid then it must have been done in conjunction with the previous option, i.e. measuring the distance between the rising and setting of a near-circumpolar star.

Whatever the solution, the Stretching of the Cord ceremony was not simply a practical process. It was essential to the cosmic harmony experienced by the pharaoh, not only during his reign, but also in the afterlife, when the accuracy of his alignment to true north might well determine whether or not he reached his ultimate destination. Thus any stars or asterisms used in establishing the meridian line would have been revered as guardians of the afterlife, and this was indeed the case with respect to the four stars forming the 'bowl' of Ursa Major. These, Wainwright realized, were identified in ancient Egyptian funerary texts as the 'Four Northern Stars',[35] synonymous with the 'Four Children of Horus'. They are named as 'Imsety, Hapi, Duamutef, Qebhsenuf ... who are behind the Foreleg in the northern sky'.[36] As the offspring of Horus the Elder (the powerful, mature god, as opposed to his infant form, Horus the Younger), they were seen as protectors of the deceased's internal organs, which were placed inside canopic jars representing these four lesser deities. Thus, Wainwright concluded, that in the absence of a Pole Star (the last one being Thuban, *alpha* Draconis, which had moved too far away from the celestial pole by *c.*2780 BC), Ursa Major, as the ox thigh, had been used to determine true north and thus the north-south meridian line.[37]

The Work of Zába and Stecchini

No one really picked up on Gerald Wainwright's findings regarding the interplay between Cygnus and Ursa Major in Old Kingdom times until 1953, when the subject was reviewed by Egyptologist and astronomer Zbyněk Zába of the Czechoslovak Academy in Prague. Having accepted that true north could have been achieved during the Pyramid Age using circumpolar, or near-circumpolar, stars, he concluded that the 'Stretching of the Cord' ceremony must have involved the use of Cygnus as the falcon-headed god Dwn-'nwy, his outstretched arms obviously representing the meridian line.[38] Zába proposed that four minor stars in this constellation (*chi*, *iota*, *theta* and *zeta* Cygni) were used for this purpose.[39]

Lending support to this theory is the work of Livio Catullus Stecchini (1913–1979), a mathematician and metrologist, and former Professor of Ancient History at William Patterson College in New Jersey. Among the many discoveries to his credit was compelling evidence that the ancient Egyptians calculated latitude and longitude, and incorporated this knowledge into setting the boundaries of Upper and Lower Egypt, as well as determining the dimensions of the Great Pyramid.[40] Stecchini was one of the greatest minds ever to have turned his attention to the subject of ancient Egypt, and so what he had to say about the manner in which the pyramid builders calculated true north should not be dismissed lightly.

In an extraordinary *magnum opus* entitled *A History of Measures*, compiled in stages and available online,[41] Stecchini agreed in principle with the findings of Zába concerning the use of Cygnus as the premier constellation involved in determining true north during the Pyramid Age. However, he swept aside Zába's suggestion that this was achieved using four minor stars, and instead asserted that it must have involved Deneb, 'because except for this most brilliant star there would not have been any reason to select this constellation as indicator.'[42]

Stecchini did accept, however, that a second star in Cygnus must also have been used, since together they would have formed the outstretched cord or spear held in the hands of the falcon-headed god. To find out which star, he turned his attentions to Ursa Major, and calculated that the meridian was most probably determined by dropping a line from Deneb through the natural divide between the four stars that form the bowl and the remaining group of three. This, he found, passed between *delta* and *epsilon* Ursae Majoris, meaning that the second star used in Cygnus must have been *zeta* Cygni, which lies in the celestial swan's upper right wing. By lining up these four stars, two in Cygnus when on its upper transit of the meridian and two in Ursa Major on its lower transit, true north might easily have been obtained using the *merkhet* measuring instrument.

Yet Stecchini noted something else of significance regarding the northern group of constellations. The ox-thigh constellation was often shown tied like a balloon to a rope being held by the hippo as the celestial personification of Draco, the dragon. This, like the Great Mooring Post alluded to earlier, related to a time when Thuban, *alpha* Draconis, came to within seven arc minutes of the celestial pole, something Stecchini calculated had occurred between *c.*3000 and *c.*2780 BC. During this period it would have seemed like the celestial ox thigh was revolving around the hippo as if on a leash. Thereafter *alpha* Draconis drifted too far away from the position of the celestial pole to count as Pole Star, and so was replaced as a meridian marker by the stars of Cygnus and Ursa Major.

Despite what Stecchini had to say in this respect, in the end he declined to assert what he believed was used to align the Great Pyramid and its neighbours, both at Giza and on the other pyramid fields attached to the ancient city of Memphis. In his favour, he readily admitted that he did not have all the necessary data concerning the foundation dates of pyramids and the necessary positions of stars to make such judgments. Stecchini's honesty is commendable, yet his vindication of Wainwright and Zába's earlier work confirms that whatever method was used to align the Great Pyramid, a north-south meridian line symbolically created by the stars of Cygnus and Ursa Major certainly fits the bill.

There is little question that over and beyond the worship of a plethora of different deities from both Upper and Lower Egypt, there existed an indigenous sky-religion with a profound stellar basis that almost certainly stretched back into prehistory. This was certainly the conclusion of Stecchini, who wrote: 'Considering the Egyptian way of thinking, it is possible that there was a cosmology [during the Pyramid Age] that assumed a world ending to the north of Egypt in the Mediterranean.'[43] In other words, the ancient Egyptians acknowledged a northerly-placed sky-world, a conclusion I concur with entirely.

Recently, the idea that circumpolar stars revolving around the northern celestial pole were used to determine the meridian line during the Pyramid Age has had a revival. Kate Spence of the Faculty of Oriental Studies at the University of Cambridge proposed in 2000 that the stars Kochab in Ursa Minor and Mizar in Ursa Major were used to achieve true north.[44] The following year Juan Antonio Belmonte of the Astrophysics Institute of the Canary Islands (IAC) highlighted serious problems with Spence's theory, and proposed instead that true north was determined using the stars Merak (*beta* Ursa Majoris) and Dubhe (*delta* Ursa Majoris).[45]

The Key to Ascension

Whatever the answer, and clearly there are differences of opinion even among the experts in archaeoastronomy, in the sky-religion of the ancient Egyptians it was the falcon-headed god Dwn-'nwy (Cygnus) and the ox-thigh Mšhtyw (Ursa Major) who were the hidden guardians of the meridian line, and as such were the key to ascension. This is a concept connected in the Pyramid Texts, and later funerary texts, with a sky-rope, ladder or cord that linked this world with the northern celestial pole and is seen in the outstretched arms of Dwn-'nwy.

We read, for instance, in a so-called 'ascension' text how the gods of the sky and earth got together to 'make a ladder for you that you may ascend on it to the sky, the doors of the sky are opened to you, the doors of the starry firmament (*Shdw*, or *Sehedu*, meaning a starry entity or region) are thrown open for you.'[46] Another utterance from the Pyramid Texts is a full 'invocation of the ladder to the sky', constructed in order that 'Osiris [i.e. the deceased] might ascend on it', and on which 'my bones are assembled for me, my limbs are gathered together for me, and I leap up to the sky into the presence of the god the Lord of the ladder'.[47] Here it is referred to several times as the 'ladder of Seth' (Set), and once only as the 'ladder of Horus', suggesting that, since Set most obviously presided over the ox thigh constellation, the Horus mentioned here might be linked with Dwn-'nwy as Cygnus. Gerald Wainwright had much to say about this ascension symbolism in the Pyramid Texts, observing: 'The ancient Egyptian considered a ladder as a good means of climbing the steep ascent of heaven. It made part of the star worship of Egypt, for it assists the Pharaoh "in order that he may sit among the stars of heaven."'[48]

The Road to Heaven

What is so intriguing about the concept of the sky-ladder is that it features universally in shamanic tradition, where it has always been viewed as 'the road of the dead', associated specifically with 'ascension'.[49] According to world-renowned expert on shamanism Mircea Eliade, 'countless' examples exist of 'shamanic ascent to the sky by means of a ladder'.[50] Moreover, the 'same means is also employed to facilitate the gods' descent to Earth or to ensure the ascent of the dead man's soul.'[51]

Eliade ably showed that the ladder motif is found among the peoples of the Indian archipelago, the Mangar tribes of Nepal, the Malay tribes of the southern Philippines, the Dudun of Borneo and the Russians of Voronezh, to mention just a few.[52] It was present also in the religious mysteries surrounding the god Mithras in the Roman world, while the means of ascension by ladder was known as well in ancient Greece, Africa and North America.[53] Then, of course, there is the biblical story in which Jacob falls asleep and sees a ladder on which angels ascend and descend between heaven and Earth (Genesis 28:11–22), and the ladder that the Prophet Muhammad witnesses rising from the Temple of Jerusalem to heaven, with angels on either side. On this ladder the souls of the righteous ascend to heaven.[54]

In all cases the sky-ladder, as Eliade pointed out, was thought to connect heaven with the *axis mundi*, the perceived centre of the world,[55] meaning that those ladders alluded to in Egyptian funerary texts derive most probably from a shamanic-based religion of Predynastic origin. Moreover, as Wainwright suspected,[56] it formed part of an original star cult that was absorbed into the rising solar religion – a subject we shall return to in Chapter Fourteen.

The Place of Judgment

The concept of ascension achieved via the meridian line as a sky-ladder was displayed also on the ground. Some 17 kilometres (10.5 miles) due north of Giza is Ausim, the site of the ancient city of Khem, or Sekhem, the Greek Letopolis. Several references in the Pyramid Texts connect Letopolis specifically with the ladder of ascension. One speaks of the Four Sons of Horus 'of Khem', i.e. Letopolis, tying a 'rope ladder for this King', and making firm 'the wooden ladder for this King',[57] showing that there were actually two types of ladder in the Egyptian sky-religion.

The Pyramid Texts speak also of the deceased achieving ascension via the 'doors of the sky',[58] which the *Book of the Dead* tells us were reached via Letopolis: 'the gates which are in Sekhem [Letopolis] are opened unto me.'[59] It appears in a chapter that earlier hails the 'Thigh [Mšhtyw, i.e. Ursa Major] which dwellest in the northern heaven ... which art seen and diest not', and goes on to speak of the deceased having journeyed from Earth to heaven in order to join 'a boat in heaven'.[60] Yet it speaks also of the god Shu having made him vigorous 'by the two sides of the Ladder, and the stars which never rest ...',[61] i.e. the circumpolar stars of the northern night sky.

Thus the ladder, rope, or meridian, was seen as ascending from a ground zero point at Letopolis, exactly north of Giza. It almost seemed as if the deceased interred at Giza was expected to exit northwards and then journey in a straight line until they reached Letopolis where, in some alternative realm, judgment of the soul took place and the ascension process began. As Wainwright observed: 'Letopolis was not only a place where the dead were judged and rebels repelled by fire, but it was also a place whence the justified soul ascended to heaven.'[62]

Opening of the Mouth

Not only is Letopolis the mythical home of the Four Children of Horus, as well as the form of Horus known as *kehnty-irty*, but its chief priest was called 'Opener of the Mouth', denoting that he presided over what was known as the 'Opening of the Mouth' ceremony.[63] This was a rite performed on the wrapped and embalmed mummy (or sometimes a statue representing the deceased), whilst it was upright in its coffin immediately prior to burial, as is depicted in various tomb paintings and funerary texts.

The Opening of the Mouth ceremony was meant to awaken the mummy as a vessel for the *ka*, or 'spirit-double', of the deceased. In addition to purification, sensing, anointing and incantations, a ritual adze was used symbolically to 'open' the mouth, so that it might speak and eat again. At the same time the instrument was used to touch other parts of the mummy, such as the eyes, ears and nose, so that it might, respectively, see, hear and breathe again. Moreover, the right leg of an ox specially slaughtered for the ceremony was sometimes extended towards the mummy, recalling mšhtyw, the ox-thigh constellation. This same cosmic influence was reflected also in the hook-like adze, which resembled the pattern made in the night sky by the seven stars of Ursa Major (and also by Ursa Minor, the Little Bear, which was occasionally identified as a second celestial adze).[64]

In ancient Egyptian myth, the Opening of the Mouth ceremony was first carried out by Horus on his father Osiris, after he was murdered by Set. During the pharaonic age, the ceremony was performed on the deceased's body by his or her heir, who would take the honorary title of 'Opener of the Mouth'.

During the Predynastic and Protodynastic periods (*c.*3500–*c.*3100 BC), the instrument used in the Opening of the Mouth was a forked flint knife, but this was replaced in Dynastic times by an adze usually made from meteoric iron (*bja*), which was seen to have celestial qualities, and to have come forth out of 'Setesh', a form of the name Set, god of disorder and chaos, associated with the ox thigh constellation.[65] The Greek biographer and moralist Plutarch (d. AD 50) even comments that the Egyptians called iron the 'bone of Typhon', the Greek name for Set.[66] In the Pyramid Texts *bja*-iron is intimately associated with the concept of heaven, since its vault, its gates as well as the heavenly throne on which the deceased sits, are all said to have been made of it.[67] Moreover, there is every indication that the ancient Egyptians saw the stars themselves as made of *bja*-iron, and that the bones of the deceased were fashioned from this same celestial substance.[68]

Meteoric iron was associated with thunderbolts and lightning, which were seen by the ancient Egyptians as the most powerful forces in nature, capable of splitting, blasting and smiting.[69] Thus, as Wainwright in a paper entitled 'Iron in Egypt' (1931) concludes, '*bja* with which the mouth was opened was of stellar, that is to say, meteoric origin. It was the thunderbolt.'[70] Of interest here is the fact that the Four Children of Horus were said to have opened the mouth 'with their fingers of *bja*', i.e. meteoric iron.[71]

A special ceremonial adze made of meteoric iron was said to have been kept in the temple at Letopolis, 'the thunderbolt city',[72] and if this was in use during the age of Khufu or any of the other Fourth Dynasty pharaohs who built their monuments on the Giza Plateau, then Letopolis's 'Opener of the Mouth' would have made the journey due south, along the line of the meridian, bringing with him the sacred adze so that it might be used, 'to cut open even that which was sealed in death'.[73]

Since meteoric iron was so much associated with Letopolis, the home of the

Four Children of Horus, it seems only fitting that it should have become the place of the Opening of the Mouth ceremony. Furthermore, Letopolis's connection with Horus is also revealing, for the root of his name (*Hor* or *Har* in Egyptian) is *hr*, or *her*, which can mean 'upper' or 'above', and is generally used as a determinative of 'sky', implying something like 'belonging to the sky', or 'of the sky' – suggesting once again a place of ascension.

Thus Letopolis – targeted exactly by the Great Pyramid's northerly-aimed entrance passage – was seen as reflecting the celestial power of Ursa Major in the form of the sacred adze. This statement is confirmed in the knowledge that the symbol for the nome, or district, of Letopolis, situated immediately north of Memphis, was the ox thigh.[74] Even further confirming the close relationship between Letopolis and Giza (*see Chapters Thirteen and Fourteen*) is that the hieroglyphs denoting the name Dwn-'nwy, the falcon-headed god of the northern group of constellations, feature in certain forms of the name used to describe the sacred adze used in the Opening of the Mouth ceremony.[75]

Yet if Letopolis represented Ursa Major, was there somewhere on this meridian line that represented the falcon-headed god identified with the stars of Cygnus? The clue is in the fact that Dwn-'nwy might well have another identity – one that resonates directly with the Giza necropolis.

CHAPTER THIRTEEN

In Search of Sokar

According to the eminent British Egyptologist Sir Ernest Alfred Wallis Budge (1857–1934), the curator of Egyptian Antiquities at the British Museum for thirty years and the translator of many ancient Egyptian texts, the falcon-headed god Sokar (or Seker) was 'probably the oldest of all the gods of the dead' in Egypt.[1] Although Sokar's growing influence was cut off in its prime by the burgeoning cult of Ptah, the creator god of the royal city of Memphis, his role as guardian of the deceased in the underworld would remain strong, particularly at his primary cult centre of Rostau (or Restau), meaning 'mouth of the passages', which, we find, turns out to be ancient Giza.[2] His connection with the location was very ancient indeed. It is mentioned in the Pyramid Texts,[3] *c.*2400 BC, although it probably goes back to the very beginnings of Egyptian history.

Certainly by *c.*3000 BC, Giza was being used as a northern extension of the Memphite necropolis, over which Sokar was divine protector, for it was at this time that a large north-south orientated tomb known as Mastaba V was constructed here. It dates to the reign of a First-Dynasty pharaoh named Djet, and was discovered in 1904 some 2.5 kilometres (1.5 miles) south-southeast of the current pyramid field. When excavated, it was found to be surrounded by the graves of no less than 56 retainers, showing the importance of the individual buried there.[4] Why exactly this unnamed official chose Giza as his burial place is not known. Yet records show that twice during the reign of Djet's father, Djer, the all-important festival of Sokar took place.[5]

Since tradition asserts that Djer built the royal palaces of Memphis,[6] there is every reason to suspect that the earliest known festival of Sokar took place within its necropolis, arguably even reaching the Giza plateau, which is likely to have been a cemetery by this time. Such a conclusion is evident from the discovery here of pottery jars and other contemporary artefacts pre-dating the foundations of Dynastic Egypt, including four intact ceramic vessels unearthed just west of the

Great Sphinx in 1907.[7] They were almost certainly buried as grave goods and belong to the so-called Buto-Maadi, or Maadian, culture, which thrived in the area of Cairo and the Nile Delta during the Chalcolithic, or Copper, age (*c.*3900–*c.*3200 BC). In all, twelve Buto-Maadi sites have been detected, including a cemetery at Heliopolis, northeast of modern Cairo.

Evidence of even earlier occupation on the Giza plateau comes from the discovery of a Late Neolithic stone tool found *in situ* close to the causeway of the Third Pyramid.[8] In addition to this, retouched chert flakes thought to date to a similar age have been picked up by the author on two occasions in an exposed gravel layer close to the base of the Maadi Formation, the hill-ridge running east–west a few hundred metres southwest of the Third Pyramid.[9]

Sokar as Cygnus

Sokar is usually depicted as a falcon-headed man either seated on a celestial throne or as a mummy, signifying new life through astral flight. Livio Stecchini saw him as the god who presided over the establishment of the geographical limits of Upper and Lower Egypt, based on units of measure which showed that the ancient Egyptians were aware of the latitude and longitude of the Earth.

Sokar was thus seen as extending his two wings to embrace, or cover, the geographical extent of Egypt. It was in this role that he gained the title 'great god with his two wings opened',[10] which is so similar to Dwn-'nwy's own title of 'he who unfolds two wings' that the two are surely one and the same, which, if correct, means that in astronomical terms Sokar is Cygnus. This relationship between the two falcon-headed deities is confirmed in the knowledge that both Dwn-'nwy and Sokar seem to have featured in the 'Stretching of the Cord' ceremony,[11] while in the Pyramid Texts both gods are identified with Osiris, lord of the dead, and thus with the deceased in their role as Osiris.[12]

In addition to this, Sokar, like Horus, was god of artisans, craftsmen and blacksmiths.[13] In the Pyramid Texts Sokar is linked specifically with *bja,* meteoric iron, a principal theme of the stellar religion, from which he fashions the bones of the deceased.[14] One utterance speaks of him splitting open the *bja* shell of the sun-egg, inside which is the new-born king in the form of Horus the Younger, who rises to avenge the murder of his father Osiris.[15] As we saw in the last chapter, meteoric iron was linked both with the adze used in the Opening of the Mouth ceremony, and through this with the cult centre of Letopolis.

Sokar is additionally connected with the *Benben,* a sacred egg-like stone symbolizing cosmic creation, which might also have been of meteoric origin.[16] This link between Sokar and the Benben is found in the Pyramid Texts, which state that the egg-like stone 'is in the Mansion of Sokar'.[17] Elsewhere it is said to have been kept at the ancient cult centre of Heliopolis (the Egyptian *Iunu* and biblical 'On'), situated northeast of modern-day Cairo. The Benben-stone was placed, most probably, on a pedestal within a structure known as the 'Mansion of the Phoenix'. The word 'phoenix' is the Greek form of the Benu, the Heliopolitan name for the bird of creation in its role as the grey heron. It is invariably shown perched on the Benben-stone, or on a sacred mound, just as the heron makes its nest on the temporary mud islands that appear in the River Nile after the annual inundation.

Fig. 32. Graeco-Egyptian magical gem of unknown date showing the Phoenix as the Benu bird, standing on a crocodile, probably representing Set, the Greek Typhon.

In Graeco-Egyptian art, i.e. Egyptian-inspired Hellenic art, especially on various magical gems, the Phoenix, having evolved into a bird of cosmic creation following its association with the Benu-bird, is shown on its mound with a crocodile beneath it. On other occasions the Phoenix is seen actually standing on a crocodile.[18] Almost certainly the crocodile signifies the god Set, the Greek Typhon, who was very often depicted in this reptilian form during his struggle against Horus the Younger.

Since the crocodile is seen on the back of the celestial hippo, Reret, in Egyptian star maps, it is likely that in Graeco-Egyptian art the crocodile represents the constellation Draco, the celestial dragon. All this suggests that the Phoenix, which here takes the place of Horus the Younger as victor over Set, god of darkness and chaos, was identified, like Horus and Sokar, with the nearby stars of Cygnus. This connection between Cygnus and Draco is also found in Olmec and Maya astronomy (*see Chapter Six*) where there also seems to have been a strong interplay between these two constellations.

The Festival of Sokar

The connection between Sokar and both meteoric iron and the sun-egg not only demonstrates his stellar attributes, but also his relationship to the northern group of constellations, the 'Great Ones' as they were known. In fact, we find that during the festival of Sokar, the king would enter the 'Halls of Sokar' and identify with the god, equated already with Osiris, after which he would undergo symbolic funerary rites including the 'Opening of the Mouth', through which he was renewed and made 'triumphant'.[19] This celestial aspect of the falcon-headed deity is expressed also in a New Kingdom inscription from the temple of Medinet Habu in southern Egypt, which proclaims, 'Opened are the doors of heaven, that the god [Sokar] may come forth',[20] which exactly echoes the understanding of Cygnus as the Bird's Foot constellation by the native peoples of North America (*see above, page 50*).

During this event the pharaoh, symbolized by a statue of Sokar, would be taken aboard the *henu*-barque, the falcon-god's personal vessel, which sported a conical roof on which was mounted a falcon head, as well as an antelope head prow that gazed backwards at a ceremonial 'chapel' or cabinet. The statue would remain in its own 'room' as the barque was paraded on a sled around the boundary walls of the city or temple complex in question. After ten days of ceremonies and processions, the festival would climax with the symbolic resurrection of Sokar, reflected in the inevitable transition from death into new life that the king would ultimately make.

Gatekeeper in the Darkness

Unquestionably, the *henu*-barque was the role model for the later solar barques that enabled the deceased to reach the afterlife. Both at Giza and at Abydos (the great cult centre of Osiris and necropolis in southern Egypt), large numbers of boat burials have been unearthed in specially dug out pits, positioned next to tombs or pyramids. Entire seagoing vessels were placed in the ground, either whole or dismantled. It was a practice that went back to the very foundations of Dynastic Egypt, and clearly it was believed that those interred in the accompanying tombs could use the astral doubles of the boats to reach the sky-world.

However, before this great voyage could be undertaken the soul of the deceased in ancient Egypt had first to *go underground* in order to navigate the mythical realm known as the *Duat*, or underworld, which resembled a labyrinthine cave system. Personified as the sun-god, or as the mummified Osiris, he or she was required to traverse twelve divisions expressed in terms of the twelve 'hours' that the sun takes to journey from dusk till dawn. Clearly, these were not real-time hours, merely symbolic periods lengthened or shortened depending on the duration of the night.

In the Duat's chthonic realm – which was thought to exist both underneath the earth, where the sun was seen to go during the night, and also in the complete darkness of space, where no light can penetrate – the deceased had to navigate a whole host of supernatural obstacles and combat its spectral denizens. Only when these had been mastered with the help of his attendants – who towed the 'night-barque' through the different hours – could the soul of the deceased be born anew. This was envisaged in the solar religion in terms of the sun-god switching in the pre-dawn light to the 'day-barque' in order that he might journey to the Imperishable Stars and Sekhet-Aaru, the Field of Reeds, along the 'Winding Waterway'. This was the ancient Egyptian name for the Milky Way, which, through its identification with the mythical river known in Classical tradition as the Eradinus, the Stream of Ocean, or River of Heaven,[21] was seen as the celestial counterpart, or even an extension, of the Nile.[22]

How exactly the deceased might successfully navigate the Duat was the theme of a number of texts either inscribed on the walls of tombs, sarcophagi and coffins, or recorded on papyri that were deposited in the tomb. Several works are known to have existed, with names such as the *Book of Gates*, the *Book of Caverns*, the *Book of Coming Forth by Day* (better known by its more popular name, the *Book of the Dead*), and the *Shat-ent-am-Duat*, or *Am-Duat*, the *Book of that which is in the Duat* or the *Book of the Secret Chamber*.

What is most interesting about the contents of the *Am-Duat* text, the oldest of these 'books of heaven and hell' – as Budge, their English translator, referred to them – is its description of the so-called Fourth and Fifth Hours of the night. These two particular 'hours' have an entirely different feel about them, and it has been suggested that they contain interpolations derived from a separate theology associated directly with the cult of Sokar.[23] The two 'hours' in question relate to an area of the underground domain referred to as the 'kingdom', 'land', or 'house' of Sokar in Rostau (also transliterated as Restau and Rosetau), the 'mouth of the passages' to the underworld, which was, of course, Giza.[24] In this role, the falcon-headed god came to personify the darkness of a coffin or tomb deep beneath the earth, from which the deceased might exit in order to reach the light offered by the sky-world.[25]

Sokar was 'god of death, and the *refuge* of the souls of the dead [author's emphasis]',[26] reflected perhaps in the name Sokar itself, which has connotations of 'a place shut in, the coffin', or 'to put to silence'.[27] He was 'the great god who snatcheth away the soul', as well as the 'gatekeeper in the darkness',[28] and 'an Earth-god whose abode was as black as night.'[29] As we shall see in Chapter Twenty, this concept of a totally dark, deep cave environment used in order to navigate otherworldly realms and encounter supernatural beings, becomes crucial to our understanding of the origins of the Cygnus mystery, and at Giza this concept is nowhere more apparent.

In the Fifth Hour, at the very heart of the Duat – underneath the image of a hollow mound and a fiery orange bell-shaped object, on which perch two falcons –

the deceased finally encounters Sokar. He is seen riding a two- or sometimes three-headed serpent, with a bearded human head on the end of its tail. With outstretched arms, Sokar holds open his wings, reminding us that he is the 'great god with his two wings opened'. Both Sokar and the serpent are supported by an oval made of sand, signifying, according to Budge, 'an oval island in the river of the Tuat [Duat]'.[30] It is guarded by a double-headed lion, and named as the 'Land of Sekri', another form of Sokar, which is described as: 'The horizon of the hidden country of Sekri, which guardeth the hidden body (or, flesh).'[31]

Who exactly the serpent represents is not clear, although an accompanying legend next to Sokar reads: 'His work is to protect his own form',[32] which, along with further clues, points towards the falcon-god being a victor in combat over the serpent, like Horus the Younger's victory over Set, paralleled also in the Graeco-Egyptian magical gems showing the Phoenix, or Benu-bird, triumphant over the crocodile. It is made clear also that the night barque is unable to pass through this realm of darkness guarded solely by Sokar. Instead, it has to pass over the top of the underground mound that seems to protect this even deeper realm. All this hints at some kind of hidden domain removed even from the rest of the Duat, where not even the sun-god is able to enter. Whatever the purpose of this strange, clearly interpolated imagery in the *Am-Duat* text, it exists separately and, as we shall see, resonates with Giza's mythological origins as a place of the dead.

Did the Duat, with its 'Land of Sekri', ever exist on a physical level, or was it all just a mind-fantasy meant to be used only as a spiritual aid to entering the afterlife? If it did exist, could it hold the key to understanding Cygnus's true role at ancient Giza? What we can say is that an important shrine to Sokar, known as the Shetayet, once existed there.[33] The so-called Dream Stela, or Sphinx Stela, commissioned by the Eighteenth-Dynasty king Thutmose IV (ruled *c.*1413–*c.*1405 BC), alludes to just

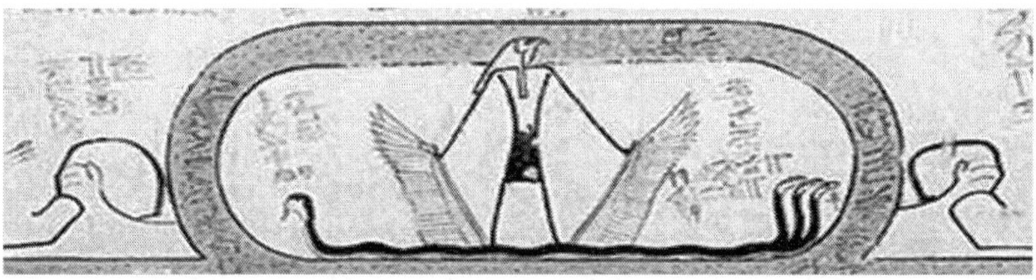

Fig. 33. The falcon god Sokar in his role as the underworld guardian of Rostau, ancient Giza, from the tomb of Thutmose III (*c.*1490–*c.*1436 BC) in the Valley of the Kings, Western Thebes (Luxor).

such a shrine. Found between the paws of the Great Sphinx, where it can still be seen, this enormous upright stone slab bears an inscription that records how, whilst out hunting one day, the then Prince Thutmose rested in the shadow of the Sphinx. He fell asleep and dreamt that Harmakhis (Egyptian *Hor-em-Akhet*, 'Horus in the Horizon, a form of Horus), the *genius loci* of the Sphinx monument, addressed him, saying that if he cleared away the sand that choked it, he would become pharaoh. The young prince did so, and indeed succeeded as pharaoh. What is important here is that the text speaks of 'Harmarkhis, beside Sokar in Rosta [i.e. Rostau]',[34] indicating that by New Kingdom times, at least, a well-known shrine, temple or even an idol honouring the falcon-headed god was located nearby. Yet where was it, and what is known about its origins and function? Although originally the Great Sphinx was carved with a human head representing, according to current Egyptological thinking, the pharaoh Khafre (builder of the nearby Second Pyramid), by New Kingdom times the monument had come to be associated with the falcon-headed Horus the Elder, rather than an individual monarch. Was this identification connected somehow with the presence on the plateau of the cult of Sokar?

Island of the Egg

Up until recently no hard evidence had emerged to pin down where at Giza the Shetayet of Sokar might exactly have been located, even though it was generally assumed to have been south of the plateau. Neither was it known whether Rostau's Duat-underworld, under the control of the falcon-headed god, might have had any tangible reality. However, as we shall see, coming at the problem from a different angle has proven to be the key, finally, to cracking this age-old enigma.

It began with a review of cosmological records found on the walls of the temple of Horus at Edfu, some 87 kilometres (54 miles) south of Luxor in southern Egypt. Known as the Edfu Building Texts, they tell of the foundation of Egypt's first temple, the dimensions and proportions of which were incorporated into every subsequent temple built in the kingdom. This included Edfu's own temple, which in its present form was begun as late as 237 BC, and had not been completed by 57 BC, when building work ceased.

The Edfu Building Texts speak of a primeval mound known as the 'Island of the Egg' that emerges from the primordial waters, like Silbury Hill in distant Britain. Like the Land of Sekri, it is said to be encircled by a 'channel' of water,[35] arguably a river, and on its shores, among the 'field of reeds', a sacred domain known as Wetjeset-Neter (or Wetjeset-Hor) comes into existence.[36] Here are placed *djed-*

pillars, or posts, used as 'perches' by the island's first 60 inhabitants,[37] known as the *Drty*-Falcons, or Sages. Their leader is named as an individual called the *Pn*-god, or, simply, 'This One'.[38] All this occurs during a mythical age referred to as the 'First Occasion' – *Sep Tepi* – when the world is still uncultivated.[39]

Lord of the Perch

Eventually, after a period of violent conflict and destruction, caused by an 'enemy snake', called the 'Great Leaping One' (*Nhp-wr*),[40] rising waters reclaim the island, destroying Wetjeset-Neter and killing the inhabitants, who are subsequently referred to as *ddw*-ghosts. Afterwards, the island re-emerges and a second building phase occurs. A single *djed*-pillar is preserved from the earlier period,[41] but even this eventually is replaced by a new one constructed for a mythical leader called 'the Falcon', known also as 'Lord of the Perch' and 'the Winged One'.[42] The mound is renamed the Island of Trampling, the Island of Combat, and the Island of Peace, reminders of the earlier destruction and the fact that it has now become the burial place of the original inhabitants of Wetjeset-Neter.[43] This includes the *Pn*-god, who as a chthonic deity is considered to be the first deceased god in Egyptian mythology, personified as the above mentioned figure named as the Falcon.[44]

Collectively, this sacred domain, known only as the 'homeland', takes the name *Bw-tepi*, the First Place or Place of the First One. More crucially, a building is erected called the 'Temple of the Falcon', after its glorious leader.[45] This structure is said to have been '30 cubits west to east, and 20 cubits from south to north', with a large courtyard containing a series of smaller buildings.[46] Here a series of mythical groups take up residence, including the 'Crew of the Falcon', the 'Shebtiw', and the 'Eldest Ones'.[47]

Czech-born Egyptologist Eve A E Reymond (1923–86), one of the only scholars ever to have made a detailed study and commentary on the Edfu Building Texts, was in no doubt that the Island of the Egg and Temple of the Falcon actually existed. Indeed, she cited philological evidence to show that the accounts originated not in the area of Edfu in southern Egypt, but within the nome, or district, of Memphis, which included the Giza plateau. In her words, the Edfu Building Texts 'preserve the memory of a pre-dynastic religious centre which once existed near to Memphis, on which the Egyptians looked as ... the homeland of the Egyptian temple.'[48] This assumption on her part was probably helped by the fact that the original Edfu stemple was said to have been constructed by Imhotep, the architect of Djoser's step pyramid at Saqqara, 'according to a plan dropped down from heaven to earth near the city of Memphis'.[49]

Does any of this material make sense of the Land of Sekri, the hollow mound and island associated with Sokar and Rostau in the Fifth Hour of the Duat (*see above, page 148*), and might the multiheaded snake he stands upon represent the Falcon's eventual defeat of the 'enemy snake', which caused the destruction of the first phase of building at Wetjeset-Neter, killing all its inhabitants at the same time? I believe there is every reason to consider that Sokar was one and the same as the mythical being from the Edfu Building Texts called the Falcon, who was responsible for the creation of the Temple of the Falcon, most probably an early shrine to Sokar, perhaps even the god's lost Shetayet. This assumption is supported by the fact that the deity known as the Falcon was considered Egypt's first deceased god, a reference most assuredly to Sokar of Rostau, described, as we have seen, as Egypt's 'oldest of all the gods of the dead' and as 'an Earth-god whose abode was as black as night'. These are connections that will now lead to a more direct link between the stars of Cygnus and the Giza plateau.

Underworld of the Soul

The Edfu Building Texts go on to speak of a chthonic domain known as the 'Underworld of the Soul' (*Duat-n-Ba*) that existed *within* the Island of the Egg.[50] It contained something called the *bnnt*, 'embryo',[51] or 'seed'[52], called also the 'Great Lotus', or 'throne', that was said to emit a 'radiance',[53] a concept equated with something known as the 'Sound Eye' (*Wdat*), seen by Reymond as perhaps 'the name of the centre of the light which illuminated the island'.[54]

The word root *bnnt* is simply the feminine form of the masculine *bnn*, linked closely to Benben (or *bnbn*), which can be translated as 'to copulate, to beget, to be begotten, virile, phallus', linked also with the word *weben*, 'to rise in brilliance' or 'shine'.[55] Thus the term 'Island of the Egg' must allude to the sun-egg seen as being made of *bja*-iron and split by Sokar, as well as the fiery bell-shaped object pictured above Sokar in the Fifth Hour of the Duat-underworld.

In the Fourth House of the Duat, the *Am-Duat* text refers to the 'road of the secret things of Re-stau [Rostau] … by which entereth the body of Seker [Sokar], who is on the sand, the image which is hidden, and is neither seen nor perceived.'[56] Repeatedly, ancient texts speak of a 'secret chamber' or 'secret cavern' of Sokar which existed at Rostau,[57] while an official during the reign of the pharaoh Pepi I (ruled *c.*2300 BC), bore the title of 'Chief of Secrets of the Chamber of Sokar'.[58]

What exactly was this 'secret chamber' or 'secret cavern', and could it be found today? It has been suggested that it was some kind of 'Sokar-Osiris tomb'.[59] However, a better clue lies in the alternative name for the 'Underworld of the Soul' given in the Edfu Building Texts. This is *Bw-hmn*,[60] which Reymond interpreted as 'Place of the Well',[61] although the suffix *hmn* can also mean 'to construct', as in 'to bring something together'. Thus Bw-hmn seems to imply an underground construction, like a physical representation of the Duat. Indeed, Reymond suggested it was a reference to some kind of 'primeval well' that might once have existed near Memphis, and thus arguably even at Giza.[62] This was a tantalizing thought, and in my earlier book *Gods of Eden* (1998) I proposed that perhaps it was 'some kind of underground complex accessed via a stairwell located on the mound-like island'.[63]

As we shall see, these have proved to be prophetic words indeed, making complete sense of Mircea Eliade's envisaged shamanic origins of ancient Egypt's funerary religion, and its relationship to the universal cult of Cygnus. If Sokar is Cygnus, the falcon-headed god in the northern group of constellations, then as Letopolis exuded the stellar influence of Ursa Major, the ox thigh constellation (*see above, page 140*), Giza must somehow reflect Sokar/Cygnus's celestial potency as Egypt's most ancient god of death and the underworld. Yet where might one start looking for clues, and what exactly was I looking for? The answer came in a quite revelatory fashion.

CHAPTER FOURTEEN

The Road to Rostau

It was at this juncture in my researches into the possible influence of Cygnus in the Pyramid Age that Rodney Hale experienced an unexpected insight. Unable to sleep one night in early January 2005, he recalled how, when the ground-breaking book *The Orion Mystery* by construction engineer Robert Bauval and writer Adrian Gilbert first appeared in 1994, he had tried in vain to superimpose the belt stars of Orion over the three pyramids of Giza – a ground-sky correlation they proposed as part of a dramatic reappraisal of ancient Egyptian astronomy.

It was easy enough to match two of the stars – Alnitak and Al Nilam – with the pyramids of Khufu and Khafre, but when it came to aligning the third belt star, Mintaka, with Menkaure's pyramid, it was clearly off to one side. Extending this ground-sky overlay to include other pyramids of the Memphite necropolis – which the authors felt marked other stars both in Orion and the nearby constellation of Taurus, which includes the smaller asterism known as the Hyades – Hale was disappointed still further, for the match was even worse. It did not even make good geographical sense.

Lying in bed, Hale now had a flash of inspiration. What if the stars of *Cygnus* were to be superimposed over the Giza pyramid field? Eager to check out his hunch, he rose early and used computer graphics to overlay the Cygnus star field on the Giza plateau. What he saw amazed him, for the three stars that make up the bird's inner 'wings', the crossbar of the Northern Cross Gienah (*epsilon* Cygni), Sadr (*gamma* Cygni) and *delta* Cygni, matched *exactly* the placement of the three key pyramids of Khufu, Khafre and Menkaure. In order to verify this extraordinary revelation, he synchronized in all, four different photographs of Cygnus with the Giza pyramid field, and each time the match was near-perfect, without any obvious deviation.

As to the orientation of the pyramids with respect to the position on the ground of the three stars of Cygnus, I noted that during the Pyramid Age, Deneb – positioned in the Cygnus-Giza overlay on the edge of the Old Kingdom mastaba field north-west of the Second Pyramid – set at an azimuth of roughly 313 degrees, two degrees off of northwest. If an observer on the plateau were to imagine that the stars, instead of setting beneath the horizon, were now moving across the landscape, as if projected on to the desert by some giant lantern, they would 'arrive' eventually at Giza in the same position as Rodney Hale's proposed ground-sky correlation, a fact which could conceivably have influenced the placement of the pyramids. Strangely, as Cygnus sets, its four main stars, called the Triangles by astronomers, have the distinct appearance of a perfect four-sided pyramid, a casual observation which is unlikely to have been missed by Old Kingdom astronomer-priests.

Cygnus at Saqqara

Aware that Bauval and Gilbert had been criticized for not having examined other pyramid fields to see if their Orion correlation might be found elsewhere, Rodney Hale next turned his attentions to Saqqara, which, as part of the greater Memphite necropolis, may have been named in honour of Sokar (although medieval Arab chronicles suggest that the name was derived from a local Arab tribe). Superimposing the three cross stars of Cygnus over the main group of three pyramids – those of Djoser, Userkaf and Teti – created a near perfect match. Whether by chance or design, the level of correspondence was stunning. Overlaying the three belt stars of Orion on the same three pyramids at Saqqara resulted in nowhere near the same degree of accuracy.

At the front of Djoser's step pyramid at Saqqara is a sealed stone room known as a *serdab*, in which the *ka*, or spirit-double, of the deceased was placed, usually in the form of a lifesized statue. Inside was found Djoser's statue, today replaced by a replica, which looks out through two eye-holes in the north wall towards the meridian, as if watching to ensure the safe passage of his *ba*, or soul, as it enters the afterlife. This said, Djoser's *serdab* would appear to be orientated around five degrees east of north, suggesting that he looked out on a rather askew meridian line. Curiously, *c.*2650 BC, when the pyramid is thought to have been constructed, just such an askew meridian line could have been achieved by dropping a vertical line from Sadr (*gamma* Cygni) through the centre point of the bowl in Ursa Major – a means of marking true north that Marion Popenoe Hatch surmised was utilized by the proto-Olmec of Mexico as early as 2000 BC (*see Chapter Six*).

Gebel Ghibli

Returning to Giza, I was intrigued to see that the position of Albireo (*beta* Cygni), a bright double star, with magnitudes of 3.5 and seven, falls just south of the summit of a curious rocky knoll called Gebel Ghibli (Arabic for 'southern hill'). Located some 300 metres due south of the Great Sphinx, it sticks up out of the desert like some kind of primeval hill. At a time when the Nile was much further west, the river's annual inundation would have caused the waters to lap around its base, making this hillock an ideal personification of the Mound of Creation, as well as the Island of the Egg referred to in the Edfu Building Texts (*see Chapter Thirteen*). Moreover, I was aware that others had already investigated this rock outcrop, sensing that it held the key to locating the Shetayet, the lost shrine of the god Sokar, and was perhaps a 'gateway' into Giza's hidden dimensions.[1]

The Lehner Line

In addition to the above Cygnus-related correlations, another now revealed itself. Having calculated the rising of Cygnus in the Pyramid Age, *c.*3000–*c.*2500 BC, I found that in the same era Deneb would have appeared on the northeastern horizon at an azimuth of 46.6 degrees, and would have been seen by the time it reached an azimuth of 47.6 degrees. Indeed, if atmospheric refraction were taken into consideration, it could conceivably have been visible in the sky even earlier.[2] This happened to be the precise position on the horizon of the ancient cult centre of Heliopolis, which lies across the Nile Valley around 28 kilometres (17.5 miles) northeast of Giza.

Wanting to learn more, I decided that the only way to take the matter further was to conduct an onsite inspection of the plateau, which I finally reached in May 2005. One of the first things I checked was the clear northeast to southwest alignment of the southeast corners of all three pyramids, which are said to target Heliopolis. This alignment, first noted by American scholar Mark Lehner during his leadership of the Giza Mapping Project (1984–6) and subsequently dubbed the 'Lehner line',[3] starts from a rocky hillock some 400 metres southwest of the Third Pyramid, below which I found the Late Neolithic retouched chert flakes (*see above, page 145*).[4] Forming part of the Maadi Formation hill range, this so-called 'back sight' line has been used by engineers and scholars to propose that the three pyramids were built as part of a grand design, or unified plan, originally conceived by Khufu and strictly adhered to by his successors.[5]

Certainly, a sacred road very likely existed between Giza and Heliopolis, since one is mentioned on the Dream Stela of Thutmose IV, found between the paws of the Great Sphinx (*see above, page 149*). Its inscription refers to 'the splendid place of the beginning of time, over against the lords of Kheraha, the sacred road of the gods to the necropolis west of On [Heliopolis].'[6] Although the exact context here of 'the splendid place of the first time' is lost, it alludes almost certainly to the existence of an extremely ancient ceremonial route that once ran between Giza and Heliopolis.

Tree of the Virgin

Unfortunately, the Lehner line does not stand up under close scrutiny, for the Third Pyramid is misaligned slightly to the southeast, or looking at it another way, the Second Pyramid is out slightly to the northwest. When all this is taken into consideration, the average deviation east of north presented by the overall design of the three pyramids corner to corner, tip to tip, is approximately 44 degrees, which is over two degrees off the rising of Deneb as seen from Giza *c.*3000–*c.*2500 BC. Although this line does target a re-erected granite obelisk that stands on the location of the former Dynastic temple of Atum at Heliopolis, the truth is that the city covered a wide area, with some of the oldest sections, including an Old Kingdom cemetery, being located in the vicinity of the ancient village of Matariyeh.

Here can be found an ancient sycamore fig, known as the Tree of the Virgin, that casts its shadow over a sacred spring, venerated as the place where the Virgin Mary sheltered the Christ child during the Holy Family's flight into Egypt. This spring recalls the Arabic name for Heliopolis, which is *'Ain Shams*, meaning the 'Eye of the Sun', or 'Fountain of the Sun', suggesting that the site was so important that it retained its significance as a holy place even after the end of Dynastic Egypt. Thus the knowledge that the proposed 'Road to Rostau', the route to the Duat or world of the dead (*see Chapter Thirteen*), once ran between Giza and Matariyeh, enables us to calculate a more accurate azimuth bearing, which turns out be 46.5 degrees east of north, exactly the same (certainly within a degree or so) as the rising of Deneb if viewed from the plateau in *c.*3000–*c.*2500 BC.

Guardian of the Meridian

Some kind of sacred connection existed between Giza and Heliopolis, due most assuredly to the fact that both were ancient cult centres important to the stellar doctrine outlined in the Pyramid Texts. More significantly, there was an intervisibility between the two sites. The observer gazing towards Heliopolis from the eastern edge of the Giza plateau anytime *c.*3000–*c.*2500 BC would have seen Deneb rise up from the position of Matariyeh. To them, I suspect, it signified the first appearance of Sokar as Dwn-'nwy, i.e. Cygnus, the falcon-headed deity associated, ritualistically at least, with the act of finding the meridian line during the ceremony known as the 'Stretching of the Cord' (*see Chapter Thirteen*).

I will go further and propose that the rising and setting of Deneb was used also to determine true north, utilizing the false horizon method first suggested by I E S Edwards (*see above, page 136*). This, I believe, is recalled in the fact that from Giza during the Pyramid Age, Deneb could be seen to rise from the position on the horizon corresponding to the location of Heliopolis. Although it might not have been the brightest near circumpolar star (Vega would have been easier to use), Deneb I feel was chosen because of its clear connection with ancient Egyptian funerary practices and because the stars of Cygnus were seen as one of the celestial guardians of the meridian. This, of course, was what the falcon-headed god Dwn-'nwy held between his outstretched arms either as a cord or spear, just as Sokar holds apart the wings of the multi-headed serpent in the Fifth Hour of the Duat or underworld, as described in the *Am-Duat* text.

There is no doubt in my mind that the alignment between Giza and Heliopolis was the true 'road of the secret things of Re-stau', the true Road to Rostau, with the word 'road' being used in a very fluent sense; 'pathway' perhaps being a better description.

I realize that any scholars of Egyptology who might read these pages will argue that there is nothing special about the Giza pyramid field over and above any other in the Memphite necropolis. The others are equally old, and before the rise of Dynastic Egypt it might be said that the east bank of the Nile was more important than the west bank, where the Memphite necropolis is to be found. Moreover, they will point out that Giza is not unique in its monuments targeting Heliopolis, since the straight line created by the northwest corners of the main pyramids of Abusir, situated some 13 kilometres (eight miles) south-southeast of Giza, are also thought to target the sun-god's ancient abode. However, in my opinion, the implications of the Giza-Heliopolis alignment targeting the rising of Deneb are quite extraordinary.

Age-Old Alignments

French Egyptologist Georges Goyon draws attention to the clear triangular relationship between Giza, Letopolis and Heliopolis, the last two locations being on the same latitude.[7] We know too that Letopolis exuded the celestial influence of the ox thigh constellation as well as that of the sacred adze, both of which were representations of Ursa Major (*see Chapter Twelve*). So should the Giza-Cygnus correlation hold up to scrutiny, then in Giza and Letopolis we have two sites, one north of the other, which reflect the dual relationship respectively of Cygnus and Ursa Major, used in unison to highlight the meridian line, and by virtue of this the path to ascension.

It would have been great to say that the Giza pyramids targeted the rising of Deneb during the epoch of their construction. But however precisely they are aligned to true north, their geometrical relationship both to the horizon and to each

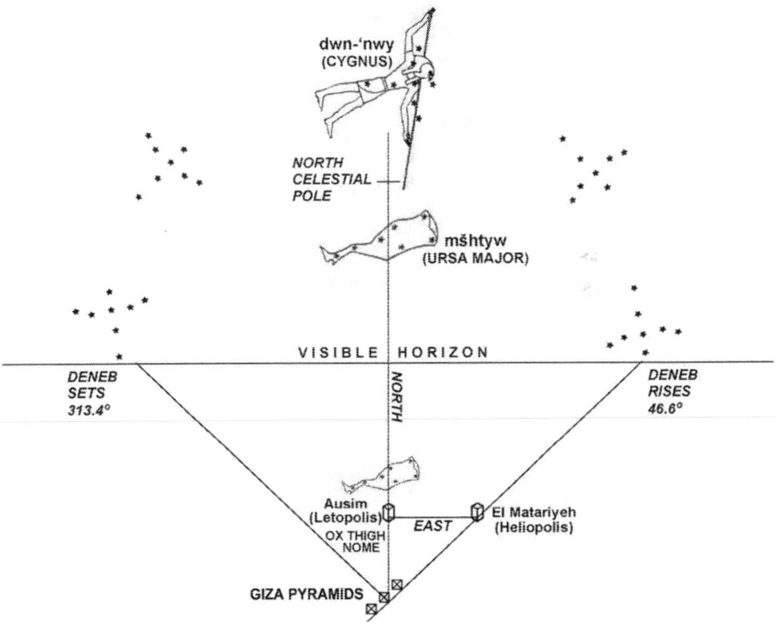

Fig. 34. Geometry of Giza, Ausim (Letopolis) and el-Matariyeh (Heliopolis) in relationship to the meridian and the rising and setting of Cygnus in conjunction with Ursa Major in 2600 BC.

other is irregular and remains a topic of fierce debate, and I feel unable to enter such a technical quagmire at this stage. Suffice it to say that the pyramids' strange placement, reflecting the positions of the three cross stars of Cygnus, along with the plain fact that their entrance passages exactly target the meridian, confirms their servitude to this important constellation.

As we have seen, the stars of Cygnus vary their declination very little from century to century, meaning that they alter their relationship to the visible horizon extremely slowly indeed. By examining the rising point of Deneb across the centuries I found that very, very slowly it shifts further south. Should the involvement of Deneb in the proposed Giza-Heliopolis alignment also prove meaningful, then the fact that the alignment becomes even more precise the further one goes back in time suggests that it is slightly older than the time-frame under examination here. Furthermore, since we know that the Buto-Maadi culture used both Giza and Heliopolis as burial grounds, *c.*3900–*c.*3200 BC, this becomes a tantalizing possibility.

Giza's Best Kept Secret?

So is the Cygnus-Giza overlay real? Is it any more valid than the Orion-Giza correlation proposed by Bauval and Gilbert back in 1994? During the Pyramid Age various funerary religions vied for superiority in the ancient Egyptian royal court. The Great Pyramid itself seems to embody stellar alignments that target, via its so-called air-shafts, no less than four different stars, including Sirius, the brightest star in the night sky, and either Alnitak or Al Nilam, 'belt' stars in the Orion constellation. Yet on the ground it becomes clear that for centuries before the southern cult of Orion began dominating the Egyptian funerary religion, the kingdom of Lower Egypt – governed by the pharaoh from the royal capital at Memphis – practised a much older shamanic-based sky-religion. This centred around the northern group of constellations, the so-called Great Ones, who, as we have seen, were celestial personifications of the Imperishable Stars as well as guardians of Sekhet-Aaru, the Egyptian concept of heaven.

Crucial to this religion was the falcon-headed deity Dwn-'nwy, personified in the night sky as Cygnus, joint guardian with Mšhtyw, the Ox/Bull or ox thigh – i.e. Ursa Major – of the meridian line, the path of ascension. The answer as to whether the Cygnus-Giza overlay is any more valid that the Orion-Giza correlation lies in the fact that the match between the cross stars of Cygnus and the pyramids of Khufu, Khafre and Menkaure is precise and meaningful. It is a perfect expression of the celestial influence on the ground of Dwn-'nwy, who as Sokar is also ancient Egypt's oldest funerary deity, whose abode was Rostau, Giza itself. Indeed, there is every reason to conclude that he was the bird-like mythical being of the Edfu Building Texts known as the Falcon (*see above, page 151*), seen as responsible for the foundation – most likely in the vicinity of Gebel Ghibli, the site of the double star Albireo – of Egypt's first ever temple. Yet if this was so, then did it also mean that other elements of the Edfu Building Texts were historically accurate, and might the newly discovered Cygnus-Giza overlay help us to find the true whereabouts of the Duat, the Underworld of the Soul, entered via the 'Place of the Well'? It is another of Cygnus's guises in ancient Egypt's rich collection of creation myths that provides the key to unlocking Giza's greatest secret of all.

CHAPTER FIFTEEN

The Well of Souls

Creation myths found at different ancient cult centres throughout Egypt speak of a cosmic goose called *Gengen-wer* (sometimes written *Negneg* or *Kenken-wer*), meaning the 'Great Cackler'. This magical bird was said to have brought about cosmic creation by emitting a great honk, cackle or call. This broke the eternal silence that existed in the void of nothingness, causing the manifestation of an egg, out of which the universe, and all that it contains, took shape.

One of those cult centres was Thebes (modern Luxor) in southern Egypt, where the priests of the god Amun, the Hidden One, saw the Great Cackler as the method by which their god 'awoke' creation.[1] The goose thus became the totem or avatar of Amun, the role it played also in the cult of the god Atum in Heliopolis, which also claimed the Great Cackler as its own. Here the goose was said to have laid the egg that became the primeval mound, in other words the Benben stone (*see above, page 145*), from which emerged the Benu, the first living spirit or essence of the universe, seen in terms of the grey heron and the Graeco-Egyptian concept of the Phoenix. It is also the basis behind the Island of the Egg that emerged from the primeval waters, according to the Edfu Building Text.

As the Primeval Being, or Primeval One, the goose features in Egyptian funerary texts where the deceased either guards or becomes at one with the cosmic egg.[2] Indeed, in some instances he or she actually takes the form of the goose in order to reach the Imperishable Stars, apparently the reason why geese, and also swans, were pictorially represented on the walls of New Kingdom tombs. Swans, it must be added, played a little understood role in ancient Egyptian funerary practices from at least the Fifth Dynasty onwards,[3] although the complete lack of textual evidence relating to their purpose makes it difficult to assess their greater significance in this respect.

In the Coffin Texts the deceased is identified with 'the great falcon which came into existence in the egg',[4] recalling here the role of Sokar as creator of the egg of *bja* (meteoric iron). In one Coffin Text, the Great Cackler becomes synonymous with Sokar in his capacity as divine artificer. Spell 223 equates the deceased with the egg and refers to Sokar as 'he who splits iron', i.e. *bja*-iron of the sky, in other words the egg's meteoric shell. Since Sokar was also a guardian of the Benben stone, then it becomes obvious that his role parallels that of the cosmic goose, an important point to remember as we now go in search of the Great Cackler's celestial identity.

The Dendera Zodiac

The significance of the goose in ancient Egyptian astronomy is unclear before its appearance on the round 'zodiac' of Dendera in Middle Egypt, which dates to the middle of the first century BC. Originally positioned in the ceiling of the East Osiris Chapel on the roof of the fabulous Ptolemaic temple of Hathor, it was discovered in 1799 by the scientific mission that accompanied Napoleon to Egypt, and was removed to France in 1822. Today it can be seen at the Musée du Louvre in Paris (a replica is in place at Dendera). As the name suggests, the stone-carved zodiac, known as Dendera B, is circular, like a disc. Another zodiac made up of a series of rectangular panels – designated Dendera E – can be seen on the ceiling of the outer hypostyle hall.

The round zodiac attempts faithfully to reproduce the entire night sky in a manner not previously recorded in ancient Egyptian astronomy. Mythical figures, animals, humans and inanimate objects, all parade anticlockwise around the heavens. Included are the planets, the twelve zodiacal constellations as well as the sequence of 36 stars and asterisms used from the Middle Kingdom onwards to divide the night into divisions called decans, based on the order of their appearance, starting with Sahu, the 'Far Strider', identified as the constellation of Orion. In addition to this, we see the Great Ones, the now familiar group of circumpolar or near-circumpolar constellations associated specifically with the northern heavens.

Mace-Man and Goose

Of particular interest on Dendera's round zodiac is a male figure, his legs apart as if walking, who sports a ceremonial tail and holds in his right hand a pear-shaped mace. Beneath his feet is a goose, and on his left side is a double sign, showing a falcon standing on an ibis, the latter being the bird of creation at the cult centre of Hermopolis, sacred to Thoth, the god of the moon. The ibis is also a hieroglyph representing the *akh*, the glorified spirit of the deceased that has taken its place among

Fig. 35. The Dendera round zodiac, after Aubourg. Note the mace-wielding man with the goose beneath his feet, marking, respectively, Cygnus and Aquila.

the Imperishable Stars. No accompanying inscription offers any additional information, either regarding the mace-wielding man or the significance of the goose, which is almost certainly the Great Cackler. Yet by determining where these figures are placed in the heavens we will be able to decide which Western asterism, or asterisms, they represent.

The Dendera zodiac shows mace-man, as I shall call him, in opposition to Mšhtyw, the Ox/Bull or ox thigh. This constellation is placed just beyond its central region, occupied by two distinct figures. One, arguably covering the centre point and thus marking the celestial pole, is a walking jackal, which can be identified as

Wapwawet (or *Upuat*), the 'Opener of the Ways'. He was said to aid the other jackal-headed god Anubis in performing the Opening of the Mouth ceremony. Indeed, both deities were thought to accompany the deceased into the afterlife. The other central figure is the hippopotamus, Reret, personifying the stars of Draco, the dragon.

In the knowledge that the ox thigh is Ursa Major, then it seems certain that the walking jackal is Ursa Minor. If so, and I would not be the first to make this connection,[5] then it makes perfect sense of why Wapwawet was chosen for this purpose. Its star pattern is so close in appearance to that of Ursa Major, the Plough or Big Dipper, that it very easily came to signify a second celestial adze, the hook-like tool used in the Opening of the Mouth ceremony (*see above, page 141*).

Mace-man and his goose are to be found in an area of sky between the northern celestial pole and the constellations Sagittarius and Capricorn, which are both clearly represented on the line of the ecliptic just beneath them. This narrows down the field, although the biggest clue as to their identity is perhaps the fact that mace man occupies the position elsewhere taken by Dwn-'nwy, the falcon-headed god of the northern group of constellations, who is noticeably absent from the round zodiac. This we can tell from the temple's rectangular zodiac – Dendera E – where Dwn-'nwy replaces mace-man in the region between Capricorn and Sagittarius. This surmise offers the tantalizing possibility that mace-man is in fact Cygnus, an assumption confirmed when one looks at a modern planisphere, which shows that the position on the round zodiac of the ox thigh, hippo, walking jackal and mace-man correspond exactly to the locations of, respectively, Ursa Major, Draco, Ursa Minor and Cygnus, an observation in line with current scholarly thought.[6]

This leaves the identification of the goose, which, since it is placed between mace-man and the zodiac constellations of Sagittarius and Capricorn means that it can only be Aquila, the Eagle – a conclusion reached by astrophysicist Éric Aubourg, who has made a detailed study of the original Dendera zodiac in the Louvre.[7] Interestingly, the goose was first identified with Aquila as early as 1862 in an incredibly forward-thinking book by the Christian writer Frances Rolleston.[8]

Why exactly the falcon-headed god Dwn-'nwy was replaced on the Dendera round zodiac with a mace-wielding man is difficult to say, especially since he appears with a falcon head on Dendera's rectangular zodiac misplaced between Aquarius and Capricorn, and here he actually *stands* on the goose. Even though he holds a sceptre and not a mace, this form of the falcon-headed god has to be the same mace-man as seen on the round zodiac, confirming his association with Dwn-'nwy. The fact that this means the falcon-headed god appears twice on the rectangular zodiac is not a problem, as it simply suggests that the Graeco-Egyptian astronomer-priests of Dendera, who created these zodiacs as late as the mid-first century BC, might have been using conflicting source maps. In one, perhaps, Dwn-'nwy appeared in his usual form, holding a cord or spear, while in another there was only a falcon-headed man with a scepter, and in a third he was replaced altogether by a mace-wielding man.

Such differences could easily have caused duplications of the type seen here. Whatever the case, the information on offer from both Dendera zodiacs more or less confirms that Dwn-'nwy is Cygnus, since mace-man occupies the exact position of this particular star group on the round zodiac.

The Role of the Goose

The goose's role in both the round and rectangular zodiacs at Dendera is as a zoomorphic avatar, or totem. He is beneath the feet of mace-man, whilst the falcon-headed god actually stands on its back. Thus it seems probable that, although representing the stars of Aquila, the goose is only meant to signify its brightest star, Altair, which is being shown here as part of an expanded Cygnus constellation.

Never before had the goose achieved such an elevated position, suggesting that there was a reason why it had gained such a distinction here. Exactly how this came about eluded me until I discovered that Dendera was seen as the 'home of the children of Geb',[9] the Earth-god, whose totemic animal was, similarly to Amun and Atum, the Great Cackler. Moreover, the village of Hamra Dun near Nag Hammadi just outside Dendera, where in 1945 a whole library of Gnostic texts was discovered, had been known anciently as Chenoboscium. The name means 'refuge of geese', or 'goose pen', which will have had a mystical as well as a practical significance.[10] So who exactly was Geb, and what was his place in this mystery?

Geb the Earth-God

In the Heliopolitan creation myth Geb was, with his twin-sister, the sky-goddess Nut, the offspring of Shu (Air) and Tefnut (Moisture), whom Atum self-created with either his spittle or semen. Before Shu separated them, Geb and Nut were joined permanently in sexual union, an act that produced two pairs of male-female twins – Osiris and Isis, and Set and Nephthys. Together, these gods and goddesses formed the Great Ennead, the nine gods of the Heliopolitan pantheon, expanded later to include two Lesser Enneads, making twenty-seven gods in all.

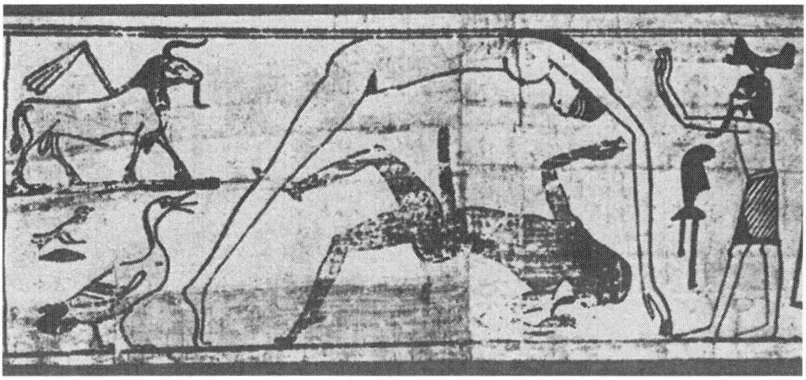

Fig. 36. The goddess Nut being prised apart from her twin Geb, with the Great Cackler at her feet. Detail from the Papyrus of Tameniu, *c.*1000 BC.

The most common manner in which Nut (or Nuit) is depicted shows her arched naked over Geb who, still with erect penis, has just been prised apart from her by Shu in order that the pair might form heaven and Earth (*see fig. 36*). When not shown in this role, Geb is depicted either wearing a white crown, symbol of the south, or as a male figure with the goose Gengen-wer on his head. Indeed, sometimes the bird is shown cackling at the feet of Nut as she arches over Geb.

The Earth-god's association with the Great Cackler is said to have come about because he too moved through the air in this form,[11] a strangely loaded claim that invokes the idea of avatarism, or bird shamanism, and makes sense of his role in the Dendera zodiac. Geb features heavily in the Pyramid Texts, and, similarly to Sokar, had 'authority over the tombs wherein the dead were laid.'[12]

Although the texts do not specify to which cult centre Geb belonged, he was intimately connected with Heliopolis. Yet he also had a foot in the door at Dendera, the great cult centre of the goddess Hathor. She was essentially an Egyptian form of the Near Eastern love goddess, who, as we have seen, went under names such as Allat, al-Uzza and Manat, who in Classical times were equated with the Greek goddess Aphrodite and the Roman Venus. Like them, Hathor governed everything from dancing through to sex, promiscuity and even sacred prostitution (a role she shared in Egypt with Isis). Curiously, both Nut and Hathor were cow-goddesses, or sacred cows, and both were associated with the female hippopotamus goddess named Apet.[13] In addition to this, the priesthood at Dendera believed that their temple was quite literally the residence of Nut, and that the birth-chamber where she brought forth Isis in the form of a dark-skinned child was to be found within its walls, under which circumstances Nut usurped even Hathor to become 'Lady of Dendera'.[14]

Mistress of the Sycamore

More significantly, both goddesses – who shared many attributes – were seen as personifications of the sacred sycamore tree, in which they were depicted offering liquid, either water or wine, from a libation vase to the deceased as his or her soul stood at its base in the form of a human-headed bird.[15] As Mistress of the Sycamore (Egyptian *nehet*, 'refuge'), both goddesses became guardians of the sun-egg laid among the plants at its base by the Great Cackler as the vehicle of Geb.

Interestingly, Nut presided over prominent sycamores to be found at both Hermopolis and Heliopolis, and in the latter case, as we saw in the previous chapter, a sycamore called the Tree of the Virgin exists in nearby Matariyeh village. At its base is a sacred spring identified with *'Ain Shams*, the 'Eye of the Sun', or 'Fountain of the Sun'.[16] The existing tree is only about 400 years old, but it replaced a much older one, which in turn probably superceded an even earlier tree, and so on, right back to Dynastic times. Linking this tree with Nut's sycamore is a tantalizing prospect especially since Egyptian funerary texts allude to a well of water at the base of these goddess trees.[17] As far back as the writing of the Pyramid Texts during the Old Kingdom, sycamores were linked both with the souls of the dead and the eastern horizon, where the Winding Waterway, i.e. the Milky Way, was seen to rise up into the sky.[18] This fits very well with the description of the Tree of the Virgin at Matariyeh, which lies at the eastern edge of the huge site of ancient Heliopolis, surrounded by various cemeteries including one from Old Kingdom times.[19]

That the gods of the lower sky, i.e. the northern group of constellations, are said to have sat in the sycamore, or sheltered beneath its branches, shows it to have been a form of the World Tree,[20] a symbol of the cosmic axis, accessed in this instance via the Milky Way. It became an alternative route to heaven, taken by the soul of the deceased in the form of a bird, since other souls were conceived of having already reached its upper branches, where they too now sat as *akhu*, or 'glorious spirits', amid the circumpolar stars.

The *Book of the Dead*

As already mentioned, Nut and Hathor shared the title Mistress of the Sycamore, or Mistress of the Tree,[21] and were shown standing among its branches. The *Book of the Dead* connects this tradition specifically with the Great Cackler. For instance, Chapter 59 of the Papyrus of Ani, preserved in the British Museum, and dating to *c.*1300 BC, is called 'The Chapter of Snuffing the Air and Having Dominion over the Water in the Underworld', and reads as follows:

> Hail thou sycamore of the goddess Nut. Grant thou to me of [the water and of] the air which dwell in thee. I embrace the throne which is in Unnu [either Hermopolis or Heliopolis], and I watch and guard the Egg of the Nekek-ur [i.e. Great Cackler]. It groweth, I grow; it liveth, I live; it snuffeth the air, I snuff the air, I the Osiris Ani, in triumph.[22]

There are elements here similar to those in one of the Coffin Texts, which reads:

> O Atum, give me this sweet air which is in your nostrils, for I am this egg which is in the Great Cackler, I am the guardian of this great prop which separates the earth from the sky. If I live, it will live; If I grow old, it will grow old; if I breathe the air, it will breathe the air. I am he who splits iron, I have gone round about the egg, [even I] the Lord of Tomorrow.[23]

Fig. 37. Vignette from the Papyrus of Ani (chapter 59), *c.*1300 BC, showing the goddess Nut pouring liquid from the sacred sycamore tree, as the deceased kneels in the waters of a well.

In both instances, the deceased takes on the role occupied by the Great Cackler in guarding the egg of creation, but only if he or she accepts to become at one with it. The vignette that accompanies Chapter 59 of the *Book of the Dead* shows Nut in the sycamore pouring liquid from a libation vase into a vessel being handed to the deceased, in this case Ani, for whom the text was written, who is seen standing in the waters of the well.

As the sycamore was seen as a point of ascent to the stars, the water became the entrance to the Duat, or underworld. Symbolically at least, the true self was seen to die in order to enter death, so as to emerge as a spirit in the next world. In this form, the souls of the dead could begin life anew. The deceased rose up in a manner compared in the ancient texts with the way Re broke forth from the cosmic egg guarded by Geb in his role as the Great Cackler. Separately, Nut herself was seen as the progenitor of Re as the spirit of the sun-egg, i.e. the solar orb itself, and, as we shall see now, she gives birth to him in a manner now becoming familiar to us from myths encountered around the world.

The Body of Nut

At Abydos, the ancient seat and cult centre of Osiris in southern Egypt, the decorated ceiling in the cenotaph temple of Seti I (ruled *c.*1309–1291 BC), spells out the Egyptian concept of the universe. Here the body of Nut extends over the Earth as the vault of heaven. Along her naked form are various stars as well as the midnight sun, and next to her is the legend:

> The uniform darkness, fount of the gods,
> The place from which birds come …
> Open to the Duat that is on her northern side,
> With her rear in the east and her head in the west.[24]

Afterwards we read that the sun enters her mouth in the First Hour of the Night, causing her to become 'pregnant'. It then sails through the darkness in the solar barque, until finally it emerges from 'her rear' at which he 'parts the thighs of his mother Nut'.[25] The sun-god then 'goes away to the sky', now in the day-barque, in order to navigate his way back towards the place of sunset, where the whole cycle can begin again.

Like a midwife, it is Geb who oversees the rebirth of the sun, affectionately described as 'the Chick' that has come forth from the sun-egg.[26] Most significant of all, the Duat, through which the sun passes, is linked directly with birds and the north, and was seen as a place where gods and men lived side by side. As James P Allen states:

> Like the sun, many of these beings are free to travel between the Duat and the world of daylight: Text 1A1 [of Seti's cenotaph] envisions some of them in the migratory birds that fly into Egypt from what were then unknown places to the north.'[27]

Moreover, it is from this same 'uniform darkness', this Duat in the body of Nut, that the morning sun comes forth into the light of the pre-dawn sky.

Lady of the Milky Way

It is not difficult to understand how the ancient Egyptians came to see the sun as being daily reborn as an egg from the body of the sky-goddess. Yet as Ronald A Wells, an archaeoastronomer and currently a computer resource specialist at the University of California, speculates, Nut can be viewed as a personification of the Milky Way, which when 'seen in its entirety over the course of a year has the appearance of a female in the thinnest of gauze robes.'[28] He noticed also that at the position of Cygnus, the Milky Way bifurcates due to the presence of the Great Rift, causing what he sees as the parting legs of this anthropomorphic being. At the figure's feet the sun crosses the ecliptic in the vicinity of Sagittarius and Scorpio, while a swelling can be seen in the Milky Way close to Gemini, where the ecliptic crosses it on the

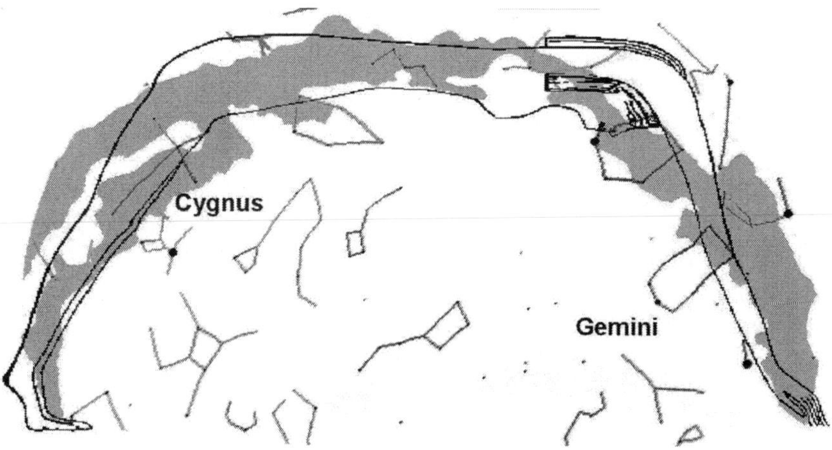

Fig. 38. Ronald A Wells' concept of the Milky Way representing the goddess Nut. Notice the stars of Cygnus between her thighs.

other side of the sky – this can be interpreted as her head. There is even a hint of an Egyptian-style cloth headdress, beyond which the starry stream thins out to give the impression of arms and hands reaching down to the horizon.

In published papers, Wells points out that the position of Cygnus, the Northern Cross, corresponds to Nut's crotch. As a consequence, he reasons, this might explain why in different cultures nude figurines are shown with crosses in the position of their genitalia. He cites examples,[29] yet fails to realize that the same thing can be said about the bird's foot device, which seems to have been another abstract symbol of Cygnus in its role as the vulva of the cosmic mother. Despite this, Wells notes that it is Deneb, the constellation's brightest star, that is located in the position of the sky-goddess's birth canal, with the rest of its stars directing the eye between her open thighs.

Ronald Wells realized that his controversial vision of Nut as the Milky Way might well explain why Egyptian myth talks in terms of the sun entering Nut's mouth after sunset and being born anew the following day. It is his belief that this event did not originally relate to the daily sun cycle, but to one that began at the spring equinox and culminated 272 days later at the time of the winter solstice. Based on the assumption that this celestial phenomenon was first recognized *c.*3500 BC, when Egyptian civilization had its beginnings, he calculated that Cygnus would rise in the northeast, where Nut's 'crotch' was said to have been, around two hours before sunrise, at a time when Deneb was just a few degrees above the horizon. Wells worked out that at this same moment, curiously, a 'great circle drawn from the north celestial pole through Deneb intersects the horizon at exactly the spot where the sun rises',[30] marking 'the shortest path that the infant Re would follow after exiting the birth canal at the point of its appearance on the horizon at sunrise.'[31]

This alignment between Deneb and the sun only occurred at the time of the winter solstice. More significantly, the ancient Egyptians referred to this day as *mswt Re*, 'the birth of Re',[32] which also signified the beginning of the year,[33] and, as Ronald Wells points out, the 272 days necessary for the death and rebirth of the sun is the exact period of human gestation. Thus Cygnus was seen not just as the womb of the stars, but as the point of cosmic creation, celebrated each midwinter with the rebirth of the sun-egg, 'dropped' from the cosmic birth canal of Nut, represented by Deneb.

Deneb and Userkaf's Sun-Temple

Ronald Wells attempted to understand Cygnus's possible relationship to Egyptian calendrics beyond even the theories outlined thus far, and for this he focused his attentions on a sun-temple built some 13 kilometres (eight miles) south-southeast of Giza at Abusir. This monument, commissioned by a Fifth-Dynasty king named Userkaf (ruled *c.*2480–*c.*2473 BC), took the form of a huge square platform on which was built an enormous squat obelisk seen as a representation of Heliopolis's mythical Benben stone. It is one of six known to have been built in and around Abusir during the Fifth Dynasty, of which only the remains of two survive today.

Wells' basic premise is quite simple. The priest-astronomers in the lower, or valley, temples attached to the more elevated sun-temples, where ablutions and sacrifices (two oxen and two geese daily) took place at dawn, would have needed to know of the approach of the sun in order that they might prepare themselves, before making the long climb along the causeway to the sun-temple. Wells speculates that this could have been achieved by watching for the appearance of a star that rose, say, one hour before sunrise. It could be acknowledged as it crossed the axis line of the causeway deliberately orientated with this purpose in mind.

So far, so good. However, because the slow movement of the Earth causes a star to rise earlier and earlier each night, in just 15 days the chosen heliacal star would have risen a full two hours before sunrise, making it useless for the purposes of the priests. Thus Wells proposed that every 15 days a new star rising around one hour before dawn would take the place of the old one, creating a sequence of 24 calendar stars utilized during the course of a 360-day year (with five extra days for feasting and ceremonies).[34] The choice of stars would depend on which ones rose in the northeast before climbing high enough to be targeted by the axis of the raised causeway. So after checking the declinations and luminosity of those stars that fitted the criteria, Wells concluded that in the case of Userkaf's sun-temple, the first of the six to be built at Abusir, the star chosen to lead the procession was Deneb, with Sadr (*gamma* Cygni), being the last one on the list before Deneb began a new cycle at the beginning of the next year.[35]

Despite certain criticisms of Wells' theories regarding the use of star-clocks during Egypt's Old Kingdom period,[36] his observations are very important indeed. They make complete sense of what we know about the significance of Deneb and Cygnus in the Pyramid Age. More significantly, he proposes that Deneb featured prominently in the calendar attached to Userkaf's sun-temple because the star was in some way special to that particular king.[37]

Wells's ideas are based only on his work at Userkaf's sun-temple, and he suggests that subsequent pharaohs chose different stars to lead the cosmic dance so that they might respect the religious preferences of their predecessors. However, in the knowledge that five more sun-temples were built around Abusir in the century that followed Userkaf's reign, then surely the astronomer-priests would eventually have run out of appropriate lead-stars, whether taken from the existing list, or chosen from others in the northern night sky.

In my opinion, the fact that Userkaf might have been interested enough in Deneb and Sadr to use them as calendrical markers was enough to convince me still further that Cygnus played a significant role in the stellar religion of Egypt's Old Kingdom. Remember, Userkaf, whose seven-year reign initiated the Fifth Dynasty, took the throne just three generations after Khufu built the Great Pyramid and a mere four years after the death of Menkaure, the pharaoh responsible for Giza's Third Pyramid.

Something might be made of the fact that the daily sacrifices at Userkaf's sun temple were two oxen and two geese, with the former personified in the sky as the stars of Ursa Major and the latter possibly signifying the Cygnus constellation as the Great Cackler. As we have seen, these two asterisms featured, symbolically at least, in the 'Stretching of the Cord' ceremony, and in their forms as the ox thigh and falcon-headed god they became guardians of the road to ascension.

A Trip Too Far

Aware of how close Abusir is to Giza, I wanted to determine whether the sun-temple of Userkaf might have played any additional roles in the Cygnus mystery. Yet in the knowledge that the Abusir pyramid field and its accompanying monuments are closed to tourists arriving by road, I decided that the only way of getting there was across the Western Desert. Thus on Wednesday, 25 May 2005, my wife Sue and I hired local horses from stables at Nazlet el-Samman and set off on what was for me one of the most terrifying, and yet exhilarating, experiences of my life. Having never ridden a horse before, I very nearly slid off the saddle as the feisty animal galloped along at speeds in excess of 50 km an hour (30 miles an hour), and although thankfully this did not happen, I managed to put my back out.

The Life of Hammad el-Samman

There is a reason for telling this tale of foolhardiness, of a type for which I am hardly unknown, as in the days that followed I suffered such pain in my neck that our driver took me to see a friend named Hassan (real name withheld), an export perfumer who doubled as an osteopath. He corrected my spine as best he could, and afterwards we shared tea together. Not unnaturally, the subject of the pyramids of Giza and their mysteries cropped up, at which Hassan revealed something very

Plate 1. Göbekli Tepe, designated the oldest temple in the world, built in what is now southeast Turkey, *c.*9500 BC. Here we see a circle of stone pillars.

Plate 2. Another shot of Göbekli Tepe, looking south. The corrugated roof protects the lower cult building.

Plate 3 (above). Interior of Göbekli Tepe's lower cult building, showing decorated stones – one (left) with a zigzagging serpent and the other (centre right) with mushroom caps.

Plate 4 (left). Stone pillar from Göbekli Tepe showing a leonine creature.

Plate 5 (above right). Göbekli Tepe stone pillar, showing a fox in high relief.

Plate 6 (right). Vulture head, a symbol of the Neolithic cult of the dead, found at Göbekli Tepe.

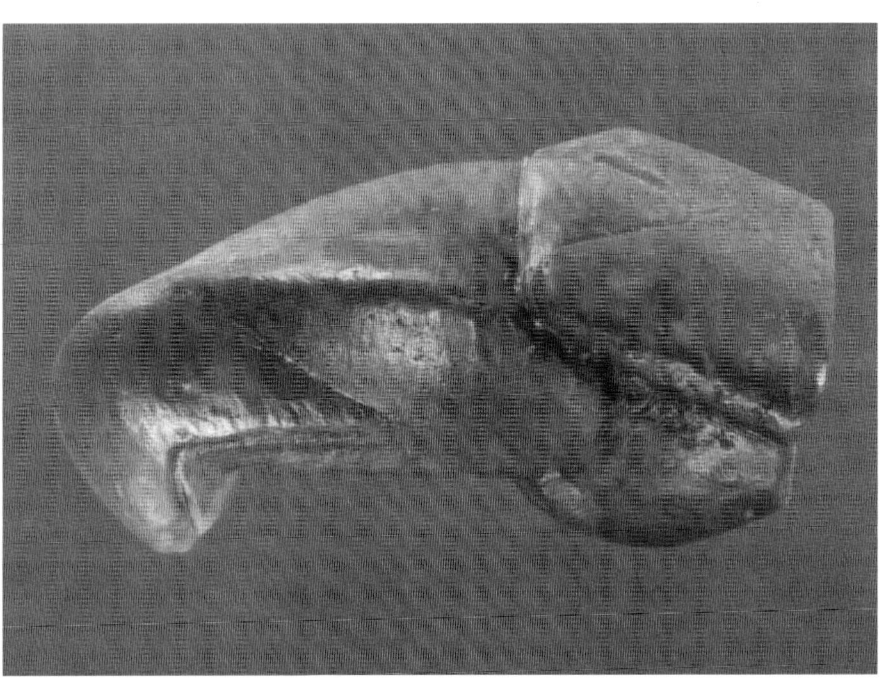

Plate 7 (above). The Astronomical Tower at Harran in southeast Turkey. It formed part of the seventh-century Great Mosque, and was used by Sabians as an observatory.

Plate 8 (below). The author stands within the doorway of Harran's Astronomical Tower.

Plate 9. Unexcavated stone row at the Early Neolithic site of Karahan Tepe, near Sogmatar in southeast Turkey, from the north.

Plate 10 (below). Mushroom-shaped stone pillar at Karahan Tepe, looking towards the northeast. Is this an indication of a local mushroom-influenced cult?

Plate 11 (left). Ground-plan of Gőbekli Tepe, showing general north-south orientation, and alignment of certain stone pillars north-northwest towards the setting of Deneb after 9300 BC.

Plate 12 (below). Cygnus as Christ Crucified on the Cross of Calvary, from an astronomical map of the Northern Hemisphere by William Schickhard (1592–1635).

Plate 13 (right). The Festival of the Sun, or Ind Raymi, which takes place each 24 June, the midwinter solstice, at Cuzco in Peru, the terrestrial form of Cygnus. The walls of the hilltop fortress of Sacsahuaman are visible in the background.

Plate 14 (below right). The Avebury monument in Wiltshire, England, built *c.*2600–*c.*2000 BC and aligned to the setting of Deneb in Cygnus.

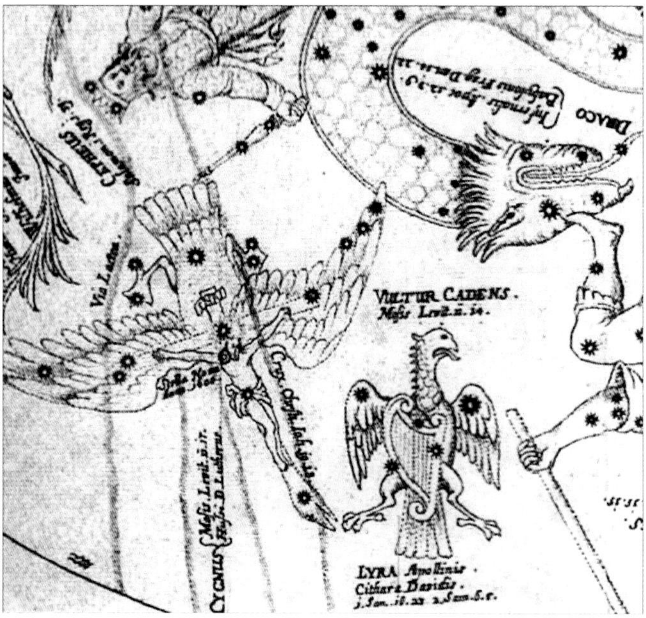

Plate 15 (left). Wayland Smithy long barrow in Berkshire, England, built *c.*3700 BC and aligned to Deneb in Cygnus.

Plate 16 (below left). Callanish stone circle on the Isle of Lewis in the Outer Hebrides, Scotland, built *c.*3000 BC. Its north-facing stone row is aligned to the rising of Sadr in Cygnus.

Plate 17 (right). Banner of the Vintners' Company Swan Warden and stuffed swan used in the annual Martinmas feast in honour of the Cygnus-linked Swan Upping ceremony on the River Thames.

Plate 18 (below). The Pyramids of Giza from the southwest. Do they reflect the age-old presence of the cult of Cygnus?

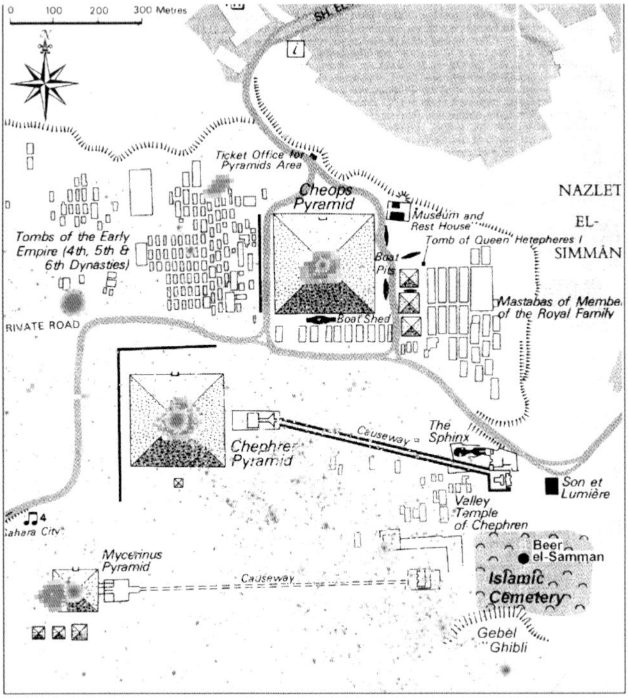

Plate 19 (left). Overlay of the principal stars of Cygnus and those of Orion on the Giza pyramid field. Note Albireo (*beta* Cygni), the 'beak star', on the south side of Gebel Ghibli, seen in the right-hand corner.

Plate 20 (below). The Giza plateau, looking south from the Great Sphinx towards the hill Gebel Ghibli and the Muslim and Coptic cemeteries.

Plate 21 (right). The holy well Beer el-Samman overlooked by a sacred sycamore tree inside the Muslim cemetery in the southeast corner of the Giza plateau. Was it seen by the ancient Egyptians as an entrance to the Duat, or underworld?

Plate 22 (below). The creator-god Brahma riding the swan-goose Hamsa, in Vedic astronomy the constellation Cygnus. From a temple at Chiang Khan, Loei province, northeast Thailand.

Plate 23 (left). Stone relief from Göbekli Tepe showing a barren female with mushroom-shaped hair. Does she symbolize a devourer of the dead, similar to the Hindu goddess Kali?

Plate 24 (below). The 'Well Scene' at the Cave of Lascaux in France's Dordogne region. The bird shaman, bison and bird on a pole have been interpreted as representing Cygnus and the cosmic axis, *c.*15,000–*c.*14,500 BC.

Plate 25 (above right). Creswell Crags in northern England, site of Britain's first Palaeolithic cave art, as it might have appeared when they were executed *c.*10,800 BC. Church Hole cave, aligned to Cygnus, is on the right-hand side of the valley.

Plate 26 (below right). Carved ibis head looking out through the entrance of Creswell Crags' Church Hole. Does it represent a bird of creation?

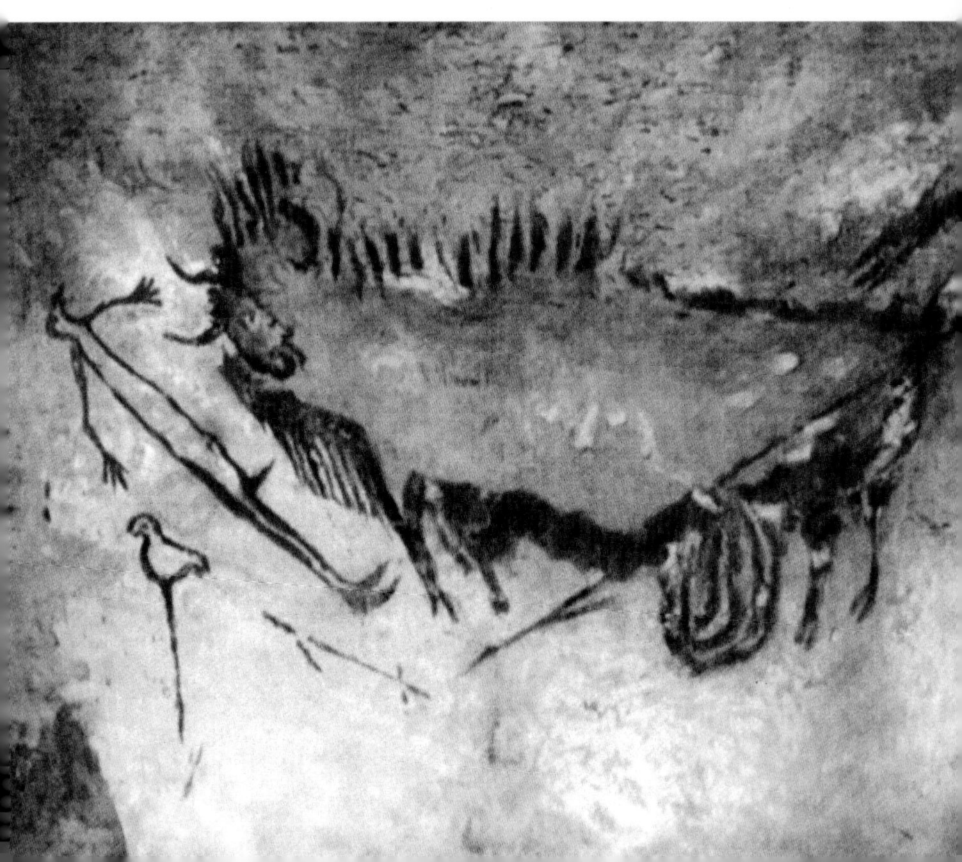

Plate 27 (left). The so-called 'swan panel' in Church Hole, Creswell Crags, showing the long heads and necks of swan-bittern chimeras.

Plate 28 (below). Image of the high-mass X-ray binary system Cygnus X-3 taken by the Chandra X-ray observatory (the sharp horizontal line is an instrument defect). Did cosmic rays produced by its relativistic jets affect human evolution during the Palaeolithic age, *c.*15,000– *c.*12,000 BC?

Plate 29 (above right). Artist's impression of a black hole/neutron star with relativistic jets accreting gas from an orbiting Wolf-Rayet star.

Plate 30 (below right). Hubble telescope image of a relativistic jet emanating from the supermassive black hole in the galaxy M87 within the constellation of Virgo. Cygnus X-3 produces similar jets.

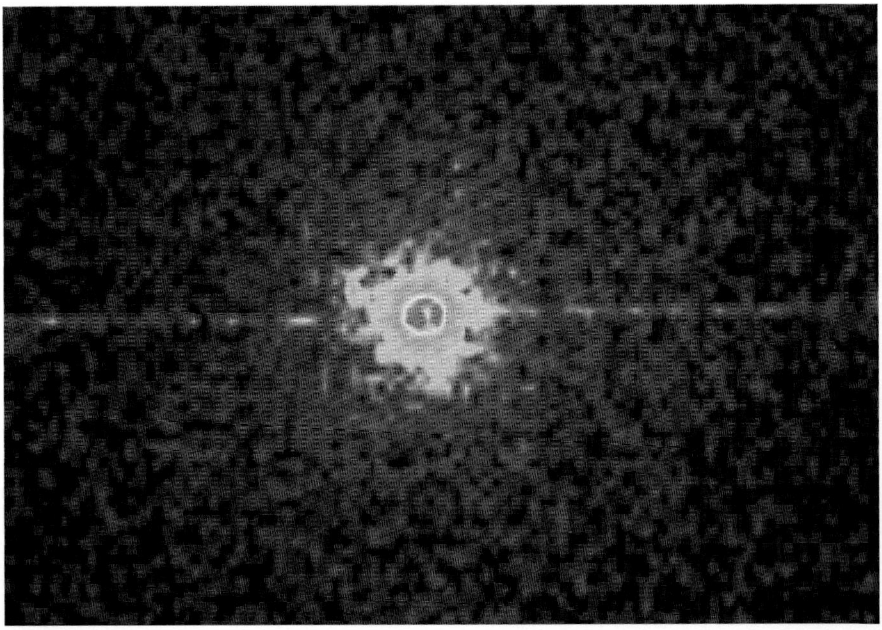

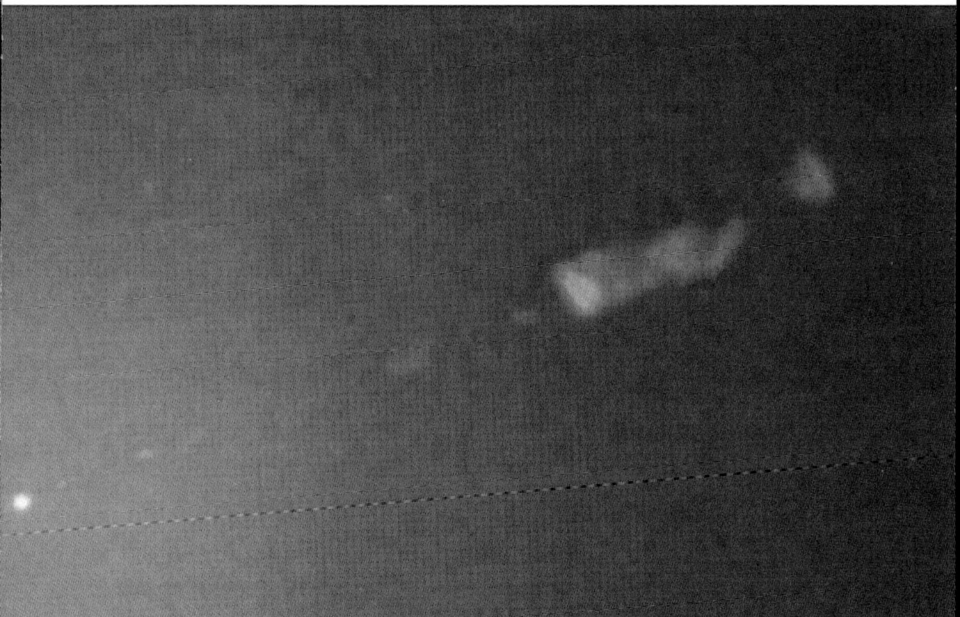

Plate 31. Photograph taken by French ethnographer Marcel Griaule in 1931 of Dogon art from the 'vault of Songo', showing the Milky Way as the north–south flowing 'blood' of Nommo.

Plate 32. Newgrange passage grave in Ireland's Boyne Valley, built *c.*3000 BC. Does its ground-plan reflect the positions of the stars of Cygnus?

interesting indeed. He voiced the often-heard opinion that there is an underground 'city' beneath the village of Nazlet el-Samman, east of the pyramid field. I thought immediately of the Underworld of the Soul described in the Edfu Building Texts and said to have been located within the Island of the Egg, as well as the Land of Sekri, the falcon god's chthonic domain at Rostau, modern Giza. In addition to this, I was aware that for the last eight decades followers of the American 'sleeping prophet' Edgar Cayce (1877–1945) have come here searching for an underground temple called the 'Egyptian Hall of Records', which, Cayce's followers claim, will reveal the secrets of a lost Atlantean race.

Hassan said that he was one of several village elders who knew the whereabouts of the entrance to this subterranean world beneath Giza. On enquiring as to where this entrance could be found, he told me that it was accessed via a well sacred to a local holy man named Hammad el-Samman.

It was a name I knew, having heard mention of this saint a few years previously. He was said to have lived in a 'hole' actually on the Giza plateau, where he guarded the gateway to an underground realm. The saint is esteemed as the founder of the village that bears his name, and as such is considered to be the ancestor of many families in Nazlet el-Samman and nearby Giza village, including that of Hassan – this being the reason why he knew so much about the saint. What is more, Hammad el-Samman is celebrated annually during a religious festival in Nazlet that has gone completely unnoticed by Egyptologists and tourists alike, even though it could hold the key to unlocking the secrets of the plateau's lost past.

Somewhat hesitantly, Hassan informed me that the well lies beneath the shadow of an ancient sycamore tree, actually a *giomez* or sycamore fig, which local tradition asserts was there at the time of the saint. This intrigued me greatly, for like Heliopolis, which had a sacred sycamore whose descendant shades a holy spring that is probably the original *'Ain-Shams*, the 'Eye of the Sun', Giza is also known to have had its own sacred sycamore. It is mentioned in the Middle Kingdom tale of Sinuhe, a court official who decides to leave Egypt when an old pharaoh dies and a struggle ensues between his sons as to which one will ascend the throne.[38] Fearing that only civil strife will now follow, Sinuhe goes into hiding, travelling incognito, until finally he reaches Syria. Years go by, and eventually he decides to return to a changed Egypt, and is welcomed back by the new pharaoh.

It is Sinuhe's early journey that is of interest here, for the account handed down to us states that he travelled first to the south, where he 'crossed Maaty near Sycamore; I reached Isle-of-Snefru'.[39] Maaty, it has been argued, refers to Giza, with the Isle of Snefru (or Snofru, founder of the Fourth Dynasty and father of Khufu) probably being the nearby pyramid field of Dahshur, where two of Snofru's three pyramids were built.[40] This meant that the sycamore in question was in the vicinity of Giza.

What is either the same, or a very similar tree, is mentioned in the Inventory Stela, an inscribed stone slab of the late Dynastic period (*c.*1087–332 BC, i.e. after the New Kingdom) unearthed at Giza and currently in the Old Kingdom room of the Cairo Museum. It bears an inscription which tells how King Khufu visited the plateau in order to assess the damage done to the Great Sphinx. The carved leonine form, along with a sycamore nearby, had apparently been struck by lightning. Fierce debate rages over the age of the text, with revisionist writers using it as evidence that the Great Sphinx was built prior to the reign of Khafre (the successor of Khufu), whose likeness the enigmatic monument is usually said to represent.

Whatever the text's age, the fact that it alludes to a sacred sycamore means that one must have existed on the plateau, very close to the Sphinx monument, at least by the late Dynastic period, and arguably much earlier still. In addition to this, there are several references in Late Period texts to Hathor as 'Mistress of the Southern Sycamore', occasionally in connection with Ptah-Sokar,[41] implying that there was a tree in the Memphis nome equivalent to the one dedicated to Nut at Heliopolis. There was a temple of Hathor at Memphis, and some scholars consider that Hathor was in fact the presiding goddess of the Giza plateau.[42]

The Well of el-Samman

This was the first time that I had heard of such a sycamore existing at the time of the holy man Hammad el-Samman. Yet what Hassan revealed next stunned me completely, for he said that the sycamore and the spring, known as Beer el-Samman, the 'Well of el-Samman', lay deep within the Islamic cemetery, which is next to the Coptic (Egyptian Orthodox Christian) cemetery beneath the north face of Gebel Ghibli, the rocky knoll located just 300 metres south of the Great Sphinx.

I recalled that the alternative name of the Underworld of the Soul was *Bw-hmn*,[43] interpreted by Egyptologist E A E Reymond as the 'Place of the Well'.[44] Indeed, she suggested that it might have been a 'primeval well', arguably in the vicinity of Giza.[45] I myself had seen it in terms of 'some kind of underground complex accessed via a stairwell located on the mound-like island'.[46] Now here was someone, a village elder and a supposed descendant of Hammad el-Samman, telling me that the entrance to Giza's Duat-underworld, the secret 'cavern' of Sokar, was via the saint's holy well, situated at the base of Gebel Ghibli.

This new information astounded me, especially since it came in such a discordant fashion, following the fateful horse ride across the desert to Abusir. Moreover, the presence on the Giza plateau of a sacred sycamore shading a spring parallels exactly the situation at Matariyeh, near Heliopolis, where the Tree of the Virgin and its accompanying holy well still resonate with the memory of an original sycamore and spring once sacred to the sky-goddess Nut. Yet here at Giza, the sycamore would seem to have been presided over by Hathor as 'Mistress of the Southern Sycamore', which I felt alluded to the direct ancestor of the present tree.

In ancient Egypt sycamores of this type were often placed among the dead, in order that the souls of the deceased could access the otherworld via its accompanying well, the waters of which would bring new life beyond death. Strangely, in Dynastic times coffins were often made of sycamore wood so as to create the sense of returning to the womb of the goddess Hathor, who was identified with the pharaoh's royal wife. Hathor's name (*Hwt-Hor* in Egyptian) means the 'House of Horus [the Elder]', which expresses her role as the divine 'mother' of every pharaoh, who is seen as an incarnation of the hawk- or falcon-headed god, once personified in the northern sky as Dwn-'nwy, i.e. the Cygnus constellation. In fact, since Hathor and Nut shared so many attributes, we can see in Hathor another personification of the Milky Way, with her birth canal, from which comes the original Horus child, marked by the stars of Cygnus. If correct, then this would make perfect sense not only of her patronage of the Giza plateau, which was always more than just a necropolis, but also that of Horus the Elder, equated by the time of the New Kingdom with the Sphinx monument.

Sycamore figs are connected with the symbol of the female vulva, due to the distinctive shape of their fruit, while Hathor – intimately associated with intoxication and the cult of the psychoactive blue water lily – stands in the tree and pours forth an unknown liquid from a jar. If not simply water, then maybe it was part of a process whereby initiates would enter the astral form of the Duat-underworld, arguably in a state of intoxication, in order to learn of its mysteries prior to death. Beyond this, they might well have emerged into the light, or radiance of the new dawn, to be projected skywards to a perceived point of creation, where, symbolically at least, souls were seen either as stars in the cosmos or as birds seated within the upper branches of the World Tree.

As above, so below. As the tree headed upwards to heaven, symbolizing perhaps the Milky Way, the Well of Souls went downwards, like the tree's roots, to the Duat-underworld. Yet whichever route was taken, both led ultimately to cosmic rebirth. To find there is a sycamore tree and holy well at Giza, which even today is seen as the sole entrance into a secret realm, its entrance guarded in the past by a solitary Muslim saint, seemed quite incredible. I vowed to find a way of visiting the cemetery, and that chance came on Saturday, 28 May, 2005.

As can be imagined, the Muslim cemetery is strictly off-limits to non-Muslims. Indeed, it serves only those families who were born in Nazlet el-Samman, and one must have a relative interred there to go beyond its gates. However, through a complicated series of negotiations, Sue and I were eventually able to secure local help in slipping past the secret police who now mingle unnoticed among the tourists and street traders guarding the Sphinx entrance, and thus gain access to the nearby cemetery. Five minutes later, and with a little less money in our pockets, we were being shunted along a path between countless box tombs towards the object of our visit.

Beer el-Samman turns out to be a deep artesian well, from which comes crystal clear water drunk by all who frequent the place. The sycamore that shades it is not even the largest, or the most important. This lies some 50 metres south-southwest in the direction of Gebel Ghibli, the jagged cliff face of which is clearly visible above the unsightly concrete wall that now divides the cemetery from the edge of the plateau as part of an ill-conceived anti-terrorist measure. Only a few days beforehand we had been on the other side of that fence searching for clues as to the rocky knoll's greater importance. Now at last we had some answers.

No one seems to be aware that the well and sycamore exist on the plateau, simply because very few people have ever taken any notice of the Islamic cemetery, which occupies quite a large chunk of its southeastern corner. Beer el-Samman is lined with brick and stone, which is unlikely to allow anyone entrance to Giza's otherworldly domain. The 'gateway' to the Underworld of the Soul, is not a staircase, or a descending passageway, but a 'primeval well', next to which is a modern-day representation of the World Tree, a metaphor for the Milky Way, a route of access into the afterlife.

I see a certain irony in the fact that what is arguably the most authentic entrance to Giza's Duat-underworld is protected by the sanctity of an impenetrable Islamic cemetery. In many ways, there could be no better place of protection for somewhere that might otherwise become just another tourist attraction for the coach-loads of camera-hugging tourists who flock onto the plateau every day of the year.

The Beak Star

The discovery of Beer el-Samman and the sacred sycamore now throws a whole new light on nearby Gebel Ghibli, the rocky knoll already proposed as the most likely location of both the Shetayet of Sokar and Giza's primeval hill. There seems every likelihood that it is the physical representation of the Edfu Building Texts' Island of the Egg, in which the Underworld of the Soul was said to have been located. If correct, then Beer el-Samman, represents, in my opinion, an echo of the *Bw-hmn,* 'Place of the Well', reflected in Giza's ancient name Rostau, meaning 'Mouth of the Passages'. I find it curious therefore that in the Cygnus-Giza overlay proposed within these pages, the double star Albireo (*beta* Cygni), the Arabic *al-Minhar al-Dajajah*, 'the Hen's Beak', or 'Beak Star', falls on the south side of Gebel Ghibli. As the mouth, or gullet, of the celestial bird, this would be an apt description of the entrance to a holy well thought to access the chthonic realms governed by Sokar, once seen as the 'gatekeeper in the darkness'. Remember too that at Newgrange in Ireland, the star Albireo is considered to mark the mouth or entrance to its Neolithic passage grave, penetrated by the first rays of the sun each winter solstice (*see Chapter Eleven*).

The fact that with the discovery of Beer el-Samman we now have two sacred sycamores and two holy wells, one at Heliopolis and the other at Giza, one dedicated to Nut and the other to Hathor, strengthens the connection between the two ancient cult centres, as well as the proposed Giza-Heliopolis sighting line targeting the rising of Deneb. Many more mysteries could hold us in Egypt, but it is time to move on now to India, where the cosmic call of the Great Cackler resounds once more in the Hindu mythos surrounding *kalahamsa*, the Swan-Goose of Eternity.

PART FIVE

ORIGINS

CHAPTER SIXTEEN

The Swan-Goose of Eternity

Each October-November, around the full moon day of Kartik Purnima, crowds of pilgrims, Hindu devotees of Lord Brahma, make their way to the sacred lake of Kanishtha Pushkar, located some 11 kilometres (seven miles) from Ajmer, in the state of Rajasthan in northwest India.[1] Its sanctity goes back to the age of the gods, for legend recalls how Brahma was out searching for a suitable place to conduct a *yagna,* or fire sacrifice, when a lotus tumbled from his hand and fell upon the earth, causing water to spring forth from three separate places. One was Pushkar, which means 'the lotus that bloomed in mud', and here the *yagna* was conducted. In gratitude, Brahma then blessed the lake, and asserted that everyone who bathed there would achieve salvation, since its waters had the power to destroy all evil within and allow the dead access to the 'three worlds'. Thus the town, which now boasts 500 temples, became the ultimate pilgrimage site for Hindus across Rajasthan.

Around the sacred lake are 52 ghats, or bathing step-ways, and once the pilgrims have immersed themselves in its waters, they are drawn to the temple of Lord Brahma, constructed in the fourteenth century. Here a series of marble steps leads the visitor through the entrance arch into the inner sanctuary, where embossed into the mosaic floor is a silver turtle, an avatar or incarnation of Lord Vishnu. In the Hindu myth known as the Churning of the Ocean, the Devas and Asuras use the poisonous snake Vasuki as a rope to churn the cosmic mountain that rests on the back of Vishnu in the form of a turtle, in order to extract the *amrita*, or nectar of the gods. It expresses the nature of the heavens, and the manner in which the cosmic axis links the Earth with the northern celestial pole.

So holy is Pushkar's image of the turtle that pilgrims have embedded hundreds if not thousands of silver coins between gaps in the floor. Many more have been pushed between spaces in the walls, a custom thought to bestow good luck. Both Vishnu (the Preserver) and Shiva (the Destroyer) are also venerated in the Brahma temple, with Shiva even having his own cave-like shrine. Ironically, Vishnu and Shiva are more favoured by visitors here, since Brahma has long been considered too remote from the day to day needs of worshippers. Yet regardless of his fate, for us Brahma and his first wife Saraswati are crucial to the Cygnus mystery.

Brahma – God of Creation

The *Mahabharata*, one of the great Sanskrit epics of India, tells of how Brahma emerged from a lotus that sprang from the navel of Vishnu, seen in terms of the sacred lake at Pushkar. Other accounts speak of him as the first conscious mind of the universe, existing within the 'Golden Nucleus' (*Hiranyagarbha*), which germinated after being 'sparked off' by a mysterious First Cause.[2] On awakening, Brahma took his first breath, at which the physical universe came into being. The entire act of creation is said to have proceeded from *Shabda-brahman*, the 'sonic absolute', conveyed by the process of *Naada-brahmam*, the 'primordial sound or vibration of Brahma'. This is thought to fill the entire expanse of the universe and becomes audible to yogins, or ascetics, when they achieve higher states of consciousness. It is symbolically expressed in terms of the conch shell,[3] perhaps reflecting the age-old belief that shells contain the sound of the primordial ocean.

So holy is Brahma that his followers assert that he does not need temples where devotees might worship him like other gods. This is why the fabulous building at Pushkar is so special, for it is one of only two places dedicated to his devotion, the other being the temple of Khed Brahma at Kerala in southwestern India. However, since Brahma is also an incarnation of Vishnu and Shiva – the reason why statues show him often with three heads and six arms – he is permitted a shrine in their temples. These are placed usually in the north wall,[4] for it is believed that Brahma's celestial abode, called *Brahmaloka*, 'World of God', lies north beyond Mount Meru (or Sumeru). This is the mythical *axis mundi* or World Mountain, which Hindu tradition asserts is the god's earthly abode.

Scholars will argue that the north for Hindus is simply the direction of Mount Kailas (or Kailash), a holy mountain in southwestern Tibet thought by many Hindus to be the original Mount Meru, even though the two are referred to separately in early texts. Mount Kailas is close to the sources of four great Asian rivers – the Ganges, Indus, Brahmputra (Tsangpo), Sutlej, as well as the now lost Saraswati (see below). Because of this the mountain is associated with many aspects of Indian and Tibetan religious cosmology, and remains a site of great pilgrimage for Hindus, Jains, Buddhists and followers of the Tibetan shamanic religion known as Bon. Yet we might argue that the significance of the north, the place of Brahma's celestial abode, is merely an extension of creation ideologies found worldwide, which see the north as the direction of cosmic life and death.

Hamsa the Swan-Goose

At Brahma's temple in Pushkar an enormous swan-goose embraces the entrance gateway, crowned by a red spire. The bird's presence is not without significance, for we read that Brahma was aided in his act of creation by *Hamsa* (also written *Hansa*), a swan-goose, although the word *hamsa* is used also for either a swan or goose. Versions of Brahma's birth found in early Sanskrit writings, including the religious texts known as the Puranas, speak of him gestating in a golden egg (the *Brahmanda*, or 'Egg of Brahma'), laid by Hamsa, through which he came to be known as *Kalahamsa* (or *Kalahansa*), the 'Swan-Goose of Eternity', or 'Swan-Goose in Space and Time'.[5] Other stories talk of how Brahma came to Earth either on the back of the swan-goose, or on a chariot drawn by seven swans. Indeed, he is said to have been in his swan-chariot when the lotus dropped from his hand, creating three water sources, one of which being Pushkar's sacred lake.

As the Hiranyagarbha or Golden Nucleus, the Egg of Brahma is seen as a seed which germinates, and even as a cosmic atom, from which the physical and mental universe took its form ('I am the Gander [Hamsa]. I am the Lord [Brahma]. I bring forth the universe from my essence and I abide in the cycle of time that dissolves it.').[6]

Similarly to the Great Cackler of ancient Egyptian myth, Kalahamsa manifests the universe by letting out a divine call, in this case the AUM, or OM (the *a* and *u* become *o* when said together), the *Pranava*, or Sound of the Infinite. This is an expression of the composition of the universe as a whole, and not in individual parts as we perceive it in the physical world.[7] The AUM, which forms the basis for all sacred mantras,[8] is expressed as the Kalahamsa, with the A considered to be its right wing; the U its left wing; and the M its tail.[9] The more familiar sign used to express the OM symbol in both Hinduism and Buddhism was originally the cosmic egg, or seed, emerging from a moon-like crescent. In the *Rig Veda*, the ancient body of Sanskrit literature which dates back in its present form to the third millennium BC,[10] the AUM becomes the sound of the sun, as well as the sound of light, seen as an upwards movement that lifts the soul, like the call of an eagle or falcon.

Saraswati

After Pushkar was chosen as the site of Brahma's fire sacrifice, the other gods were invited to witness this prestigious event, and once they had arrived, their wives were asked to join them. Yet Brahma's wife Saraswati tarried in the celestial abode, for she would hurry for no one. Losing patience, her husband chose a milkmaid in her stead, whom the god Indra purified by placing her head in a cow's mouth, thus enabling the ritual to go ahead. When Saraswati finally arrived with Lakshmi, Indrani and other of the gods' wives, and saw that her place had been taken by a milkmaid, she cursed her husband, telling him that she would not be worshipped anywhere else but at Pushkar, and then only on one day of the year. So in rage she departed for the stark, conical hill of Ratnagiri, which rises out of the bare landscape just a few kilometres away from the sacred lake. Here, on the summit, her temple was built, and to this day it remains one of only a few dedicated to Saraswati in the whole of India.

Statues and painted images of the four-armed goddess depict her always as a young, serene and very beautiful woman. She is shown seated on a lotus, and wears only white, the colour of purity and serenity. She is said to have manifested out of Brahma's head, and even though this made Saraswati his daughter he still desired her. At first she managed to avoid his gaze, but then he grew a new face on every side of his head so that he might follow her wherever she went; he even grew one on the top of his head, making five in total. Finally, she consented to marry him, and out of this union came every living creature in the world.

Saraswati (whose name means 'abundance of lakes') is seen to be the personification of all knowledge, from the creative arts and crafts to the sciences. In her form as the goddess Vak, or Vach, she is patron of sound and speech, the reason why statues show her holding a wooden string instrument known as the *veena*. Because Saraswati governs what might be termed the creative impulse, found in such things as music, beauty and eloquence, we find that writers, artists and others of a creative nature flock to Pushkar from all over Rajasthan to gain divine inspiration, in the same way that the Greeks looked towards the Muses for theirs. It is for this reason that Saraswati holds in one hand a book, since she is said to have inspired the writing of the Vedas and to have been the creator of the Sanskrit language. Indeed, Saraswati and Brahma's daughter is Brahmi, the name also of an ancient script that was the ancestor of most South Asian writing systems, including Devanagari (used for Hindi and most other Indian dialects) and Tibetan. In addition to this, it may well relate to the ancient written language of the little understood Saraswati civilization of western India and the Indus Valley civilization centred on neighbouring

Fig. 39. The goddess Saraswati on her swan vehicle. She is seen as a personification of both the Saraswati River and its celestial extension, the Milky Way.

Pakistan (which today are grouped together by some Indian scholars under the all-embracing title of the Saraswati-Sindhu culture, with Sindhu being the Sanskrit and Hindi name for the Indus river).[12] It is the former of these, the Saraswati civilization, that was most likely responsible for the composition of the Vedas (see below).

Saraswati holds also a sacred *mala*, or rosary, used by Hindus and Buddhists alike to count the number of mantras recited. It is made up of 108 beads on a string, with a 109th bead hanging separately. This final one is said to represent Sumeru, the Buddhist name for the cosmic mountain, around which the pilgrim is expected to walk 108 times if he or she wishes to attain enlightenment.

Beyond all this is the fact that Brahma gained the power to think and create the universe through the influence of Saraswati. More crucially, we find that she was responsible for enabling her husband to hear the Naada-brahmam, the primordial sound seen as the essence of all creation, encapsulated by the fact that she wears conch shells as earrings. In this aspect, she became absorbed in the AUM vibration, which holds together the entire universe. An understanding of the sacred syllables that form the AUM – which relate to the three states of waking, dreaming and sleeping – leads the initiate to the higher realm of *turya*, represented by silence, on which one must meditate in order to hear the primordial sound that fills the universe.

The greater significance of Saraswati is that her avataristic form is that of Hamsa, the swan-goose, the reason why she becomes the divine swan-maiden. Representations of Saraswati show the goddess sitting on her 'vehicle' (*vahana*), i.e. Hamsa, playing the *veena* instrument. Sometimes she is associated not just with the swan-goose, but also with the peacock, the royal bird of India, reminding us of the Yezidi's belief in the power of the Peacock Angel (*see Chapter Three*). Indeed, images of peacocks, as the vehicle of Saraswati, adorn the walls of Pushkar's temple to Brahma.

The Celestial River

Legend has it that at one time all five, or seven, sacred rivers of India rose in the Himalayas and flowed through the town of Pushkar. One of these was the Saraswati, interpreted in this sense as 'the flowing one', seen as an extension of the goddess herself. It is said to have come down from the mountains past the northern city of Patiala, and then followed a course between Punjab and Haryana, before flowing through Rajasthan and emptying finally into the Arabian Sea. What is believed once to have been its route, originally green and lush due to the river's lifegiving waters, is marked today by the Thar or Indian desert, a barren world where once a civilization thrived.

In the *Rig Veda* the Saraswati River was seen as the terrestrial counterpart of the Milky Way,[13] which, as one commentator put it, was regarded as 'flowing down from heaven about the time of the winter solstice: it thus opened, with its two branches touching the northeastern horizon, the "gate" to heaven.'[14] No more specific details are given, although these words recall the rising of Deneb, and thus the Milky Way, on the northeastern horizon during this epoch. Such ideas would make the 'two branches' of the Milky Way the Great Rift, with the 'gate' being the very tip of the dark nebulous region where the stars of Cygnus are to be seen.[15] Interestingly, in Vedic tradition the Milky Way was equated with the World Tree (an *ashvattha* or peepal) located at the centre of heaven and Earth, the Saraswati River being its mirror-like counterpart on the landscape.[16]

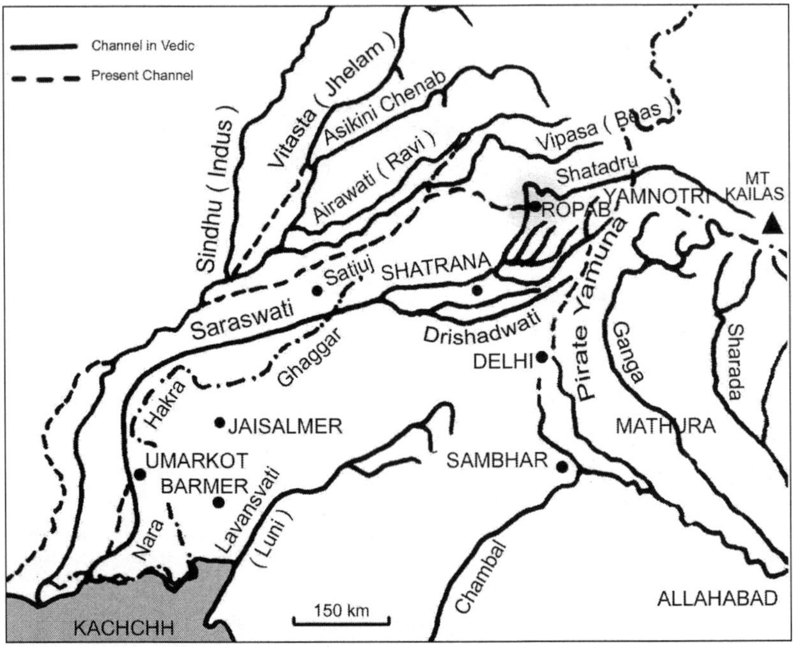

Fig. 40. The river systems of western India and eastern Pakistan, showing the possible course of the Saraswati River, with its source in the region of Mount Kailas in Tibet. According to one theory, its culture was responsible for the compilation of the Rig Veda.

Thus through her personification as the starry river the goddess Saraswati can be compared with Nut, the ancient Egyptian sky-goddess, while her patronage of music and the arts makes her very much like the goddess Hathor. Indeed, there are many comparisons that can be made between Saraswati and the Near Eastern love goddess, who went on to become the Venus-Aphrodite of Classical tradition. Her worship was widespread across Central Asia, and in Afghanistan a beautiful third-century AD ivory engraving of a naked love goddess accompanied by a swan-goose was found during excavations at Begram, the former summer capital of the Kushan empire.[17]

That Saraswati's avataristic form is, like Brahma, the swan-goose Hamsa struck me as strangely relevant to the Cygnus mystery, especially in the knowledge that Saraswati herself is known as a star-goddess. Whenever a baby arrives, the grandmother of the household uses a little honey to make a five-pointed sign called

'Saraswati's star' on the child's tongue, which is considered the organ of speech. In this way, the infant is thought to become attached to Saraswati's star from an early age, enabling them to learn more easily the gift of speech, one of the attributes of the goddess. I am reminded here of another swan-linked star-goddess back in Britain. The star of Bride, or Bridget, we shall recall, was affixed to corn dollies called *Brideog*, meaning 'Little Bride'. Like Saraswati's milkmaid rival alluded to earlier, Bride-Bridget was also once a lowly milkmaid, an allusion most probably to the supposed lacteous qualities of the Milky Way.

Lake Manasarovar

In India generally, swans were always seen as incarnations of divine beings and royal dynasties. One place in particular seems to have been a focus for swan legends, and this was Lake Manasarovar, or Manasa, which lies within sight of Mount Kailas in southwest Tibet. In one Buddhist story,[18] Brahmadatta, the king of Varanasi (Benares), devises a plan to lure Dhritarashtra, the king of the swans, his commander-in-chief Sumukha and the entire swan population of Lake Manasarovar, to his kingdom in east India. For this, King Brahmadatta orders the construction of a beautiful lake in a forest that in every way resembles the swans' abode in the Himalayas.

There are various accounts of what transpires when this comes to pass, and of how the swan-king, his commander-in-chief and the rest of the flock arrive at Varanasi, staying there long enough for them to forget completely about Lake Manasarovar. Sometimes the contents of such tales vary, but always they revolve around the existence of a dynasty of swan-kings living in the region of Lake Manasarovar, who are enticed to artificial lakes in different parts of India. Such accounts seem to preserve within them a transference of sacral power from the Himalayas to the various Indian kingdoms in question, as if in an attempt to legitimize their own royal dynasty, simply by the presence of the swan-king and his flock.

Exactly what might have been going on at Lake Manasarovar is explored below, yet suffice it to say that India's tales of swan-dynasties can be compared with the legends of swan-knights, swan-lineages and swan-maidens found not only in Europe, but also among the shamanic-based societies of central and northeastern Asia and northern Europe cited in Chapter Five.

Is it possible therefore that the original sources behind the more formalized cosmologies preserved in the Hindu and Buddhist traditions of India and Tibet were originally shamanic in nature? Were the creation myths that speak of Brahma, as

Kalahamsa, bringing the universe into manifestation derived from information achieved during shamanic journeys, like those so familiar to us from other parts of the world? This might be so, yet only in the Hindu and Buddhist traditions are the creation myths so complex that they might almost be mistaken for some modern quantum theory regarding the origins of the universe. How is this possible, and what does it tell us about the identification of Kalahamsa, the Swan-Goose of Eternity?

What we can say is that the seven swans which draw Brahma's chariot are probably linked with the seven swans that are believed to fly down from heaven and land on Lake Manasarovar, near Brahma's terrestrial abode on Mount Kailas in southwest Tibet. They are said to be the Seven Rishis, enlightened poets or priests, who on rising to heaven became the seven stars of Ursa Major. They assume the role of swans to visit the place where the Vedas were thought to have been conceived, i.e. in the Himalayan hills and mountains around Lake Manasarovar, one of the sources of the Saraswati River.[19]

Vedic Astronomy

In the knowledge that Saraswati was a personification of the Milky Way, there has to be a good chance that Hamsa was, and still is, seen as an asterism somewhere in the general area of both Ursa Major and the Milky Way. I searched through several Indian star charts and found that the stars of Cygnus are indeed seen in terms of a great bird, although from the artistic representations I looked at it seemed to resemble not a swan or goose, but a hen or cock. However, I subsequently found out that this connection only came about through the influence of Greek and Babylonian astronomy on Indian star lore. Much earlier, there had existed an indigenous astronomy, alluded to in the *Rig Veda* and other sacred texts.[20]

What I needed to establish was the identification of individual constellations during *this* period, and not their names in later times. For this I turned to the work of astrophysicist and astronomer Dr P K Kunte of India's Space Physics Group. He is an expert on Vedic astronomy, and derides the fact that Greek and Babylonian asterisms corrupted India's original view of the sky-world. I read his identification of known star clusters, and was stunned to find that he identifies Hamsa, and thus Kalahamsa, with the stars of Cygnus, saying that this knowledge was 'known [a] long time back'.[21] However, except in its modern form as Cygnus, the swan-goose is no longer recognized as the basis for the star group, a point which Dr Kunte is at pains to point out.[22]

If he is right – and more research is needed into the substance of Vedic astronomy – then we can conclude that in India the Cygnus constellation was viewed as the celestial manifestation of the Swan-Goose of Eternity, as well as the source of cosmic creation, a fact emphasized by the location of Brahma's celestial abode north, beyond Mount Meru. If this abode is to be identified as Mount Kailas, which was certainly the case in later times, then the knowledge that the Seven Rishis in the form of seven swans were associated directly with nearby Lake Manasarovar links this sacred body of water, associated so strongly with divine swans, with star lore relating to Ursa Major.

That Hamsa can be connected through the symbol of the swan-goose with Cygnus, Ursa Major's age-old sparring partner in the northern night sky, brings to mind the worldwide use of these two constellations to define the celestial meridian, which, as we have seen, was considered a pathway or ladder to the sky-world. Moreover, was Saraswati simply an expression, like Nut and Hathor in Egypt and Bride-Bridget in Britain, of the Milky Way and the stars of Cygnus in particular? That Saraswati's totem or vehicle was the swan, like Brahma and the love goddesses of the Near East, seems to confirm this fact.

Saraswati-Sindhu Culture

In the knowledge that Saraswati also inspired the creation of a major Indian civilization, responsible very possibly for the *Rig Veda*, only adds to her significance. Over 1,200 archaeological sites have so far been recorded in the putative Saraswati basin, and these are providing dates in the region of *c.*3100–*c.*1900 BC,[23] close to those of the Indus Valley civilization, leading some scholars to speculate that this culture used the Vedic knowledge of geometry, algebra, astronomy, geography, shipbuilding and navigation to achieve its greatest potential, and even to trade with Egypt and Mesopotamia.[24] Yet such knowledge of civilization had to have come from more inspired origins. Thus I strongly suspect that the seemingly advanced culture of the Saraswati River,[25] was the vehicle for a more ancient shamanic-based society responsible not just for the contents of the *Rig Veda*, but also for introducing the concept of Hamsa, the avatar of both Brahma and his wife/daughter, the goddess Saraswati. I feel also that this knowledge of the cosmos, so close to that accepted by science today, derived from otherworldly journeys to achieve absolute enlightenment in the realms of Brahma. Such notions are not held back by current anthropological thinking, which sees the presence of death trance states, as well as examples of ascending sky-poles to heaven, as present in Vedic texts.[26]

Links exist also between Vedic imagery and Saraswati-Sindhu sacred art. For instance, a seal showing two birds looking at one another across the branches of an *ashvattha* or peepal (sacred fig) tree,[27] recalls a Vedic story in which a seer-bard speaks of two birds, 'friends joined together' on a tree, one of whom tastes the fruit while the other only looks on.[28] Interpretations of the account vary, but one bird is thought to express the individual soul, or spirit, while the other is the universal spirit, reminding us of Hamsa, in its role as the divine bird at the top of the sky-pole.

Strange too that in India, as in Egypt, the sycamore fig was an important symbol of the mythical World Tree, and by virtue of this the Milky Way. Here it was a symbol of Indra, while under its shade (as the Bodhi tree), the Buddha sat to gain enlightenment (*bodhi*). In addition to this, its wood was said to kindle the fire with which gods granted knowledge to the human race.

Aside from the World Tree, another symbol of the universe in Vedic tradition was the fire altar, sacred to the fire-god Agni. A great many such altars have been excavated throughout the Indus Valley, but by far the most intriguing group came to light at the possible former confluence of the Saraswati and Drishadvati rivers. Seven examples, rectangular in shape, were found standing in a row, aligned north-south, next to which was a well.[29] In cosmological terms, this is perfect evidence of the Vedic interest in the north as the direction of both the cosmic axis, seen in terms of the World Tree or fire altar, as well as Brahma's celestial abode. If this was thought to be accessed via Mount Kailas, then it is not surprising that we find next to it the source of the Saraswati River, which became the lifeblood for one of the most advanced civilizations of the ancient world.

Despite the allure of other rich and varied cultures, past and present, which also possess creation myths and star lore that might help provide further clues to the Cygnus mystery, it was time to go back to the very root of the matter. I wanted to examine the earliest known evidence of shamanism, expressed in the Upper Palaeolithic cave art of western Europe, in the hope of discovering why even by *c.*9500 BC there existed megalithic sites in Upper Mesopotamia that appear to reflect an interest in the stars of Cygnus in a manner that was already thousands of years old. But in order to do this, I needed first to go to China, to examine why some scholars have believed that its stellar-based calendar is at least 17,000 years old.

CHAPTER SEVENTEEN

The First Astronomers

Following a lengthy examination of Chinese astronomy for his French-language book *Uranographie Chinoise* ('Chinese Star Charts', 1875), the noted Dutch Orientalist, philologist and ethnologist Gustave Schlegel (1840–1903) came to a quite staggering conclusion. According to him, China's extremely ancient stellar-influenced solar calendar reflected the night sky of the Northern Hemisphere as it appeared around 15,000 BC, when Deneb, the brightest star of Cygnus, was Pole Star.[1]

Schlegel's findings were afterwards cited rather disparagingly in various books, including M. Camille Flammarion's weighty tome *Popular Astronomy* (1897). He declared that the 'distinguished' author's proposals were 'not convincing', and that there was nothing to suggest that Chinese astronomy was 'very much anterior to the reign of the Emperor Hoang-Ti [or Huangdi]', the legendary 'Yellow Emperor', *c.*2700 BC, and certainly no earlier than the age of Fou-Hi (Fuxi or Fu-hsi), the legendary first ruler of China, who according to Chinese tradition reigned *c.*2852–2738 BC.[2] Clearly, no one was going to accept Schlegel's findings gladly, even though *Uranographie Chinoise,* which has never been translated into English, is still considered a masterpiece of its genre, and is referenced constantly in academic books on Chinese astronomy.

What we can say about Gustave Schlegel is that he was no madman. He travelled extensively in the Indian subcontinent acting as a Dutch interpreter, and in his spare time examined the relationship between Oriental astronomy and that established in the West by the Greeks and Babylonians. On his arrival in the Far East during the 1860s Schlegel embarked on an ambitious project to create the first Dutch-Chinese dictionary, using the Southern Min dialect. It appeared as a four-volume set (1886–90), and remains an essential reference work to this day.[3] He also wrote various other books on Chinese history and culture, which, like his other academic works, were accepted into mainstream literature. They included the first ever work on the Hung (Hong) League, the earliest known incarnation of the modern-day Triads, published at Batavia on the island of Java in 1866.[4]

Although Schlegel's ideas on the greater antiquity of Chinese astronomy have been largely ignored by all, they were belatedly endorsed by American astronomer Julius D W Staal, FRAS, who, until his death in 1986, was Planetarium Director of the Bradley Observatory at Agnes Scott College, Decatur, Georgia, as well as the author of various books on popular astronomy, including *Patterns in the Sky* (1961) and its revised edition *The New Patterns in the Sky* (1988). Staal was a great supporter of Schlegel's work on Chinese astronomy, and wrote a highly underrated book featuring his findings entitled *Stars of Jade* (1984).[5]

China's Topsy-Turvy World

Schlegel's ideas are scholarly and complex, and need to be understood from the perspective of the very basics of Chinese astronomy. They divide the celestial sphere into four heavenly sectors – east, south, west and north – with each governing a particular season, respectively spring, summer, autumn and winter. The problem is that these quadrants are presided over by enormous super-constellations composed of star clusters that do not reflect the season they are said to represent.

For example, the sector called the Blue Dragon of Spring, positioned in the east, is made up of stars from Virgo, Libra and Scorpio, which rise with the sun in the autumn, while the stars of the White Tiger of Autumn, connected with the west – that is Andromeda, Pisces, Aries, Taurus and Orion – are all spring constellations. In contrast, the Black Warrior (or Tortoise) of Winter, positioned in the north, is correctly marked by stars featured in the Western constellations of Sagittarius, Capricorn, Aquarius and Pegasus, through which the sun currently passes during the winter months, while the Red Bird of Summer, associated with the south, is marked by Gemini, Cancer, Leo, Hydra and Corvi, all summer signs, which is also correct.

Yet if the Blue Dragon – with its stars of Virgo, Libra and Scorpio – does mark the entry of the sun in spring, then it would imply that the next season, expressed by the Red Bird of Summer, should by Chinese reckoning be represented by the stars of Sagittarius, Capricorn, Aquarius and Pegasus, which are in fact associated with the Black Tortoise of the North. Moreover, if the White Tiger – with its stars in Andromeda, Pisces, Aries, Taurus and Orion – marks the autumn, then it should mean that the winter season, symbolized by the Black Warrior, should be marked by the stars of Gemini, Cancer, Leo, etc, which in fact belong to the Red Bird of Summer.

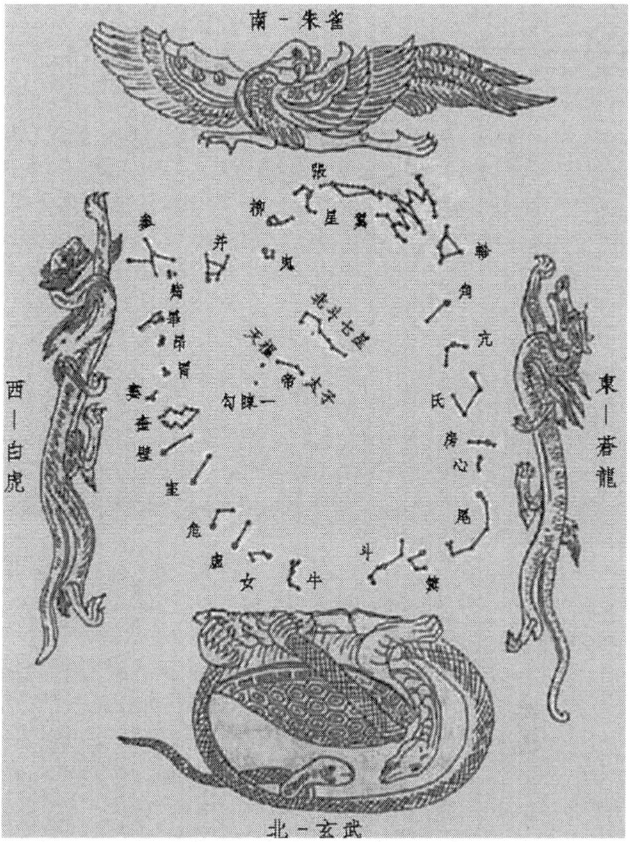

Fig. 41. Ground view of the four beasts of Chinese astronomy – Green Dragon, Red Bird, White Tiger and Black Warrior, complete with constellations.

China's entire astronomical calendar is completely topsy-turvy, with a heaven full of constellations – Schlegel recorded no fewer than 670 – that are completely opposite to what they should be with respect to their relationship to the sun's yearly course. Let me give just one example, bearing in mind that both Schlegel and Staal cite dozens more such anomalies. The constellation known as Fang, which means 'The House', comes under the rule of the Blue Dragon of Spring, with the 'House' being the House of the Sun. It is said to herald the arrival of the spring equinox, which is why it became known as the 'Great Opener', since it enabled the sun to pass from the Southern Hemisphere into the Northern Hemisphere.[6]

Fang was seen also as a relay station, where the chariot of the sun could obtain new horses for the uphill journey from the equinox to the summer solstice. Moreover, Fang was known, along with a neighbouring star group called Sin, as the Ming Tang, or 'Hall of Light', the heavenly representation of the temple complex of this name at Mount Tai (*see below*), since it was in March that the emperor offered sacrifices to ensure that the sky-father, lord of light, watched over the growth of crops during the summer season.[7] As an asterism, Fang can be found in the stomach area of the Blue Dragon, and yet, like neighbouring Sin, it is composed of stars belonging to the Western constellation of Scorpio, which rises with the sun not in spring, but in autumn.

Something was clearly out of kilter, and Schlegel realized this from the outset. He therefore used basic mathematics to precess the skies back to an age when the ancient Chinese calendar fitted precisely the sun's course through the seasons. His conclusions are startling in their implications, for he determined that its astronomy made no sense whatsoever unless you turned back time to *c*.15,000 BC, when the equinoctial sun rose each spring in the sign of Scorpio. Schlegel found support for his theory in ancient Chinese records that allude to a foundation of its solar calendar 16,916 years before the present time, give or take 900 years.[8]

Schlegel acknowledged that during this distant epoch the northern celestial pole was closest to the star Deneb. This made sense of Chinese astronomy, which speaks of an important asterism called *Tianjin* (or *T'ien-tsin*), 'Ford of the Sky', composed of nine stars from the constellation of Cygnus. It is conceived of as a junction where the Milky Way, seen as the 'celestial river', or 'river of stars', divides into two due to the presence of the Great Rift.[9] Chinese writings from the early fourth century AD saw the celestial pole as lying in the proximity of the Great Rift, which Schlegel took to be an allusion to Deneb.[10] It was for this reason that Tianjin became known as the 'ultimate star'.[11]

In addition to this Schlegel wanted to know why Tianjin came under the rule of Hiu, the ox, a constellation formed by the stars *beta* Aquarius and *gamma* Equulei (i.e. Equuleus, the foal). Schlegel investigated the matter, and calculated that in 15,000 BC Hiu made its midnight meridian transit at its highest point on midwinter's eve, the same time that Tianjin did the same. Thus he concluded that the meridian transit of Cygnus as the heavenly ford was used in this distant epoch to mark the arrival of the winter solstice sunrise, the shortest day of the year, when the sun starts its course back towards the spring equinox.[12] Once again, this conforms to a now familiar pattern encountered in various other countries of the world, where

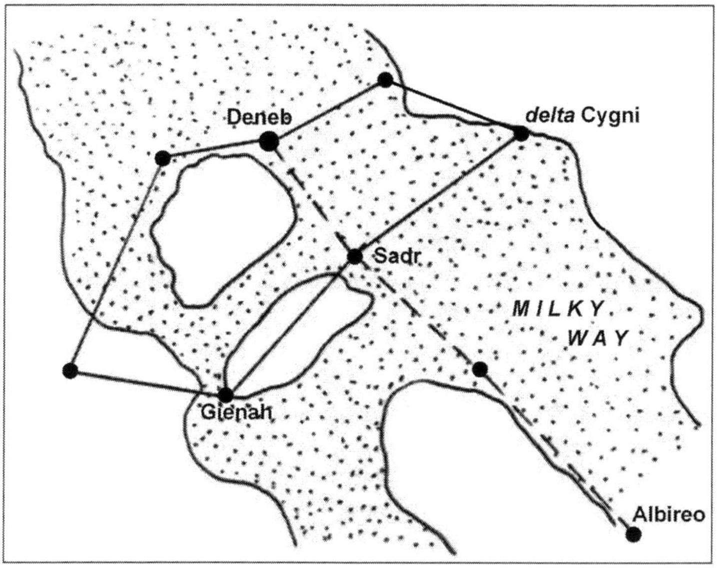

Fig. 42. Tianjin, the Ford of the Sky, formed by the stars of Cygnus.

Deneb and the stars of Cygnus were, or are, seen as heralding the arrival of the midwinter sunrise (and sometimes the summer solstice).

Staal's Confirmation

Julius Staal's own work in this field, outlined in *Stars of Jade*, led him to propose a three stage development of the Chinese astronomical system, beginning with the introduction of several key asterisms, including Tianjin, *c.*15,600 BC,[13] with more being added *c.*12,900 BC.[14] Finally, sometime *c.*2700 BC, the entire calendar was revamped by Chinese astronomers to incorporate hundreds of new constellations. In his final assessment of the evidence, Staal concluded that 'the four great sky animals, their houses (i.e. divisions) and paranatellons (or 'co-risers', neighbouring constellations which rise or set with the houses) would not make the slightest sense if the sky were not of the period which we have been discussing ... namely 15,600 BC'.[15]

He felt that this necessitated the existence of a Chinese 'civilization' during that age, although more likely is that its ancient astronomy was the creation of a shamanic elite that studied the stars and their movement, and existed somewhere on the Eurasian continent during the Upper Palaeolithic era. As bold a statement as this might seem, there will be reasons given for this conclusion.

Staal's dating of the Chinese stellar calendar to *c.* 15,600 BC, along with Schlegel's proposed time-frame of *c.* 15,000 BC, fitted precisely with my own suggested start-date for an interest in Deneb and the stars of Cygnus as the destination of the soul in the afterlife. Thus Schlegel and Staal's work seemed to confirm that during this epoch something of quite incredible significance had been taking place in the ancient world, either among all peoples collectively or among groups in isolation, and whatever it was it had somehow managed to catalyze the emergence of what we know today as astronomy.

The Magpie Bridge

Before we leave China in order to pursue these revelations more fully, there is one further piece of the puzzle that must be put into place. Both Schlegel and Staal recognized the importance of a folktale found in various forms throughout the Far East that seems to encode valuable astronomical knowledge of a bygone epoch. It is the story of Zhi Nü, the Weaver Princess (also called the Weaving Maid and Spinning Damsel), who was the daughter of the sun-king, the King of Heaven or 'Jade Emperor'.[16]

One day, whilst at her spinning wheel or loom, she saw from a window of the celestial palace her father's herdsman, or ox driver, Jian Niu, also called Niu Lang, who was at the time driving his master's flock along the banks of the Milky Way, the celestial river. Their eyes met, and very soon the couple fell in love, and saw each other as often as they could. The Jade Emperor consented to their marriage, and finally the happy day came, but so in love were they that each began neglecting their duties. Zhi Nü left her spinning wheel idle, while Jian Niu allowed the royal animals to roam free.

Following repeated requests that they resume their duties forthwith, all of which were ignored, the Jade Emperor decided to separate the lovers. He sent Zhi Nü to one side of the celestial river, while Jian Niu remained on the other. Yet those who lived in the palace of heaven were so grieved by this sad situation that they persuaded the Jade Emperor to allow the lovers to come together once every year. Thus from that time onwards, on the seventh day of the seventh month, all the magpies of the world fly up to the celestial river where they gather (or provide twigs) to form a bridge on which the Weaver Princess and the royal herdsman are able to fall into each other's arms.

There is, of course, an astronomical basis to this touching story. The Jade Emperor, or King of Heaven, and his celestial palace are placed somewhere in the vicinity of the Pole Star, since the emperor of China, the so-called 'Son of Heaven', was seen as its terrestrial counterpart.[17] The famous temple complex known as Ming Tang ('Hall of Light'), built at the base of Mount Tai by the emperor Wu in 109 BC, was known as the Palace of the Shangdi [Heavenly Ruler] of the Tai Wei, or North Star, and had a northerly placed shrine known as the Temple of the Sovereign Heaven.[18] Moving on to Zhi Nü, the Weaver Princess, although her spinning wheel, or loom, was located in the celestial palace, i.e. the Pole Star, she represents the star Vega in Lyra. Meanwhile, Jian Niu, the herdsman, is identified as the star Altair in Aquila, his animals possibly other asterisms in the northern night sky; while the bridge formed each year by every magpie in the land is Cygnus, the Chinese asterism known as Tianjin, the ford of the sky.

Thus in China we find that, once again, the Cygnus star group was, and still is, linked with a bird, in this case the magpie. The birds came together to form a bridge across the Milky Way, which might be compared with the celestial bridge that the Mandaeans of Iraq and Iran (*see Chapter Three*) saw as located at the northern most extreme of the Milky Way, arguably in the vicinity of the Cygnus constellation.

Magpies are scavengers belonging to the same genus as crows, ravens and jays. Yet unlike in Britain and most of Europe, where the bird is generally seen as an ill omen, in China it is considered a sign of good fortune and happiness. This said, if any magpies are spotted on the seventh day of the seventh month, when they should be helping their brethren create the 'bridge of magpies', it has been acceptable in China to pelt them with stones, since they are seen as being lazy and disrespectful to the Weaver Princess.

Yang and Yin

Chinese astronomy is also reflected in microcosm within the subtle flow of *qi* (*ch'i*) energies around the human body, and here we again encounter the Magpie Bridge. A chance conversation with friend and colleague Yuri Leitch, a British practitioner of the Chinese art of *taiji quan* (*t'ai chi ch'uan*), revealed this quite astonishing fact. Many readers may be aware of the Indian concept of *chakras*, energy 'wheels' or vortices, said to exist along the spine from the coccyx to the crown of the head. These regulate the flow of vital energy to every part of the body, like the neurological pathways of the central nervous system.

In Taoism, however, the system is somewhat different, and instead of the main

Fig. 43. The Weaver Princess, Zhi Nü, standing on the Magpie Bridge, represented in Chinese astronomy by Tianjin, the celestial ford (the Western constellation of Cygnus).

energy artery being solely up the spine, it is in two halves. One, considered *yang* (male, active), flows from between the genitalia and anus around to the back, and then up the spine before going over the head to end at the upper lip. The other line, seen as *yin* (female, passive) flows from the same starting position, up over the front of the body to terminate on the lower lip. Thus a gap exists between the two lines where the mouth is, and only by the act of using the tongue to touch the upper palette behind the front teeth is the circuit, seen as a 'ring', made complete. This enables the bringing together of the male and female energies, *yang* and *yin*, creating a perfect balance in both body and mind. Yet most astonishing is the fact that the mouth, where the ring is completed, is known as the Magpie Bridge, and is unquestionably associated with Tianjin, the 'Ford of the Sky', since the ring of energies is seen in terms of the complete circle made in macrocosm by the Milky Way.

Making the mouth and tongue of the *taiji quan* practitioner synonymous with the Cygnus constellation allows us to perceive of it as the place from which the first word was spoken, as in the Logos or Word of God in Judeo-Christian tradition. In other words the asterism becomes the source of the divine sound or vibration that brought the universe into manifestation, a concept met with previously in association with Egypt's Great Cackler, India's Swan-Goose of Eternity, and the Anfar of the Yezidi, which emits a loud cry that breaks the pearl and causes the formation of the primeval sea.

One is reminded also of the Opening of the Mouth ceremony in ancient Egyptian funerary tradition (*see Chapter Twelve*). This we found to be associated with the stars of Ursa Major, as the heavenly counterpart of the ceremonial adze used to conduct this ceremony. Its principal function was to give the soul of the deceased the power of speech in the afterlife, although it is very possible that the mouth here, as in *taiji quan*, was synonymous with the stars of Cygnus. Interestingly, the adze-like shape made by the stars of Ursa Major (known in China as the 'bushel') also features as a move in *taiji quan* called 'Stepping up with Seven Stars' where its shape is formed by the outstretched arms and head of the practitioner. Furthermore, I learnt that another move which involves leaning forward before spinning, jumping and then coming to a halt represents Zhi Nü, the Weaver Princess, taking up her position as the star Vega, the final twist being an expression of the turning of the celestial pole.

Shifting Poles

Schlegel and Staal saw in the tale of the Weaver Princess more than simply the use of the three stars that make up the Summer Triangle – Deneb in Cygnus, Vega in Lyra and Altair in Aquila – which have independently been determined in the orientation of at least one megalithic site in nearby Japan.[19] Not only did both authors suggest that the Weaver Princess represented Vega as the Pole Star *c.*13,000–*c.*11,000 BC, but it was realized that by *c.*12,300 BC both Vega and Altair made their upper meridian transits together at midnight in late December, showing that Chinese astronomy must be at least this old.[20] Moving forward to the present day, we find that both Vega and Aquila cross the meridian around midnight on the seventh day of the seventh month, which falls in August (remember, the Chinese new year starts either in late January or early February depending on the year in question).[21] This can be taken as the lovers coming back together again.

Beyond this is the simple fact that the banishing of the Weaver Princess to one side of the Milky Way with Jian Niu, the herdsman, being cast to the other side, implies some kind of axial shift of the celestial pole due to precession. This is self-evident from the fact that the spinning wheel, or loom, in the celestial palace, located in the proximity of the Pole Star, is left idle. Yet then once the lovers are parted, she presumably continues her spinning duties from the position of Vega, as the herdsman resumes his role as the star Altair. These are movements which strongly, although awkwardly, hint at the shift of the celestial pole from one star to another, in this case from the position of Deneb on the Milky Way, the location of the celestial palace to the proximity of Vega, the personification of the Weaver Princess. To find that this ancient astronomical knowledge, at least 15,000 years old, is encoded even today within the graceful actions of *taiji quan* is quite extraordinary.

Ice Age Star Map

There the matter might have remained – wholly unsubstantiated, but intriguing – had it not been for a chance discovery made in January 2005. Browsing online, I unexpectedly found myself viewing a BBC News story dated 9 August 2000. With the headline 'Ice Age star map discovered', it began 'A prehistoric map of the night sky has been discovered on the walls of the famous painted caves at Lascaux in central France. The map, which is thought to date back some 16,500 years, shows three bright stars known today as the Summer Triangle.'[22]

The story revealed that Dr Michael Rappenglück of Munich University had concluded that the Upper Palaeolithic cave art in the famous Lascaux cave, near Montignac in France's Dordogne region, discovered as recently as 1940, was a veritable prehistoric planetarium. The main focus of attention was the image of a 'bird-man' in a falling position, along with an accompanying bison being 'killed' with arrow-like spikes, and a bird seen on a pole. All are found in a part of the cave known as the Well Shaft, and were being interpreted as abstract representations of, respectively, the stars Deneb, Lyra and Altair (actually, not Altair but Rotanev in Delphinus – *see Chapter Eighteen*). In addition to this, a series of spots seen over the shoulder of a painted bull found near the cave mouth have been identified by Rappenglück as the Pleiades star cluster, making the bull very likely a representation of the Taurus constellation, which occupies the same relative position in the night sky.[23]

Naturally, I was amazed, not simply because the story had been floating around in cyberspace for over four years without it coming to my notice, but I too had come to realize that the bird-man frieze at Lascaux, which probably dates to *c.*15,000–*c.*14,500 BC, encoded valuable astronomical knowledge concerning the epoch in which it was painted. It was a conclusion I reached after noticing the strange bird on a pole, which immediately reminded me of the Yezidi bird totem known as a *sanjak* (*see above, page 21*). I was reminded also of the sky-poles used by shamans to reach the sky-world in many parts of Asia, and especially the wooden swans in flight affixed to the top of slim poles erected in association with open-air altars by the Tungus of northeast Asia. Then there is the swan-topped sky-pole being climbed by a shaman seen among the rock art at Perinos on the southern cape of Lake Onega in Russia. They all confirm the inevitable conclusion that the example at Lascaux is most likely a shaman's pole, meaning that the bird at its apex provides us with firm evidence that by at least 14,500 BC the Cygnus star group was seen in terms of a celestial bird.

The accompanying bird-man at Lascaux has four 'fingers' on each hand, showing that they might in fact be bird's claws. He falls backwards, arms and legs together, in a manner that reminds me of the cartoon cat Tom being knocked out cold by Jerry. The bird-man is acting dead, even though he appears ithyphallic, i.e. he has an erect penis. Somehow the approaching bison seems connected with his death-like state, as if the bird-man is overwhelmed by its presence, even though the beast is being 'killed' by spears, and its entrails hang from its belly. It might even be considered that the bison's own death is mimicked by that of the bird-man. So what exactly is going on in this picture? What does it really represent, and what does death have to do with accessing the celestial realms of the spirit? More pressingly, how did Palaeolithic bird shamans like the one depicted at Lascaux come to view Cygnus as a celestial bird positioned at the top of the sky-pole? We will examine these questions in the following chapter.

CHAPTER EIGHTEEN

The Point of Creation

There is now overwhelming anthropological, epigraphical and scientific evidence to demonstrate that a high percentage of Upper Palaeolithic cave art in western Europe probably depicts shamans in altered states of consciousness. It shows also their hallucinations, which include everything from abstract geometric forms to chimeras (purely animal hybrids), therianthropes, (human-animal hybrids) and other types of perceived spirit intelligences. What is more, there is every reason to suppose that these encounters were initiated by the oral ingestion of psychedelic plants and/or mycetes, i.e. mushrooms.[1]

This dramatic new theory to explain the meaning behind Palaeolithic cave art derives from the fascinating work of J David Lewis-Williams, Professor of Cognitive Archaeology and Director of the Rock Art Research Unit of the Department of Archaeology at Johannesburg University, and his colleague Thomas A Dowson. In a breakthrough article published in *Current Anthropology* in 1988 the two researchers compared the geometric signs in Upper Palaeolithic art with the rock art of, firstly, the San bushmen of South Africa, which ranges datewise from *c.*25,500–*c.*23,500 BC (the age of several painted rock slabs found in the Apollo 11 cave in southwest Namibia) through until the early twentieth century, and, secondly, that of the Shosshonean Coso peoples of the Californian Great Basin.

Williams and Dowson then compared this new knowledge with existing historical epigraphical evidence that records the shamanic ceremonies, mythology and symbolic art of the San and Shosshonean Coso, and concluded that a very similar mindset had been present among the Palaeolithic cave artists. Moreover, neuropsychological research indicates that the cave art itself displays all three levels of entoptic phenomena (visual effects within the eye itself) resulting from the three-stage descent into a hallucinogenic trance state. In the case of the art belonging to the Upper Palaeolithic peoples and the Shosshonean Coso, this was inspired by psychedelic experiences brought on by the use of psychoactive (or psychotropic) substances. In the case of the San bushmen, the chosen form of inducing trances in order to communicate with the spirit world is thought to have been a lengthy process known as the trance dance.[2]

Flesh of the Gods

In western Europe, where almost all of the continent's Palaeolithic cave art can be found, it is likely, as writer Graham Hancock has recently established, that our Palaeolithic ancestors, *c.*40,000–*c.*8000 BC, used the mushroom *Psilocybe semi-lanceata,* commonly known as the Liberty Cap, as their drug of choice. It belongs to the Psilocybe group, which has been indigenous to Europe since the last Ice Age.[3] The property shared by many types of Psilocybe is that they contain high doses of active alkaloids including psilocybin, psilocin, baeocystin and nor-baeocystin. Oral ingestion invariably brings on vivid psychedelic experiences, if, that is, they are consumed in sufficient quantities.

Although it is merely conjecture as to whether our Palaeolithic ancestors did use mushrooms of the Psilocybe group, we know that its psychedelic effects were understood in the past. For example, in Spain during the Middle Ages witches were accused of using such mushrooms to induce hallucinations, while in the Swiss Alps nomads referred to them as the 'dream mushroom'.[4] This said, it was only following the European conquest of the Americas in the fifteenth and sixteenth centuries that the world really became aware that mushrooms of the Psilocybe group were being used by shamans and 'medicine men' to enter the spirit world.

Mushroom cults have been found among the indigenous peoples in countries such as Colombia, Ecuador, Guatemala, and, particularly, Mexico, where Psilocybe mushrooms are known as *teonanacatl,* 'flesh of the gods'.[5] Obviously, the Catholic Church in Latin America attempted to stamp out these ungodly practices, and were highly successful in doing so. It was thus a complete surprise when in 1955 amateur mycologist and writer R Gordon Wasson travelled to Mexico and discovered a 'magic mushroom' cult still thriving in secret among the remote mountain tribes in the south of the country. He took part in a mushroom-related ritual with a 65-year-old female shaman. His entire experience was written up and published in 1957 in *Life* magazine, complete with graphic pictures of the ceremony.

In European folklore the entire concept of the fairy realm is attached to mushroom lore, in particular the much more toxic *Amanita muscaria,* better known as fly agaric, distinguished by its familiar red cap with an even distribution of snow-like white warts. Since we know that there is a powerful overlap between fairy lore and folklore surrounding swan-maidens and swan shamanism, this connection needs to be explored more fully to understand its relationship to the Cygnus mystery.

The Earliest Mushroom Imagery

The earliest artistic evidence for the ingestion of hallucinogenic mushrooms comes from rock art in the Central Sahara Desert, and belongs to a long vanished hunter-gatherer society that thrived in the region when the climate was more equatorial, thus as long ago as *c.*7000–*c.*5000 BC.[6] Among the thousands of examples of rock art to be found on cliff faces and overhangs at Tassili-n'Ajjer and Hoggar in southern Algeria, are many themes including hunters, game, giant 'Martian' gods, chimeras, geometric forms, hands, dots, 'masks' and shamans either floating in space or in one of the stages of transformation into a therianthrope.[7]

Some frescoes clearly show figures in the context of what appears to be mushroom ingestion. One example from a rock art location named Tin-Tazarift depicts a series of masked dancers (or spirits) surrounded by geometric forms and spots. Each holds a mushroom-like object, linked in some instances to the figure's head via a parallel line, as if to emphasize some kind of neuropsychological association.[8]

Another example of rock art from a site named Matalem-Amazar in southern Tassili shows a hybrid with big ears, insect-like eyes and a stripy nose resembling that of an aardvark.[9] Surrounding it is an intense aura of the sort experienced during psychedelic experiences. Look closer and you will see that the therianthrope holds psilocybe-style mushrooms, which also seem to be sprouting from every part of its body. There is no question that this represents the spirit of the mushroom, envisioned during the psychedelic journey. Various other examples have also been found at Tassili, including a fish between two mushrooms that seem attached to its body, as if by cord-like stems.[10]

This invaluable rock art is contemporary with the latest art of Europe's Upper Palaeolithic era, and, indeed, there are some remarkable similarities in the styles, particularly the portrayal of human forms with thick-set brows and protruding jaws.

Other examples of possible mushroom-inspired prehistoric rock art come from the Pegtymel river in Siberia, which, like the Tassili rock art, were produced by a hunter-gathering society of probable Bronze Age origin.[11] Here figures are shown quite literally with mushrooms on their heads. These are thought to depict shamans

Fig. 44. Rock art from Tin-Tazarift in the Tassili-n'Ajjer region of southern Algeria, *c.*7000–*c.*5000 BC. Dancing figures hold mushroom-like objects, some linked to their heads via dotted lines.

Fig. 45. Rock art from Matalen-Amazar in the Tassili-n'Ajjer, this example showing a figure with bunches of mushrooms in his hands, and others surrounding his body.

under the influence of fly agaric mushrooms, used since time immemorial by Tungus reindeer shamans, whose Tunguso-Manchurian language gives us the modern term 'shaman', meaning 'one who knows'.

These examples of Palaeolithic cave art certainly show that psychedelic mushroom usage might well have been important to prehistoric societies both in North Africa and many parts of Asia, while the mushroom cults on the American continent date back at least 4,000 years, and are arguably much earlier still. Thus we can assume that the artists and shamans responsible for the Palaeolithic cave art of western Europe, might also have used very similar substances to achieve deep trance states in cave settings. If mushrooms were not used, then there is every chance that these individuals utilized psychotropic plants of a far heavier nature, such as henbane, mandrake and belladonna (deadly nightshade).[12] Certainly, henbane and nightshade are listed as one of the ingredients of the so-called 'witches' unguent', or 'flying ointment',[13] used in late medieval and Tudor times supposedly to achieve magical flight on broomsticks. The effects of ingesting such highly toxic substances through the skin would have brought the user quite literally to the point of physical death – a state obviously intended if the Lascaux 'Well Scene' is to be read as evidence of a shaman transforming into a bird-man, in order to enter the spirit world.

Back at Lascaux

As early as 1952, forward-thinking cave art specialist Horst Kirchner interpreted the celebrated relief at Lascaux as showing a bird-headed individual in a 'shamanic trance'.[14] Mircea Eliade, the great pioneer in our understanding of shamanism throughout the ages, agreed, writing: 'Europe offers evidence for the earliest forms of shamanism (Lascaux) with the plastic representations of the bird, the tutelary spirit, and ecstasy',[15] while at the same time admitting that the cave's motif of a '"bird perched on a post" is extremely archaic.'[16] To him, the frieze signified the achievement of magical flight, in which shamans adopted the mantle of a bird and were able 'to fly to the World Tree to bring back "soul-birds"',[17] a matter familiar to us from other countries of the world.

The biggest clue to the shamanic nature of Lascaux's Well Scene is its placement. To access it the visitor has to navigate their way beyond the main gallery, where at the end of the chamber a kind of stone lip leads the way down to a foreboding pit nearly five metres (14.4 feet) deep, and accessed only by a rope. Indeed, the fossilized remains of a rope cord, almost certainly used for this purpose, were found in the alluvial deposits at the base of the well shaft.[18] Here, on the wall, is the bird-man panel, which is about two metres (6.6 feet) in height. To the left of it is the image of a woolly rhino; its purpose is not clear, although it could relate in some way to virility, since rhino horns have universally been seen not only as phallic symbols, but also, when powdered, as aphrodisiacs, bringing us back to the bird-man's apparent erection.

The sexual nature of hallucinogens – species of Psilocybe mushrooms in particular – is well-known to any user. During the earlier stages of a 'trip', a male will experience a virtual burning sensation in the groin, combined with sexual urges, which can and frequently do lead to inappropriate erections, a condition known as priapism. It occurs shortly before the user enters into a more calming, trance-like phase during which time the psychedelic experience begins in earnest.

So the implications are clear. In the darkest part of the Lascaux cave is a unique frieze which suggests, very strongly, that shamans of the Upper Palaeolithic age, *c.*15,000–14,500 BC, came here to enter a death-like trance, induced most probably by a powerful psychedelic substance. In such states they were able, as Eliade proposed, to ascend to the cosmic axis, via the sky-pole or World Tree, symbolized, for example, by the actual rope found at Lascaux. As we have seen, the celestial bird, identified as Cygnus, marked their place of destination – the gateway, or 'hole' into the sky-world, the realm of the soul. Here they might encounter other human souls, or otherworldly denizens, who were seen to exist on a quite separate level of existence.

Yet how might this Palaeolithic death cult be linked with the builders of the subsurface stone temples in southeast Turkey, who as early as 9500 BC would appear to have revered the Cygnus constellation as a celestial vulture expressing the concept of cosmic life and death?

Egg-Head and Mushroom Serpents

Although no hard evidence for the presence at any of the Early Neolithic sites of Upper Mesopotamia of mushroom spores has ever come to light, there does exist a considerable amount of abstract art suggesting the proliferation of mushroom-related practices. For example, at the cult centre of Jerf el-Ahmar in northern Syria, which dates to *c.*9500–*c.*7300 BC, Professor Danielle Stordeur and her team from CNRS-Université,[19] Lyon, France, unearthed various portable stone tablets in the mid-1990s bearing pictographs that are now being hailed as the earliest known evidence of a symbolic written language.

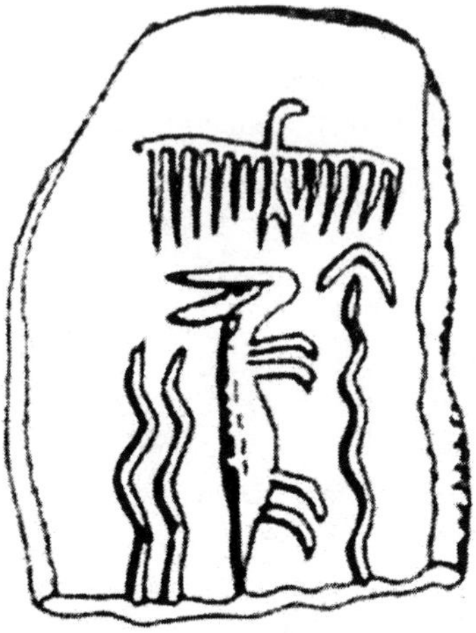

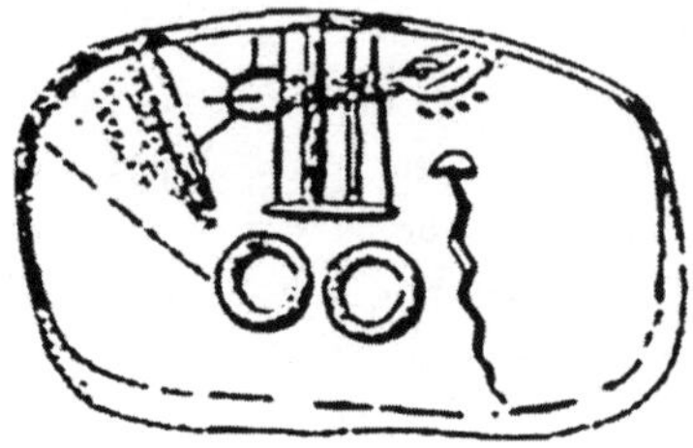

Figs.46a and 46b. Two examples of inscribed tablets from the Pre-pottery Neolithic site of Jerf el-Ahmar in northern Syria, *c.*8000–*c.*7300 BC (after Stordeur et al.), showing a clear relationship between mushroom imagery and the cult of the dead.

In at least two instances (*see figs. 46a and b*) these symbolic engravings include what appear to be mushroom caps with long flexuose stems, closely resembling a species from the Psilocybe group. One particular example depicts the 'mushroom' next to a) an upward moving snake, seen universally during psychedelic experiences; b) a vertically positioned rhino, which, as already proposed, can represent the sensations of male virility; and, incredibly, c) a stylized vulture with its wings outstretched, which rises away from the other three symbols.

This extremely important stone tablet expresses, in my opinion, the outward journey of a shaman achieving release from the body following the ingestion of psychedelic mushrooms, linking this whole process not only with Palaeolithic cave art, but also the Neolithic death cult, showing perhaps that there is a common origin here.

Moving on to Nevali Çori, constructed during the same epoch by the same faceless individuals, we come now to the discovery by Harald Hauptmann of the German Archaeological Institute at Istanbul of the life-sized human head, shaped very much like an egg.[20] As you will recall from Chapter Three, it was discovered perched upright within a niche in the northeast wall of the site's square-plan cult building. Even though the face is missing, the rear of its bald head – the side found facing out into the room – is of great interest. It sports what looks like a ponytail in high relief, although peer a little closer and you will see it is in fact a curling serpent that ends, like the engraved pictographs from Jerf el-Ahmar, in a mushroom-like cap. De-focus the eyes a little, and the whole ponytail/serpent/mushroom can additionally be mistaken for a penis.

The fact that the north would appear to have been a direction of veneration among the earliest Neolithic stone temples of the region does suggest that the Nevali Çori stone head symbolized some kind of personification of what German archaeologist Klaus Schmidt referred to, in connection with Göbekli Tepe, as a personalized deity, a 'non-terrestrial being'.[21] We do not know what that was, but from the head's egg-like appearance and its placement in the northwest wall of the cult building, the chances are that it expressed their view of cosmic life and death, what the Sabians (*see Chapter Three*) called the Primal Cause.

Fig. 47. Stone head found at Nevali Çori, Turkey, showing snake-like ponytail.

Egg, head, serpent, mushroom and penis all combine to suggest a multifaceted interest in cosmic creation, and a knowledge of it obtained arguably through the ingestion of psychedelic mushrooms. Yet this is by no means the only mushroom-related imagery to be found in the region, for at Göbekli Tepe one of the T-shaped pillars has on its side a series of serpents with mushroom-shaped heads, four winding their way downwards and a fifth one climbing up to meet them.[22] Moving around to the flat front face of the pillar we see a 'tapestry' of interwoven serpents with mushroom-like caps, eight emerging at the top and nine at the bottom.[23] There is little doubt that were such imagery to feature in Upper Palaeolithic cave art it would instantly be classed as entoptic phenomena. Curiously, beneath the interlace is the carving of a ram, which might well be another symbol of virility.

Aside from this compelling T-shaped pillar, a stone slab found at Göbekli Tepe bears a striking engraved image of a thin-armed naked woman whose sagging breasts suggest that she is meant to be seen as a hag or crone.[24] More significantly, her genitalia are not only exposed, but over-emphasized, while her head of hair is the exact shape of a hemispherical mushroom cap. Now, this could be an example of an idiosyncratic art style familiar to the Early Neolithic artists of the region, even

Fig. 48. A standing pillar at Göbekli Tepe, Turkey, showing interlace tipped with mushrooms on its front face (left) and mushroom-headed serpents on its side (right), *c.*9500–*c.*7300 BC, after Harald Hauptmann.

though nothing quite like it has been found elsewhere. On the other hand, it might well be that she represents some kind of matriarchal spirit encountered during psychedelic experiences, perhaps even a devourer of the dead, like the Hindu goddess Kali, whose mythos and cult also includes quite powerful sexual elements.

I identified all this striking mushroom-related art among the Early Neolithic world of Upper Mesopotamia simply by personal observation, and so I was pleasantly surprised to find that others had already detected similar examples not too far away. For instance, writer and philosopher Terence McKenna in his book *Food of the Gods* (1992) draws attention to a curious item unearthed on the Konya Plain, near the site of the Neolithic city of Çatal Hüyük in southern-central Turkey, and now in the archaeological museum at Kayseri in Cappadocia.[25] It is a strange idol of a man with a discoid body on which are two mushrooms in high relief that sprout from an oval-shaped area. Strangely, the mushrooms have eyes and mouths, suggesting that they might signify their spirits, a theme found among the statues of mushrooms produced by the mushroom-eating peoples of Central and South

America. Although the Konya idol is thought to be only 4,000 years old, it expresses the repeated use of so-called twin symbolism common among the portable art found at the nearby Neolithic city of Çatal Hüyük, *c.*6500–*c.*5500 BC.

McKenna also cited the discovery of carved mushrooms fashioned from green stone produced by the Vinça culture, which thrived along the course of the Danube *c.*6000–*c.*3000 BC.[26] Found in Yugoslavia, they are yet further evidence of a mushroom cult among the Neolithic peoples.

The Sacred Mushroom and the Cross

Despite the lack of hard evidence of mushroom consumption during the Early Neolithic era, noted Semitic-language scholar and Dead Sea Scrolls expert John Allegro (1923–1988) put his career on the line when he announced that he had found widespread philological evidence of mushroom use by the Sumerians and their close neighbours the Akkadians. As mentioned in Chapter One, their civilization, arguably the oldest anywhere in the world, sprang from the Early Neolithic culture responsible for sites such as Jerf el-Ahmar, Nevali Çori, Göbekli Tepe and Karahan Tepe.[27]

Allegro's far-reaching book *The Sacred Mushroom and the Cross* (1970) explored the cryptic symbolism behind the perceived mushroom cult of Mesopotamia, and concluded that two of its principal motifs were the stork – an obvious symbol of fertility and new life – and, more significantly, the swan. For him its long curved neck represented the vaginal passage, its white body the uterus and its outstretched wings the fallopian tubes. The Latin *cygnus* and Greek *kuknos* (also written *kyknos*), both meaning 'swan',[28] he saw as deriving from the Sumerian word *gug-nu*, meaning 'seed pod', or 'womb pod', which he ably demonstrated related to the psychedelic mushroom.[29]

Allegro felt that this cosmic connection was played out in the story of Jupiter/Zeus taking the form of a swan and lying with Leda, the wife of Tyndarus. It was a union that produced two cosmic eggs, from one of which hatched Helen and Pollux, and from the other came Clytemnestra and Castor. The first pair were seen as the offspring of Jupiter, while the second pair were attributed to Tyndarus.[30] For Allegro, this was mushroom-inspired symbolism connected with twin mythology of the sort first displayed in the portable art found at Neolithic cult centres such as Çatal Hüyük, and dated to *c.*6500–*c.*5500 BC.

Extending the connection still further, Allegro cited the fact that the Hebrew *kotereth*, Akkadian *katarru*, both meaning 'mushroom', are used also to describe a 'mushroom-shaped capital of a pillar'.[31] This immediately brought to mind the T-shaped pillars found at Early Neolithic cult centres such as Göbekli Tepe and Karahan Tepe. Although these stones are seen by archaeologists as simply decorative roof supports, the resemblance of some of them to mushrooms is undeniable (*see Plate 10*). Possibly connected here is the fact that, as Allegro points out, the Latin word for a T-shaped implement used for measuring the depth of furrows is *ciconia*, which also happens to be the Latin for 'stork', the bird most commonly associated with the arrival of newborn babies in European folklore (a role, as we have seen, attributed to the swan by the inhabitants of the Baltic). The word *ciconia*, Allegro claimed, derives from the Sumerian *gig-ia-u-na*, meaning 'pod of fertility', a reference once more to the sacred mushroom.[32]

John Allegro cited dozens of philological examples from a plethora of ancient textual sources to support his claim that the Sumerians and Akkadians were sampling the delights of magic mushrooms, and that this was the basis of their cosmic religion, which appears to have revolved around the cult of Cygnus. If correct, then he arguably decoded part of the root language behind the Neolithic cult of cosmic life and death, practised by those responsible for the emergence of the earliest civilizations of Mesopotamia, which began with the building of prehistoric cities such as Eridu at the mouth of the Euphrates sometime *c.*5500 BC.

Rappenglück's Vision

Exactly how all this related to Michael Rappenglück's vision of Lascaux's Well Scene was not fully appreciated until he kindly sent me copies of his papers on the subject.[33] In these he observes that the northern celestial pole remained in the vicinity of the Milky Way from *c.*20,500–*c.*13,200 BC, reaching its greatest depth within it in *c.*15,500 BC, when it was in the vicinity of Deneb.[34] He considers that this celestial river was seen even in Palaeolithic times to have distributed the fertility of the heavens via the points at which it crosses the ecliptic, i.e. between Sagittarius and Scorpio on one side and in Gemini on the other side of the sky.

Rappenglück argues that the Solutrean and Magdalenian sub-cultures of the Palaeolithic era, *c.*20,000–*c.*9,000 BC, possessed a shamanic worldview that 'could connect their concepts of astral travelling to the point of creation with this extraordinary situation in the sky.'[35] Moreover, he argues that: 'Human beings ... (kings and shamans in particular – and [in death] ... souls and ghosts) tried to get in contact with the original point of creation, to bring down the essence of life to the earth.'[36]

Rappenglück goes on to identify the concept of celestial poles as 'special places of descent and ascent, disembodiment and embodiment, pictured as gaps, holes, canals, gorges and doors.'[37] They relate originally to a timeframe when the first conceived celestial pole was attached to the Milky Way. Then, when finally the two parted company due to precession, Rappenglück says that universal myths speak in terms of the 'world mountain' tipping over, or the 'world mill' being destroyed (and the spindle or loom being left idle, as in the story of the Weaver Princess – *see Chapter Seventeen*).[38]

One ancient Chinese myth speaks of *Buzhou*, the world mountain, as originally touching the River *Tianhe*, or Milky Way. Through its turning, it was said to have 'drilled' a hole in the river bed, i.e. up from underneath it, causing water to fall to Earth as an inundation of rain. Then some time later, the damage was repaired, and the rains no longer came, in that the mountain no longer 'drilled' the celestial river.[39] This is a reference, Rappenglück argues, to a time when the celestial pole was in the proximity of the Cygnus constellation, for after this time it shifted away from the Milky Way towards Vega in Lyra.

This whole concept is displayed in the bird-man scene in Lascaux, when the stars of Cygnus occupied the position at the top of the sky-pole, providing a date of construction no later than 14,500 BC, by which time, of course, Deneb had given up its role as Pole Star to *delta* Cygni. According to Rappenglück's calculations, the bird on a stick, symbol of the 'world axis', 'points to the northern sky-pole at the latitude of Lascaux', which is 45 degrees 1 minute. In this knowledge, he concludes: 'All over the world, symbols, myths and rites of shamanism illustrated the notion of the Milky Way as a path to the origin of creation', and that in this trance state the shaman (or his soul) was able to 'travel through the levels of the cosmos along the Milky Way'.[40]

Having pointed out that the star *delta* Cygni (on the left-hand 'wing' of the swan) stood just a few degrees away from the celestial pole at this time, Rappenglück proposes that the eyes of the bird-man, the bird on top of the pole and the bison form a triangle, made up of the stars Deneb, Vega, and Rotanev (*beta* Delphini), the second brightest star in Delphinus, the celestial dolphin.[41] This, of course, is similar, although not the same, as the Summer Triangle of today, whereby Altair in Aquila replaces the star Rotanev. All this would make the bird-man a huge super-constellation with the upper body embracing the stars of Cygnus and Vulpecula, the fox, and the lower part shaped by the stars of Aquila, Ophiuchus the serpent bearer, Hercules, and Sagitta, the arrow.[42]

The Real Area of Creation

Although I might doubt the extent of Rappenglück's bird-man as a star constellation, choosing instead to assume that at Lascaux Cygnus was represented simply by the bird on a pole, the implications of his discoveries are staggering, and could not be put better than by the German archaeoastronomer himself:

> The bird-man can be understood as a shaman who travels in a state of ecstasy through the layered cosmos along the world-axis and the Milky Way and reaches the realm of the other world, the area of the circumpolar stars and the pole of the sky in ... Cyg[nus], which was situated in the Milky Way in 14,500 BC and therefore marks the real area of creation according to [the] archaic mind.[43]

Here was perfect confirmation of everything I had been attempting to convey in words throughout this book, and had first recognized following our visit to see the world's oldest stone temples in southeast Turkey in May 2004 (*see Chapters One and Two*). Somehow, I sensed that, although created *c.*9500–9000 BC, these monuments expressed a shamanic worldview that reflected a far older cosmological mindset which saw Cygnus as the bird of creation atop the sky-pole. I became convinced that this was the assumed destination of the shamanic journey, as well as the deemed place of cosmic creation, a gut feeling now borne out by Michael Rappenglück's fascinating work.

If all of this was correct, then it strongly hinted that Cygnus and its stars retained their importance in ancient cosmologies across the globe due to their role as polar stars *c.*15,000–*c.*13,000 BC. As a result of this belief, cultures and civilizations worldwide embraced, knowingly or otherwise, creation myths that related to the celestial heavens not in their own epoch, but when ice covered large areas of the Earth and the Americas were physically linked to the Eurasian continent.

The Gift of Soma

As we saw in Chapter Sixteen, the civilizations of the Saraswati and Indus rivers likely responsible for the creation of the *Rig Veda* were very probably shamanic in origin. In this knowledge, it is intriguing to find that these sacred texts, with their deep cosmology, refer constantly to the virtues of ingesting a mythical elixir, an ambrosia of the gods, called *Soma*, which was seen in terms of a god.

R Gordon Wasson examined the *Rig Veda* and concluded that Soma was in fact the extracted juices of the *Amanita muscaria* mushroom,[44] even though this theory has been challenged in recent years.[45] Whatever the true identity of Soma, it is very possible that the extraordinary cosmic knowledge outlined in the *Rig Veda* derived from direct communications with perceived otherworldly intelligences encountered by initiates in the course of Soma-inspired psychedelic journeys during a much earlier age.

What Happened 17,000 Years Ago?

When John Allegro drew philological links between the mushroom experience, the shape of the swan and the human reproductive organs, he was insinuating that this was knowledge of cosmic creation known to the peoples of ancient Mesopotamia. Such knowledge, I now realize, did not originate with them, but came via the Early Neolithic world from the same human epoch that gave us as its legacy the Upper Palaeolithic cave art of western Europe. Whatever group might have been behind this crucial phase of human history was, I feel, responsible not only for the invention of astronomy *c.*17,000 years ago, but also for spreading the Cygnus-linked cosmology across the Eurasian continent and into the Americas prior to the submergence of the Beringia land-bridge at the end of the last Ice Age.

It is even possible that this profound cosmological knowledge was carried across the ice-bound Atlantic by Solutrean peoples responsible for Palaeolithic cave art in parts of southern France and northern Spain between 20,000–15,000 BC. They, as we saw in Chapter Four, are now thought to have been behind the introduction into North America, *c.*15,000 BC, of a very specific kind of flint-knapping technology that matches the style and manufacture of bifaced points of the slightly later Cactus Hill and Clovis cultures. Did the Solutreans carry with them an understanding of cosmic life and death that included knowledge of the greater significance of the Cygnus constellation?

I am not necessarily implying here that all of these peoples were of the same race or culture, or that these ideas developed in one place alone, only that there was a cosmopolitan understanding of the heavens that spread rapidly across the Eurasian continent and into the Americas.

I am also not presuming that everything *began* 17,000 years ago, or that Cygnus is the only candidate for a source of cosmic creation, since there are always going to be rival ways of understanding life's origins, and its place in the cosmos. Nor am I denying that some rudimentary knowledge of the night sky was worked out prior to this age, for there is evidence of a bear cult with possible astronomical overtones among the Neanderthal peoples who inhabited the Swiss Alps *c.*43,000 years ago.[46] What I *am* saying is that a major acceleration in our knowledge of the cosmos occurred sometime *c.*17,000 years ago, and that this kick-started something that reverberated down through the ages, and is still being felt by us today.

Clearly, the interpretation of one Upper Palaeolithic cave scene by a single academic does not prove everything. However, Dr Rappenglück tells me that a whole new generation of archaeoastronomers not only accept his work as valid, but are now finding representations of Cygnus, and, of course, other star groups within the Upper Palaeolithic cave art and rock art of Europe.[47]

Rappenglück himself admits that his own inspiration to think with this new mindset came from a lecture by his mentor Dr Felix Schmeidler of the Faculty of Natural Sciences at Munich University. At a conference on Palaeolithic cave art on 19 November 1984, Schmeidler asked the university audience: 'Is astronomy 17,000 years old?' Rappenglück set out to explore this loaded question, and from his work and the evidence presented here now, I am pretty sure that the answer is going to be yes, since I believe we can now show how and why Deneb became so important to our early ancestors.

Yet now comes a dilemma. Did Cygnus only become important to our Palaeolithic forebears because they wanted to create a meaningful sky-world to satisfy the spiritual needs of their communities worldwide? Did their descendants unwittingly perpetuate a religious ideal that had become outdated within just a few thousand years, in the same way that our own outdated concept of the astrological zodiac reflects the sky as it appeared over 2,000 years ago? Or was there some deeper-rooted reason why our ancestors believed that the human soul came from, and would ultimately return to, a heaven accessed via a single point in the night sky? Simply to *begin* to answer this question, we must now return to where we left off in Chapter One, with Jeremy Narby under the influence of the psychedelic brew *ayahuasca* in a rainforest clearing somewhere in the Peruvian Amazon.

PART SIX

COSMOS

CHAPTER NINETEEN

The Secret of Life

There are over 100,000 different plant species in the South American rainforest, and yet somehow the Ashaninka Indians of the Peruvian Amazon were able to isolate an MAO (monoamine oxidase) inhibitor which blocks the body's natural enzymes that normally make *ayahuasca*'s active ingredient, DMT (N,N-dimethyltryptamine), ineffective when consumed orally. This, and the fact that, along with so many other tribes of the rainforest, the Ashaninka have a pharmaceutical knowledge of thousands of plants and herbs, utilized for everything from a simple headache to accelerating the healing of wounds, prompted anthropological student Jeremy Narby to enquire as to how they accumulated their incredible understanding of the natural world.[1]

The answer the village elders gave was simple. The information was conveyed to the *ayahuasqueros*, the drinkers of *ayahuasca* ('vine of the dead'), by the spirit world, or more correctly the spirits of the plants themselves. Narby didn't believe a word of it, and so went back to studying the tribe's indigenous lifestyle as part of his doctorate in anthropology at Stanford University. He thought no more of the matter until one day his own niggling back problem was instantly cured by a special concoction prepared for him by one of the tribe's medicine men. This got him thinking, and so finally he accepted their invitation to experience what it was that the *ayahuasqueros* saw under the influence of *ayahuasca*.

Television of the Forest

The evening came, and after beginning the proceedings by accepting a toke from a rolled cigarette called *toe*, which he later found contained extracts of a highly toxic variety of thorn apple, Narby quickly gulped down the foul-tasting *ayahuasca* cocktail that was handed to him. Not unexpectedly, the concoction made him hallucinate fairly rapidly. His entire body, including his hands, arms and internal organs were now glowing red, as if he could see through his own pale skin. Suddenly feeling ill, he staggered away from the clearing and was immediately sick. The contents of his stomach exited his mouth as a fire-red snake, an image found among the amazing psychedelic art of Peruvian *ayahuasca* drinker and shaman Pablo Amaringo,[2] and also amid a writhing mass of finger-drawn serpents on the ceiling of the 'Serpent Dome', a chamber of Palaeolithic cave art in the Grotte de Rouffignac, near Lascaux in the Dordogne.[3]

For Jeremy Narby, the visions then began in earnest. Unexpectedly, he saw before him two rainbow-coloured snakes, giant boa constrictors with bodies that seemed as much as two metres thick. They were aware of his intrusion into their world, and conveyed to him the idea that he was 'a mere human being', puny in comparison to the greater universe. Wanting to get back to the clearing, Narby more-or-less stepped over the pair of boas, and stumbled across to where the *ayahuasqueros* awaited his return. They asked him whether he had now seen the 'television of the forest', the understated term they use to describe *ayahuasca* visions. When he told them what he had just witnessed, they simply joked that everybody saw snakes, and that he would get used to it.

But Narby did not get used to it. This and other subsequent experiences with *ayahuasca* – including one occasion when he actually felt himself becoming a large feline complete with a taste for blood (he was a vegetarian at the time) – left him unable to explain what was truly going on, a sentiment that remained with him even after his return home to Switzerland. For several years the experiences plagued his memory, as he began to read up on everything he could find on the neuropsychological, biological and philosophical effects of drug use among indigenous cultures worldwide. He also explored the works of psychedelic gurus, and studied the symbology of shamanism in his search for an answer. When it finally came it was stunning in its simplicity, yet far-reaching in its consequences.

Narby concluded from his researches that the *ayahuasca* experience was independent and real, and that the twin snakes were the key to understanding why. Everywhere in art, mythology, alchemy and religion, serpents are shown intertwined, like those that curl around the Caduceus, the wand of the Classical god Hermes/Mercury. Moreover, he found that twin serpents are universally seen by shamans during psychedelic experiences (once again, see the extraordinary visionary paintings of Pablo Amaringo), as are ropes, cords, vines, and ladders which, as we have seen, are familiar visual aids used to enter or leave the sky-world.

The Genetic Code

All these symbols, Narby felt sure, were created by human consciousness in order to convey a specific message regarding their true nature, which he felt could be explained in just three letters – DNA (deoxyribonucleic acid), the hereditary gene molecule that adopts the form of the double helix and carries within it the instructions for making up our entire bodies, creating who we are and what we look like.

Despite its vital function in the body, DNA is not known to possess any kind of self-awareness or consciousness. Yet Narby noted that there is always intelligence at work on a cellular level. Gene cells are always sending signals between themselves in the form of proteins, and this basic data tells other cells either to divide or not divide, and at any one time a cell is receiving hundreds of incoming signals, and it has to make the right decision, and this is how intelligence works.

What Narby began to ask himself is whether or not it is possible that DNA not only has a sense of purpose, but is also able to communicate with DNA outside of its own cellular environment, arguably between one living organism and another. As a functioning consciousness, it might act collectively to convey coded information between species, in order to relate specific ideas, such as which plants are deadly, edible or psychedelic; or how they might best be grown. This empathic link would thus exist between any life form – humans to plants, animals to trees, even humans to animals, or *vice versa*, exchanging fundamental information and consciousness – explaining why Narby had on one occasion felt himself becoming a large feline creature with an overwhelming blood-lust.

Signal Nonlocality

Such an idea is made possible by the quantum theory of 'signal nonlocality', which holds that certain subatomic particles, when separated, will continue to communicate with each other even if placed at opposite ends of the universe. A kind of unbreakable bond exists between them whereby information is conveyed as instantaneous signals, causing a two-way action-reaction process. On its own, signal nonlocality is an interesting curiosity at best, but should these signals between particles be multiplied indefinitely, then it creates a means of consciousness-generation and information-transference on a subatomic level without any obvious link between the two parties, whether we are talking about DNA molecules or fully formed life forms such as ourselves.

So the *ayahuasqueros* of the Upper Amazon might well have been correct when they said that the 'spirits' of the plants were responsible for providing them with their extensive pharmaceutical knowledge. Narby proposes that it is not spirits in the true sense of the word that provide us with this information, but some kind of quantum consciousness of DNA, received and interpreted by our minds as visual or emotive communication with 'real' spirits. Very often this knowledge-transfer will come, he suspects, with symbolic imagery that mimics DNA's double helix structure, seen in terms of intertwined serpents, ropes, vines or ladders, which feature in shamanic traditions worldwide.

The True Gods of this World

I read Jeremy Narby's groundbreaking book *The Cosmic Serpent* (1995) just after my return from southeast Turkey in 2004. Indeed, it was recommended to me in the wake of my observations regarding the suspected mushroom cult evidenced from the Early Neolithic art of the region. I was astonished by Narby's theories. However, it was the deeper implications of his findings that really excited me.

Those who undergo psychedelic experiences very often believe that the alternative realities they enter and the sentient intelligent beings they encounter are objectively real. For example, anthropologist Michael Harner experienced the effects of *natemä* (the Ecuadorian form of *ayahuasca*) with Jívaro Indians of the Ecuadorian Amazon, and gave the following account of his experiences:

> I found myself, although awake, in a world literally beyond my wildest dreams. I met bird-headed people, as well as dragon-like creatures who explained that they were the true gods of this world. I enlisted the services of other spirit helpers in attempting to fly through the far reaches of the Galaxy. Transported into a trance where the supernatural seemed natural, I realized that anthropologists, including myself, had profoundly underestimated the importance of the drug in affecting native ideology.[4]

What makes a respected man of Harner's calibre come to such far-reaching conclusions? Did he really fly 'through the far reaches of the Galaxy' as he imagined, and meet 'bird-headed people' and 'dragon-like creatures', whom he felt were the 'true gods of this world'?

The Machine Elves

Years beforehand, philosopher and writer Terence McKenna and his brother Dennis travelled to the jungles of South America where they met with shamans, ingested magic mushrooms and drank and smoked *ayahuasca* in 'heroic' doses. Very quickly they became convinced that psychedelic substances such as psilocybin and *ayahuasca* were vehicles that enabled the mind to interact with other life forms in the universe, either in inner space – 'hyperspace' as Terence McKenna called it – or in outer space. He was also amazed at the consistency of the experiences, with many users of DMT entering a strange realm inhabited by what he came to refer to as the 'self-transforming machine elves', seen as jewel-encrusted, crystal-like spheres that were constantly morphing, i.e. changing shape. When extracted, purified and then smoked, DMT caused the user to enter a realm that bore the appearance of a brightly lit medical room, where dwarfish entities immediately began examining them in a manner reminiscent of the classic 'alien abduction' scenario.

Room 531

Due to US drug laws forbidding research into illegal substances, very little work has been conducted into the true potential of hallucinogens extracted from plants and mycetes. Nevertheless in 1990 Dr Rick Strassman, Associate Professor in Psychiatry at the University of New Mexico's School of Medicine in Albuquerque, instituted the first new research in the United States on the effects of psychedelic substances on the human brain for over twenty years. He invited subjects to experience the effects of DMT, and in just five years administered around 400 doses of DMT to sixty volunteers from different walks of life. Their experiences were meticulously recorded and analyzed.

What Strassman found during his experimental work in Room 531 – where subjects received their prescribed dosage and then waited to see what happened – was entirely unexpected. A high percentage of the volunteers consistently entered what they perceived as parallel realms, where elfish entities or mechanical insectoids awaited their arrival. They often communicated and interacted with them in futuristic medical rooms where the entities would frantically expunge all impure parts of the body, recreating a form of astral excarnation. Although some of the imagery experienced by Strassman's subjects was culturally or circumstantially motivated, much of it was unique with its own separate existence.

In his controversial book *DMT: The Spirit Molecule* (2001), Strassman summed up the nature of his subjects' seemingly objective encounters with separate realities in the following manner.

> I believed that these experiences were hallucinations, albeit rather complicated ones ... However, research subjects tenaciously resisted biological explanations because such explanations reduced the enormity, consistency, and undeniability of their encounters. How could anyone believe there were chunks of brain tissue that, when activated, flashed encounters with beings, experimentation, and reprogramming?[5]

The subjects also resisted other logical explanations for the experiences. They denied that they were either waking dreams, or mere hallucinations with symbolic meaning and purpose, based on wishes, fears or unresolved issues. Some volunteers did simply shrug their shoulders and accept that it was all just the effects of the drug, but many others remained wholly convinced that they had undergone real and very vivid experiences in some alternative reality that coexisted with our own, leading Strassman to admit:

> How could their imagination generate a scenario that felt more real than waking consciousness? If it were 'real,' how does one now live his or her life, knowing that existing right now are multiple invisible realms inhabited by intelligent life-forms? Who are those beings? What is the nature of their relationship to the volunteers now that they had made 'contact'?[6]

Strassman is an academic who started off believing that DMT trips were simply hallucinations. Eventually, however, he came to the conclusion that what his subjects had experienced was real indeed. What is more, the sensation of entering another world and communicating with supernatural entities is so common in psychedelic experiences that we can be sure that such encounters have been taking place among indigenous cultures worldwide for many thousands of years. Moreover, if we accept this, then there is no reason to doubt that our Early Neolithic forebears in Upper Mesopotamia experienced the same thing during their assumed journeys to the sky-world, accessed via the cosmic axis envisaged as synonymous with the Cygnus constellation. Even before them the Palaeolithic shamans of western Europe must have been encountering very similar supernatural entities and coexistences, hence the cave images of chimeras, therianthropes, snakes and anthropomorphs (human-like figures). Although they would not have seen some things that we might be preconditioned to see under such circumstances, the core experiences, I surmise, would have been almost identical.

Exploring Panspermia

If Narby is correct and some form of two-way non-local communication can occur between the collective consciousness of DNA in different life forms, then what if, as scientists are now coming to believe, life did not originate on Earth? What if DNA arrived on this planet complete, with genetic instructions to create and evolve new life to its ultimate end? This thought-provoking theory is known to the world as panspermia (which means 'seeds everywhere'), a concept proposed as far back as the fifth century BC by the Greek philosopher Anaxagoras (*c.*500–428 BC) of Clazomenae, a town near the city of Smyrna (Izmir) in what is today southern Turkey. He believed that the seeds of life swarm throughout the cosmos, and are not exclusive to Earth.[7] More intriguing is that Anaxagoras, who was an influence on Socrates and thus Plato, envisaged these 'seeds' not as molecular in nature, but as actual seeds containing the essence of life itself.

Panspermia would have been accepted as the true origins of life back then had not the philosopher Aristotle (384–322 BC) come up with the theory of spontaneous generation of life on Earth, which was preferred by the more rationally minded, and remained a workable theory through until the nineteenth century, when it was finally disproved by the French chemist Louis Pasteur (1822–1895).

In the wake of Pasteur's work into microbiology (which included determining that infectious diseases were caused by germs), various ideas were proposed on the origins of cellular life, but it would not be until 1903 that the idea of panspermia would raise its head again. In that year Swedish physical chemist and Nobel Prize-winner Svante August Arrhenius (1859–1927) wrote that life on Earth emerged from microscopic spores that were propelled across space by what he saw as the radiation pressure of star light.[8]

Arrhenius's theories received a fuller treatment in his book *Worlds in the Making* (1908). It answered key criticisms of his theory, including the belief that potentially lethal ultraviolet light rays would kill any microscopic spores that existed in deep space. He was optimistic that at low temperatures the spores could remain intact for extremely long periods of time, and in his final opinion, 'all organisms in the universe are related and the process of evolution is everywhere the same'.[9]

Spreading Spores

Strangely, hard evidence for panspermia has been around for almost half a century. In 1961, a meteorite examined by Spanish-American biochemist Juan Oro was found to contain micro-fossils of an algae-like organism known as adenine, as well as the component nucleic acids of RNA (ribonucleic acid) and DNA, enough to produce ATP (*Adenosine triphosphate*), a major energy-releasing molecule in living cells.[10] Then in 1969 a meteorite that landed in Victoria, Australia, was determined to possess a complex series of organic compounds, including some of the nitrogen bases and amino acids that are the building blocks of DNA. Subsequent tests by Dr Ron Brown of Melbourne's Monash University revealed there were 'formations in the meteorite reminiscent of a very primitive form of cell structure'.[11]

All this is, of course, aside from the now famous five-pound (2.5 kilogram) meteorite ALH 84001 discovered in the Antarctic in 1984, which was subsequently examined and found to contain a variety of organic chemicals, including carbon molecules formed in water and created by single-celled organisms, remaining as 'fossil-like impressions of micro-tubular and other organisms.'[12] This example was, as we know, determined to have been ejected from Mars, reigniting the age-old debate as to whether or not there is, or was, life on the red planet.

Hitching a Ride

Panspermia is a theory that has had some heavyweight scientific support over the years. During the 1970s, renowned British astronomer Fred Hoyle (1915–2001) and his Sri Lankan-born colleague Chandra Wickramasinghe put their combined efforts behind the theory, proposing that complex organic compounds might well have evolved within interstellar dust clouds.[13] They wrote that interstellar spores or micro-organisms have continued to rain down on Earth in the form of flu viruses and other diseases which seem to develop spontaneously without any kind of common mutation from an existing strain. These micro-organisms, they argued, initially settle in the Earth's upper atmosphere, where they become caught up in the jet stream. Eventually they mix with lower winds rising up over mountain ranges such as the Himalayas, which take them down on to the plains of neighbouring countries, where the viruses are soon transferred to birds, animals and, finally, human beings.

Sugar and Space

In 2004, a bizarre new twist in the panspermia debate came in the form of a quite revelatory press release from NASA.[14] The story claimed that using the Green Bank Telescope in West Virginia astronomers had detected faint radio emissions, giving the signature of a sugar called glycolaldehyde. They were coming from a giant interstellar gas cloud dubbed Sagittarius B2, located close to the centre of the galaxy. Since glycolaldehyde – an eight-atom molecule made up of carbon, oxygen and hydrogen – can react to create the simple amino acids necessary to form life, NASA now felt it extremely likely that the building blocks of life existed first in deep space, and were then transported here by a comet. This discovery came just two years after the spectral 'fingerprint' of glycine, a simple amino acid, was detected in three interstellar gas clouds, one of which was Sagittarius B2.[15]

For a space organization of the calibre of NASA to have released such information meant that panspermia was now being taken very seriously indeed. Yet it took until October 2005 for NASA to announce finally that organic compounds called PAHs (polycyclic aromatic hydrocarbons) were not only 'abundant in space' but, more significantly, had more in common with life on Earth than had previously been recognized. *New Scientist* magazine reported that Douglas Hudgins and his colleagues at the NASA Ames Research Center in Moffat Field, California, initiated a search for PAHs using the Spitzer Space Telescope, launched from Cape Canaveral, Florida, on 25 August 2003. Their initial findings revealed that not only do PAHs exist everywhere in the galaxy, but that a high percentage contain nitrogen.[16] As plain as this discovery might seem, nitrogen-containing compounds are found in chlorophyll, DNA and haemoglobin, a fact which more-or-less confirms that carbon-based organisms evolved originally in deep space, and only afterwards made the journey here.

Crick's Great Secret

As astounding as some of these notions might seem, they will become directly relevant to the Cygnus mystery in due course, but for the moment it is time to examine the case of someone whose entire creative genius owes a great debt to psychedelic exploration: namely Francis Crick (1916–2004), the Nobel Prize-winning co-discoverer, with his brilliant American colleague James Watson, of DNA's double helix structure in 1953.[17]

Following his death at the age of 88 in July 2004, the news media revealed what had been common knowledge for some time. The fact is that Crick not only used 'small doses' of LSD (Lysergic Acid Diathylamide), colloquially known as 'acid' – a synthesized substance replicating the psychedelic alkaloids present in fungi such as ergot, which grows on rye – but he was also 'high' when he cracked the DNA code.[18] Indeed, according to a former colleague of Crick 'Cambridge academics used LSD in tiny amounts as a thinking tool, to liberate them from preconceptions and let their genius wander freely to new ideas. Crick ... perceived the double-helix shape while on LSD'.[19]

Such an admission – which in life Crick kept secret, light-heartedly threatening to sue any newspaper that printed the story – is stunning in itself, even though it has prompted a fierce reaction from his friends and family, who deny this was the case. What is not so well known is that Crick became a fervent supporter of what he called 'directed panspermia', writing a key essay on the subject in 1973 with his colleague Leslie E Orgel.[20] The Nobel Prize-winner went on to author a popular book on the subject entitled *Life Itself: Its Origin and Nature* (1981).

Crick's theory – which he stood by even after admitting in 1995 that the book 'might have been misguided' and a 'mistake to do'[21] – was that the Earth had been seeded originally by micro-organisms sent here from outer space. Crick speculated that whole colonies of micro-organisms were sent out, perhaps even by a race of intelligent life forms, realizing that their own race would eventually be destroyed, and knowing that most would fail to reach a planet that possessed the necessary amino acids to create life. Yet if only one found its target, then a complete eco-system might be created that would one day replicate the life found on the planet of departure.

For Crick, life on Earth formed part of a bigger cosmic picture, leading him to comment 'we may be part of a cosmic wildlife park ... Perhaps we are under some sort of discreet surveillance by higher beings on a planet of some nearby star. It is not clear how these cosmic game-wardens would do this without our detecting them ...'[22] In a similar breath, he asked: '... perhaps they are trying to send us signals of some sort', before adding, finally: 'This is too complicated a topic to develop fully here.'[23]

How did Crick come to believe in such fantastic theories, which clearly did not go down well among his contemporaries? As Graham Hancock has similarly suggested in his book *Supernatural* (2005), is it possible that he was himself 'rewired' through his extensive use of psychedelic substances, which, among other things, revealed to him the structure of DNA, the secret of life itself?[24] I am certain that it was under very similar conditions that he came to believe in directed panspermia, and also that the human race were part of a much greater plan that involved the existence of highly intelligent entities that he saw as watching over us like a shepherd looking after his flock. And what did he mean by suggesting that these life forms might be attempting to send us 'signals'? The answer probably lies in the fact that the true key to our cosmic origins might be found much closer to home.

Messages in our DNA

DNA is the hereditary molecule, present at the heart of genes in every life form. Yet it is a fact that almost all DNA is considered scientifically useless. The human genome (i.e. DNA and all its genes) has three billion (3,000,000,000) base pairs of nucleotides, which make up the chain-like structure of DNA and RNA, and these are arranged to form the familiar double helix, although just three per cent represent functional genes. The remaining 97 per cent are seen as 'junk DNA', simply because their function remains unclear. This is not just 97 per cent of DNA in human beings, but a high percentage of DNA in all life forms (the amount varies from species to species). Junk DNA is simply that which does not produce proteins, since it contains no blueprint to do so. Only the other three per cent of DNA is able to transform itself into RNA in order to produce the proteins that make us what we are.

The exact nature of junk DNA remains an enigma to molecular biologists, but in August 2004 a groundbreaking article in *New Scientist* by physicist and writer Paul Davies proposed that encoded 'messages', countless millions if not billions of years old and of extra-terrestrial origin, might well be contained in the genomes of terrestrial organisms.[25] Here they will remain dormant until something triggers the encoded 'message' into revealing itself. Davies speculated that these messages, Crick's 'signals', are sparked into life by 'carefully crafted viruses', which infect host cells containing the 'message-laden DNA'.[26]

Since the DNA molecules that instruct normal living cells to grow are prone to mutation, messing about with them could cause random errors in their genetic sequence, making them completely unsuitable for revision. Thus in order to minimalize the effects of mutations, unchanging segments of DNA would have to be used, and this, claims Davies, is where junk DNA comes in, for it has recently been established that certain types are conserved in exactly the same format across *millions* of years.[27] Thus it could well be primed with all kinds of 'genetic oddments', without it affecting the performance of other living cells, which operate entirely independently. As Davies concludes, 'If ET has put a message into terrestrial organisms, this is surely where to look'.[28]

Expansion of the Brain

Paul Davies' views on the existence of these hidden messages seem to me too materialistically deduced, based on Hoyle and Wickramasinghe's own dark vision of the panspermia epidemic. Surely, it would be simpler to propose that these messages or signals preserve knowledge regarding the cosmic origins of life, and how we might link with it today. Such ideas are already being contemplated by left-field astrobiologists such as Rhawn Joseph, Ph.D., of the Neurodynamics, Brain Research Laboratory. He writes that human beings are on the verge of a 'cerebral metamorphosis and expansion of the brain', caused by the activation of some hidden facet of junk DNA.[29] This brings to mind the overriding effects of the psychedelic experience, including the possibility of contact with other worlds and perceived supernatural intelligences. Is it possible, therefore, that psychedelics open up what the philosopher and writer Aldous Huxley (1894–1963), author of *A Brave New World* (1932) and renowned mescaline experimenter, referred to as the 'doors of perception'?[30] Is it such substances, and not 'carefully crafted viruses', that spark the 'message-laden DNA' into action?

Quantum Tunnels

In my opinion, it is some inert quality of the junk DNA which, when unleashed, creates neural transmissions that open up previously dormant subatomic pathways, and even quantum tunnels that enable unmitigated signal nonlocality to take place. This allows the brain to function as a receiver of new information, or 'messages', not accessible to normal human consciousness. As bold a theory as this might seem, similar ideas concerning junk DNA being utilized to link all life forms via hyperspace were proposed as early as 2001 by two groundbreaking German science writers, Grazyna Fosar and Franz Bludorf.[31]

Inspired by the work of Finnish physicist Matti Pitkänen into the concept of magnetic 'wormholes',[32] perceived quantum tunnels linking two different places in space-time, Fosar and Bludorf now view junk DNA as like antennae, using the mysterious force of gravity as a bond to contain microscopic wormholes, which act like a fibre-optic network, a process they refer to as 'hypercommunication'.[33] Moreover, they see incoming information and data as being received by junk DNA, and then transmitted via the body's neural network to the brain, which transforms it into very real human experiences of the type triggered most usually during altered states of consciousness.

Opening the doors of perception to allow such hypercommunication via quantum tunnels would be like unzipping and configuring a computer program, opened only when the correct mental stimulus is given. If correct, then what more obvious stimulus can there be than psychedelic substances, freely available in plants and mycetes that grow all over the world. Indeed, it might be argued that such plants exist simply to supply us with these substances, which, as Jeremy Narby was informed, were made known to the indigenous peoples of the Peruvian Amazon by the plant's alleged 'spirits' (*see above, page 220*).

Quite literally, the psychedelic experience is the key to unlocking what might be described as 'personal cosmic consciousness', and if this is correct then the possibilities are endless. Inner space communications of this order could result in a much greater acceleration of evolution as new universal data and information is projected into the human mind like some kind of organic program download.

I was intrigued by the statements of some of Rick Strassman's subjects (*see above, page 224*) who felt as if the entities encountered during their DMT experiences were changing or transforming them in some way. One account, from a person named 'Rex' reads as follows:

> When I was first going under there were these insect creatures all around me. They were clearly trying to break through ... the insectoids began to feed on my heart, devouring the feelings of love and surrender ... There was no feeling of space. Everything was so close ... I don't know if they were male or female or something else, but it was extremely alien, though not necessarily unpleasant. The thought came to me with certainty that they were manipulating my DNA, changing its structure. And then it started fading. They didn't want me to go.[34]

Interestingly, it was the American astronomer and science writer Carl Sagan (1934–1996) – a regular user of marijuana – [35] who first proposed that 'perhaps the [ETI, extra-terrestrial intelligence] messages are already here, present in some everyday experience that we have not made the right mental effort to realize'.[36] This idea was later explored by two Japanese biologists, Hiromitzu Yokoo of Kyorin University, Hachioji City, and Tairo Oshima of the Mitsubishi-Kasei Institute of Life Sciences, who speculated that these 'messages' might well be carried in the DNA of a simple organism, such as a bacterium.[37] So they tested a bacteriophage called øX174, a virus that inhabits the human gut, looking for an ETI message, but after studying a prominent section of its DNA, they concluded that there was nothing there.

It now looks as if these Japanese biologists were searching in the wrong place. Had they looked more closely at junk DNA, then there is every chance that they would have made some remarkable discoveries. Sagan himself went on to use the idea of instant communication with ETI through a symbolic and geometric interface in his novel *Contact* (1985), subsequently made into a Hollywood movie with Jodie Foster playing the lead role. Did this inspired idea, so close to Paul Davies' own theory regarding junk DNA, come from Sagan's regular use of marijuana? I feel the answer is going to be yes.

Life's Origins Elsewhere

During the 1970s, UFOs were big news, and the likelihood of some kind of extra-terrestrial contact being made was a thrilling prospect. Unfortunately, however, modern UFO encounters and abductions, although of huge scientific interest, have failed to confirm the popularly-held view that extra-terrestrials exist, or that they have visited the Earth using conventional hardware. More damning still is that nothing so far discovered in the archaeological record argues for the intervention of alien beings in the evolution of humankind. This is unfortunate, and yet the connection between life on Earth and the cosmos is something that our prehistoric ancestors categorically accepted and, in the West, would have continued to do so if it had not been for Aristotle's more 'rational' theory of the spontaneous creation of life on Earth.

In Chinese mythology some of the earliest kings of China were said to have been sons of star-gods,[38] while the kings of ancient Sumer and Akkad (in what is now Iraq) bore a star symbol after their names indicating that they were the product of a divine union with sky-beings. Beyond this is the view shared by ancient peoples all over the world that even though we might have been born on Earth, and are the descendants of a putative first human couple, our true self, our soul, originates elsewhere, and upon its release at death it will be free to return whence it came. This recalls the magico-religious beliefs of the shamanic-based societies of Asia, who considered that the souls of children sat in the upper branches of the World Tree where they await a shaman to draw them into incarnation, or even the European folk belief in storks, or swans, bringing newborn babies into the world.

In Chapter Three we saw how the Mandaeans of Iraq and Iran believed that the human soul passed beyond the North Star, identified here as Deneb in Cygnus, where it would join a sky-boat that would take it across the celestial river, arguably the Milky Way, to one of the countless 'worlds of light', home to their dead kin.[39] In these blissful realms, governed by 'great spirits of light', they would encounter their purified souls as well as their own '*dmutha* or over-soul'.

Then there is the work of cultural historian William Sullivan, who, as we saw in Chapter Seven, highlighted the Andean belief that: 'In this world we are exiled from our homeland in the world above [*hanaq pacha*]',[40] which is 'up there',[41] in the northern night sky, once again in the direction of Cygnus (even though Peru is in the Southern Hemisphere). He compared this native concept with that of the semi-nomadic Naskapi of Labrador in Canada, who 'speak of the possibility of contact between worlds along the Milky Way, which they call "ghost trail," or "dead person's path."'[42] Sullivan pointed out that for these indigenous peoples, 'the souls of the living originated in the sky, where they "rest in the firmament until they become reincarnated."'[43] Similar ideas about the transmigration of the soul lay at the heart of almost all ancient religions, such as that of Dynastic Egypt, inspiring the belief in a celestial heaven, somewhere that was accessible not just to spirits or souls of the dead, but also shamans who, as we have seen, believed that they could enter the sky-world via a 'hole', door or gate beyond the northerly placed cosmic axis.

In the Indonesian archipelago, several island cultures are said to be directly descended from sky-beings. The Posso-Todjo Toradja, for example, say that they are the children of Lasaeo, the 'sun-lord', who married a Toradja woman. Eventually, he 'returned to the sky', and his people departed from Pamona and founded a line of chiefs at Waibinta Luwu.[44] In Taiwan, the non-Chinese Tsalisen people say that their ancestors came out of the moon,[45] while the Kayan and Kenyah say that sky-beings made the first man and woman in the form of stone images.[46] The Totemboan say that To'ar, a 'sun-lord', married their daughter Lintjambene, while her son Si Marendor was said to have been half sky-born and half made of stone.[47]

These examples are given simply to demonstrate how across the world indigenous cultures have believed that their entire existence is as a result of life on Earth having been seeded from elsewhere whatever way their creation myths might have interpreted such information. Many other examples might be cited, such as those Native Americans who point towards a star and say it is their original homeland, or the African peoples, including the Dogon of Mali (*see Appendix: The Dogon Mystery*), who likewise claim to be descendants of sky-beings.

The Dark Between Stars

The importance here is not to assume the reality of such accounts, but simply to acknowledge that in the past there was no stigma attached to the idea that life came originally from the sky. Indeed, I sense it was the norm. The celestial abode was not only the homeland of the sky-beings, but also the place of cosmic creation, where life, or souls at least, originated, and would return in death, as in the Judaeo-Christian concept of heaven. So how did the world come to believe such views of life's cosmic origins – which were invariably attached to the stars of Cygnus as the cosmic axis and northern apex of the Milky Way?

From the evidence presented in this book, I suspect it was as a result of the shamans or priestly elite of prehistoric communities telling their people exactly this, since it was through the shaman's contact with otherworldly agencies that the ancients most probably came to accept life's universal nature, the ancient concept of panspermia. What is more, the possibility that psychedelic substances can enable the human mind to achieve a state of DNA-linked cosmic consciousness allows us to perceive of the shamanic experience as authentically real.

The prospect of extra-terrestrial contact on a neuropsychological level alone makes perfect sense. With our clumsy space technology, SETI-inspired radio telescopes scanning tiny fractions of the night sky for incoming 'alien' signals, and well-lit landing pads ready to welcome incoming UFOS, we are unlikely to make contact with ETI any time soon. This will not be for lack of trying, but simply because we are dealing with enormously vast distances between stars. As Carl Sagan pointed out in his book *Broca's Brain* (1974), the epic journeys of spacecraft such as Pioneer 10 and 11 and Voyager 1 and 2, sent up from Earth and boosted by gravitational assistance from Jupiter, will take tens of thousands of years to travel interstellar distances. 'Unless some special effort is made to redirect them,' he said, 'they will never enter another planetary system in all the tens of billions of years of future history of the Milky Way Galaxy. The star-to-star distances are too large. They are doomed to wander forever in the dark between the stars.'[48]

The universe is quite simply too large to cross using conventional nuts-and-bolts spacecraft, and the theory that we might one day be able to create 'wormholes' or produce 'hyperdrives' in order to cross the galaxy is at present no more than theory. And this is not simply our problem, for if there really are other intelligent beings out there, then wouldn't you think that they also face the same dilemmas, no matter how technologically advanced they might have become?

Because of this sober conclusion, it is obvious that any highly evolved ETI 'out there' would have created a means of communication and/or contact with distant planets that was more or less instantaneous. So if we are to accept panspermia and the idea that junk-DNA triggered by psychedelic experiences has the ability to 'wire' us into cosmic consciousness, then it means that human beings have always been capable of contact with intelligences anywhere in the universe, and that this might well be a necessary part of our evolution.

I am not proposing that the human mind is able to project itself through space to communicate with some alien intelligence in another star system. What I am saying is that there exists *some kind of universal consciousness* that can link together the brains of carbon-based life forms, wherever they are. It exists not in outer space, but in inner space, that is inside our heads, and can be imagined like some kind of neuropsychological Internet chat room, where we appear as ourselves, and the consciousness (or 'spirits') of visiting entities, both terrestrial and non-terrestrial, can interface with us either in their own natural forms, or as 'morphians', shape-shifters, beings that take whatever form our minds deem acceptable for the purposes of communication. These links occur in a coexisting higher dimension that exists beyond the space-time so familiar to us, just like the avataristic identities that users assume in an Internet virtual world. And like the Internet, it is always available to us, its 'activation' or 'online facility' occurring via our DNA under the correct circumstances, most obviously during the psychedelic experience.

Judging by the achievements of ETI-advocating drug users such as Francis Crick and Carl Sagan we need to understand this process, which could be important to human evolution. Moreover, we should recall also the concluding words (*see above, page 232*) of Rick Strassman's subject 'Rex', who proclaimed that the entities he encountered 'were manipulating my DNA, changing its structure'. If this is what really happens to us under such circumstances, then our entire genetic make-up becomes altered in some way, either temporarily or even on a more permanent basis.

The Place of Emergence

If non-local contact with supernatural beings and worlds is available through the activation of junk DNA, then it is a process that has been going on since time immemorial, or at least since humanity first began ingesting psychedelic substances. Although this might well coincide with the appearance of anatomically modern human beings in Ethiopia as much as 195,000 years ago, the most concrete evidence for its emergence comes from the Upper Palaeolithic cave art of western Europe between 32,500 and 11,000 years ago (the oldest pre-San rock art in Africa dates to *c.*25,500–*c.*23,500 BC).

We must, however, acknowledge the Neanderthal bear cult, with its possible astronomical associations, sometime around 43,000 years ago, as well as the recent discovery in South Africa's Blombos cave, which overlooks the Indian Ocean, of a piece of red ochre with a flat surface on which are incised parallel lines between which is simple cross hatching. It is the oldest recorded example of prehistoric art, and was unearthed in a layer that has provided a date in the region of 77,000 years BP (before the present).[49]

Somehow, deep caves were extremely important to the evolution of rock art and religion among our Palaeolithic forebears. It was an environment they sought out time and time again, and the quite novel manner in which this might have come about will, at last, begin to provide some real answers as to why our earliest ancestors came to view Cygnus as the source of cosmic life and death.

CHAPTER TWENTY

Cosmic Swansong

Why did the Upper Palaeolithic cave artists paint some of their most beautiful and enigmatic frescoes deep underground, often several hundred metres from the entrance? For instance, at the Grotte de Rouffignac in the Dordogne, where the room known as the Serpent Dome has a ceiling writhing with finger-painted snakes, there are frescoes up to 735 metres (0.46 miles) from the entrance. At nearby Lascaux the Well Scene showing the bird-man, bison and bird on a stick, identified as a 17,000-year-old image of Cygnus, are within a five metre (16.5 feet) pit, deep underground.

At the Grotte de Niaux in France's Ariège, there is no art until several hundred metres into the cave. To witness the paintings at Font-de-Gaume in the Dordogne, a crawl along a narrow passage for 130 metres (427 feet) is necessary to reach its best examples, while the discoverer of a cave at Montespan in the Haute Garonne had to navigate an underground stream for nearly 1200 metres (0.75 miles) before coming upon its Ice Age art. Finally, at Tuc d'Audobert in the Ariège its decorated caverns are only accessible following tortuous journeys, and even then the art is to be found in the remotest chambers.[1]

Beyond this is the fact that the most revered cave art is almost always found in the deepest part of the caves, where very little human activity ever took place.[2] Unlike cave art nearer the surface, it was never defaced, a fact which led Jean Clottes – an eminent French prehistorian who has written extensively on Palaeolithic cave art – to observe that 'the images of the walls retained their power and … the surfaces on which they had been drawn also remained "sacred."'[3]

Clottes noted also that starting from the so-called Early Magdalenian period, a sub-division of the Upper Palaeolithic era, *c.*15,000–*c.*13,000 BC, there was a new-found trend in using and painting the deepest sections of caves, which peaked in the Middle Magdalenian period, *c.*13,000–*c.*11,000 BC, and then began to wane in the Late Magdalenian phase, *c.*11,000–*c.*9000 BC.[4] It seemed like the Magdalenians, unlike their predecessors, the Gravettians, made the decision to paint far inside the caves and to constantly explore 'mile-long caves, such as Niaux, Montespan and Rouffignac.'[5]

Deepest, Darkest

Something curiously powerful went on in the deepest, darkest regions of the caves, and there had to be a reason why. An obvious answer is that it was connected somehow to the idea of natural acoustics, whereby some sections of the caves would resonate with the human vocal chords better than others. Investigations within various cave complexes have revealed that there are meaningful patterns of overlap between the placement of key paintings and the chamber's natural resonance. For instance, hoofed animals can often be seen where the place resounds with clattering echoes, while other more spacious rooms reflect a lower resonance, triggered simply by humming. Deeper inside, stalactites have been identified as lithophones, stones that when struck make ringing sounds.[6] Even though I am certain that sound, and rhythmic chanting in particular, would have been important to the Palaeolithic mindset, this theory does not explain the predominance of paintings in the farthest reaches of the caves.

Sensory depravation might also have played a role in the choice of where the art was created and shamanic experiences carried out. The further one goes into a cave system, especially in virtual or total darkness, the more disorientated the mind becomes, and the more a distinct sense of detachment is felt from the real world. This in itself might have helped the shaman to achieve a suitable altered state of consciousness, even without the use of psychedelic substances.

Other possible factors such as the need to find suitable canvases for painting (not always easy), a reduced threat of attack from wild animals (always a problem), or simple privacy (from those who might wander in from nearby rock shelters) might all have played some role in the placement of murals, and the choice of sacred space used. Yet in the knowledge that communication with otherworldly realms and entities would invariably have played a part in shamanic trance states, made me consider other possibilities as well. What if the shamans had been told specifically by the spirits where to go, where to carry out their rituals? It is worth recalling Jeremy Narby's concept of a DNA-linked collective consciousness, and the fact that it was the spirits of the plants that directed the ayahuasqueros as to which ingredients they should use in order to create medicines, as well as the chemically-complex *ayahuasca* brew. What if similar communications took place in the Palaeolithic caves of western Europe?

Food of the Dead

Although our Palaeolithic forebears have long since vanished, we can gain some insight into their approach to the supernatural by examining legends and stories concerning the relationship between caves and drug-related spirit communications. For instance, the story of the discovery of *iboga* (also known as ibogaine), a powerful psychoactive plant with the botanical name *Tabernanthe iboga,* used by followers of the native Bwiti religion of Gabon and Cameroon in Equatorial Africa in their Christian-style (i.e. missionary friendly) 'services', is relevant to this debate.

According to their foundation story, Bandzioku, a pygmy woman of the forest, lost her husband when he fell from a great tree in the forest.[7] Inconsolable at being unable to find his remains, she reluctantly accepted the custom of her people, which was to marry her brother-in-law. Finally, the bones of her first husband unexpectedly turned up in a net she was using to catch fish from a boat. Yet on going ashore the remains were stolen by an animal, forcing her to follow it into the Kakonangonda cave. Inside, she heard the spirits of the dead calling out to her, 'Bandzioku, do you want to *see* us?' 'Yes' she said, and so the spirits told her to eat of the root of the plant that grew in the 'corner', and this was how *iboga* came to be known to humanity.

Thereafter she could see as well as talk to the spirits of the dead, among which was her first husband. She returned to the cave on several occasions, until one day her second husband followed her, thinking that she was going there to meet someone. Hearing his wife in conversation inside the cave, he became upset because he could see nothing. So she told him about the *iboga* plant, and after eating of its roots he too could see the spirits including his dead brother. At that moment, the spirits requested the obligatory *okandzo*, or offering, but what he had brought with him was not enough. He was left with no choice but to give up his wife, who was sacrificed in their honour. After returning to the village, the man created the first Bwiti temple, and officiated as its priest, although soon human sacrifice was abolished, as chickens were offered in its place.

In some versions of the story the spirits of the dead inside the cave tell Bandzioku to place the *iboga* root on top of a large mushroom known as *duna* before either the *iboga* or both are consumed.[8] A mushroom called *duna*, or *dune*, is known to have been used in sorcery by the Fang, the main tribal group that practise Bwiti in Gabon and Cameroon. The fungus apparently resembles the size and shape of a human head (a symbol of the soul), in which capacity it was seen as the brain of the 'first man to die',[9] recalling the use of skulls in the Neolithic cult of the dead. Unfortunately, a lack of knowledge regarding the exact species of mushroom has meant that its psychoactive properties have not been fully understood. This said, Italian ethnobotanist and ethnomycologist Giorgio Samorini, who has made a personal study of the Bwiti religion, was able to establish that *duna* is ingested with other vegetables in order to induce visions during sleep.[10]

Although this foundation story of the Bwiti religion is quite obviously mythological in nature, Samorini believes it to be based on an indigenous cult of the dead (indeed, the word *bwiti* might simply mean 'ancestor'[11]), one presumably focused around the significance of primordial caves as places of direct communication with the spirit world. He speculates also that the use by the Bwitists of plant roots such as *iboga* might have replaced an earlier mushroom cult, linked with the descendants of those responsible for the Tassili rock art of Algeria, which corresponds in age with the tail-end of western Europe's cave art period.[12]

Clearly, the significance of the Bwiti account is that spirits who supposedly haunt a cave instruct the woman how she might see them if she ingests the *iboga* root that grows in the 'corner' of the cave. Was it simply the spirit of the plant instructing her on its importance, and how best it might be used inside the mythical Kakonangonda cave? All we can say is that the Bwitists consume huge amounts of the substance during their bizarre services, where initiates can be spoon-fed *iboga* for up to four days at a time. Interestingly, the areas of the temple, or 'church', are laid out to represent the human body. The altar, where the *iboga* is administered, corresponds to the skull, which is another tell-tale link to an ancestral cult of the dead.

The God of Dreams

Caves, visions and drugs feature also in Classical myth. According to the Roman writer Ovid (43 BC-AD 18) in his *Metamorphoses*, Somnus ('Sleep'), son of Nox ('Night'), the Roman goddess of night and darkness, was said to have lived in a dark cave where the sun 'can never come'. At its 'doors', i.e. mouth, poppies 'bloom in abundance, and innumerable herbs, from the juice of which the humid night [Nox] gathers sleep, and spreads it over the darkened Earth.'[13] Somnus himself was represented as a sleeping figure on a bed of feathers, surrounded by black curtains. Around him lay countless 'unsubstantial dreams' (*somnia*).[14] Apparently, the Lacedaemonians (Spartans) of ancient Greece would place an image of Hypnos, the Greek form of Somnus, near that of his brother Thanatos, god of death,[15] showing a relationship between dream visions and the influence of death.

In this myth, we find a reference to the psychoactive poppy, from which is extracted opium, as well as an allusion to herbs that induce sleep. What is more, an emphasis is placed on them growing 'before the doors [i.e. mouth] of the cavern'. Somnus's son Morpheus, god of dreams, was said to have watched over his father with a bunch of poppies in one hand, further establishing the link with opium. He would appear to dreamers in whatever guise their minds could receive him, meaning that he was a morphian, a shapeshifter, reflected in the etymology of his name, which derives from the Greek *morphe* (hence also *morphine*, an alkaloid extracted from the opium poppy used also to make heroin).[16] This word generally means 'shape', 'form', 'face' or 'look'. Yet, more tellingly, *morphe* can also mean 'training', 'teaching', 'instruction', 'education' and 'learning', all perfect expressions of what might be expected through interaction with otherworldly intelligences encountered in altered states of consciousness, including dream states.

The Sound of Silence

Somnus's subterranean palace is said to have been a dark cave where the sun 'can never come', and Morpheus makes sure that no noise ever wakes his father ('No wild beasts, no cattle, no boughs waving with the breeze, no loud outbursts of the human voice, there make any sound; mute Rest has there her abode ... There is no door in the whole dwelling, to make a noise by the turning of the hinges; no porter at the entrance.'[17]). Why the emphasis here on silence? Silence is, of course, extremely important to mystical practices. For instance, the great Tibetan yogi and poet Milarepa (1052–1135) was noted for his many years of meditation inside a sacred cave during which time he cupped his hand, placed it to his ear and listened 'to the sound of the universe', in which manner he is depicted in Tibetan Buddhist art.[18]

The Prophet Muhammad is said also to have retired for solitude to a cave, where the archangel Gabriel appeared to him. Over the next 23 years, Muhammad received the word of Allah through Gabriel, who would either grace him with his presence or sound a bell, whereupon his voice would become audible. This is how the holy *Qur'an* ('Recitation') came into existence.

Saraswati enabled Brahma to hear the Naadabrahmam, the primordial sound, symbolized by the AUM vibration, which holds together the universe. The AUM (or OM), personified as the swan-goose Hamsa, or Kalahamsa, the 'Swan-Goose of Eternity', relates to the states of waking, dreaming and sleeping, and understanding its divine purpose leads the devotee to the higher realm of *turya*, represented by total silence. It is only in this state of meditation that an initiate might come to hear the primordial sound that fills the universe. We should recall also ancient Egypt's

Great Cackler, the goose that laid the egg of creation and brought the universe into manifestation with its honk or call. Was any of this linked to the fact that the English name 'swan' (German *schwan*) is related to the Sanskrit root *svanash*, meaning 'tone, sound',[19] found also in the Latin *sonare*, 'to sound', and *sonus*, the source of the word 'sound' itself?[20]

As early as the sixth century BC, the Greek fabulist Aesop expressed the obviously already-held belief that, having remained silent all its life, the swan lets out a fearful cry (some say a beautiful song) at the moment of death.[21] Although this piece of folklore, perpetuated by Socrates in Plato's *Phaedo*,[22] is of course a fable, it attributes the swan with a special sound connected directly with the attainment of physical death, the very state of existence that a shaman strives to mimic when in trance. Among the Ainu of Japan the swan was also connected with death, or more particularly death rites, for it was said that the peculiar wail that women let out whenever a death occurs mimics the cry of the swan.[23] Was this in some way linked with the ultimate relationship between the celestial swan and the deep cave setting for the shamanic experience?

Cosmic Microwave Background Radiation

It is tempting to see the repeated reference to sound in the creation and maintenance of the universe as a subtle awareness of Cosmic Microwave Background Radiation (CMB). This is the residue of giant electro-magnetic waves, peaking in the microwave range, created by the blazing matter that filled the universe shortly after its formation 13.7 billion years ago. It was detected by accident for the first time in 1965, even though its existence had been predicted as early as 1948. Bizarrely, its presence even today can be recorded quite easily. Just turn on your television and de-tune it to white noise, and a few per cent of the 'snow' between channels is CMB!

John G Cramer, popular science writer and Professor of Physics at the University of Washington in Seattle, has determined that the 'Big Bang' was more like a deep hum than a bang, following his own research into the nature of CMB. Indeed, he has created audio files which he says replicate the sound heard throughout the universe during its first 760,000 years, when it was a mere 18 million light years across.[24] At the time, he says, the microwave radiation would not have been audible, and so in order to hear them he has had to scale up the frequencies 100,000 billion billion times.

Cramer's audio files are available online,[25] and the resulting effect actually sounds like a jumbo jet flying directly overhead, after which the strangely pleasant cacophony reduces to a low pitched hum as it gradually fades into the distance. This replicates the manner in which the frequency levels dropped as the universe expanded and the sound waves became more and more stretched. Even now this process continues, since the CMB has imprinted itself into its very fabric as temperature variations, which can still be detected today.

Life on earth is embedded in cosmic radiation and I suspect that our distant ancestors not only became aware of CMB, but also came to associate it with the creation and maintenance of the universe. It may well be this that was 'heard' in the absolute silence of deep caves by yogins such as Milarepa. Yet even though it is extremely possible that enlightened figures of the past were aware of CMB, an understanding of what it represented most probably came from their interaction with cosmic consciousness during shamanic trance states, perhaps induced by psychedelic substances or sensory deprivation. In other words, there is every reason to believe that this knowledge might have been gained through perceived supernatural experiences.[26]

The true source of the CMB, so ably reproduced on audio files by John G Cramer, is everywhere. Any religious ideals which might have directed this influence to a particular area of the sky were misguided by our ancestors' own Earth-orientated understanding of the cosmos, which saw Cygnus as marking the point of creation. Having stated this, it does explain the preponderance of creation myths that feature birds emitting some kind of sound or call that brings the universe into manifestation. What is more, it provides us with a possible solution as to how the swan gained its ancient Sanskrit name, for as Kalahamsa, identified in Vedic astronomy with the stars of Cygnus, it became an active expression of the sound of the universe.

It is possible that links between swans, caves and sound long predated the *c.*15,000 BC (17,000 BP) horizon under scrutiny here (*see Chapter Twenty-Two*), for two of the oldest flutes so far discovered were made from swan bones, one at least coming from a whooper swan (*Cygnus cygnus*). These were uncovered inside a cave in the Ach Valley of the Swabian Jura in southwest Germany at a level corresponding to 35,000 BP (+/- 2,000 years), close to where another example, this time made from the tusk of a woolly mammoth, was later found.[27] An even older flute, made from a hollow bear femur and dating to 45,000 BP, was discovered during 1995 in a cave once occupied by Neanderthal peoples in the Idrijca Valley of western Slovenia.[28]

The existence of the two swan flutes certainly suggests an older link between this species of bird and the use of sound, if only because their bones were suitable for the creation of musical instruments. What is more, it could be that the connection between swans and Cygnus also goes back further than the time-frame suggested in this book.

Siberian Swan Cult

What initially seemed like evidence of an even earlier interest in Cygnus as the celestial swan was discovered in 1928 at the site of a Palaeolithic settlement at Malta, in the district of Bratsk, some 85 kilometres (53 miles) from Irkutsk in Siberia's Angara Valley. Here a large number of carved pendants in mammoth ivory were found, each fashioned into the appearance of a swan in flight, with elaborately carved head and necks, truncated wings, and a drilled hole in the tail so that it might be worn around the neck. The pendants range in size from 15 to 4.5 centimetres (6 to 2 inches), and were originally estimated to be around 22,000 years old.

Given the knowledge that swan shamanism in Siberia was widespread – and there is evidence that they recognized Cygnus as a celestial swan[29] – then the existence of the Angaran swan pendants would have been important evidence of a pre-15,000 BC cult of Cygnus, especially as one example was found placed in a child's grave, tentatively linking it with the transmigration of the soul. However, following further excavations at the Malta site in 1968, Carbon-14 evidence from organic materials indicated that it thrived *c.*15,000 years ago, around the time that

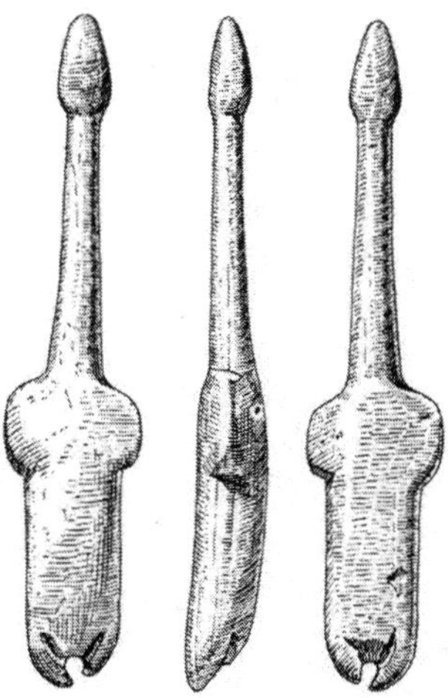

Fig. 49. Example of one of the many bone swan pendants found at the Palaeolithic site of Malta within Siberia's Angara Valley. They have been dated to *c.*15,000 BP.

Vega took over from *delta* Cygni as Pole Star. Even so, this impressive art collection is hard evidence that the Siberian cult of the swan is unquestionably Ice Age in origin. What is more, there is now evidence that by the end of the Palaeolithic age the north was recognized as the direction of the land of the dead.

Cave of the Swans

In 2003 the first ever verifiable examples of Upper Palaeolithic cave art were found in Britain (*see plates 25–27*). They consist of a series of engravings, once enhanced with a magnesium-based pigment, created *c.*10,800 BC inside a cave named Church Hole at Creswell Crags. This is an east–west orientated river valley, containing several Ice Age caves, situated between the counties of Derbyshire and Nottinghamshire in the north of England. Clearly visible are line images of an ibex, horse and bison, as well as the beautifully carved head of an ibis with its distinctive curved beak.

The sole engravings found in the long birth canal-like tube at the rear of the cave, around 17 metres from the entrance, and well beyond the reach of sunlight, are a group of standing birds with extremely long necks, their heads craned skywards. One of them is unquestionably a bittern, a species known for raising its neck in this way. Yet to its left is a bird with chimeric (hybrid) qualities, which although it has a bittern-style head, also possesses a long curved neck like that of a swan. Other birds in the group are so abstract that identifying their species becomes impossible. However, palaeontologists have themselves noted the swan-like appearance of the 'bird panel', leading Sheffield University's Paul Pettitt, one of the team that discovered the Church Hole cave art, to comment: 'Given the presence of points of swan bone in the Creswellian [horizon, *c.*13,000–*c.*10,000 BC] at Creswell, perhaps their imagery is not surprising.'[30] He added that the presence of the points, used as awls, might also have meant that swan feathers were used for 'symbolism and waterproofing'.[31]

Directly opposite the bird panel, on the other side of the wall, is an oval-shaped niche, positioned horizontally, inside which are two smaller circular holes. Although the function of this apparently artificial feature is unknown, it probably symbolized an egg-like device. This suggestion is made more likely by the knowledge that just behind the ibis head, near the cave mouth, is an outlined oval in high relief that could easily be construed as an egg, which, like the ibis in ancient Egyptian cosmology, arguably signifies cosmic creation. What is more, at least two examples of 'triangular vulvae'[32] have been recorded among the cave art. However, I found these more to resemble the classic bird's foot symbol, composed of three strokes converging together, which probably served a dual symbolic function.

This was the conclusion of Lithuanian-born prehistorian and archaeologist Marija Gimbutas (1927–1994), who determined that the abstract signs on Old European and West Asian portable objects from the Neolithic period were in fact a symbolic written language. She identified the bird's foot as a primary device used since Palaeolithic times as an abstract representation of the Great Goddess.[33] 'Like the regenerative triangle and hourglass,' she recorded, 'isolated bird's feet were also symbols imbued with the potency of regeneration.'[34] In other words, it was not simply an abstract symbol of the Great Goddess's avian attributes, but also a visual metaphor for the vulva.

Church Hole's cave art is not simply a random selection of zoomorphic and geometric images. To start with, two creatures portrayed – the ibis and ibex, a species of wild goat – were not indigenous to Britain, suggesting some kind of link with continental Europe, most probably southern France and/or northern Spain. Yet such migrations by semi-nomadic hunter-gatherers make little sense, for at the end of the last Ice Age, Creswell Crags was on the very edge of the northerly ice fields that had covered much of Britain and the Northern Hemisphere for anything up to 30,000 years. Why should these people from warmer climes have wanted to come here in order to create continental-style cave art?

If, on the other hand, the art was executed by the local Creswellians, then what were they doing depicting creatures from foreign parts, for surely if groups of them had migrated across to what are now France or Spain (remember, there was no English Channel at this time), they are hardly likely to have returned without good reason. All this suggests that Creswell Crags was in some way important to them, perhaps for no other reason than its position in the extreme north, beyond which was only an inhospitable wasteland.

The biggest clue comes from the fact that only the caves on the north side of the valley would seem to have been utilized as places of communal habitation. In contrast, those on the south side, of which Church Hole is the best example, have produced almost no evidence of occupation, just the aforementioned engraved art, and a few portable artefacts unearthed during excavations in the nineteenth century. This conundrum led Paul Pettitt to speculate, quite cryptically, on 'whether the north side of the gorge was the land of the living, whereas the south side was something very different.'[35] Without realizing it, he was in fact suggesting that the caves on the south side of the valley might have been reserved for ritualistic activity associated with the realms of the dead. If correct, then this was perfect confirmation that the peoples of the Upper Palaeolithic recognized the north, towards which Church Hole faced, as the direction of the otherworld.

Curiously, the only engraving so far found on the north side of the valley is a classic three-pronged bird's foot, its 'talons' pointing upwards, the manner in which it appears universally (except for the bardic Awen symbol, which is reversed). This is to be seen in Robin Hood's Cave, a large rock shelter thought to have been used as a place of communal occupation.

Facing North, the Stars of Cygnus

On entering Church Hole for the first time in September 2005, I realized immediately that it is orientated due north, and that from the interior of the cave, even with a floor level lower than in Palaeolithic times, a small window of vision is created above the cliff face opposite. Subsequent calculations ably demonstrated that Deneb, then circumpolar at this latitude, would have been visible from the cave as it crossed the meridian on its lower transit at a date of *c.* 10,800 BC.[36] Could this realization be linked with the likelihood that the cave was quite probably used for ritual practices involving the realms of the dead? The superbly carved ibis head gazes eternally northwards, the carved egg-like device visible behind it. Did these images signify the direction of cosmic life and death, and if so why?

It is easy to imagine this rocky crag still gripped by icy cold winters, with swans migrating here on a yearly basis, most probably from southern France and northern Spain. By *c.* 10,800 BC, when the art was created, I suspect that the swan had already become associated with Deneb, seen by the Creswellian peoples as the ultimate North Star. Studies into bird migrations have revealed that certain species – particularly those which, like swans, fly mostly at night (the reason why swans are commonly associated in European folklore with the moon[37]) – recognize and use certain star groups to navigate in order to reach their northerly breeding grounds.[38] This input of information is used to recalibrate the birds' internal magnetic compass during rest stops. Indeed, if they do not get enough rest on the long journey, then there is every likelihood that they will get lost.

Rather curiously, astronomers have come to realize that the Milky Way has its own magnetic field, with a strength somewhere in the region of five microgauss, directed along the galaxy's spiral arms. Even though the Earth's own, much stronger magnetic field would almost certainly get in the way, it is a fact that were we to produce a compass sensitive to this galactic magnetic field, it would point directly towards the Cygnus constellation, and not to galactic centre as some might have thought.[39] So if one of the circumpolar constellations used by swans and other migratory birds to reach their northerly destinations is Cygnus, then we can begin to understand why shamans of the Upper Palaeolithic epoch might have come to associate this star group with the symbol of a swan.

Thus in the same way that Jeremy Narby was able to feel himself transforming into a large feline after taking *ayahuasca* in the Peruvian Amazon, it is possible that shamans living around flocks of swans were able to attune to the bird's own vision of the night sky. As we have seen, swan shamanism is a very archaic practice, which survived until fairly recently in many parts of Asia.

Even though Church Hole is merely one of the many hundreds of European cave sites with Upper Palaeolithic cave art, it almost certainly exemplifies the concept of shamanic communications in sacred caves using specific bird symbolism to represent cosmic life and death, as well as the clear connection, once again, with the stars of Cygnus.

Everything made sense – the Palaeolithic cult of Cygnus, their adoption of the swan as its totemic representation, and why the bird came to be associated with the primordial sound that brought the universe into creation. Yet I now looked beyond these facts for some more direct reason why the peoples of the Early and Middle Magdalenian eras, *c.*15,000–*c.*11,000 BC, suddenly began gravitating towards the use of deep caves, as if responding to some prehistoric call to prayer.

I sensed it had to be something more than simply the caves' orientation towards the stars, or the fact that they were used for conducting supernaturally inspired vision quests, or listening to the sound of the universe. Portraying symbolic representations of specific star groups on cave walls implied a powerful connection between the night sky and cave settings, something that was acknowledged by the Palaeolithic shamans who frequented such places. Somehow they came to recognize a certain quality about deep cave environments, one that drew them back again and again. They either sensed changes going on within themselves, or came to accept that the caves were having some profound effect on their lives. It was, I felt, a sense of recognition, or acceptance, seen in terms of a presence perceived as the cosmic source of life and death.

Yet I needed to find out what this might have been – what it was that so influenced their beliefs and practices, and caused them to take such an interest in the Cygnus constellation. For a while I wasn't quite sure what I was looking for, but after much searching, I finally found what I believe to be the answer.

CHAPTER TWENTY-ONE

Children of the Swan

Something quite fascinating happened during the 1980s – something that challenged everything physicists knew about the nature of the cosmos. At the time various deep underground particle detectors in Europe and the USA were being used in long-term experiments to track the predicted decay of protons – subatomic nuclei at the heart of every atom. If any nucleon decay could be detected, then it would have helped prove the then popular Grand Unified Theory (GUT) of physics, which asserts that all primary forces of the universe have a single unifying source and interaction.

Even though these underground facilities failed to achieve evidence of proton decay, they did come across something entirely unexpected. In addition to the very occasional decay of neutrinos – subatomic particles released through nuclear fusion reactions in the sun, or within supernovae – they repeatedly registered the presence of powerful cosmic rays from deep space. This was despite the fact that the location of the detectors, several hundred metres below the Earth's surface, should have shielded them from any form of cosmic radiation, the reason why they had been built at such depths in the first place. Yet repeatedly these facilities began tracking the disintegration of inexplicable particles that simply should not have existed.

One such experiment was NUSEX – actually a 150–tonne cube of metal plates and photomultiplier light sensors that register the decay of sub-atomic particles deep inside Mont Blanc in the French Alps. It began tracking these strange cosmic rays in 1983.[1] On the other side of the Atlantic, Soudan I, another newly operational proton-decay detector, built in a disused iron mine over 500 metres (a third of a mile) beneath the surface of Minnesota, also began to detect the presence of the same cosmic particles.[2]

In addition to this, at least two ground-based detectors of so-called extensive air showers (EAS) of cosmic radiation likewise began tracking the path of these highly unique, ultra high energy (UHE) and high energy (HE) cosmic rays, which would often occur coincident to the detection of *gamma*-rays coming from the same source. One of these facilities was the Fly's Eye, built in a remote part of the Utah desert under the control of the University of Utah. When it became operational in 1981 it consisted of 67 1.5 metre diameter mirrors pointing in different directions in order to cover the entire night sky. Each of the mirrors was focused upon clusters of 12 or 14 highly sensitive photomultipliers, set to record the passage of charged particles in the air showers through their excitation of atmospheric nitrogen.[3]

Along with the Kiel extensive air-shower (EAS) array in West Germany,[4] the Fly's Eye recorded erratic bursts of incoming cosmic radiation between 1981[5] and 30 October 1985, when, without warning, they simply stopped. Realizing that something quite amazing was going on, physicists began focusing their attention on further detecting these unique cosmic ray 'signal events'.

The Mystery of Cygnus X-3

Their source was easily determined, since the bursts of activity fluctuated with a cycle, or periodicity, of 4.8 hours, the unique 'fingerprint', or 'signal', previously recorded in connection with *gamma*-ray and X-ray emissions from a binary star system (i.e. two stars in orbit around each other) called Cygnus X-3. Indeed, Cygnus X-3 – situated around 30,000 light years from Earth – is one of the brightest sources of high energy *gamma*-rays in the entire galaxy (*see plate 28*).[6] Additionally, it is one of the strongest X-ray sources, as well as the loudest source of radio waves associated with an X-ray binary. It lies in the middle of the galactic plane, which is a dense band of stars and interstellar gas clouds in the central region of the Milky Way. With a declination of 40 degrees 57 minutes, and a right ascension of 20 hours 32 minutes, Cygnus X-3 – which is invisible to the naked eye – is located in the vicinity of Sadr (*gamma* Cygni),[7] the star at the very centre of Cygnus's cross-like pattern.

Cygnus X-3 was discovered in 1967, following the advent of *gamma*-ray astronomy. At the time of the anomalous 'signal events' of the 1980s, astronomers wrongly believed that it was a low-mass X-ray binary star system. However, during the 1990s infrared spectroscopy (a measurement technique for collecting infrared spectra) led astrophysicists to reclassify Cygnus X-3 as a high-mass binary consisting of two distinct components. One is what is termed a 'Wolf-Rayet star', a truly massive star, with a mass ten times that of the sun and a fast stellar wind. Its outer envelope of hydrogen gas is being systematically robbed by the intense gravitational field of its companion, a compact high-mass object situated closer than the diameter of the larger star. This process of 'accretion' (i.e. stealing from its companion), which heats

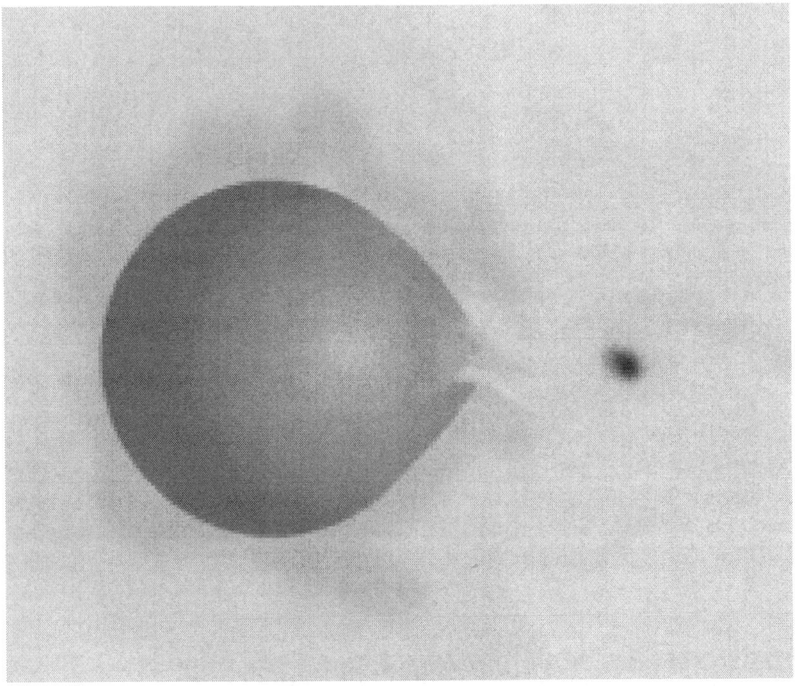

Fig. 50. Artist's impression of a high-mass X-ray binary system like Cygnus X-3. The compact star (either a black hole or neutron star) accretes mass from its enormous companion.

the gas to millions of degrees, results in the liberation of extreme amounts of X-rays, a form of cosmic radiation easily detected down here on Earth.

Although minute by comparison, the second object in Cygnus X-3 is a collapsed stellar core (known as a 'collapsar'), that has become either a 'neutron star' – quite literally an immensely dense mass of neutrons, with a diameter of only about 15–20 kilometres (9–12.5 miles) – or a black hole. The Cygnus X-3 star system can be pictured in terms of a lightweight gym ball (the Wolf-Rayet star) linked via a curved trail of luminous gas to a bright glowing Frisbee (the disc of accreted gases with the neutron star/black hole at its centre), which spins the gym ball around once every 4.8 hours, a quite astonishing sight by anyone's standards.

The Cygnet Mystery

The bigger problem for physicists was determining the nature of the cosmic rays coming from Cygnus X-3, which quickly gained the name 'cygnets', quite literally 'Children of the Swan', an expression that was certainly used in the 1980s by at least one popular science writer.[8] The fact that they seemed to be coming directly from Cygnus X-3, and had not been pulled off course by the galactic magnetic field,[9] meant that they had to be neutral particles,[10] which, like a neutrino, have no charge, and are therefore unaffected by magnetism. Because they do not interact on their journey here with the tiny traces of interstellar hydrogen that occupy the otherwise vacuum of space, they must also possess virtually zero mass.[11]

Such a conclusion, however, was always going to be controversial, for it meant that cygnets had to be travelling very close to the speed of light, one of the reasons why the cosmic rays retain their unique 4.8-hour periodicity across such a vast distance of space. The significance of this is that according to Einstein's special theory of relativity, no particle can go faster than the speed of light, since the greater the velocity you achieve, the quicker time passes in the outside world. In other words, although a cygnet travelling from Cygnus might take some 30,000 light years to reach here (with one light year – the distance light travels in a vacuum in one year – reckoned at approximately 9.46 trillion kilometres or 5.88 trillion miles) in normal time, just 10 to 15 minutes will have elapsed in the life of the particle.

Stranger still were the incredible kinetic energies being recorded in connection with cygnets. This was estimated to be 20 million times greater than the mass energy of a proton at rest, or 20,000 times stronger than any particle created in an accelerator.[12] John G Cramer, Professor of Physics at the University of Washington, put it this way back in 1985: 'The raw energy dumped by Cygnus X-3 is ten times greater than that seen by any other identified source of high energy particles.'[13] Some

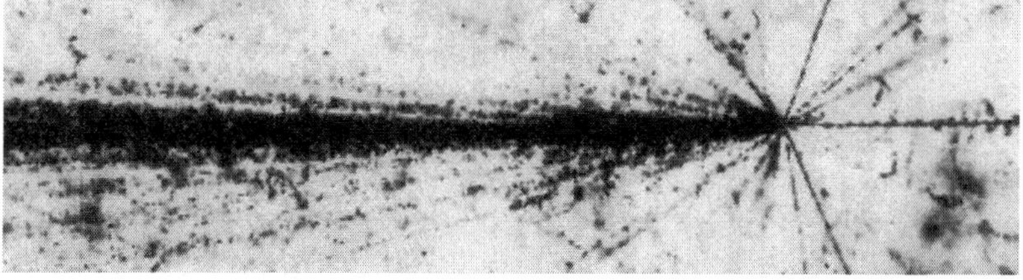

Fig. 51. Micrograph of a cosmic ray tracked on emulsion.

astrophysicists suggested that this level of energy could only have been accelerated into space by an intense 'proton beam' incident on the surface of a neutron star, causing 'a significant amount of material in the form of a fountain of gas' to be ejected outwards.[14] One group even described it as the 'first direct sign of ... cosmic-ray acceleration within the galaxy'. These were all poignant observations that, as we shall see, proved to be strikingly accurate.[15]

As to what cygnets might actually be, four suspects were on offer – photons, neutrinos, neutral atoms and neutrons. Yet none of these matched all the criteria,[16] leading one physicist to admit that the cygnet profile 'cannot be fit by any known particle.'[17] More exotic explanations followed. Hypothetical particles with names such as gravitinos, photinos, axions, winos, gluinos, monopoles, quark nuggets, squarks and R-odd particles were all proposed as candidates for the cygnet, but not one made absolute sense.[18] More conservatively, it was theorized that cygnets were simply a more energetic form of high energy *gamma*-rays, although these usually produce just 1/300th of the secondary particles generated by cygnets (see below).[19]

One challenging theory concerning the identity of the cygnet was the proposal that it might be the hypothetical 'Higg's boson',[20] a neutral particle with zero spin, which combines with charged particles called W and Z vector bosons to produce a 'Higg's field', seen as the mechanism for the production of mass. It is for this reason that the Higg's boson has become known as the 'God particle', since it is quite literally the unseen force behind the creation of the building blocks of matter.

So what then, you might ask, is the significance of Cygnus X-3 and its mysterious 'cygnets' to the theories presented in this book? The answer is simple, for if such unique cosmic rays were registered during the 1980s and, as we shall see, through at least until 2000, then unquestionably this was not the first time that they have bombarded the planet, nor will it be the last. If this is the case, it might have been the presence of cygnets in caves during past ages that was affecting the behaviour patterns and mindset of our Palaeolithic forebears, leading them to single out the Cygnus star cluster as significant in some way, most probably during intense shamanic experiences conducted deep underground.

I See No Cygnets

So fantastic was the entire concept of cygnets penetrating the Earth's atmosphere that, following their sudden cessation on 30 October 1985, sceptics immediately began to cast doubts on their very existence. It was pointed out that whilst some deep underground detectors and ground-based air-shower arrays did find cygnets, other similar experiments geographically close to these facilities recorded nothing. More damningly, new ground-based particle detection experiments, established with cygnets in mind, failed to detect anything unusual. This included the CYGNUS Experiment, an extensive air shower detector in Los Alamos, New Mexico, built in 1986 to monitor incoming high-energy *gamma*-rays from sources such as Cygnus X-3 and Hercules X-1, which is an X-ray pulsar that also produces high-energy cosmic rays, although at nowhere near the same energy potential.

Despite the assertion by Marvin Marshak, a leader of the University of Minnesota's Soudan I experiment, that different geologies and equipment set-ups would have hampered the chances of other experiments recording incoming cygnets,[21] the doubters persisted. There were even suggestions of professional misconduct on the part of the facilities in question, leading to the whole subject being swept quietly under the carpet. Today many particle physicists simply do not believe in the existence of undefined cosmic particles called cygnets, while astrophysicists steer away from the subject realizing what a hot potato it has become. Indeed, for them the official line is that nothing can be proved, and there is no consensus on whether or not Cygnus X-3 is one of the first confirmed sources of cosmic rays in the galaxy.

Feeling that there was a greater story to be told here, I read numerous articles and reports on the history of cygnets, and began piecing together a whole different story. To begin with, too much corroborative evidence exists simply to deny the fact that underground and ground-based experiments around the world were not detecting anomalous cosmic rays with Cygnus X-3's unique 4.8–hour periodicity during the 1980s.

Of even greater interest is the way in which the cygnet events were detected by the underground experiments. Normally, incoming primary particles, or high-energy nucleons, from any one of a number of galactic or extra-galactic sources, split up as they collide with atom nuclei in the Earth's upper atmosphere. As a result, neutrons and electrons break away from the atom nuclei, causing the destruction of the primary particle and the birth of short-lived secondary particles, including so-called mesons or muons. These then cascade down to Earth as 'air showers', their final disintegration hopefully being tracked by one of several ground-based air shower arrays scattered around the world. Very few mesons or muons have a chance to penetrate the ground, the reason why particle accelerators can operate free from cosmic ray intrusions deep underground.

What was different about cygnets is that they not only produced phenomenal amounts of muons in the upper atmosphere, which would uncharacteristically pierce through rock down to the level of the detectors, as was reported at Los Alamos occasionally in connection with Hercules X-1, but some of the *primary* particles, direct from Cygnus X-3, were penetrating solid rock to a depth of at least a 'few hundred meters',[22] before they themselves collided with atom nuclei to produce secondary particles. The creation of muons deep underground was confirmed by their angle of spread, which was unlike anything tracked before by nucleon-decay detectors.[23] This was an incredible discovery, for, as previously mentioned, the only other cosmic particles usually tracked at such depths are neutrinos either from the sun or supernovae, which pass through the Earth and us without any noticeable interaction. No other stellar body has so far produced such exotic particles as Cygnus X-3, singling them out as apparently unique in physics.

In addition to these mysteries, I discovered that at least two other underground experiments appear to have registered anomalous incoming cosmic rays from Cygnus X-3 between 1986 and 1994. One was the Ohya air shower detector in Japan, situated in a tunnel 33 metres (108 feet) underground,[24] and the other was the Gotthard underground detector, located beneath 1,460 metres (4,790 feet) of rock in a cave on one side of the St Gotthard road tunnel, deep in the Swiss Alps.[25] Moreover, Soudan II, the successor to Soudan I, reported an all too familiar flurry of muon activity coincident with the appearance of large radio flares from Cygnus X-3, initially in January 1991[26] and then again in April 2000.[27] Indeed, in 1999, the Soudan II collaboration concluded in a published paper that during the first ten years of the experiment's operation, from 1989 to 1999, they had regularly tracked incoming cosmic particles from Cygnus X-3, which they saw as 'either exotic interactions of known primaries, exotic primaries or very large fluxes of neutrinos or photons.'[28]

However, even the Soudan II team admitted that interest in the topic had virtually died away, with no other reports published on the subject for five years, and interest in Cygnus X-3 switching back to monitoring its somewhat erratic record of X-ray, *gamma*-ray, infrared and radio emissions. Then suddenly everything changed.

Microblazar – Found!

In 1997, Mike McCollough of NASA's Marshall Space Flight Center produced a high-resolution radio map of Cygnus X-3 using the Very Long Baseline Array (VLBA), described as a 'continent-sized radio interferometer', which is a series of telescopes all pointing in the same direction that combine their signals to produce stronger results. In the case of the VLBA, it is made up of ten radio-telescope antennas, each with a dish 25 meters (82 feet) in diameter, spread out from Mauna Kea on Hawaii's Big Island to St Croix in the US Virgin Islands, a distance of just over 8,000 kilometres (5,000 miles).

What McCullough saw intrigued him greatly, for it showed a one-sided particle jet about 50 milliarcseconds in length (this is a measurement of parallax, the apparent shift of an object against a background due to a change in observer position relative to distance), produced by Cygnus X-3's neutron star/black hole as it insatiably accretes gas-fuelled stellar wind from its companion star. Such 'relativistic jets', as they are called, were already known to astrophysicists (*see plate 30*). They are in fact narrow magnetic beams of plasma, i.e. ionized gas, and particle radiation produced by gas-accreting black holes and neutron stars.

These particle beams, considered to be one of the most violent forces in the universe, can retain their tubular or conical forms across light years of space, due to the presence of powerful magnetic sheaths. They are like unimaginable searchlights, which when turned on destroy everything in their path, causing powerful radio emissions in the process. They might also be likened to cosmic gun barrels, shooting out particle barrages that can cross entire galaxies, retaining their velocity, force and momentum virtually indefinitely. Only when they are pulled off course by the galactic magnetic field, or broken up by constant collisions with the tiny amounts of interstellar hydrogen that exists in the emptiness of space is their progress finally halted.

Although exciting news for a radio astronomer, there was nothing too special about this discovery by McCollough. Two days later, however, Cygnus X-3's relativistic jet had extended to a length of 120 milliarcseconds, an increase of apocalyptic proportions, before it simply vanished from view. McCollough and his colleagues were now *very* excited, for they had witnessed what was for them one of the most amazing events ever recorded in the history of astronomy. These findings led McCollough to announce, through an official NASA press release in February 2000, that Cygnus X-3 was a microblazar (a term explained below) since 'we were looking straight down the jet',[29] in other words its particle jet had been aimed straight at the Earth.

Such energetic phenomena connected with a high-mass binary system usually defines it in astronomical terms as a 'microquasar', an appellation that Cygnus X-3 therefore justly deserves[30] (*see plate 29*). Yet so powerful did its one-sided jet seem to Mike McCollough that he controversially felt compelled to compare it with those produced by Active Galactic Nuclei (AGN), which are thought to be supermassive black holes at the centre of every galaxy. This includes our own galaxy, the Milky

Way, even though its AGN is thought to have been dormant for tens of thousands of years. AGNs are known to produce relativistic jets (such as M87 (Virgo A) in the constellation of Virgo – *see plate 30*), and when these particle beams are directed our way, in other words their central axis is aligned towards the Earth, astrophysicists term them galactic blazars (such as 3C279, an active galaxy also in Virgo).

Even though several neutron stars and black holes in our own galaxy have spectacularly produced relativistic jets (such as the microquasar SS433 in Aquila), none had so far been discovered with a jet aimed right at us, classifying it as a microblazar (i.e. the kid brother of a much larger galactic blazar). Thus if Cygnus X-3 is to be classed as a microblazar, then it is unique in being the only one observed in our galaxy. Yet to learn that the most powerful cosmic accelerator in the galaxy, with an acknowledged violent disposition and penchant for cosmic pinball, is aimed at the Earth, might not be the news that everyone wants to hear.

The exact mechanism involved in producing such powerful relativistic jets remains unclear, while it is still not known whether the smaller object forming part of the Cygnus X-3 binary system is a neutron star or a black hole, for it cannot, in theory, be both (although some astrophysicists now argue that it is either a neutron star with an exotic core of what is known as 'strange matter', composed of sub-atomic particles called quarks, or even that it might be a 'quark star', an even more compact collapsar, just a few kilometres in size, composed wholely of 'strange quark matter'[31]). Moreover, there exist some teething problems with regards to McCollough's findings, for in October–November 2000, just eight months after his dramatic announcement that Cygnus X-3 was a microblazar, radio astronomers working for the National Radio Astronomy Observatory (NRAO) in the United States managed to take three pictures of what appear to be bipolar jets emerging from either side of Cygnus X-3's active core.[32] This is in contrast to McCollough's VLBA observations, which clearly show a one-sided relativistic jet aimed at the Earth.

Nothing can explain this discrepancy, other than the suggestion that the accretion disc wobbles to such a degree that it causes jets constantly to shift position, like some Hollywood laser show. If this is not the case, then somehow Cygnus X-3 manages to shoot out jets on more than one axis, a suggestion hinted at by the fact that in 2002 radio astrophysicists confirmed that it might well possess two types of jet – twin-particle beams that emerge from either side of the central axis, and a single-sided particle jet that erupts separately.[33]

It is almost certain that Cygnus X-3's frequent relativistic jets are the true source of its unique cosmic rays and high-energy *gamma*-rays, which are projected through deep space without any effect from the galactic magnetic field, until, finally, they penetrate the Earth's atmosphere. In fact, the idea of Cygnus X-3 being a microblazar makes complete sense of much of what was recorded or predicted in connection with cygnets, including the violent manner in which they were able to pierce solid rock for the first 'few hundred meters', before splitting to form short-lived muons.

More significantly, the signal events from Cygnus X-3 which feature the arrival of cosmic rays generally coincide with intense bursts of energies across a wide band of electromagnetic frequencies that are known to accompany the production of relativistic jets. For instance, in October 1985, the cosmic rays detected around the world coming from Cygnus X-3 (*see above*) coincided with intense bursts of high energy *gamma*-rays and radio emissions,[34] while the unusual muon activity registered by the Soudon II experiment between 1991 and 2000 invariably coincided with the production of large or intermediate radio flares.[35]

All of this says that when Cygnus X-3 shoots out its extremely narrow, magnetically-driven particle jets at close to the speed of light, the Earth will almost always be showered with different types of electromagnetic radiation, from radio waves through to X-rays, *gamma*-rays, infrared radiation and the truly mysterious cosmic rays called cygnets.

There were two major radio flares in 2001,[36] but since then Cygnus X-3 has been relatively quiet, although the results of a seven-year study into the fluctuations of its high-amplitude X-ray emissions showed that, while erratic, the pulses display an underlying oscillation pattern of precisely 71 days.[37] Monitoring continues, and the great 'explosion' of activity predicted in 2000 by McCollough, described by one science writer as 'the next Big Bang',[38] is still expected (and see the Postscript for news on Cygnus X-3's more recent activities). When, finally, it comes, perhaps it will at last provide the vital evidence needed to confirm that Cygnus X-3 is one of the most exotic star systems in the whole of the galaxy.

Cosmic Rays in the Ice Age

The question we must now ask is exactly how powerful cosmic rays from sources such as Cygnus X-3 might have affected the Palaeolithic mindset, and caused them to revere deep caves as the cosmic source of life and death. A date of *c.*17,000 BP for the beginning of a dramatic upsurge of interest in Cygnus by our earliest ancestors coincides with the turning-point of the last Ice Age, after which time the ice sheets that had covered the Earth for tens of thousands of years very slowly began to recede. What is more, it has long been considered that a relationship exists between cosmic ray activity and glacial cycles. For example, an international group of scientists recently announced that the intensity of cosmic rays reaching the upper atmosphere might affect cloud production, leading to changes in the Earth's climate.[39] This would mean that the planet becomes more vulnerable to cosmic rays at certain times in its long term climatic cycles, reflected in the onset and cessation of ice ages.

Scientists are able to determine increases and decreases in cosmic rays hitting the Earth, due to the presence in the geological record of a cosmogenic isotope with a half-life called Beryllium-10 (Be-10), produced as a by-product when incoming cosmic rays collide with the atomic nuclei of atmospheric nitrogen and oxygen. These secondary particles then settle in ocean or lake sediments, or within polar ice, or even inside forming stalagmites and stalactites. For instance, Be-10 detected in a stalagmite removed from an underwater blue hole, a deep water cave, in the Bahamas has revealed that between 45,000 and 11,000 BP, when the blue hole would have been above sea-level, the Earth was bombarded by twice the amount of cosmic radiation as it is today.[40]

On this same theme, an ice core extracted from Summit, in Greenland, and examined by the Greenland Ice Core Project (GRIP)[41] for levels of Be-10, has revealed that there was a dramatic increase in cosmic rays reaching the Earth's atmosphere, beginning *c.*40,000 BP and lasting for around 1,500 years. This information correlates with data from another ice core from Vostok in Antarctica, which shows a similar peak of activity *c.*39,000–*c.*37,000 BP.[42] Although the GRIP collaboration felt it unnecessary to check for Be-10 between *c.*18,000–*c.*11,000 BP, there is a hint that another wave of activity began *c.*20,000–19,000 BP and was destined to rise to a peak *c.*17,000–*c.*14,000 BP. This seems certain from the Vostok ice core results, which highlight a later spike of activity that seems to commence *c.*16,000 BP and end close to 13,000 BP.

Although the above data derives from just two ice cores extracted from sites at opposite ends of the globe, they serve to indicate that there were at least two periods of intense cosmic ray activity during the last Ice Age,[43] If this is correct, then there is a high probability that some percentage of what was going on, especially during the later spike of activity, *c.*17,000–*c.*14,000 BP involved Cygnus X-3 in its role as the first proposed microblazar. Certainly, we know that the smaller object in the binary system has functioned in its present capacity as a neutron star/black hole, rapidly accreting gas via its giant companion's stellar wind, for anything up to 700,000 years.[44] This would mean that Cygnus X-3 has been firing out relativistic jets in the direction of Earth for a very long time indeed. So, has Cygnus X-3 really had some influence on human evolution?

Cosmic Irradiation and Human Evolution

Cosmic particles, such as neutrinos, pass through us all the time, and in almost all cases they will not affect us. However, depending upon their type, mass, and kinetic energy, the secondary particles they create, generally in the upper atmosphere, called muons do frequently make contact with our cell nuclei, and when this happens they can irradiate, i.e. damage or alter, our DNA, causing genetic mutation or even deletion in healthy genomes. This is what happens when UV-radiation from the sun produces malignant tumors, or when people become seriously ill after intense exposure to other forms of radiation such as X-rays, geologically produced radon gas (*see below*), and industrial radiation leaks, such as the high profile accidents at the Three Mile Island Nuclear Generating Station in Pennsylvania, USA, in 1979 and Chernobyl in the Ukraine in 1986.

For some time, there has been concern over the increased risks of cancer and leukaemia to those who spend prolonged periods in the upper atmosphere, where cosmic rays are at their most intense. Astronauts and flight crews have been singled out as particularly vulnerable to cosmic rays and *gamma*-rays, not only with regards to their own safety, but also due to the fact that DNA mutations might occur in their ova or sperm, which will then be transferred to any offspring, a conclusion denied in a recent official study of the effects of cosmic rays on living cells.[45]

Obviously, the human body has the ability to repair or replace damaged cells, and it is always possible that exposure to cosmic radiation might cause more subtle changes to occur over a much longer period of time, especially underground, where its effect would have been less severe, and so might have had a more positive effect. It is my belief that long term exposure to increased levels of cosmic rays out in the open would have had a quite different impact on the human body – more intense and ultimately far more harmful. Although those outside on the surface will have been irradiated in the same way as those underground, it is likely that any genetic changes in the human body would have occurred too rapidly, too soon.

Radon Health Mines

One is reminded here of what are known as radon 'healing mines', which are found today in various countries including the United States, Britain, Germany and Russia. Radon is a radioactive gas, produced by the natural decay of uranium in rocks and soil. Exposure to it for prolonged periods can kill or damage living cells, causing genetic mutations and cancer. Indeed, it has been regularly cited as a major cause of lung cancer in people living in areas with radon-producing rock. In contrast, however, short-term exposure to the odourless gas can be beneficial, alleviating or even curtailing painful ailments such as chronic rheumatism and arthritis, as well as respiratory problems and skin diseases. It is also believed to cause miraculous cures of the sort that might be expected from a trip to the cave grotto at the pilgrimage centre of Lourdes in France.

It is for this reason that certain old uranium mines around the world, which still produce low levels of radon gas, have over the past 50 years become health spas for those seeking miracle cures. Visitors to places such as Montana's Merry Widow Healing Mine in Boulder, or the Earth Angel Radio Gas Mine in nearby Basin, descend underground, where they remain in specially prepared healing rooms for prescribed periods, usually from one to three hours (with return visits allowed on consecutive days). In many cases a series of exposures will keep long-term illnesses at bay for up to a year, leaving the patient free from medication. Yet afterwards symptoms might start to come back, necessitating further visits to the mines, with many people ideally returning yearly or even every other year.

How exactly low doses of a radioactive substance like radon might accelerate the body's natural healing processes is a complete mystery. Some have claimed that the gas stimulates nerves, which enable the healing process to quicken. Others suggest that it stimulates the pituitary gland into producing health-giving hormones and natural steroids. Many see the whole process simply as a miracle of God. More significantly, from our point of view, it is not only miraculous cures that are claimed. Some visitors speak of experiencing a sense of well-being and exhilaration, almost as if they are undergoing some kind of religious transformation.[46]

The reason for introducing this subject here is to demonstrate how, even though high levels of radiation – whether terrestrial or otherwise in origin – invariably causes harmful effects to the human body, much lower doses can have lasting beneficial effects. This includes cellular regeneration and healing, as well as an influence on the parts of the brain responsible for producing religious experiences, most likely in the temporal lobe region. Probably, our Palaeolithic ancestors would quickly have realized that caves producing what we know today as radon gas should be avoided, since prolonged periods in these only made a person sick. Short-term exposure within them might have been more beneficial. However, there would have been many other caves to serve their purposes, and these would only ever have been affected by incoming cosmic particles.

It is therefore extremely likely that an exposure to low doses of cosmic radiation, such as that which might be experienced deep underground from point sources such as Cygnus X-3, will have had long-term beneficial effects which would probably not have been available from massive exposure to cosmic radiation on the surface. Did this include subtle changes in the biological, chemical and neurological make up of the human body, arguably across many generations, with 70 (i.e. around 1,500–2,000 years) being the minimum amount needed for what is known as a germline mutation to occur? Such changes might have included alterations in behaviour and actions, as well as an increase in capability and intelligence, along with advances in creative and artistic skills. All of this might have inspired a strong connection with deep caves, which thus became places of great sanctity, since they were seen quite literally as the essence of life itself.

It was a bold and extraordinary theory, and just as I was preparing to put forward Cygnus X-3 as the possible source of incoming cosmic rays during this distant epoch, *c.*17,000–*c.*14,000 BP, came news of an American scientific team proposing almost exactly the same thing. As we shall see in the final chapter, they too now believe that relativistic jets originating from a microblazar were responsible for a rapid acceleration in human evolution at the height of the last Ice Age.

CHAPTER TWENTY-TWO

The True God Star

Dr Aden Meinel, Professor Emeritus of the College of Optical Studies at the University of Arizona, Tucson, and formerly of the Jet Propulsion Laboratory (JPL) at the California Institute of Technology, Pasadena, is a co-founder of the Meinel Institute, a scientific think-tank based in Las Vegas, Nevada. In a key-note presentation delivered to 500 archaeologists and students on the opening night of TAG 2005,[1] the conference of the Theoretical Archaeology Group held in Sheffield, England, between 19–21 December that year, he pointed out that the 40,000 BP spike in cosmic rays traceable in the Beryllium-10 records of the Greenland ice core examined by GRIP (*see previous chapter, page 260*) coincided with the extinction of certain species of Ice Age animals and the sudden emergence of others.

Turning then to human evolution, Aden Meinel reminded the somewhat sceptical audience that up until *c.*40,000 BP Europe and Asia had been the domain of Neanderthal man (*Homo sapiens neanderthalensis*), who was well adapted to the cold, rugged conditions. Then along came our own species, modern humans (*Homo sapiens sapiens*), at just about the same time that our Neanderthal cousins disappeared from the fossil record. With this knowledge, Aden Meinel proposed that cosmic irradiation over the course of 70 or so generations – around 1,500 years – caused the Neanderthals to mutate into anatomically modern humans. In other words, the 40,000 BP 'event', as he was calling it, signalled the emergence of *Homo sapiens sapiens*, and the death knell of the Neanderthal race.

As bold a theory as this might seem, it is, however, fraught with problems, not least of all the discovery of Neanderthal remains in small pockets across Europe, which have provided dating evidence as late as 30,000 BP,[2] showing that the race co-existed with our own for anything up to 10,000 years after we entered the landmass. More damning, however, is the fact that the fossil record clearly supports the theory first put forward some 15 years ago by Professor Chris Stringer, Head of the Human

Origins Programme at London's Natural History Museum, that our earliest modern ancestors emerged out of Africa, where the race had remained in isolation for anything up to 150,000 years, and quickly began populating Europe and Asia *c.*60,000–*c.*70,000 years ago.[3] Accordingly, groups of modern humans, who had previously only ever experienced warm, temperate climates, made the decision to enter much colder regions close to the edge of the ice fields, exploring fresh hunting grounds beyond their usual territories, perhaps in quest of such large beasts as mammoth and bison. Others simply followed coastlines in their eternal search for new seafood resources, reaching the Middle East first, before moving into southern Asia and, finally, Australia in less than 10,000 years.

Having said this, the sudden appearance across western Europe of sophisticated cave art, *c.*32,500–*c.*30,000 BP (see below), is a complete mystery, tending to suggest that changes in human behaviour relating to creativity and symbolic representation had occurred extremely rapidly indeed, especially as the oldest confirmed rock art outside of Europe are the painted slabs of stone found in the Apollo 11 Cave in southwest Namibia, which date to *c.*25,500–*c.*23,500 BP. Attributed to the ancestors of the San (Bushmen), there is then a massive gap in African rock art with the next oldest examples, found in the Cave of Bees at Matopos in Zimbabwe, dating to *c.*10,500 BP. The oldest rock art in Australia, which has been accurately dated to *c.*30,000–*c.*25,000 BP, is to be found in the rock shelters of Cape York, northern Queensland. Even earlier rock art might well exist in parts of Australia, although exact dating becomes difficult for examples earlier than 30,000 BP.

Despite the early age of rock art in Africa and Australia, it is clear that European cave art developed dramatically several thousand years beforehand, creating impressive subterranean chambers filled with mesmeric paintings. The earliest known cave art, dating to *c.*32,500–*c.*30,000 BP, is to be found in the Ardèche region of southeast France. Here in the Chauvet cave, discovered as recently as 1994, hundreds of beautiful representations of cave bears, horses, bison, cave lions, mammoths and rhinos cover the walls. There is even an abstract naked female torso, a 'Venus', painted on the curved surface of a stalactite.

Thereafter European cave art remained at the same level of sophistication until the Early Magdalenian, *c.*17,000–*c.*15,000 BP, when there was a dramatic increase of interest in the deepest recesses of cave complexes, mostly in France and Spain. It was a process which, as previously mentioned, reached a climax in the Middle Magdalenian, *c.*15,000–*c.*13,000 BP, before gradually waning in the Late Magdalenian, *c.*13,000-11,000 BP.

Even though the Meinels' claim that *Homo sapiens sapiens* evolved from the

Neanderthal race is untenable, given the evidence presented above, the idea that our distant ancestors might have undergone genetic changes through exposure to cosmic rays, *c.*40,000–*c.*37,000 BP, is worth considering further, especially with the flowering of cave art in Europe shortly after this time. So let us now examine their evidence for this 'event' a little closer.

The Meinel group determined from the Be-10 records of the Greenland ice core that the greatest level of irradiation would have been at a latitude of 65 degrees north (+/- 10 degrees), a line that embraces Canada, northern Europe and northern Asia. The influence would have decreased the further south one went, until at five degrees north the exposure would have been halved, and by 20 degrees south, a latitude that embraces South America, southern Africa and Australia, it would have diminished to zero.

As we know, the distinctive Upper Palaeolithic cave art of western Europe, which emerged first at places such as the Chauvet cave in southeast France, marked the beginning of an entirely new way of life that developed in full very quickly and underwent relatively few changes until *c.*17,000 BP, when suddenly something important happened worldwide. For instance, we find a new understanding of astronomy (at Lascaux, for instance), as well as the use of a stellar-based solar calendar (China). This time-frame also coincides with the formulation of magico-religious symbolism worldwide, the spread of a universal cosmology regarding the existence of the cosmic axis, presided over by a 'bird of creation' (i.e. Cygnus), and possibly even transoceanic travel (the Solutrean peoples reaching North America).

This sudden burst of human activity towards the end of the last Ice Age led eventually to the emergence of agriculture, metalworking, fired pottery, beer, wine, a symbolic written language, and everything we associate with the Neolithic evolution, *c.*12,000–9000 BP, which occurred first on the Euphrates river of Upper Mesopotamia, i.e. southeast Turkey and northern Syria. Here in the biblical land of Eden was the fabled 'garden' in which mankind's putative first parents were beguiled into temptation by the Serpent, seen as a symbol of the Watchers in the Book of Enoch. These mythical individuals of tall stature and pale complexion were said to have revealed to mortal kind the arts and sciences of heaven. Here too, in Upper Mesopotamia, the earliest stone temples were constructed by a faceless people *c.*11,500–11,000 BP, and these must be seen as the precursors of all subsequent rectilinear and curvilinear structures built anywhere in the world. Something very profound went on in southeast Turkey and northern Syria during this period, and there seems little question that it acted as a transitional phase between the achievements of the Palaeolithic cave artists who created the wonderful art in western

Europe, *c.*32,500–11,000 BP and the rise of civilization down on the plains of Iraq's Fertile Crescent around 7,500 years ago. Could it be possible that the intervention of cosmic rays during the Later Upper Palaeolithic age, *c.*17,000–14,000 BP (and arguably earlier), was behind not just the acceleration in human evolution during this period, but also for catalyzing the events in Upper Mesopotamia responsible for the birth of civilization itself?

If all this is correct then it makes some sense of the findings from the Greenland ice core, which suggest that this later period of acceleration roughly coincides with the *c.*17,000–*c.*14,000 BP peak of activity highlighted by its Be-10 levels (*c.*16,000–*c.*13,000 BP in the Vostok ice core). Even though the Meinel group see no relevance in this data, since an examination of the *c.*18,000 to *c.*11,000 BP phase of the Greenland ice core has yet to be carried out by GRIP,[4] their findings regarding the proposed *c.*40,000 BP event echo exactly what I am saying regarding the period *c.*17,000-14,000 BP, when a second phase of acceleration in human evolution would seem to have taken place. Could there have been two periods of rapid growth caused by a sustained exposure to incoming cosmic radiation, the first between *c.*40,000-37,000 BP and the second sometime *c.*17,000–*c.*14,000 BP? If so, then did the Earth simply become more susceptible to incoming cosmic rays at these times, due to changes in the climatic cycles, or had some special event occurred in space on two separate occasions?

A Glint in the Cat's Eye

In order to try and answer these questions, the Meinels examined a 60,000–year window of cosmic ray activity, *c.*80,000–*c.*20,000 BP, comparing it with the Earth's precessional cycle, which they take to be 23,000 years instead of the more usual 26,000 years. By combining the results with the predicted impact of sustained cosmic rays on the Earth's magnetic field, it provided them with a suspected angle of declination for the stellar object they felt might have been responsible for the cosmic irradiation. They then calculated the other vital astronomical coordinate – the so-called 'right ascension', which is celestial longitude measured in hours using the northern celestial pole as the turning point of the heavens. This enabled them to isolate a 20-degree diameter search area in the region of Draco, the dragon, which borders the Cygnus region. Here they scanned the skies looking for a microblazar, i.e. a microquasar with a relativistic jet aimed at the earth, that might have been responsible for the cosmic rays that caused the increased levels of Be-10 present in the ice cores. They found just one possible candidate, and this was a planetary nebula called the Cat's Eye (NGC 6543), unanimously accepted by astronomers to be around 3,300 light years from Earth,[5] even though the Meinels argue fiercely that it is just 130 light years away.[6]

A planetary nebula has nothing to do with planets. It is a mass of glowing, nebulous clouds of gas and dust spread out across the equivalent of hundreds or even thousands of solar systems, created by a dying central star, which in the case of the Cat's Eye is most probably a Wolf-Rayet 'O'-type star.[7] Around 1,000 years ago, its outer layer burst, creating two oval-shaped gas clouds that interlink at right angles to give the nebula a flower-like appearance. Beyond these are up to nine faint concentric rings, or shells, thought to be the debris of a series of regular convulsions in which the core puffed out even older layers over a period of around 13,500 years. As a nebula the Cat's Eye is small, its dust cloud calculated as having just 1.17 times the mass of our own sun. Its central star, although currently inactive, is destined one day to go supernova before collapsing to form a super-dense 'white dwarf'. However, it does still possess some interesting properties. For instance, the Cat's Eye is known to produce soft X-ray emissions,[8] while it would also appear to produce bipolar lobes, or jets, which scatter the nebulous clouds in the polar regions of the inner shell.

The Meinels propose that the Cat's Eye is a tight binary system with a jet-producing black hole accreting mass from the dying central star. They cite its active period, deduced from an evaluation of the nebula's outer halo of gas and dust, as being *c.*80,000–*c.*20,000 BP, which they say fits precisely with the cyclic levels of Be-10 preserved in the Greenland ice core. Moreover, because they view the nebula as just 130 light years away, the slim magnetic sheath that holds together the jet would easily, they believe, have penetrated the solar system, irradiating the Earth in the process. Thus, in their opinion, it becomes the likeliest candidate for what they see as the 1,500-year peak of activity *c.*40,000 BP, which they consider to have accelerated human evolution.

'Planetary Nebulae are Wimpy Objects'

However, this drastic reappraisal of the Cat's Eye finds little support among leading academics in the field. For instance, You-Hua Chu, Professor and Chair of the Astronomy Department of the University of Illinois, who has studied the Cat's Eye nebula for 20 years, is unable to see it as any closer than 3,300 light years from Earth. She finds no convincing evidence for it being a binary system, or that its nebulous clouds conceal a black hole. Furthermore, she points out that its bipolar lobes, not really jets, are shown in X-ray photographs as emerging from either side of the central flower-like region 'meaning that we are not seeing them pole-on'.[9]

Chu further makes it clear that these bipolar lobes are not to be confused with relativistic jets of the sort produced by microquasars or galactic blazars (*see Chapter Twenty-One*). Although the Cat's Eye's bipolar lobes might reach velocities of hundreds or even thousands of kilometres per second, relativistic jets reach velocities in the range of 300,000 kilometres (180,000 miles) per second, close to the speed of light.[10] What is more, Chu is certain that the nebula does not produce cosmic rays. 'No, it's not powerful enough,' she says, adding, curtly: 'Planetary nebulae are wimpy objects.'[11] Indeed, she fails to see why anyone would want the Cat's Eye 'to be responsible for things it was not able to do'.[12]

Chu's opinions are echoed by her Illinois colleague Dr Robert Gruendl, a research scientist who in 2001 formed part of the team assessing the nature of the Cat's Eye's X-ray emissions using the Chandra X-ray observatory.[13] In his words:

> I don't think the Cat's Eye (or more specifically the star that formed the Cat's Eye) will work for this. The time scale might work out for the star going through pulsations and throwing off its outer layers but I don't think that cosmic rays in any substantial quantity would be generated when this happened. In the current 'best' models the wind shocks associated with those layers being thrown off might be sufficient to generate X-rays (but not cosmic rays).[14]

Gruendl admits that a potential microblazar, such as Cygnus X-3, would work much better, although he is unsure about how close the source would need to be in order that the acceleration of particles produced by relativistic jets might reach the Earth.[15] However, as we have seen, distance is no object, since Cygnus X-3's unique, long-lasting neutral particles are unaffected by the galactic magnetic field. They travel at relativistic speeds and, since they have more or less zero mass, these moving particles rarely interact with the minute background levels of interstellar hydrogen to be found on their path between Cygnus X-3 and here.[16]

But is the Cat's Eye a Binary System?

The Meinels' belief in the energetic potential of the Cat's Eye nebula has other detractors. Noam Soker, at the Faculty of Physics at the Technion (the Israel Institute of Technology) in Haifa, is one of the world's leading theorists on the structure and formation of planetary nebula. He has much to say about the Meinels' interpretation of the Cat's Eye, and has set down his comments in a private paper.[17]

Soker argues that all planetary nebulae of irregular shape, as opposed to those with a spherical appearance, are binary systems. Their central dying star would be accompanied by a so-called main-sequence star, like our own sun, with others possessing a neutron star or even a black hole.[18] In the case of the Cat's Eye, he sees it as a binary system consisting of a burnt-out supergiant (the progenitor of the nebula) and a star similar to our own sun, the latter being the point source of the X-ray emission discovered by Chu and her team using the Chandra X-ray observatory.[19]

In Soker's opinion, the Cat's Eye's diffuse X-rays are 'similar in nature to other nebulae', and began once the main-sequence star became magnetically active, something that occurred as it was set spinning by drawing mass and momentum from the dying central star. This is firm evidence, he says, that the companion cannot be a black hole, and so can never have produced powerful jets of the sort proposed by the Meinels.[20]

These views are supported by Romano Corradi, another top theorist on planetary nebulae.[21] He says that although the Cat's Eye is a binary star system at present not fully understood, the nebula possesses neither the mechanics nor the energy to have irradiated the Earth.[22] That said, he finds the Meinels' theories fascinating, and definitely worth pursuing by all open-minded scientists.

Despite these serious flaws in their chosen candidate for the 40,000 BP cosmic ray event,[23] the Meinels' allegiance to the Cat's Eye remains unshakable.[24] Their rigid stance is understandable, especially since by their own admission it is the only 'unusual object' within their chosen search area of the sky.[25]

In email correspondence with the Meinels, I have discussed the strengths and weaknesses of their theory, and they admit to finding my own proposals concerning Cygnus X-3's possible influence on human evolution 'very interesting'.[26] In fact, before coming upon the beguiling sight of the Cat's Eye – one of the most beautiful objects in the galaxy – they admit to checking neighbouring Cygnus for a possible candidate. However, they 'didn't see any object likely to be producing a jet of cosmic rays',[27] which I see as a major oversight on their part. Their principal reason for rejecting Cygnus X-3 as a likely candidate for the incoming cosmic rays is that it lies outside their designated search area, and, in their opinion, the Cat's Eye fits all the criteria they have set out to establish the true source of the cosmic rays that they see as bombarding the Earth *c.*40,000 BP.

In my opinion, Cygnus X-3 is a better candidate by far for at least a percentage of the high levels of Be-10 recorded in the Greenland and Vostok ice cores during the last Ice Age. It adheres to the estimated declination of the search area offered by the Meinel Institute (+65 degrees north +/- 10 degrees) in the time-frame concerned, and fits exactly the source of the cosmic rays that the Meinels see as irradiating the Earth during the last Ice Age. Furthermore, we know that Cygnus X-3 has been active in this capacity for up to several hundred thousand years, meaning that it has been out there causing chaos for a very long time indeed.

In the end there are two theories that come out of this ground-breaking research concerning the possible accelerated evolution of the human race owing to cosmic rays. Firstly, it may have increased the speed of evolution of the entire human race (i.e. from Neanderthals to *Homo sapiens sapiens* – the Meinels' contention), or, more likely, it resulted in enhanced evolution among only some humans, qualifying them for the role of shamans/priests, communicators deep underground with the perceived cosmic source of life and death. Either solution might prove to be correct, yet far more research is needed before any final answers might be forthcoming (although see the Postscript below for a review of the extraordinary work of British anthropological writer Denis Montgomery, who in two books argues persuasively that cosmic rays originating from the Cygnus region helped accelerate human behaviour and evolution during the last Ice Age).

Uttering the Logos

If such intense cosmic ray activity had contaminated the Earth in a former age, causing noticeable changes in human evolution, then it is extremely unlikely that Palaeolithic shamans would have been able to determine the direction it was coming from above ground. But deep beneath the earth it might have been a different story. As we have seen, aside from neutrinos, the only primary particles known to penetrate rock down to great depths come from Cygnus X-3. If this had been the case in the epoch under question, *c.*17,000–*c.*14,000 BP, it is possible that its unique fingerprint became known to those who entered deep caves to commune with the 'great divine' (the signal events from Cygnus X-3 wax and wane in accordance with the rising and setting of the star group, and since its cosmic activity has also shown an underlying 71-day periodicity, this cycle might have been recognized unconsciously by our Palaeolithic ancestors. It is a particularly appealing prospect in the knowledge that 5 x 71 days equals 355 days, the length of a lunar year, when not 354 days.[28] Lunar cycles were especially important during the Palaeolithic age, as the number of lunar notations found on portable artefacts from this epoch has shown.[29] Moreover, the swan was often a symbol of moon gods and the night,[30] while *kuu*, the name given by the original inhabitants of Greece and Italy to the moon, along with the Estonian *kukene*, 'Little Moon', might well have a root in common with *kuknos*, the Greek for 'swan' [the Latin *cygnus*.] [31]).

It is possible that the proposed unzipping of the pre-existing program within our junk DNA, causing the release of information regarding the cosmic origins of life (*see Chapter Nineteen*), was first effected during periods of high intensity cosmic ray activity, enhanced perhaps by the use of psychedelic substances in radiation-charged cave environments. If so, then I suspect this enabled humans to perceive the existence not only of supposed parallel realms and realities, but also of the entities that frequented these places, some of which might well have been visual or emotional expressions of very real life forms present in inner space. I doubt if these non-terrestrial beings would have manifested in a manner that we might expect today, as space aliens, spirit guides, fairies, angels or demons. More likely is that they appeared as animal-human hybrids (therianthropes), perhaps like Michael Harner's 'bird-headed people' (*see page 223*); imaginary animals (chimeras), perhaps Harner's 'dragon-like creatures' who were 'the true gods of this world'; or even as shape-shifters (morphians), assuming whatever form the mind deemed acceptable. Were these non-terrestrial 'beings', accessed via the achievement of a personal state of cosmic consciousness (*see Chapter Nineteen*), able to provide information on the cosmic origins of life, as well as knowledge concerning the greater significance of the Cygnus constellation? I sincerely believe this to have been possible, given the astonishing evidence presented in this book.

Most probably the ancients of *c.*15,000 BC would have looked towards Deneb, the brightest star in the Cygnus group as well as the Pole Star, as the guiding light for any connection with this asterism, but in many ways it simply acted as a herald for Sadr, the true 'God star', placed at the dead centre of the great cross in the sky, pin-pointing the location of the invisible Cygnus X-3. Remember, its influence would have diminished the further south one went, until finally Cygnus X-3 would no longer have been circumpolar. Instead, it would have risen and set each day, and disappeared altogether below the horizon at certain times of the year. It is clear that under such circumstances, the Cygnus star cluster would soon have become identified as the cosmic source of life and death through the more or less religious experiences it might have been seen to induce in those situated deep underground.

The First Call to Prayer

The emergence of astronomy, cosmology, a stellar-based solar calendar and maybe even transatlantic journeys *c.*15,000 BC all argue for something major having taken place around this time. If this was connected in some way with the effect of cosmic rays, then it goes some way to explaining why during the Early to Middle Magdalenian epochs, *c.*15,000–*c.*11,000 BC, there was a dramatic increase in the specific use of deep caves for magico-religious purposes. It was, as I suggested in Chapter Twenty, like the first call to prayer, recalling the significance played in this story by the Sabians of Harran. They were drawn to the city's mesmeric Astronomical Tower, not just to give praise to the Primal Cause, but also, like their most distant ancestors, to embrace the significance of a single star in the night sky.

In many ways deep caves were the first places of worship, the forerunners of all shrines, temples, synagogues, churches and mosques. Yet, as with all religious beliefs, original concepts tend to get distorted, confused, or simply watered down. This would explain why, despite its meagre size, Church Hole in the north of England functioned as a very real shrine to the cosmic source of life and death, complete with all the right symbolism (birds, eggs, vulvae) and the correct orientation towards the stars of Cygnus. Yet even by the time of the Church Hole cave art, *c.*10,800 BC, the true potential of deep cave environments had been lost, here in Britain at least.

Just fifteen hundred years later, the Ice Age was over, and those priest-shamans whose ancestors had arguably evolved rapidly as a result perhaps of their exposure underground to cosmic rays, became the new priestly elite of the earliest Neolithic communities in southeast Turkey, perhaps remembered as the 'Watchers' and 'Nephilim' of the *Book of Enoch*. Here the whole concept of the cosmic signal being experienced in the deep cave setting was, I sense, purposely replicated in the construction of subsurface structures that teemed with exquisitely carved stone pillars and sculpted statues. This new form of high relief replaced the cave art, which often accentuated natural surfaces on which they were created. A similar effect was achieved at Göbekli Tepe with the carving of the large feline that seems to flow around the shape of the almost flag-like pillar on which it appears.

Yet like Church Hole in England and the stone rows at Karahan Tepe, the first temples anywhere in the world, such as Göbekli Tepe, were directed north towards Cygnus, the direction of the Primal Cause. It was a relationship with the heavenly cross, or celestial bird, a concept which even before this time had rippled around the globe, either springing up spontaneously in different places or being carried from landmass to landmass by our Palaeolithic ancestors. I believe that these shamans' entire mindset, as well perhaps as their physical appearance (for instance, radiation-induced germline mutations can cause higher instances of albinism, as is now happening among the swallow population around Chernobyl[32]), was altered by long-term exposure to cosmic rays, especially deep underground where more subtle effects from sources such as Cygnus X-3 might have been felt. This in turn helped draw attention to the constellation's greater role, aided dramatically by the fact that Deneb and later *delta* Cygni occupied pole position between *c.*16,000–*c.*13,000 BC.

I suspect that it was for these reasons that Cygnus featured so strongly in later epochs within the alignments of sacred structures that celebrated cosmic life and death through various forms of swan shamanism. Avebury, Newgrange, Wayland Smithy and Callanish all targeted its key stars, while Cygnus would seem also to have been at the heart of Egypt's oldest sky-religion. The significance of the deep cave setting was preserved not just in the concept of the soul of the deceased having to pass through the cavern-like Duat-underworld in order to achieve ascension, but also in the construction of the inner chambers of the pyramid. They invariably targeted the meridian – symbolized by the sky-rope or ladder guarded by the falcon-headed god that represented the stars of Cygnus. The very placement of the three main pyramids of Giza might even have reflected the star group's potency, as well as the site's relationship to the ancient cult centre of Heliopolis.

It was a similar story all around the world, from North America to Mexico, Peru, Siberia, China, India and, as we shall see in the Appendix, in Africa as well. Everywhere Cygnus became associated with the cosmic source of life and death, and the transmigration of the soul. Very likely, the true significance of why this particular asterism was so important was lost to even the wisest of astronomer-priests, until eventually its stars were seen only as celestial time-markers, sparring around the northern celestial pole opposite those of Ursa Major.

In time, the concept of the cosmic cave degenerated into the interior of a long barrow, and eventually the crypt of a cathedral or, indeed, the holy of holies in a temple, which – with the exception of religions such as the Sabians, Mandaeans, Yezidi and Brethren of Purity – were now generally orientated east-west instead of north-south. Yet the true significance of the north, the Pole Star, and the stars of Cygnus could never be truly eradicated, even after the northerly-placed heaven was transformed into a place of hell, and the north was denounced as the direction of darkness and the devil. Ironically, Christianity's ultimate symbol of faith, the cross on which Christ died before ascending to heaven, is also a basic representation of the Cygnus constellation in its role as the Greek mystery god Orpheus. In addition to this, Allah, who became the god of Islam, was in all likelihood originally represented by the pagan Arabs as a bird idol at Mecca that expressed the Sabian concept of the Primal Cause, celebrated in the Mystery of the North.

All of this is as a result, I am sure, of Cygnus X-3's role in human affairs towards the end of the last Ice Age. Had its influence not been felt on Earth, or its source never been established, then I am convinced that Deneb's function as the ultimate North Star, marking the 'gateway to heaven', would simply not have happened.

Time-Wave Zero

Any further speculation on Cygnus's possible influence on the prehistoric mindset will now have to wait (although see the Appendix on the Dogon of Mali), but one last fact *has* emerged during this research project, which takes us back to the voyage of discovery undertaken by psychedelic guru Terence McKenna. As alluded to in Chapter Six, following his own *ayahuasca* experiences in South America he used mathematical computations – based on the Chinese divination system known as the *Yijing* (*I Ching*) – to determine what he referred to as Time-Wave Zero, which was derived from the notion that time is a fractal wave, highlighting periods of 'novelty'. McKenna used this time-wave principle to determine its culminating 'Zero Point', or 'eschaton', signalling the end of the present wave cycle. That date fell within a few days of 21 December 2012, the completion date of the Mayan Long Count calendar (*see Chapter Six*).

As I have attempted to demonstrate in this book, the eschatological phenomenon symbolized by 2012 aligns precisely with everything we know about Cygnus, not just as a celestial time-marker, but also as the original point of creation and 'birth canal' of the cosmic source of life and death, personified in the night sky as the Milky Way. From the Great Rift in Cygnus, where lurks Cygnus X-3, the sun will emerge on 21 December 2012, signalling a new beginning in cosmic time cycles. It is an event, I am sure, that will be marked quite spectacularly around the world.

'The Finger of God'

Finally, we might ask ourselves this: is it merely by chance that Cygnus X-3's one-sided jet came to be directed at the Earth? Pastor David Drach-Meinel, the son of Aden Meinel, has already suggested, in a radio interview in Britain following his father's appearance at the 2005 TAG conference, that the microblazar's one-sided jet, perhaps tens of light years in length, could be the 'finger of God' pointing towards the Earth.[33]

Of course Drach-Meinel would have had the Cat's Eye nebula in mind, rather than Cygnus X-3, when he made this bold suggestion. And as a Christian minister, he is naturally interested in the idea of 'intelligent design'. But whatever standpoint we are coming from, we can only speculate on what science might, in the future, have to say about the nature of the compelling binary system Cygnus X-3 and its unique cosmic rays. In the same way that our Palaeolithic ancestors might have looked towards the Cygnus constellation as the cosmic source of life and death, one day some people might indeed come to believe that a higher intelligence intervened in order, quite literally, to evolve the human race and create who we are today. But whether we think in such terms or not, we might even now gaze at these stars and come to realize that life almost certainly does indeed exist elsewhere and that we are part of a much greater whole, for which reason our world will never be alone.

Only the fact that such great distances exist in space prevents us from spending all our time and effort pursuing life's cosmic origins through till their ultimate end. In the future, our descendants, with more advanced technologies and a better understanding of the cosmos, will eventually crack what I have termed 'the Cygnus mystery'. And yet this *could* happen today, if only we realized that all the tools we will ever need to provide us with some meaningful answers are there to be awakened – inside us all.

Postscript: April 2006

Further developments continue to occur in the Cygnus mystery even as this book goes to press. Following a period of inactivity, Cygnus X-3 has recently burst back into life with its first major radio flares since 2001. These were detected by the Ryle Telescope at Cambridge in England on 7–8 March 2006, with a series of lesser fluctuations in the days that followed. Flares of this kind are likely to be connected with the production of relativistic jets (*see Chapter Twenty-One*), and I understand that Mike McCollough is currently examining new data regarding synchronous emissions from Cygnus X-3 on multiple frequencies, which occurred on these same dates.

At the same time, news reached me of further speculation that human evolution might have been affected in Palaeolithic times by cosmic rays originating from the Cygnus region. The story, featured in the March 2006 issue of *Astronomy Now*,[1] cites the findings of British anthropological writer Denis Montgomery, who in 1995 proposed that high levels of Beryllium-10 in the Antarctic and Greenland ice core records (*see Chapter Twenty-One*), for a period of 2,000 years *c.*35,000 BP, argue in favour of a connection between cosmic ray activity and the relatively sudden transitions in human behaviour patterns around the same time. Most obviously, this includes the flowering of cave art in western Europe *c.*32,500–30,000 BP. The piece in *Astronomy Now*, written by Adrian Berry, the Consulting Science Editor for Britain's *Daily Telegraph* newspaper, compared this sudden emergence of modern humans with the opening sequence to the movie *2001: A Space Odyssey*, where a tribe of ape-men encounter a mysterious black obelisk that appears unexpectedly in their midst, and instantly transforms their thinking and behaviour patterns. For 'alien obelisk' in the film read 'directed cosmic rays' in real life – the cosmogenic process outlined in this book and referred to by Montgomery as the 'Cygnus Event'.

Based on suggestions made by American and Russian scientists working on the aforementioned ice cores at the beginning of the 1990s, Montgomery outlined his opinion that the source of the cosmic rays was a close supernova, most likely the one that caused the beautiful stellar debris photographed by the Hubble space telescope and known to astronomers as the Cygnus Veil, or Cygnus Loop. Located in the right wing of the celestial swan, the shock waves of this cosmic event were thought to have ripped open the Earth's protective layer of ozone, causing cosmic rays and ultraviolet radiation from the sun to rain down on the unsuspecting world beneath. For many years the exploding star would have been brighter than the full moon, making it a blinding light source that turned night into day.

Premature deaths, cancer and mutations on a massive scale would have been experienced by both animals and humans. Yet very gradually the supernova would have burnt out, and an immunity achieved by the human survivors, our own *Homo sapiens sapiens* ancestors, who were the successors of the less adaptable Neanderthal peoples.

It is a brave vision of a Palaeolithic holocaust and post-apocalyptic nightmare, although it is difficult to equate this scenario with the known facts. Even though the 35,000 BP cosmic event highlighted by the Be-10 levels in the ice cores alluded to by Montgomery is the same as the one proposed by the Meinel Institute of Las Vegas, and said by them to have taken place *c.*40,000 years ago, the suspected source of the cosmic rays is unlikely to be the Cygnus Veil, or Loop. This is now believed to have been created when a dying supergiant in this suspected binary system exploded in a supernova just 5,000 to 8,000 years ago. Moreover, this spectacular event, which would have made it temporarily one of the brightest sources in the night sky, was far too distant to have affected life on Earth.

This reassessment of the Cygnus Veil comes from new data regarding its distance, which is now thought to be around 1,400 light years away, instead of the presupposed 150 light years bandied around in the early 1990s. Thus there is nothing firm to link the Cygnus Veil with the assumed supernova of *c.*35,000 years ago. Moreover, no other similar event is known to have occurred around this time, even though close supernovae cannot be ruled out as the cause of mass extinctions on Earth, either in the past or in the future.[2]

As if to emphasize this possibility, on 18 February 2006 NASA's Swift satellite picked up a *gamma*-ray burst (GRB) lasting an amazing 2,000 seconds.[3] The longest such GRB ever recorded, it was caused when jets of radiation were suddenly blasted out by a supermassive star which, having come to the end of its life, exploded in a supernova. Immediately after the GRB, a flux of X-rays was registered for a period of 3,000 seconds, portending the visual discovery of the supernova, now designated GRB 060218, which is located in a galaxy 440 million light years away in the constellation of Aries. Even though this record-breaking GRB is seen to have been 'fairly weak',[4] it is once again a stark reminder of the unpredictable nature of the cosmos, and how similar events much closer to home might well be catastrophic for life on Earth.

Having contacted Denis Montgomery, and explained to him the latest data regarding the Cygnus Veil, he has been happy to revise his two electronic books – both available for download online and thoroughly recommended[5] – to include other possible sources of cosmic rays that might have irradiated the Earth in Palaeolithic times. They include Cygnus X-3, which the Meinel group now publicly acknowledge as a proposed point source of cosmic rays reaching Earth during the Palaeolithic age, even though they go on to dismiss it in favour of the Cat's Eye nebula.[6] Their criticisms of Cygnus X-3 as a cosmic accelerator are fully addressed in a scholarly paper prepared by myself,[7] which is available for download on my website, where this debate is likely to run and run.

Despite some questions arising from his overall theory, Denis Montgomery must be credited for having pioneered the idea of cosmic rays influencing human evolution, and for concluding that their point source was in the Cygnus region – a road which he admits has been a long and often solitary one.

Yet we leave you, finally, with the words of astronomer and scientific writer Carl Sagan who, I lately find, proposed as early as 1973 that cosmic rays have been essential to the evolution of the human species. In his ground-breaking book *The Cosmic Connection*, he wrote:

> Cosmic rays fall on the Earth's atmosphere... the more energetic particles, the ones produced by supernovae or neutron stars, penetrate to the surface of the Earth. And here they collide with life. Some cosmic rays penetrate through the genetic material of life forms on the surface of our planet. These random, unpredictable cosmic rays produce changes, mutations, in the hereditary material ... The vast bulk of mutations are harmful, but the small fraction of mutations that are an improvement provide the raw material for evolutionary advance... Thus ... life on Earth is intimately bound to stellar events. Human beings are here because of the paroxysms in dying stars thousands of light-years away.

APPENDIX

The Dogon Mystery

The concept of a DNA-linked cosmic consciousness is offered in *The Cygnus Mystery* as a possible mechanism by which Palaeolithic shamans might have become aware of both the Cosmic Microwave Background radiation (the 'sound of the universe') and the apparent importance of the Cygnus constellation in human evolution. Support for this idea might be provided by the claimed astronomical knowledge of indigenous cultures worldwide. For instance, in the 1950s the Efé tribe of pygmies of the Ituri Forest in Central Africa told Belgian sociologist Jean-Pierre Hallet, who spent eighteen months in their company, that to them the planet Saturn was the 'star of nine moons'.[1] It does, in fact, have ten moons, although the smallest one is only 200 kilometres (124 miles) across. On the other side of the world, the Maori of New Zealand call Saturn *Parearu*, which means 'caught in the band', since their ancestors believed it had a ring around it. This information was recorded by anthropologist Elsdon Best in the 1920s. Even though there was some query over the exact identity of Parearu, the fact that it also bore the title 'puller of the Milky Way', seemed to confirm it was Saturn since this was seen as the outermost planet, and thus the closest to the outer galaxy.[2]

Then there is the mystery of the Dogon tribe of Mali in West Africa. They were studied by French ethnographer Marcel Griaule between 1931 and his death in 1956. He gained the trust and confidence of the Dogon elders, and after many years of trying finally got them to open up about the cosmological background to their magico-religious system, the details of which were published in his book *Conversations with Ogotemmêli* (1965).[3] A further series of deep conversations followed on the tribe's complex creation myths, which included an intimate knowledge of the cosmos. The Dogon, too, were seemingly aware that Saturn possessed a ring, and that Jupiter had four little 'stars' around it. Even though we now know that Jupiter in fact has twelve moons, only four of them are of any size, with the rest being 'mini-moons' or simply fragments of space debris.

Such claims of indigenous astronomical knowledge among the Efé pygmies of the Ituri Forest, the Maori of New Zealand and the Dogon of Mali might be dismissed by sceptics. Most probably, these tribal peoples were able to observe either the rings and satellites of Saturn or the moons of Jupiter, or such information was conveyed to them by European travellers. However, the Dogon informants of Griaule went further by alluding to the existence of two companion stars, *po tolo* and *emme ya tolo,* orbiting Sirius (*sigu tolo*), the brightest star in the night sky. They drew him a diagram showing their relative positions, and explained how the first companion, *po tolo*, circled Sirius once every 50 years, and was the 'smallest thing there is', comparing it to the tiny seed *Digitaria exilis.*[4] It was also a 'heavy star', said to weigh as much as all the iron in the Earth, so that 'all earthly beings combined cannot lift it'.[5] In 1950, a paper written on the subject by Griaule and his colleague Germaine Dieterlen was published under the title '*Un Système Soudanais de Sirius*' ('A Sudanese Sirius System', with 'Sudanese' used here in its ethnographical sense of the region south of the Sahara).[6]

This initial article was followed by a mammoth book entitled *Le renard pâle* (*The Pale Fox*), which greatly expanded on the Dogons' cosmological ideals, found also among three other Sudanese tribes – the Bambara and Bozo in Segou and the Minianka in Koutiala.[7] Griaule unfortunately died whilst it was being compiled, and so the project was completed by Dieterlen. The work was published in 1965, with an appendix entitled 'The Companion of Sirius', which at last identified *po tolo* with Sirius B, first discovered in 1862. Griaule and Dieterlen pointed out that, like *po tolo*, Sirius B does indeed orbit Sirius A every 50 years (in fact, 49.5 years). Moreover, as a superdense white dwarf, Sirius B can indeed be described as an extremely 'heavy star'.[8] At the time, the presence of a Sirius C had only be hinted at in astronomical circles, and not until 1994 would its existence be finally confirmed, only then making sense of the Dogon's claim that a second companion called *emme ya tolo* also encircled Sirius A.[9]

All of this information might have been lost in the pages of ethnographical and anthropological journals had the subject not caught the attention of historical writer Robert Temple, who embarked on a fresh study of Griaule and Dieterlen's Dogon material, resulting in the publication in 1976 of his bestselling book *The Sirius Mystery*. It proposed that the Dogon gained their cosmological knowledge, including the information regarding the existence and properties of Sirius B (Sirius C had still not been confirmed), from amphibious extra-terrestrials alluded to in great detail within Griaule and Dieterlen's *The Pale Fox,* published for the first time in English in 1986. Temple asserted that Dogon myth spoke clearly of the arrival here from the Sirius star system of eight sky-beings led by a fish-like creature called Nommo. Since there exist accounts of similar amphibious beings in Babylonian myth, and the ancient Egyptians venerated Sirius as a goddess, Temple concluded that these great civilizations of the past also benefitted from Nommo and his companions' divine wisdom.

Here at last was supposed evidence of direct contact between an extra-terrestrial race and humanity, which, of course, was news that was not going to be greeted too kindly by the sceptics of this world. They tore *The Sirius Mystery* apart, and utilized some serious criticisms of Griaule's working procedures[10] to convince the world that the entire Dogon mystery was a complete confabulation. This is a shame, for as much as some people might like to see this subject swept quietly under the carpet, the fact is that from my own research into Dogon cosmology I would say that in essence it is genuine, and that there was no major collusion on the part of Griaule and Dieterlen to mislead the world. That said, I have to admit that Robert Temple's interpretation of the Dogon mystery *is* misleading in places.

Terraforming the Earth

Let me begin by stating that although the Dogon do indeed talk about a cosmic journey made on an 'ark' by a sky-being called Nommo, who arrived on Earth with four pairs of twins, nowhere can I find it stated in any of Griaule and Dieterlen's published works that the sky-beings came from a planet in the Sirius star system. Indeed, the star *sigi tolo*, i.e. Sirius A, was only 'born' out of the emasculation of Nommo, who along with his trickster twin Ogo, the 'pale fox', were the first beings brought forth by the creator god Amma. The reason for this death was in order to sweep away the darkness previously brought upon the face of the Earth by Ogo.[11] Nommo's resurrection and journey to Earth led to the sun and Sirius meeting for the first time, out of which came the star's first heliacal rising.[12]

In other words, there was no way that Nommo could have been 'born' on a planet orbiting Sirius A, since it did not exist until he was killed by Amma. Furthermore, it is made clear in *The Pale Fox* that the newly resurrected Nommo descended to Earth not from Sirius, but from 'Amma's womb'.[13] The ark came out through the opening he had left in the placenta for the emergence of the sun with everything needed to create life in this world, including animals, reptiles, sea-creatures, even metals and sand dunes.[14] In fact, we might see Nommo's mission as a complete terraforming exercise, reminding us once more of the ancient cosmological view that life on Earth originated in the sky, the modern theory of panspermia.[15] Very little of this is brought out in Robert Temple's *The Sirius Mystery*.

The fantastic nature of the Dogons' creation myth, and I have done its complexity and grace nowhere near justice, suggests to me that it is little different from the claims of many indigenous peoples worldwide concerning the seeding of life on Earth. In fact, it is more likely that such profound knowledge preserved by the Dogon derives, not from spacemen or aliens, but from trance-induced communications, where contact with *perceived* otherworldly intelligences would have been assured.

If this is also the method by which the Dogon came to learn of invisible stars such as Sirius B and Sirius C (if indeed they *are* Sirius B and Sirius C, for there are some doubts[16]), then it provides an answer as to how an abstract awareness and understanding of Cygnus might have been gained by the shamanic elite of the Palaeolithic world. Interestingly, there is some evidence to suggest that the earliest known ancestors of the Dogon were a semi-nomadic Libyo-Berber race (recalled as the Garamantes in Classical myth) who came from what is today the Libyan Sahara.[17] If correct, then their southerly migration route would have taken them very close to Tassili and Hoggar, rock art locations that display evidence of a mushroom cult, *c.*7000–*c.*5000 BC (*see Chapter Eighteen*). What is more, there is one final twist in this story, highlighted by Griaule and Dieterlen's spin on Dogon cosmology, that I feel compelled to reveal.

Path of the Blood

In the sacred village of Upper Ogol in the Sanga Valley of the Bandiagara region, some 300 kilometres (186 miles) south of Timbuktu in Mali, Griaule and Dieterlen recorded the existence of a series of altars placed in a north–south line on the so-called 'terrace of Lebe'.[18] According to their informants, each altar represented a different star or planet, which together signified Nommo's trail of flowing blood,[19] following his emasculation by Amma.

What became known as *illi ozu*,[20] the 'path of the blood', was seen to pass directly overhead from the perceived head of Nommo in the north to his feet in the south, hence the line of altars. Indeed, it turns out that *illi ozu* is the Milky Way, with the stars placed along its course being the bones, limbs and blood of the Emasculated One.[21] For the Dogon, it was seen as the driving force of the stellar world, directly influencing life on earth, like a celestial representation of all the functioning parts and arteries of the human body. *The Pale Fox* contains illustrations of what appears to be *Illi ozu*, including a photograph taken by Griaule as early as 1931 of a forked river of flowing red and white blood that was painted on the roof of a rock shelter called the 'vault of Songo' (*see Plate 31*).[22]

The Fork of Space

The northern axis of the 'path of the blood', i.e. the Milky Way, was, according to Griaule and Dieterlen, the 'seat' of *amma talu*, the egg of the creator god Amma,[23] who is occasionally represented in ceremonies honouring the dead by a dancer wearing a crane-beaked *kanaga* mask.[24] It was from here that he brought the universe into manifestation by his 'word',[25] or vibration, which pierced the wall of the placenta, or womb,[26] within the egg, represented in Dogon ritual by an ostrich egg.[27] All this took place in the original darkness, when the manifest universe was still just a thought in Amma's mind.[28]

According to Griaule and Dieterlen, Amma's Egg was held in position by the 'Fork of Space',[29] known also as Amma's Fork, a cosmological device symbolized by a piece of iron shaped like a stake.[30] It acted as a cosmic axis upon which the creator 'span' to manifest the 'world', and with it the physical universe. Thus around the Fork of Space the movements of creation were seen to take place. It is a role shared with *po tolo*, seen as the first created star.[31] Indeed, the Fork of Space would seem to have connected the northern celestial pole, known to the Dogon as *aduno giru* ('eye of the world'), with *aduno giru ley* ('second eye of the world'),[32] identified as the southerly placed star constellation we know today as Crux, or the Southern Cross.[33]

There is no question that in Dogon star-lore the Milky Way was seen to link the Pole Star of the north with the Southern Cross in the south.[34] This meant that the Fork of Space had to correspond with some celestial marker in the vicinity of both the celestial pole and the northern end of the Milky Way. The drawing of the Fork of Space contained in *The Pale Fox* shows it with a long vertical stem, most likely signifying the Milky Way, on top of which is an oval shape representing Amma's egg. From this emerges four spokes, roughly equidistant apart from each other, that terminate in small flower-like rays, which I take to be stars.

The moment I saw this illustration it reminded me of the arrangement of five of Cygnus's key stars – Gienah (*epsilon* Cygni), Deneb (*alpha* Cygni), *delta* Cygni, *eta* Cygni and Sadr (*gamma* Cygni). The first four form the flower-like devices on the end of stems, while the fifth star, Sadr, corresponds to the position of Amma's Egg. Rodney Hale kindly overlaid a photograph of the Cygnus stars upon the Fork of Space diagram and the match was pretty close indeed.

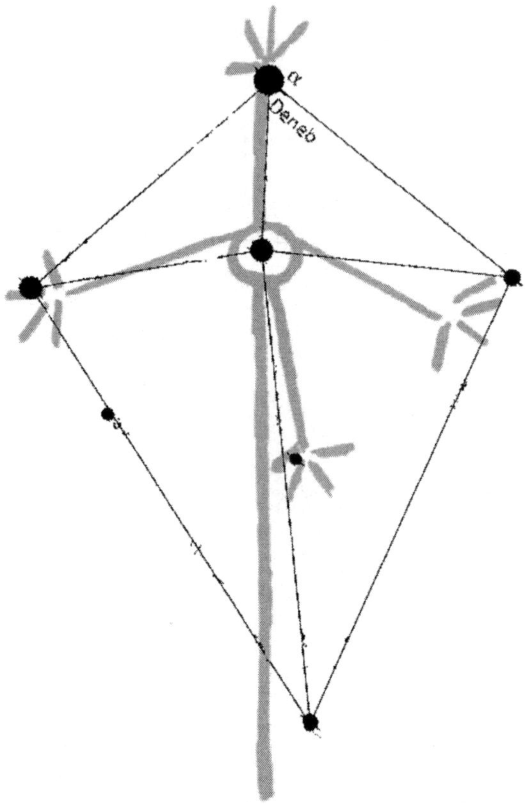

Fig. 52. The Dogon concept of the Fork of Space, the seat of the creator god Amma, overlaid with the principal stars of Cygnus.

Thus it seemed that according to Dogon cosmology, Amma's egg, the Dogon point of creation and 'axis' of the universe, was located in the proximity of the star Sadr, which, of course, also marks the position of Cygnus X-3. In addition to this, the term Fork of Space, or Amma's Fork, was surely a reference to the Milky Way's Great Rift. Indeed, when I looked again at the example of Dogon rock art photographed by Griaule in 1931, and seemingly depicting the 'path of the blood', it bore a striking resemblance to the section of the Milky Way that includes the Great Rift.

From North to South

The cosmological relationship between the Southern Cross and the Cygnus constellation as the Northern Cross has already been noted among the Inca of Peru and the Neolithic peoples of Britain. Yet in Dogon cosmological tradition the Milky Way is seen to flow directly overhead, from the head of Nommo in the north to his feet in the south, hence the line of altars at Upper Ogol.

If the Skyglobe computer program is consulted, we find that only once in a precessional cycle of 26,000 years does the Milky Way align north-south, so that it passes directly overhead when viewed from anywhere in the Northern Hemisphere. However, the last time this occurred was between *c.*16,000–*c.*15,000 BC. In addition to this, we find that from a latitude corresponding to the North African continent, the Milky Way would have been seen to flow from Cygnus in the extreme north, where Deneb occupied pole position, to the Southern Cross in the extreme south. If all this is correct, then it would seem that the Dogon have preserved an understanding of the cosmos which, as is the case in China and so many other places around the world, can only have been created by our Palaeolithic ancestors some 17,000 years ago.

BIBLIOGRAPHY

If two dates are given for a title, the first relates to the publication date of the first edition, the second to the edition consulted. Abbreviations: AA: *Astronomy and Astrophysics*; AJ: *Astrophysics Journal*; AJL: *Astrophysics Journal Letters*; ALC; *Astrophysics Letters and Communications*; AN: *Astronomy Now*; ARP: *Annual Review of Physiology*; AS: *Anatolian Studies*; AT: *Aquarian Theosophist*; BCA: Book Club Associates, London; BIFAOC: *Bulletin de l'Institut Français d'Archéologie Orientale, Cairo*; BMMA: *Bulletin of the Metropolitan Museum of Art*, New York; BSOAS: *Bulletin of the School of Oriental and African Studies*, London; *c.*: *circa* (as in date of publication); CA: *Current Anthropology*; CC: *Culture and Cosmos*; CUP: Cambridge University Press; DE: *Discussions in Egyptology*; DU: *Die Umschau*; EJVS: *Electronic Journal of Vedic Studies*; IJO: *International Journal of Osteoarchaeology*; IMHMST: *International Magazine of the History of Mathematics, Science and Technology*; JE: *Journal of Ethnopharmacology*; JEA: *Journal of Egyptian Archaeology*; JGR: *Journal of Geophysical Research – Oceans*; JHA: *Journal for the History of Astronomy*; JLAL: *Journal of Latin American Lore*; JNES: *Journal of Near Eastern Studies*; JPGNPP: *Journal of Physics G: Nuclear and Particle Physics*; JSA: *Journal de la Societe des Africanistes*; MAA: *Mediterranean Archaeology and Archaeometry*; MD: *Migration and Diffusion*; MDAIK: *Mitteilungen des Deutschen Archäologischen Instituts (Abteilung Kairo)*; MNRAS: *Monthly Notices of the Royal Astronomical Society*; MT: *Mammoth Trumpet*; nd: no date given; NS: *New Scientist*; OUP: *Oxford University Press*, Oxford; PAPS: *Proceedings of the American Philosophical Society*; PNAS: *Proceedings of the National Academy of Sciences*; PR: *Physical Review*; PRL: *Physical Review Letters*; SA: *Scientific American*; SAK: *Studien zur Altägyptischen Kultur*; SN: *Science News*; SSA: *Studien sur Altägyptischen*; TDE: *Trabajos de Egiptología – Papers on Ancient Egypt* (Madrid); VBP: *Vigyan Bharati Pradeepia*; WA: *World Archaeology*; ZDM: *Zentralblatt für Didaktik der Mathematik*.

Aesop's Fables – *see* Gibbs.

Albîrûnî, *The Chronology of Ancient Nations: An English Translation of the Arabic Text of the Athâr-ul-bâkiya of albîrûnî*, trans and ed Dr C Edward Sachau, Wm H Allen, London, 1879.

'Alien life seems yet more likely', NS 188: 2522 (22 October 2005), p.22.

Allegro, John M, *The Sacred Mushroom and the Cross*, 1970, Abacus, London, 1974.

Allen, James P, *Genesis in Egypt: The Philosophy of Ancient Egyptian Creation Accounts*, Yale Egyptological Studies 2, Yale University, New Haven, CT, 1988.

Allen, Richard Hinckley, *Star Names: Their Lore and Meaning*, 1899, Dover, New York, NY, 1963.

Allison, W W M, G J Alner, D S Ayres, W L Barrett, C Bode, P M Border et al, 'Cygnus X-3 revisited: 10 years of muon and radio observations', Proceedings of the 26th International Cosmic Ray Conference (ICRC 99), Salt Lake City, Utah, 17–25 Aug 1999.

Al-Nadim, *The Fihrist of al-Nadim*, ed and trans Bayard Dodge, Columbia University Press, NY, 1970.

Anderson, Flavia, *The Ancient Secret: In Search of the Holy Grail*, Victor Gollancz, London, 1953.

Armstong, Edward A, *The Folklore of Birds*, Houghton Mifflin, Boston, MA/Riverside Press, Cambridge, 1959.

Arrhenius, Svante, 'The Propagation of Life in Space', DU 7 (1903), pp.481. Reprinted in Goldsmith, pp.32–3.

Arrhenius, Svante, *Worlds in the Making*, Harper and Brothers, London, 1908.

Ashpole, Edward, *The Search for Extra-terrestrial Intelligence*, Blandford, London, 1989.

Aubourg, Éric, 'La date de conception du zodiaque du temple d'Hathor à Dendera', BIFAOC 95 (1995), pp.1–10.

Aveni, Anthony F, *Archaeoastronomy in Pre-Columbian America*, University of Texas Press, Austin, TX, 1975.

Bachelor, Rev John, *The Ainu and their Folk-Lore*, Religious Tract Society, London, 1901.

Bacon, Edward, ed., *Vanished Civilizations: Forgotten Peoples of the Ancient World*, Thames and Hudson, London, 1963.

Bauval, Robert, *Secret Chamber: The Quest for the Hall of Records*, Century, London, 1999.

Bauval, Robert, and Adrian Gilbert, *The Orion Mystery*, Heinemann, London, 1994.

Bayley, Michael, *Caer Sidhe: Vol 1 – The Celtic Night Sky*, Capall Bann, Chieveley, Berks, 1997.

Bellows, Henry, *The Poetic Edda, translated from the Icelandic with an Introduction and Notes*, 2 vols in one, Princeton University Press, Princeton, NJ/American Scandinavian Foundation, New York, NY, 1936, available at sacred-texts.com.

Belmonte Arilés, Juan Antonio, 'On the Orientations of the Old Kingdom Egyptian Pyramids', JHA 32 (2001), No 26, pp.S1–20.

Belmonte Avilés, Juan Antonio, 'Some open questions on the Egyptian calendar: an astronomer's view', TDE (2003), pp.7–56.

Benest, D, J L Duvent, 'Is Sirius a triple star?', AA 299 (1995), pp.621–8.

Berezinsky, V S, 'Time delay of the PeV *gamma* ray burst after the October 1985 radio flare of Cygnus X-3', *Nature* 334 (11 August 1988), pp.506–507.

Berry, Adrian, '2001 replayed', *AN* 20:3 (March 2006), p.21.

Billing, Nils, 'Writing an Image – The Formulation of the Tree Goddess Motif in the Book of the Dead, Ch. 59', SSA 32 (2004), pp.35–50.

Blackham, *The Soul of the City: London's Livery Companies*, Sampson Low, Marston & Co, London, nd (*c.*1931).

Blavatsky, H P, 'The Hindu Theory of Vibration as the Producer of Sounds, Forms and Colors', AT 5:6 (17 April 2005), pp.1–6.

Blavatsky, H P, *The Secret Doctrine: The Synthesis of Science, Religion, and Philosophy*, 1888, 2 vols, Theosophical Company, Los Angeles, CA, 1974.

Bocquet-Appel, Jean-Pierre, and Pierre Yves Demars, 'Neanderthal contraction and modern human colonization of Europe', *Antiquity* 74:285 (September 2000), pp.544-52.

Bower, B, 'Doubts Aired over Neanderthal Bone Flute', (and Reply by Musicologist Bob Fink) SN 153 (4 April, 1998), p.215.

Brandon, Jim, *The Rebirth of Pan: Hidden Faces of the American Earth Spirit*, Firebird Press, Gretna, IL, 1983.

Breasted, James Henry, *Ancient Records of Egypt*, ii, University of Chicago, IL, 1906.

Brown, Robert, *Researches into the Origin of the Primitive Constellations of the Greeks, Phoenicians and Babylonians*, 2 vols., Williams and Norgate, London, Edinburgh and Oxford, 1899.

Budge, E A Wallis, *An Egyptian Hieroglyphic Dictionary*, 2 vols, 1920, Dover, New York, NY, 1978.

Budge, E A Wallis, *The Book of the Dead*, 3 vols, Routledge & Kegan Paul, London, 1960.

Budge, E A Wallis, *The Egyptian Heaven and Hell*, 3 vols, Kegan, Paul, Trench, Trübner, London, 1906.

Budge, E A Wallis, *From Fetish to God in Ancient Egypt*, 1934, Dover, New York, NY, 1988.

Budge, E A Wallis, *The Gods of the Egyptians*, 2 vols, 1904, Dover, New York, NY, 1969.

Buhl, Marie-Louise, 'The Goddesses of the Egyptian Tree Cult', JNES 6 (1947), pp.80–97.

Bullinger, Ethelbert W, *The Witness of the Stars*, 1893, Eyre and Spottiswoode, London, 1911.

Burl, Aubrey, *Prehistoric Avebury*, BCA, 1979.

Burl, Aubrey, *The Stone Circles of the British Isles*, 1976, Yale University Press, New Haven, CT, and London, 1977.

Burton, Capt Sir Richard, *Personal Narrative of a Pilgrimage to Al-Madinah and Meccah*, Tylston and Edwards, London, 1893.

Calame-Griaule, Geneviéve, 'On the Dogon Restudied', CA 32:5 (December 1991), pp.575–7.

Carmichael, Alexander, *Carmina Gadelica: Hymns and Incantations*, 1899, Oliver and Boyd, Edinburgh & London, vol I: 1928, vol. 2: 1928.

Cassiday, G L, et al, 'Evidence for 10^{18}-eV Neutral Particles from the Direction of Cygnus X-3', PRL 62:4 (23 January 1989), pp.383–6.
Çelik, Bahattin, 'A New Early-Neolithic Settlement: Karahan Tepe, *Neo-lithics, A Newsletter of the Southwest Asian Lithics Research,* 2,-3/00, Berlin, 2000, pp.6–8.
Chadha, Kulvinder Singh, and Keith Cooper, 'Longest gamma-ray burst signals supernova', *AN* 20:4 (April 2006), p.9.
Chamberlain, Von Del, *When Stars Came Down to Earth: Cosmology of the Skidi Pawnee Indians of North America,* Ballena Press/Center for Archaeoastronomy, Cooperative Publication, Los Altos, CA/College Park, MD, 1982.
Charles, R H, ed. *The Book of Enoch,* OUP, 1912.
Chu, Y-H, M A Guerrero, R A Gruendl, R M Williams, J B Kaler, 'Chandra Reveals the X-ray Glint in the Cat's Eye' AJL 553 (2001), p.L69.
Clottes, Jean, 'Art of the Light and Art of the Depths', in Conkey, pp.203–16.
Cole, J H, *The Determination of the Exact Size and Orientation of the Great Pyramid of Giza*, Government Press, Cairo, 1925.
Collins, Andrew, *From the Ashes of Angels,* Penguin, London, 1996.
Collins, Andrew, *Gateway to Atlantis*, Headline, London, 2000.
Collins, Andrew, *Gods of Eden,* Headline, London, 1998.
Conkey, Margaret W, *et al, Beyond Art: Pleistocene Image and Symbol,* Memoirs of the California Academy of Sciences 23, San Francisco, CA, 1997.
Cope, Julian, *The Modern Antiquarian*, Thorsons, London, 1998.
Coppens, Philip, *The Canopus Revelation: Stargate of the Gods and the Ark of Osiris,* Frontier Publishing, Enkhuizen, Netherlands/Adventures Unlimited Press, Stelle, IL, 2004.
Cowan, Thaddeus M, 'Effigy Mounds and Stellar Representation: A Comparison of Old World and New World Alignment Schemes', in Aveni, pp.217–34.
Cox, Simon, 'A Sanctuary for Sokar', in Bauval, 1999, pp.390–6.
Crawford, Anne, *A History of the Vintners' Company*, Constable, London, 1977.
Crick, F H C, and L E Orgel, 'Directed Panspermia', *Icarus* 19 (1973), pp.43–57. Reprinted Goldsmith, pp.34–7.
Crick, Francis, *Life Itself: Its Origin and Nature*, 1981, Futura/Macdonald, London, 1982.
Czapek, G, B Hahn, W Krebs and L Muller, 'Measurement of the muon flux in the Gotthard underground laboratory', JPGNPP 16:7 (July 1990), pp.1101–1108.
Dames, Michael, *The Avebury Cycle,* Thames and Hudson, London, 1977.
Dar, Arnon, 'The Threat to Life from Eta Carinae and Gamma-Ray Bursts' *Frascati Physics Series* XXIV (2002), pp.513–23.
Dar, Arnon, Jere J. Lord and R. Jeffrey Wilkes, 'Nature of the high-energy particles from Cygnus X-3', PR D33:1 (1 January 1986), pp.303–6.
Daressy, Georges M, 'L'Egypt Celeste', BIFAOC 12 (1915), pp.1–34.
Davies, Paul, 'Do we have to spell it out', NS 183:2459 (7 August 2004), pp.30–1.
Dawood, N J, trans and intro, *Tales from the Thousand and One Nights,* BCA, London, 1977.
Deane, John Bathurst, *The Worship of the Serpent*, J.G. & F. Rivington, London, 1833. Available at sacredtexts.com/etc/wos.

DeMott, Barbara, *Dogon Masks,* 1979, UMI Research Press, Ann Arbor, MI, 1982.
Devereux, Paul, *Stone Age Soundtracks: The Acoustic Archaeology of Ancient Sites,* Vega, London, 2001.
Dikov, N N, 'La pétrographie en Sibérie du Nord-Est', *Inter-Nord* 12 (1971).
Dodge, Bayard, 'The Sabians of Harran', in Sarrüf and Tamim, *pp.*60–85.
Dorsey, George Amos, 1904, *Traditions of the Skidi Pawnee,* Kraus Reprint, New York, NY. 1969.
Drijvers, H J W, *Cults and Beliefs at Edessa,* E J Brill, Leiden, 1980.
Drower, E S, *The Mandaeans of Iraq and Iran: Their Cults, Customs, Magic, Legends, and Folklore,* OUP, 1937.
Edwards, I E S, *The Pyramids of Egypt,* 1947, revised 1985, Viking, London, 1986.
Eliade, Mircea, 1957, *Myths, Dreams and Mysteries,* Harper Torchbooks, New York, NY, 1960.
Eliade, Mircea, 1951, *Shamanism: Archaic Techniques of Ecstasy,* Princeton University Press, Princeton, NJ, 1970.
Empson, R H W, *The Cult of the Peacock Angel,* H F & G Witherby, London, 1928.
Enoch, The Book of – see Charles.
Faulkner, R O, *The Ancient Egyptian Coffin Texts,* 3 vols, Aris and Phillips, Warminster, Dorset, 1973/1977/1978.
Faulkner, R O, *The Ancient Egyptian Pyramid Texts,* OUP, 1969.
Faulkner, R O, 'The King and the Star-religion in the Pyramid Texts, JNES 25, 1966, pp.153–161.
Feuerstein, Georg, Subhash Kak and David Frawley, *In Search of the Cradle of Civilization,* Quest Books, Wheaton, IL/Adyar, Madras, India, 1995.
Flammarion, Camille, *Popular Astronomy,* Chatto & Windus, London, 1897.
Flattery, D S, and M Swartz, *Haoma and Harmaline: The Botanical Identity of the Indo-Iranian Sacred Hallucinogen 'Soma' and its Legacy in Religion, Language, and Middle Eastern Folklore,* Univ of California Press, Berkeley, CA, 1989.
Forgione, Adriano, 'Il Potere dalle Stelle' *Hera* 59 (December 2004), pp.52–8.
Fosar, Grazyna, and Franz Bludorf, *Vernetzte Intelligenz: Die Natur geht online,* 2001, Omega, Aachen, Germany, 2002.
'Francis Crick', obituary, *The Times,* 30 July 2004, pp.68–9.
Freidel, David, Linda Schele and Joy Parker, 1993, *Maya Cosmos: Three Thousand Years on the Shaman's Path,* Perennial, New York, NY, 2001.
Freke, Timothy, and Peter Gandy, *The Jesus Mysteries: Was the 'Original Jesus' a Pagan God?,* Thorsons, London, 1999.
Furst, Peter T, *Flesh of the Gods,* 1972, Waveland Press, Prospect Heights, IL, 1990.
Gaballa, G A, and K A Kitchen, 'The Festival of Sokar' *Orientalia* 38 (1969), pp.1–76.
Gardiner, Sir Alan, *Egypt of the Pharaohs,* 1961, OUP, 1964.
Gettings, Fred, *Dictionary of Demons,* 1988, Guild Publishing, London, 1989.
Gibbs, Laura, trans., *Aesop's Fables,* OUP, 2002.
Gillespie, Charles, ed, *Dictionary of Scientific Biography,* xv, i, 1978, pp.706–727.
Gimbutas, Marija, *The Language of the Goddess,* Thames and Hudson, London, 1989.
Goedicke, Hans, 'The Route of Sinuhe's Flight', *JEA* 43 (1957), pp.77–85.

Goldsmith, Donald, ed, *The Quest for Extra-terrestrial Life*, University Science Books, Mill Valley, CA, 1980.
Gooch, Stan, *Cities of Dreams: When Women Ruled the Earth*, 1989, Aulis Books, London, 1995.
Goyon, Georges, *Le secret des bâtisseurs des grandes pyramides,* Editions J' ai lu, Paris, 1990.
Graves, Robert, *The White Goddess*, Faber and Faber, London, 1948.
Green, Tamara, *The City of the Moon God; religious traditions of Harran,* E J Brill, Leiden, 1992.
Gregory of Tours, *De cursu stellarum* – Haase.
Griaule, M, *Masques Dogons*, Institit d'ethnologie, Paris, 1938.
Griaule, Marcel, intro Germaine Dieterlen, *Conversations with Ogotemmêli*, OUP, 1965.
Griaule, Marcel, and Germaine Dieterlen, 'Un Systeme Soudanais de Sirius', JSA 20 (1950), pp.273–294. Republished as *A Sudanese Sirius System*, in Temple, pp.317–35.
Griaule, Marcel, and Germaine Dieterlen, *The Pale Fox*, (Originally published in French as *Le renard pâle*), 1965, trans. Stephen C Infantino, Continuum Foundation, Chino Valley, AZ, 1986.
Griffith, Ralph T H, trans, *Sacred Writings – Hinduism: Rig Veda*, Book of the Month Club, New York, NY, 1992.
Grimm, Jacob, *Teutonic Mythology*, 4 vols, Geo Bell, London, i: 1882; ii-iii:1883, iv:1888.
Guerrero, M A, Chu, Y-H, Gruendl, R A, Williams, R M, Kaler, J B, 'The Enigmatic X-ray Point Sources at the Central Stars of NGC 6543 and NGC 7293,' AJL 553 (2001), p.L55.
Guest, John S, *The Yezidis: A Study in Survival*, KPI, London and New York, 1987.
Gündüz, Nullinasi, 'The Knowledge of Life: The Origins and Early History of the Mandaeans and their Relation to the Sabians of the Qur'an and to the Harranians', *Journal of Semitic Studies Supplement 3*, OUP, 1994.
Haase, Henr. Aeonoth. Frid., ed. *Gregorii turonensis episcopi*, libro *de cursu stellarum* etc, Typis Universitatis, Vratislaviae (Bratislava/Pressburg University Press), Austria-Hungary [modern Slovakia], 1853.
Hall, R L, 'Ancient Olmec and Maya Calculation and Use of Major Eras of Time Based upon the Tropical Year and Planetary Periods', 23rd DDA/HAD Meeting, BAAS, 1992, p.1067.
Hallett, Jean-Pierre, with Alex Pelle, *Pygmy Kitabu*, Souvenir Press, London, 1974.
Hamzeh'ee, M Reza, *The Yaresan: A Sociological, Historical and Religio-Historical Study of a Kurdish Community*, Klaus Schwarz, Berlin, 1990.
Hancock, Graham, *Supernatural*, Century, London, 2005.
Harding, Luke, 'After the hunt, Ice Age man chilled out – with a flute', *The Guardian*, 17 December 2004.
Harner, Michael J, *Hallucinogens and Shamanism*, OUP, New York, NY, 1973.
Harner, Michael J, 'The Role of Hallucinogenic Plants in European Witchcraft', in Harner, *Hallucinogens and Shamanism*, pp.125–50.
Harner, Michael J, 'The Sound of Rushing Water', in Harner, *Hallucinogens and Shamanism*, pp.15–27.

Harrison, Michael, *The London that was Rome,* Geo Allen & Unwin, London, 1971.
Hart, George, *A Dictionary of Egyptian Gods and Goddesses*, RKP, London, 1986.
Hassan, Selim, *Excavations at Giza, 1934–5*, VI, Pt 1, Service des Antiquités de l'Egypte, Government Press, Cairo, 1946.
Hatch, Marion Popenoe, 'An Astronomical Calendar in a Portion of the Madrid Codex', in Aveni, pp.283–340.
Hatch, Marion Popenoe, 'An Hypothesis on Olmec Astronomy, with Special Reference to the La Venta Site', pp.1–38, reprinted from *Contributions of the University of California Archaeological Research Facility: Papers on Olmec and Maya Archaeology* 13 (June 1971).
Hauptmann, Harald, 'The Urfa Region', in Ozdogan and Basgelen, pp.65–86.
Hawkins, Gerald, *Beyond Stonehenge*, Harper & Rowe, New York, NY, 1973.
Hawkins, Gerald, *Mindsteps of the Gods*, Souvenir Press, London, 1983.
Hawkins, Gerald, *Stonehenge Decoded,* 1965, Souvenir Press, London, 1966.
Herodotus, *History*, trans. George Rawlinson, 2 vols, 1858, J M Dent, London, 1940.
Heusch, Luc de, 'On Griaule on Trial', CA 32:4 (August-October 1991), pp.434–7.
Hill, Charles, Martin Millett and Thomas Blagg, *The Roman Riverside Wall and Monumental Arch in London*, Lamas Publications, London, 1980.
Hole, Christina, *English Custom and Usage,* Batsford, London, Winter 1941–2.
Hole, Christina, *English Folklore,* Charles Scribner's Sons, New York/B T Batsford, London, 1940.
Holy Bible, The, Revised Authorized Version, OUP, 1905.
Houlihan, Patrick F, *The Birds of Ancient Egypt*, Aris and Phillips, Warminster, Dorset, 1986.
Hoyle, Fred, and Chandra Wickramasinghe, *Diseases from Space,* J M Dent, London, 1979.
Hoyle, Fred, and Chandra Wickramasinghe, *Lifecloud: The Origin of Life in the Universe.* J M Dent, London, 1978.
Hudson, Travis, and Ernest Underhay, forward by Anthony F Aveni, *Crystals in the Sky: An Intellectual Odyssey Involving Chumash Astronomy, Cosmology and Rock Art,* Ballena Press Anthropological Papers 10, Menlo Park, CA, 1978.
Hurry, Jamieson B, *Imhotep: The Vizier and Physician of King Zoser and afterwards the Egyptian God of Medicine*, OUP, 1928.
Hutton, Ronald, *The Stations of the Sun*, OUP, 1996.
Huxley, Aldous, *The Doors of Perception*, Heaven and Hell, 1954/1956, Flamingo, London, 1994.
Izady, Mehrdad, *The Kurds: A Concise Handbook*, Crane Russak, Washington, DC/Bristol, PA/London, 1992.
James, Peter, and Nick Thorpe, *Ancient Mysteries,* Ballantine Books, New York, NY, 1999.
Joseph, Isya, *Devil Worship: The Sacred Books and Traditions of the Yezidiz,* 1919, Health Research, Mokelumne Hill, CA, 1972.
Joseph, Rhawn, *Astrobiology, The Origin of Life and the Death of Darwinism*, Univ Press California, San Jose, CA, 2000.

Julius Caesar, *The Gallic War*, trans Carolyn Hammond, OUP, 1999.
'Junk DNA', NS 188:2526 (19 November 2005), p.92.
Kauffmann, Friedrich, *Northern Mythology*, J M Dent, London, 1903.
Kay, Charles de, *Bird Gods*, A S Barnes, New York, 1898.
Keeton, W T, 'Avian Orientation and Navigation', ARP 41:1 (March 1979), pp.353–66.
Keiller, Alexander, and Stuart Piggott, 'The Recent Excavations at Avebury', *Antiquity* 10:40 (1936), p.417–27.
Kirchner, Horst, 'Ein archäologischer Beitrag zur Urgeschichte des Schamanismus', *Anthropos* 47 (1952), pp.244–86.
Knappert, Jan, *Indian Mythology; An Encyclopedia of Myth and Legend*, The Aquarian Press, London, 1991.
Kolb, E W, 'Searching for Cygnets', in Aubert and L Montanet, pp.423–433.
Krupp, E C, 'Astronomers, Pyramids, and Priests', in Krupp, *In Search of Ancient Astronomers.*
Krupp, E C, *In Search of Ancient Astronomies*, Chatto and Windus, London, 1979.
Kühn, Herbert, *Rock Pictures of Europe*, 1952, Sidgwick and Jackson, London, 1956.
Kunte, Dr P K, 'Ancient India's Heritage in Observational Astronomy', VBP 1:1 & 2 (11 April 1994).
Kürkçüoğlu, Cihat A, and Zuhal Karahan Kara, *Harran: The Crossroad of Civilizations*, Harran District Governorship Cultural Publications, Şanliurfa, Turkey, 2003.
Lajoux, Jean-Dominique, *The Rock Paintings of Tassili*, 1962, Thames and Hudson, London, 1963.
Laliberte, Norman, and Edward N West, *The History of the Cross*, Macmillan, London and New York, NY, 1960.
LaViolette, Paul, *Earth Under Fire*, Bear and Co, Rochester, 1997, VT, 2005.
Legon, John A R, 'A Ground Plan at Giza', DE 10 (1988), pp.33–9.
Legon, John A R, 'The Giza Ground Plan and Sphinx', DE 14 (1989), pp.53–61.
Lehner, Mark, *The Complete Pyramids*, Thames and Hudson, London, 1997.
Lempriere, J., *A Classical Dictionary*, Routledge, London, 1919.
Lewis-Williams, J D, and T A Dowson, 'The Signs of All Times', CA 29:2 (April 1988), pp.201–45.
Lhote, Henri, *The Search for the Tassili Frescoes*, 1959, Readers Union Hutchinson, London, 1960.
Lichtheim, Miriam, *Ancient Egyptian Literature: Vol I – The Old and Middle Kingdom*, 1973, University of California, Berkeley/Los Angeles and London, 1975.
Little, Gregory, John Van Auken and Lora Little, *Mound Builders: Edgar Cayce's Forgotten Record of Ancient America*, Eagle Wing Books, Memphis, TN, 2001.
Luna, Luis Eduardo, and Pablo Amaringo, *Ayahuasca Visions*, 1991, North Atlantic Books, Berkeley, CA, 1999.
Mac Cana, Proinsias, *Celtic Mythology*, 1968, Chancellor Press, 1996.
MacDonald, Lorraine, 'Musings on Saint Brigit: Mary of the Gael', *Dalriada* 17:1 (An Fheille Bride 2002), pp.11–3.
Mackenzie, Donald A, *Ancient Man in Britain*, Blackie and Son, London, Glasgow, Bombay, 1922.

Mackenzie, Donald A, *Myths of China and Japan,* Gresham, London, n.d. (*c.*1920).
Mackenzie, Donald A, *Myths of Pre-Columbian America,* Gresham, London, n.d. (1923).
Mackenzie, Donald A, *Scottish Folk-lore and Folk Life*, Blackie, London & Glasgow, 1935.
Macleod (Wm Sharp), Fiona, *The Winged Destiny: Studies in the Spiritual History of the Gael*, Heinemann, London, 1910.
Magli, Giulio, *Misteri e scoperte dell'archeoastronomia*, Newton & Compton, Rome, Italy, 2005.
Magli, Giulio, 'On the astronomical content of the sacred landscape of Cusco in Inka times', *NNJ Architecture and Mathematics* 7:2 (2005).
Maiani, L, 'Electro Weak Interactions', presentation, EPS Int. Europhysics Con. on High Energy Physics, Bari, Italy, 18–24 July 1985 (November 1985).
Marsden, Peter, *Roman London*, Thames and Hudson, London, 1980.
Marshack, Alexander, *The Roots of Civilization*, Moyer Bell, Mount Kisco, NY, 1991.
Marshak, M L, et al, 'Evidence for Muon Production by Particles from Cygnus X-3', PRL 54:19 (13 May 1985), pp.2079–82.
Marti, J, J M Paredes and M Peracaula, 'Development of a two-sided Relativistic Jet in Cygnus X-3', AA 375 (2001), pp.476–84.
Marti J., D Perez-Ramirez, J L Garrido, P Luque-Escamilla, J M Paredes, 'Possible Hot Spots Excited By The Relativistic Jets Of Cygnus X-3', AA 439 (August 2005), pp.279–285.
Matthews, Caitlin, *The Celtic Tradition*, 1989, Element Books, Shaftesbury, Dorset, 1995.
McCluskey, Stephen C, *Astronomies and Cultures in Early Medieval Europe,* 1998, CUP, 2000.
McKenna, Terence, *Food of the Gods*, Rider, London, 1992.
McKenna, Terence, and Dennis McKenna, 1975, *The Invisible Landscape*, HarperSanFrancisco, New York, NY, 1993.
Mead, G R S, *Orpheus,* J M Watkins, London, 1965.
Meinel, Aden, and Marjorie Pettit Meinel, Barbara Meinel and David Drach-Meinel, 'Antiquity's Fingerprints in Ice: A Cosmic Encounter, A Cat's Eye, and Origin of Modern Humans', TAG 05, Sheffield University, 19 December 2005.
Meinel, Aden B, Marjorie P Meinel, David L Drach-Meinel and Barbara Meinel, 'The 250 Ky GRIP archives show the signature of a point source of cosmic rays: an analysis of the data leading to NGC 6543 as being the most probable source', paper presented at the IAU Symposium 234, Planetary Nebulae, Hawaii, April 2006.
Meinertzhagen, Colonel R, *Nicoll's Birds of Egypt,* 2 vols, Hugh Rees, London, 1930.
Mellaart, James, *Çatal Hüyük – A Neolithic Town in Anatolia,* Thames and Hudson, London, 1967.
Mercer, Samuel A B, *The Pyramid Texts in Translation and Commentary*, i, Longmans, Green and Co., New York/London/Toronto, 1952.
Michell, John, *The Dimensions of Paradise: The Proportions & Symbolic Numbers of Ancient Cosmology,* Harper and Row, London, 1988.
Milbourn, Thomas, *The Vintners' Company*, Vinters' Company, London, 1888.
Miller, Dorcas S, *Stars of the First People: Native American Star Myths and Constellations,* Pruett, Boulder, Colorado, 1997.

Mithen, Steven, *After the Ice: A Global Human History 20,000–5000 BC*, 2003, Phoenix, London, 2004.
Møller, A P, and T A Mousseau, 'Albinism and Phenotype of Barn Swallows (*Hirunda rustica*) from Chernobyl', *Evolution* 55:10 (2001), pp.2097-2104.
Moore, A W, *The Folk-lore of the Isle of Man*, 1891, Llanerch, Felinfach, Lampeter, Dyfed, 1994.
Mortensen, Bodil, 'Four Jars from the Maadi Culture found in Giza' MDAIK 41 (1985), pp.145–7.
Munn, Henry, 'The Mushrooms of Language', in Harner, *Hallucinogens and Shamanism*, pp.86–122.
Muraki, Y, *et al*, 'Search for Ultra High Energy Photons from Cygnus X-3', *Proceedings of 2nd Int. Conf. on Grational Microvensis Surveys at Paris*, 1995, pp.426–9.
Musser, George, 'Magnetic Anomalies', SA, August 2000.
Narby, Jeremy, *The Cosmic Serpent: DNA and the Origins of Knowledge*, 1995, Tarcher, Putnam, New York, NY, 1998.
Neugebauer, O, and Richard A Parker, *Egyptian Astronomical Texts: I. The Early Decans; II. The Ramesside Star Clocks; III. Decans, Planets, Constellations and Zodiacs – Text*, Brown University Press, Providence, Rhode Island/Lund Humphries, London, 1960/1964/1969.
Norbu, Namkhai, *The Crystal and the Way of Light*, Routledge and Kegan Paul, New York, NY/London, 1986.
North, John, *Stonehenge: Neolithic Man and the Cosmos*, 1996, HarperCollins, London, 1997.
Nougier, Louis-René, and Romain Robert, *The Cave of Rouffignac*, Geo Newnes, London, 1958.
O'Kelly, Claire, *Illustrated Guide to Newgrange*, John English, Wrexford, 1967.
Ott, Jonathan, 'The Post-Wasson History of the Soma Plant', *Eleusis* 1 (1998), pp.9–37.
Ovid, *The Metamorphoses* – see Riley.
Ozdogan, Mehmet, and Nezih Basgelen, eds, *Neolithic in Turkey: The Cradle of Civilization*, Arkeoloji ve Sanat Yaynlar, Istanbul, 1999.
Parker, Richard A, 'Egyptian Astronomy, Astrology, and Calendrical Reckoning', in Gillispie, pp.706–27.
Perry, W J, *The Megalithic Culture of Indonesia*, Univ of Manchester/Longmans, Green, London, 1918.
Petrie, W M Flinders, *Gizeh and Rifeh*, School of Archaeology in Egypt, University College, London/Bernard Quaritch, London, 1907.
Pillai, Thamotharam, *Iraiyanar Akapporul*, privately published, 1883.
Plato, *Phaedo*, Hackett, Indianapolis, IN, 1977.
Pogo, A, 'The Astronomical Ceiling-decoration in the Tomb of Senmut, *Isis* 14 (1930), pp.301–25.
Popul Vuh: The Mayan Book of the Dawn of Life – see Tedlock.
Rabinowitz, Jacob, *Isle of Fire*, Invisible Books, West Orange, NJ, 2004.
Rappenglück, Michael A, 'The Milky Way: Its Concept, function and meaning in ancient cultures', *Astronomy of Ancient Societies*, 2002, English language version, pp.270–6.

Rappenglück, Michael A, 'A Palaeolithic Planetarium Underground – The Cave of Lascaux Pt 1', MD 5:18 (2004), pp.93–119.

Rawson, Philip, *The Art of Tantra,* 1973, Thames and Hudson, London, 1978.

Reed, Darren S, Bruce Balick, Arsen R Hajian, Tracy L Klayton, Stefano Giovanardi, Stefano Casertano, Nino Panagia, Yervant Terzian, 'Hubble Space Telescope Measurements of the Expansion of NGC 6543: Parallax Distance And Nebular Evolution', AJ 118 (November 1999), pp.2430–2441.

Rees, Alun, 'Nobel Prize genius Crick was high on LSD when he discovered the secret of life', *The Mail on Sunday*, 8 August 2004, pp.44–5.

Reymond, E A E, *The Mythical Origin of the Egyptian Temple,* Manchester Univ Press, Manchester, 1969.

Rig Veda – see Griffith.

Riley, Henry T., trans. *The Metamorphoses of Ovid,* Geo. Bell, London and New York, NY, 1893.

Rolleston, Frances, *Mazzorath, or the Constellations,* Rivingtons, London, 1862. Available online at http://philologos.org/__eb-mazzaroth/default.htm.

Rolleston, T W, *Myths and Legends of the Celtic Race*, 1911, Geo G Harrap, London, Bombay, Sydney, 1929.

Ruddick, K, 'Model for the Underground Muons Associated with Cygnus X-3', PRL 57: 5 (4 August 1986), pp.531–4.

Rudgley, Richard, *The Lost Civilizations of the Stone Age,* The Free Press, New York, NY, 1999.

Ruggles, CLN, *Megalithic Astronomy: A New Archaeological and Statistical Study of 300 Western Scottish Sites*, British Archaeological Reports, Oxford, 1984.

Rundle Clark, R T, *Myth and Symbol in Ancient Egypt*, 1959, Thames and Hudson, London, 1978.

Sagan, Carl, *Broca's Brain*, 1974, Presidio Press, New York, NY, 1980.

Sagan, Carl, *The Cosmic Connection,*1973, Dell Publishing, New York, NY, 1975.

Salazar, Fernando E. Elorrieta, and Edgar Elorrieta Salazar, *The Sacred Valley of the Incas, Myths and Symbols*, Sociedad Pacaritanpu Hatha, Cusco Peru 1996.

Samorini, Giorgio, 'The Bwiti Religion and the Psychoactive Plant Tabernanthe iboga (Equatorial Africa)', *Integration* 5 (1995), pp.105–114.

Samorini, Giorgio, 'The Oldest Representations of Hallucinogenic Mushrooms in the World', *Integration* 2/3 (1992), pp.69–78.

Santillana, Giorgio de, and Hertha von Dechend, *Hamlet's Mill,* 1969, Macmillan, London, 1970.

Sanussi, Ashraf el-, and Michael Jones, 'A Site of the Maadi Culture Near the Giza Pyramids', MDAIK 53 (1997), pp.241–53.

Sarruf, Fuad, and Suha Tamim, *American University of Beirut Festival Book* (*Festschrift*), American University of Beirut, 1967.

Schlegel, Gustave, *Nederlandsch-Chineesch woordenboek,* 4 vols, E J Brill, Leiden, 1886–1890.

Schelgel, Gustave, *Thian Ti Hwui: The Hung-League or Heaven-Earth-League,* 1866, Banfield, Singapore, 1970.

Schlegel, Gustave, *Uranographie Chinoise,* 1875, 2 vols, Ch'eng-wen Publishing Company, Taipei, 1967.

Schirmer, Wulf, 'Some aspects of building at the 'aceramic-neolithic' settlement of Çayönü Tepesi', WA 21:3 (1990), pp.363–87.
Schmidt, Klaus, *Sie bauten die ersten Tempel,* C H Beck, Munich, 2006.
Schuchhardt, Dr D, *Schliemann's Excavations,* Macmillan, London and New York, NY, 1891.
Schultes, Richard Evans, Albert Hofmann and Christian Rätsch, *Plants of the Gods,* 1992, Healing Arts Press, Rochester, VT, 2001.
Segal, J B, 'Pagan Syriac Monuments in the Vilayet of Urfa', AS 3 (1953), pp.97–119.
Segal, J B, 'The Sabian Mysteries: The planet cult of ancient Harran', in Bacon, *Vanished Civilizations: Forgotten Peoples of the Ancient World.*
Serrano, Alejandro Jiménez, *Royal Festivals in the Late Predynastic Period and the First Dynasty,* BAR International Series 1076, Archaeo Press, Oxford, 2002.
'Sgeul gu Latha: The Coming of Angus and Bride', *Dalriada* 17:1 (An Fheille Bride 2002), pp.27–34.
Shimada, Atsuko, Akihiro Shima, Kumie Nojima, Yo Seino, and Richard B. Setlow, 'Germ cell mutagenesis in medaka fish after exposures to high-energy cosmic ray nuclei: A human model', *PNAS* 102 (11 April 2005) pp.6063–6067.
Sider, David, *The Fragments of Anaxagoras,* International Pre-Platonic Studies 4, second edition, Academia Verlag, Sankt Augustin, Germany, 2005.
Sidharth, B G, *The Celestial Key to the Vedas,* Inner Traditions, Rochester, Vermont, 1999.
Skeat, Rev Walter W, *Etymological Dictionary of the English Language,* 1879–1882, OUP, 1946.
Soker, Noam, 'The Cat's Eye (NGC 6543)', preliminary report, 2006.
Soker, Noam, and Gili Bisker, 'Bubbles in Planetary Nebulae and Clusters of Galaxies', *astro-ph*/0601032 (2 January 2006).
Solecki, Rose L., 'Predatory Bird Rituals at Zawi Chemi Shanidar', *Sumer* 33:1 (1977), pp.42–7.
Sommers, P, and J W Elbert, 'Implications of the Fly's Eye Evidence for Neutral Particles from Cygnus X-3', ALC 27 (1990), pp.397–402.
Soothill, Wm Edward, *The Hall of Light: A Study of Early Chinese Kingship,* Lutterworth Press, London, 1951.
Southwell, David, *Secrets and Lies,* Carlton Books, London, 2005.
Spaeth, Ove Von, 'Dating the Oldest Egyptian Star Map', IMHMST 42:3 (2000), pp.159–79.
Spalinger, Anthony J, ed., *Revolutions in Time; Studies in Ancient Egyptian Calendrics,* Van Siclen Books, San Antonio, Texas, 1994.
Spence, Kate, 'Ancient Egyptian Chronology and the Astronomical Orientation of the Pyramids', *Nature* 408 (16 November 2000), pp.320–4.
Spence, Lewis, *The Myths of the North American Indians,* Geo Harrap, London, 1916.
Sperlich, Dr Waltraud, 'Die erste Siedlung der Altsteinzeit', *bild der wissenschaft* (August 2000), pp.68–71.
Squier, Ephraim G, and Edwin H Davis, *Ancient Monuments of the Mississippi Valley,* vol. 1, 1848, Smithsonian Institution Press, Washington and London, 1998.

Squire, Charles, *Celtic Myth and Legend*, Gresham, London, nd (c.1912).
Staal, Julius D W, *The New Patterns in the Sky: Myths and Legends of the Stars*, McDonald and Woodward, Blacksburg, VA, 1988.
Staal, Julius D W, *Stars of Jade: Astronomy and Starlore of Very Ancient Imperial China*, Writ Press, Decatur, GA, 1984.
Staniland Wake, *Serpent-Worship and Other Essays*, 1888, Banton Press, Largs, 1990.
Stecchini, Livio C, 'Notes on the Relation of Ancient Measures to the Great Pyramid', see Tompkins.
Stephens, John L, *Incidents of Travel in Central America, Chiapas and Yucatan*, 2 vols, 1841, Dover, New York, NY, 1969.
Stevens (Mrs Drower), E S, *By Tigris and Euphrates*, Hurst & Blackett, London, 1923.
Stordeur, Danielle, 'New Discoveries in Architecture at Jerf el-Ahmar (Syria) 1997–1999', *Neo-Lithics* 1/00 (2000), pp.1–4.
Stoyanov, Yuri, 'Islamic and Christian Heterodox Water Cosmogonies from the Ottoman period – parallels and contrasts', BSOAS 64 (2001), pp.19–33.
Strassman, Rick, *DMT: The Spirit Molecule*, Park Street, Rochester, VT, 2001.
Stray, Geoff, *Beyond 2012: Catastrophe or Ecstasy – A Complete Guide to End-of-Time Predictions*, Lewes, East Sussex, 2005.
Stringer, Chris, and Peter Andrews, *The Complete World of Human Evolution*, Thames and Hudson, London, 2005.
Stukeley, Wm, *Abury, a Temple of the British Druids, With Some Others Described*, privately published, London, 1743. Available at www.avebury-web.co.uk/AburyWS/AburyWS.html
Sullivan, Wm, *The Secret of the Incas*, 1996, Three Rivers Press, New York, NY, 1997.
Tales from the Thousand and One Nights – See Dawood.
Tedlock, Dennis, trans and commentary, *Popul Vuh: The Mayan Book of the Dawn of Life*, 1985, Touchstone, New York, NY, 1996.
Temple, Robert, *The Sirius Mystery*, 1976, Century, London, 1998.
Thom, A, *Megalithic Sites in Britain*, 1967, OUP, 1979.
Thom, Alexander, Archibald S Thom and T R Foord, 'Avebury (1): A New Assessment of the Geometry and Metrology of the Ring', *JHA* 7 (1976), pp.183–92.
Thompson, R Lowe, *The History of the Devil: The Horned God of the West*, Kegan Paul, Trench, Trubner, London, 1929.
Thomsen, D E, 'A disbelief in Cygnets – Cygnus X3', SN 130:6 (9 August 1986), p.89.
Thomson, M A, et al, 'The Observation of Underground Muons from the Direction of Cygnus X-3 during the January 1991 Radio Flare', PRL B 269 (1991), pp.220–6.
Ticehurst, N F, *The Mute Swan in England*, Cleaver-Hume Press, London, 1957.
Tompkins, Peter, *Secrets of the Great Pyramid*, Allen Lane, London, 1971.
Urton, Gary, 'Animals and Astronomy in the Quechua Universe', PAPS 125:2 (April 1981), pp.110–27.
Urton, Gary, *At the Crossroads of the Earth and the Sky: An Andean Cosmology*, University of Texas Press, Austin, TX, 1981.
Urton, Gary, 'Beasts and geometry: Some Constellations of the Peruvian Quechuas', *Anthropos* 73 (1978) pp.32–40.

Urton, Gary, 'Celestial Crosses: The Cruciform in Quechua Astronomy', JLAL 6:1 (1980), pp.87–110.
Van Beek, Walter E A, 'Dogon Restudied', CA 32:2 (April 1991), pp.139–67.
Van den Broek, R., *The Myth of the Phoenix*, E J Brill, Leiden, 1972.
Vergani, Teresa, 'Ethnomathematics and Symbolic Thought: The Culture of the Dogon', ZDM 99:2 (1998), pp.66–70.
Völundarkvitha – see Bellows.
Wainwright, G A, 'A Pair of Constellations', *Studies Presented to F L Griffith*, 1932a, pp.373–83.
Wainwright, G A, 'Iron in Egypt', JEA 18 (1931), pp.3–15.
Wainwright, G A, 'Letopolis', JEA 18 (1932b), pp.159–72.
Wainwright, G A, *Sky-religion in Egypt*, CUP, 1938.
Wakefield, J D, *Legendary Landscapes: Secrets of Ancient Wiltshire Revealed*, Nod Press, Marlborough, Wilts, 1999.
Walsh, Martin W, 'Medieval English Martinmesse: The Archaeology of a Forgotten Festival', *Folklore* (October 2000).
Wasson, R Gordon, 'The Divine Mushroom of Immortality', in Furst, *Flesh of the Gods*, pp.185–200.
Wasson, R Gordon, *Soma: Divine Mushroom of Immortality*, 1968, Harcourt Brace, New York, NY, 1972.
Wasson, R Gordon, 'What Was the Soma of the Aryans?' in Furst, *Flesh of the Gods*, pp.201–213.
Wasson, Gordon R, Albert Hofmann and Carl A P Ruck, *The Rites of Eleusis*, Helen & Kurt Wolff /Harcourt Brace Jovanovich, New York, NY, & London, 1978.
Watling, Professor Roy, 'Psilocybe semilanceata – a hallucinogenic mushroom native to Europe', in Hancock, pp.614–7.
Watson, James D, *The Double Helix*, Weidenfeld and Nicolson, London, 1968.
Watt, W Montgomery, *Muhammad at Mecca*, OUP, 1953.
Weigall, Arthur, *A History of the Pharaohs: The First Eleven Dynasties*, Thornton Butterworth, London, 1925.
Wells, R A, 'The Mythology of Nut and the Birth of Ra', SAK 19 (1992), pp.305–21.
Wells, R A, 'Origin of the Hour and the Gates of the Duat', SAK 20 (1993), pp.305–26.
Wells, R A, 'Re and the Calendars', 1994, in Spalinger, pp.1–37.
Wilkinson, Richard H, *The Complete Gods and Goddesses of Ancient Egypt*, Thames and Hudson, London, 2003.
Williams ab Ithel, Rev. J, *Barddas*, Roderic/Longman, London, 1862.
Winlock, H E, 'The Egyptian Expedition 1925–1927', BMMA (February 1928), pp.32–58.
Xu, H Mike, *Origin of the Olmec Civilization*, University of Central Oklahoma Press, Edmond, OK, 1996.
Yiou, F, *et al*, 'Beryllium-10 in the Greenland Ice Core Project ice core at Summit, Greenland', JGR (30 November 1997), pp.102, No C12, pp.26, 783–26, 794.
Zába, Zbyněk, *L'Orientatation Astronomique dans l'Ancienne Égypte*, Archiv Orientální Supplementa II, Československá Akademie, Prague, 1953.

Zick, Michael, 'Derälteste Tempel der Welt', *bild der wissenschaft* (August 2000), pp.60–66.
Zimmer, Heinrich, *Myths and Symbols in Indian Art and Civilization*, 1946, Princeton Univ Press, Princeton, 1972.

ONLINE ARTICLES AND FEATURES
(All web pages active at time of writing.)

Alford, Alan, 'Egypt', The Official Website of Alan Alford, www.eridu.co.uk
Becker, Dr Alfred, 'Frank's Casket', www.franks-casket.de
Boyd, Patricia T, and Alan P Smale, 'The Long Term Light Curves of X-ray Binaries Contain Simultaneous Periodic and Random Components', AJ 612 (10 September 2004), pp.1006–17.
Boyle, Alan, 'Listening to the Sounds of Science', MSNBC, www.msnbc.com/news/372624.asp?cp1=1
Catchpole, Heather, 'Incan capital looked to heavenly puma', ABC Science Online, 14 September 2004, www.abc.net.au/science/news/space/SpaceRepublish_1198067.htm
Chalmers, Mathew, 'Amino acid detected in space', PhysicsWeb, available physicsweb.org/articles/news/7/8/7
Chandler, James, 'Clovis and Solutrean: Is There a Common Thread?', MT 16:3 (June 2001), available http://www.centerfirstamericans.com/mt.php?a=47
'Chandra Reveals The X-Ray Glint In The Cat's Eye', 8 January 2001, Chandra Press Room, available at chandra.harvard.edu/press/01_releases/press_010801.html
Chown, Marcus, 'Big Bang sounded like a deep hum', 30 October 2003, www.newscientist.com/article.ns?id=dn4320
'Chronological History Of The Newark Earthworks', a PDF file obtainable at The Ohio Historical Society – Newark Earthworks site www.ohiohistory.org/places/newarkearthworks/managementplan/managementplan.cfm
Collins, Andrew, 'Gods, Grails and Morphian Contact', available www.andrewcollins.com/page/articles/Gods,%20Grails%20and%20Morphian%20Contact.htm
Collins, Andrew, 'In defence of Cygnus X-3 as a Cosmic Accelerator: Response to Criticisms regarding its Production of Neutral Particles with Energies up to PeV', 2006, available as a PDF at www.andrewcollins.com
Collins, Andrew, 'Mothman, Mounds and Memphis', www.andrewcollins.com/page/articles/USVisit04.htm
Collins, Andrew, 'One Week in Kurdistan', www.andrewcollins.com/page/articles/kurdistan.htm
Conant, Richard, 'Mining for health', Atlantis Rising, www.atlantisrising.com%2Fissue4%2Far4mining.html
Conman, Joanne, 'The Round Zodiac Ceiling of the Temple of Hathor at Dendera', home.maine.rr.com/imyunnut/den.round.html
Cramer, John G, 'Children of the Swan, *Analog* (March 1986), www.npl.washington.edu/AV/altvw12.html
Cramer, John G, 'The Sound of the Big Bang', 10 November 2003, faculty.washington.edu/jcramer/BBSound.html

'Discovery of India: Pushkar Mela' Mera Bharat Mahan, www.merabharatmahan.org/modules.php?name=News&file=article&sid=9

Dumé, Belle, 'Did cosmic rays cause ice ages?' PhysicsWeb, 12 July 2004, physicsweb.org/articles/news/8/7/6

Encyclopedic Theosophical Glossary, Theosophical University Press, 1999, www.theosociety.org/pasadena/etgloss/ard-asr.htm

Erickson, Barbra E., 'Radiation and Health: An Overview of Radon Therapy in the United States and Europe', www.radonmine.com/pdf/radonandhealth.pdf

Fischer, Daniel, 'Cygnus X-3: Waiting for the Next Big Bang', *The Cosmic Mirror* 178 (26 February 2000), www.astro.uni-bonn.de/~dfischer/mirror/178.html

Harben, Henry A, *A Dictionary of London*, 1918, @ www.motco.com/Harben/

Hardaker, Chris, 'Towards resolving Clovis origins', MT 16:3 (June 2001), www.centerfirstamericans.com/mt.php?a=46

Jatakamala: XXII. The Story of the Holy Swan – SE Quadrant, Upper Register, Reliefs 77–80, Buddhism 101, adapted from the 19th century translation by J. S Speyer, www.borobudur.tv/jataka_022.htm

Jefferis, Marie, 'Ritual Deposition and Feather-Lined Pits in 17th Century Cornwall', revised 2005, ArchaeologyOnline.org, www.archaeologyonline.org/Feather%20Pits%20–%20revised.htm

Larson, Dana, 'Stoned Scientists' (04 Apr, 2003), CannabisCulture Marijuana Magazine, www.cannabisculture.com/articles/2783.html

LaViolette, Paul, 'Evidence for a Global Warming at the Termination I Boundary and its Possible Cosmic Dust Cause', Starburst Foundation, arxiv.org/ftp/physics/papers/0503/0503158.pdf

Magli, Giulio, 'On the astronomical content of the sacred landscape of Cusco in Inka times', arxiv.org/abs/physics/0408037

Malek, Jaromir, Diana Magee and Elizabeth Miles, *Topographical Bibliography of Ancient Egyptian Hieroglyphic Texts, Statues, Reliefs and Paintings: Objects of Provenance Not Known: Statues: Non-royal statues. LP: Man kneeling to ancestral busts,* Griffith Institute, Ashmolean Museum, Oxford, 2001, www.ashmol.ox.ac.uk/gri/s21.html

Marshak, M, 'Underground Muons Observed during the April 2000 Flare of Cygnus X-3', ICHEP 2000, ichep2000.hep.sci.osaka-u.ac.jp/abs_PA-11.html

Mioduszewski, Amy J, Michael P Rupen and Vivek Dhawan, 'Radio observations of Cygnus X-3 after the Large Radio Flare in September 2001', www.nrao.edu/~amiodusz/Cygx3head02.pdf

Montgomery, Denis, *Aquatic Man and African Eve,* 1995–2006, at www.sondela.co.uk/Aqua/Books/AquaApeA4.pdf

Montgomery, Denis, *Aquatic Man and African Eve: Book Two at African Eve at Home,* 2004, at faculty.mdc.edu/jmcnair/EveA4.pdf

Munzel, S C, and N J Conard, 'Change and Continuity in Subsistence during the Middle and Upper Palaeolithic in the Ach Valley of Swabia (Southwest Germany)', IJO 14 (2004), pp.225–243.

Murphy, Anthony, and Richard Moore, 'The Cygnus Enigma', *Mythical Ireland,* 1999–2004, www.mythicalireland.com/cygnus/

Nicholson, Philip T, 'The Soma Codes: Parts I-III', EJVS 8:3 (27 March 2002), users.primushost.com/~india/ejvs/issues.html

Pennicott, Katie, 'Carbon clock could show the wrong time', PhysicsWeb, 10 May 2001, physicsweb.org/articles/news/5/5/7

Perlman, David, 'Cave's ancient treasure 77,000-year-old artefacts could mean human culture began in Africa', *San Francisco Chronicle*, 11 January 2002, www.sfgate.com/cgi-bin/article.cgi?file=/c/a/2002/01/11/MN151227.DTL

Pettitt, Paul, 'Discovery, nature and preliminary thoughts about Britain's first cave art', *Capra* 5, www.shef.ac.uk/~capra/5/pettitt.html

'Recording Year: Autumn Migrations', BirdTrack, www.bto.org/birdtrack/recording_year/autumn_migration.htm

Ross, David J, 'The Bird, The Cross, And The Emperor: Investigations into The Antiquity of The Cross in Cygnus', CC 4:2 (12 February 2002), www.twcac.org/onlinehorizon/cross.htm

Samorini, Giorgio, 'L'Amanita muscaria nella preistoria siberiana Fiume Pegtymel', Samorini Network, www.samorini.net/archeo/tx_arc/arc_peg.html

Stecchini, Livio C, 'The Dimensions of the Great Pyramid', *A History of Measures: II – Units of Length,* www.metrum.org/measures/dimensions.htm

'Sugar in Space', 20 June 2000, Science@NASA, available spacescience.com/headlines/y2000/ast20jun_1.htm

'The Annual Taking Up and Marking of Thames Swans', *Swan Upping: A Brief History,* The Royal Windsor Website www.thamesweb.co.uk/swans/upping2.html

'The Radish: Part One', Lords of the Earth, www.mayalords.org/incfldr/nascalines.html

'The Tower', Four History www.channel4.com/history/microsites/H/history/t-z/tower8.html

Toyokazu, Watanabe, Iwakura Shinden, www.jomon.or.jp/ewatanabe.html

Unwin, G, 'London Tradesmen and Their Creditors', British History Online, Centre for Metropolitan History, www.british-history.ac.uk/report.asp?compid=33002

Vedamurthy, K, 'Ancient River', Review of The River Saraswati – Legend, Myth and Reality, by Dr S Kalyanaraman, *The Hindu*, 08 January 2002, hinduonnet.com/thehindu/br/2002/01/08/stories/2002010800120300.htm

'Vedic Saraswati', www.geocities.com/narenp/history/info/river.htm

'Waiting for Cygnus X-3', Science@NASA, science.nasa.gov/headlines/y2000/ast25feb_1m.htm

Whitehouse, Dr David, 'Ice Age star map discovered', BBC News, 9 August 2000, news.bbc.co.uk/1/hi/sci/tech/871930.stm

Windling, Terri, 'One is for Sorrow, Two is for Joy: The Magical Lore of Birds, The Endicott Studio', www.endicott-studio.com/rdrm/forbird.html

Witzel, Michael, 'Early Sanskritization: Origins and Development of the Kuru State', EJVS 1:4 (December 1995), pp.1–26, sers.primushost.com/~india/ejvs/ejvs0104/ejvs0104article.pdf

'Yezidi Religion and Society' www.geocities.com/Athens/Thebes/2153/yezidi.html

Aloian, Dr Zourab, 'Shaikh 'Adi, Sufism and the Kurds',
216.239.59.104/search?q=cache:SGrolzNaF2cJ:www.malaezdiyan.com/lalish.com/en/index2.php%3Foption%3Dcom_content%26do_pdf%3D1%26id%3D10+aloian+shaikh+adi+sufism&hl=en

OTHER WEBSITES MENTIONED IN TEXT

Cosmic Elk, www.cosmicelk.co.uk

Foundation for the Advancement of Mesoamerican Studies, Inc, www.famsi.org

The Swan Sanctuary, Shepperton, Middlesex, www.swanuk.org.uk

The Vintners' Company, www.vintnershall.co.uk

The Vintners' Company, virtual tour of Vintners' Hall www.ehouse.co.uk/virtualtours/standard5/8030258.htm

The website of Denis Montgomery, www.sondela.co.uk

Notes

Introduction

[1] Rincon, 'Space rock re-opens Mars debate', BBC News, 8 February 2006, news.bbc.co.uk/1/hi/sci/tech/4688938.stm

[2] Muir, 'It's raining aliens', NS 189:2541 (4 March 2006), pp.34–7.

[3] Lewis and Kumar, ASS arViv: astro-ph 0601022 (2 January 2006), pp.1–18.

Part One: Mystery of the North Chapter One – The Oldest Temple in the World

[1] See Zick, 'Der älteste Tempel der Welt', in *bild der wissenschaft* (August 2000), pp.60–66. Also Sperlich, 'Die erste Siedlung der Altsteinzeit', *bild der wissenschaft* (August 2000), pp.68–71. See also Schmidt, *Sie bauten die ersten Tempel.*

[2] Sperlich, p.71. See also Schmidt.

[3] Ibid.

[4] Zick, p.64.

[5] See Collins, *From the Ashes of Angels* for a full account of the Watchers, and their relationship to the Neolithic world.

[6] See Charles, R H, *The Book of Enoch.*

[7] See Note 1.

[8] To learn more about our journey to southeast Turkey in May-June 2004, see my online article 'Seven Days in Kurdistan' at www.andrewcollins.com

Chapter Two – In the Garden of Eden

[1] Albîrûnî, *The Chronology of Ancient Nations*, p.186.

[2] Ez. 27:23. All biblical quotes and references are taken from the Revised Authorised Version of 1611.

[3] Albîrûnî, p.188.

[4] Dodge, 'The Sabians of Harran', in Sarrüf and Tamim, *American University of Beirut Festival Book (Festschrift)*, p.62.

[5] Al-Nadim, i, *The Fihrist of al-Nadim*,pp.647, 661.

[6] Kürkçüoglu and Karahan Kara, *Harran: The Crossroad of Civilizations*, pp.77–8.

[7] Çelik, 'A New Early-Neolithic Settlement: Karahan Tepe, *Neo-lithics, A Newsletter of the Southwest Asian Lithics Research,* 2,-3/00, Berlin, 2000A, pp.6–8.

Chapter Three – The Direction of Heaven

[1] Schirmer, 'Some aspects of building at the "aceramic-neolithic" settlement of Çayönü Tepesi', WA 21:3 (1990), pp.363–87.

[2] Ibid, pp.382, 385.

[3] Ibid., pp.384–5.

[4] See al-Nadim, i, *The Fihrist of al-Nadim,* p.755 and Gündüz, 'The Knowledge of Life', *Journal of Semitic*

Studies Supplement 3, pp.143-8.

[5] Al-Nadim, i, pp.757–764; Dodge, 'The Sabians of Harran', in Sarruf and Tamim, *American University of Beirut Festival Book (Festschrift)*, p.70.

[6] Dodge, p.65.

[7] Gündüz, pp.142, 151–2.

[8] Al-Nadim, i, p.760.

[9] Ibid., p.63; Segal, 'The Sabian Mysteries: The planet cult of ancient Harran', in Bacon, *Vanished Civilizations: Forgotten Peoples of the Ancient World*, p.216.

[10] See al-Nadim, i, pp.746, 764; Dodge, 'The Sabians of Harran', pp.69, 72; Gündüz, pp.164–6. See also Dodge, 'Glossary', *s.v.* 'North', in al-Nadim, i, pp.918–9. However, Gündüz, p.166, makes a case for the direction of the Harranian *kiblah* being the south, while Albîrûnî states that although the Sabians of Iraq (i.e. the Mandaeans turn towards the north for prayer, the Harranians turn towards the 'south pole'. See Albîrûnî, *The Chronology of Ancient Nations*, p.188). This clearly contradicts other sources, such as al-Nadim, and since the Mandaeans and the Yezidi, who both face north, were related to the Harranians, this conclusion must be in error.

[11] See North, *Stonehenge: Neolithic Man and the Cosmos*, p.44 n. 3.

[12] See Drower, *The Mandaeans of Iraq and Iran,* p.6.

[13] Drower, p.18 n. 9. See also Stevens, *By Tigris and Euphrates,* p.215

[14] Stevens, p.209; Drower, pp.110, 216.

[15] Drower, p.110. See also Stevens, p.219.

[16] Drower, p.199.

[17] Ibid., p.95.

[18] Ibid., p.184.

[19] For information on carvings of vultures/raptors found at Nevali Çori, see Hauptmann, 'The Urfa Region', in Ozdogan and Basgelen, *Neolithic in Turkey: The Cradle of Civilization*, pp.65–86; for Göbekli Tepe, see Zick, 'Derälteste Tempel der Welt', *bild der wissenschaft,* August 2000, pp.60–66. Also Sperlich, 'Die erste Siedlung der Altsteinzeit', *bild der wissenschaft,* August 2000, pp.68–71; for Jerf al-Ahmar, see Stordeur, 'New Discoveries in Architecture at Jerf el-Ahmar (Syria) 1997–1999', Neo-Lithics 1/00 (2000), pp.1–4.

[20] Solecki, 'Predatory Bird Rituals at Zawi Chemi Shanidar', *Sumer* 33:1 (1977), pp.42–7.

[21] Ibid. Date given without recalibration.

[22] Drower, p.18 n. 9.

[23] Mellaart, *Çatal Hüyük: A Neolithic Town in Anatolia,* p.104.

[24] See Empson, *The Cult of the Peacock Angel*, pp.36, 206–9; Joseph, *Devil Worship*, pp.120–7.

[25] Joseph, pp.146–7.

[26] See Empson, p.54, for the Yezidi adoration of the Pole Star, and Joseph, p.163, for their veneration of the rising sun.

[27] Stevens, p.200.

[28] For translations of the Black Book see Guest, *The Yezidis*, pp.202–4, and Joseph, pp.36–49.

[29] A second account of this creation myth that appears later on in the Black Book gives forty years. See Joseph, p.43.

[30] Joseph, p.68.

[31] Empson, pp.191–2.

[32] For discussions on the 'eagle of the Arabians' see Drijvers, *Cults and Beliefs at Edessa*, pp.34, 41–2. 153. See also, Joseph, p.68 n. 34, 151.

[33] It is the story told in 'The Second Voyage of Sindbad the Sailor', found within *Tales from the Thousand and*

One Nights, pp.122–8.

[34] See 'Yezidi Religion and Society' online at www.geocities.com/Athens/Thebes/2153/yezidi.html, and Aloian, 'Shaikh 'Adi, Sufism and the Kurds', at www.malaezdiyan.com/lalish.com/en/index2.php?option=com_content&do_pdf=1&id=10

[35] Al-Nadim, i, pp.748–9; Gündüz, p.184; Dodge, 'The Sabians of Harran', p.73.

[36] Albîrûnî, p.187.

[37] Burton, *Personal Narrative of a Pilgrimage to Al-Madinah and Meccah*, p.174.

[38] Ibid., pp.175, 352 n. 3.

[39] Watt, *Muhammad At Mecca*, p.102.

[40] Ibid., p.106.

[41] Ibid., p.103.

[42] Izady, *The Kurds: A Concise Handbook*, p.156.

[43] Hauptmann, p.76.

[44] Ibid.

[45] Hamzeh'ee, *The Yaresan, pp.*70–1.

[46] Ibid., p.91.

[47] Green, *The City of the Moon God*, p.111.

[48] Ibid., pp.211–2.

[49] Hauptmann, p.68.

[50] Brown, *Researches into the Origin of the Primitive Constellations of the Greeks, Phoenicians and Babylonians*, i. pp.34–5, 234; ii. pp.17, 148.

[51] Allen, *Star Names: Their Lore and Meaning*, *s.v.* 'Lyra, the Lyre or Harp', pp.280–8.

[52] Segal, 'Pagan Syriac Monuments in the Vilayet of Urfa', AS 3 (1953), pp.97–119.

[53] Brown, i. p.35.

[54] Allen, *s.v.* 'Libra, the Balance or Scales', pp.269–78.

[55] For instance, in China the stars of Scorpio and Libra form part of the Azure Dragon of the East. See Ibid., *s.v.* 'Libra, the Balance or Scales', pp.269–78; 'Scorpio, or Scorpius, the Scorpion', pp.360–72. See also Staal, *The New Patterns in the Sky: Myths and Legends of the Stars*, p.225, for the stars of Scorpio as a serpent in Java and among the Tukano, Kobeua and Siusi in Brazil. As the sign of the Hebrew tribe Dan, Scorpio was also depicted as a crowned serpent or basilisk, while also in Egyptian tradition it was shown as the serpent of the autumn equinox.

[56] See Bullinger, *The Witness of the Stars*, pp.54–6, for the connection between the Hebrew *Akrab* and Scorpio.

[57] Hauptmann, Fig. 34, and also personal observation on our visit in May 2004.

Chapter Four – The Circle of Cygnus

[1] Brown, *Researches into the Origin of the Primitive Constellations of the Greeks, Phoenicians and Babylonians*, ii, p.148

[2] Ibid. Apparently, the Athenian astronomer Euktemon in 432 BC knew the stars of Cygnus as *Iktinos*, the kite, the Latin *Miluus* or *Milvus*.

[3] Allen, *Star Names: Their Lore and Meaning*, *s.v.* 'Cygnus the Swan', pp.192–8.

[4] Ibid.

[5] Ibid.

[6] Gen. 1:2.

[7] Ibid.

[8] Al-Nadim, i, *The Fihrist of al-Nadim*, p.757.

[9] Allen, *s.v.* 'Cygnus, the Swan', pp.192–8.

[10] Gregory of Tours, *De cursu stellarum*, 44, 5–6.

[11] Ibid., 46, and Haase, commentary, p.44. See also McCluskey, *Astronomies and Cultures in Early Medieval Europe*, pp.104–8.

[12] Rev. 21:6.

[13] Ross, 'The Bird, The Cross, And The Emperor: Investigations into The Antiquity of The Cross in Cygnus', CC 4:2 (12 February 2002), www.twcac.org/onlinehorizon/cross.htm.Ross

[14] For example, Minucius Felix (thrived *c.*AD 180 or 230), spoke out against those who used wooden crosses, including those 'with a man affixed to it', as did Tertullian (*c.*AD 160–240), in *Ad Nationes,* who described them as 'the object of worship', adding that 'with you [i.e. non-Roman Christians] the figure is a human one'. See Labiberte and West, *The History of the Cross*, p. 7.

[15] Freke and Gandy, *The Jesus Mysteries*, p.52.

[16] Ibid., p.53.

[17] See Ibid. which fully explores this hypothesis.

[18] Deane, *The Worship of the Serpent*, p.430.

[19] Segal, 'The Sabian Mysteries: The planet cult of ancient Harran', in Bacon, *Vanished Civilizations: Forgotten Peoples of the Ancient World*, pp.208, 214.

[20] This is a complex subject, although I would refer the reader to Mead, *Orpheus*, who certainly draws the connections between Sabianism and various of the Orphic works, particularly pp.28–9. Moreover, Orphic theogony also bears some similarities to that of Sabianism.

[21] Segal, p.217: Dodge, 'The Sabians of Harran', in Sarrüf and Tamim, *American University of Beirut Festival Book (Festschrift), p.77.*

[22] Allen, *s.v.* 'Cygnus the Swan', pp.192–8.

[23] Ibid.

[24] For discussions on the cosmic axis and its associations with death and otherworldly destinations see Eliade, *Myths, Dreams and Mysteries*, 1957, pp.59–98, and particularly Eliade, *Shamanism,* 1951, pp.259–300. For a more popular overview see Michell, *The Dimensions of Paradise,* and Santillana and von Dechend, *Hamlet's Mill.*

[25] Eliade, 1951, *pp.*269–74.

[26] Staniland Wake, *Serpent-Worship and Other Essays*, pp.14–5.

[27] Eliade, 1951, pp.272–3.

[28] Ibid., p.271 n. 48.

[29] According to Skyglobe 3.6, Deneb reached its closest point to the celestial pole at a distance of 7.1 degrees between 15,700–15,500 BC.

[30] According to Skyglobe 3.6, *delti* Cygni reached its closest point to the celestial pole at a distance of just 2.2 degrees around 14,200 BC.

[31] According to Skyglobe 3.6, Vega reached its closest point to the celestial pole at a distance of 5.1 degrees in around 12,000–11,900 BC.

[32] I will refer to the Eurasian continent simply because almost all of the activity cited in this book relates to Europe and Asia, and I dislike modern terms such as Afro-Eurasian or Euroafroasian continent. However, when using Eurasian continent I mean to include Africa, which, as we will see, also features in the Cygnus mystery.

[33] For a basic account of the Clovis-Solutrean enigma see Chandler, 'Clovis and Solutrean: Is There a Common Thread?', MT 16:3 (June 2001), www.centerfirstamericans.com/mt.php?a=47

[34] For objections to the Solutrean origin to Clovis see, for instance, Hardaker, 'Towards resolving Clovis origins', MT

16:3 (June 2001), www.centerfirst americans.com/mt.php?a=46

Part Two: America
Chapter Five – On the Wolf Trail

[1] Many thanks to Greg Little for supplying me with a copy of this image.

[2] The story is told in Spence, *The Myths of the North American Indians*, pp.201–2.

[3] Miller, *Stars of the First People*, pp.248–9.

[4] Ibid., p.252.

[5] Ibid., p.251.

[6] Ibid., pp.164, 166.

[7] Cowan, 'Effigy Mounds and Stellar Representation: A Comparison of Old World and New World Alignment Schemes', in Aveni, *Archaeoastronomy in Pre-Columbian America*, p.233.

[8] For instance, see Little, Van Auken and Little, *Mound Builders*.

[9] For a full account of our visit to the United States in July 2004 see Collins, 'Mothman, Mounds and Memphis' at www.andrewcollins.com/pages/articles /USVisit04.htm

[10] Hudson and Underhay, *Crystals in the Sky*, pp.118–9.

[11] Miller, p.255.

[12] Ibid., pp.47, 56, 60, 66, 80, 113, 127, 130, 132, 138.

[13] This information was obtained by using Skyglobe 3.6, and is based on an azimuth of 58.5 degrees east of north, a date of 100 BC and coordinates of 39 degrees 58 minutes N and 82 degrees 30 minutes W, the closest the program can get to Newark, Ohio, at 40 degrees 1 minute N, and 82 degrees 28 minutes W. The azimuth matches both the gap as viewed from Eagle Mound and also the first appearance of the solar orb from the same position on the date in question. A date of 100 BC for the construction of Great Circle is given in 'Chronological History Of The Newark Earthworks', a PDF file obtainable from The Ohio Historical Society – Newark Earthworks site at www.ohiohistory.org/places/newarkear thworks/managementplan/ managementplan.cfm

[14] See Cowan, *pp.*227–8.

[15] Ibid., p.218.

[16] Ibid., p.226 Table 1, 227, 232.

[17] Brandon, *The Rebirth of Pan*, p.222.

[18] Chamberlain, *When Stars Came Down to Earth*, pp.113–5; Miller pp.224–5. Another candidate suggested for the Bird's Foot constellation is Cassiopeia, which does fall on the Milky Way and is just outside the region of the circumpolar stars. However, the compelling evidence for Deneb being the Skidi Pawnee's North Star, and Cygnus being the Bird's Foot constellation outweighs this conclusion. Moreover, to identify Cassiopeia as a bird's foot would require having to ignore *epsilon* and *delta* Cassiopeiae, which makes no visual sense. Indeed, the Skidi Pawnee almost certainly identified the stars of Cassiopeia as an asterism known as the Rabbit. Although the Bird's Foot constellation remained unidentified among early writers who studied the Skidi Pawnee, both Chamberlain and Miller wrote that it fitted well with the stars of Cygnus.

[19] Chamberlain, p.114.

[20] Miller, p.226.

[21] Chamberlain, p.113. In Skidi Pawnee tradition the soul of the deceased was said to continue its journey towards the south, where the South Star, Midway Star or Death Star was to be

found. This is generally identified as Canopus, the second brightest star in the night sky after Sirius. Although this implies a southerly destination of the soul, the fact that the upper world is accessed via a north star identified with Deneb is the purpose of this exercise. Moreover, there would seem to have been two distinct directions of the afterlife in Skidi Pawnee tradition – one north and the other south, the final destination of the deceased being decided according to their status in life. See Miller, p.224; Dorsey, *Traditions of the Skidi Pawnee*, p.57. For anyone wishing to pursue the greater importance of Canopus in ancient religious funerary myth and legend, see Coppens, *The Canopus Revelation*.

[22] Other candidates include Capella, Vega and Polaris. However, neither Vega nor Polaris fall on the Milky Way, while Capella in Auriga, although located on the Milky Way, is well outside the region of the circumpolar stars. Only Deneb truly fits all the criteria. See Chamberlain, p.113.

[23] Ibid., p.242.

[24] Ibid.

[25] Ibid., p.226.

[26] Ibid., p.115.

[27] Ibid.

[28] Miller, p.179.

[29] Ibid., pp.179, 210. In contrast, a constellation known to the Osage as the 'Large Foot of Goose' is equated with the belt stars of Orion. See Ibid., p.234.

[30] Ibid., p.161. The Tipai of South California have a similar constellation called Chiyi, seen as the head of an eagle, formed from Altair and two other stars that are not identified. See Ibid., pp.165, 171.

[31] Armstrong, *The Folklore of Birds*, pp.14, 49.

[32] Ibid, pp.49, 112.

[33] Kühn, *Rock Pictures of Europe*, pl. xci

[34] De Kay, *Bird Gods*, p.182.

[35] Bachelor, *The Ainu and their Folk-Lore*, pp.449–51.

[36] Windling, 'One is for Sorrow, Two is for Joy: The Magical Lore of Birds, at The Endicott Studio, www.endicott-studio.com/rdrm/forbird.html

[37] Stoyanov, 'Islamic and Christian Heterodox Water Cosmogonies from the Ottoman period – parallels and contrasts', BSOAS 64 (2001), p.31.

[38] Ibid., p.30.

[39] Ibid., pp.19–33.

Chapter Six – Maya Cosmogenesis

[1] Hatch, 'An Hypothesis on Olmec Astronomy, with Special Reference to the La Venta Site', pp.1–38, reprinted from *Contributions of the University of California Archaeological Research facility: Papers on Olmec and Maya Archaeology* 13 (June 1971), p.5.

[2] Dr H Mike Xu of the University of Oklahoma believes that the north-south axis found at several Olmec sites reflects a knowledge of magnetic north, and does not relate to astronomical considerations. He does, however, accept that their cosmology featured the North Star, as it did in China, which he feels was culturally linked to the Olmec civilization. See Xu, *Origin of the Olmec Civilization*, pp.34–7.

[3] Hatch, 1971, p.8.

[4] Ibid.

[5] Ibid., p.9.

[6] Ibid.

[7] Ibid., pp.31–2.

[8] Ibid., p.11.

[9] Cowan, 'Effigy Mounds and Stellar Representation: A Comparison of Old World and New World Alignment Schemes', in Aveni, *Archaeoastronomy in Pre-Columbian America,* 1975, pp.217–34.

[10] Ibid., p.232. Cowan's argument is a little more complex than offered here, although for more information I suggest reading his paper on the subject.

[11] Hatch, 1971, p.14.

[12] Ibid.

[13] Ibid., p.17.

[14] Xu, p.33.

[15] Hatch, 'An Astronomical Calendar in a Portion of the Madrid Codex', in Aveni, 1975, pp.283–340.

[16] Ibid., p.325.

[17] Freidel, Schele and Parker, *Maya Cosmos,* p.55.

[18] Ibid., p.73.

[19] Ibid., p.76.

[20] Tedlock, commentary to *Popol Vuh,* p.237.

[21] Ibid.

[22] Ibid.

[23] *Popol Vuh,* p.237.

[24] See the website forum of the Foundation for the Advancement of Mesoamerican Studies, Inc at www.famsi.org for discussions for and against Seven Macaw being Deneb and the stars of Cygnus.

[25] Ibid., p.141.

[26] From what is known of the Olmec calendar, it would seem that they recognized a 52-year calendar cycle thought to have been anchored by a triple conjunction of Venus, Saturn and the sun on the summer solstice 810 BC. It has been proposed by R L Hall of the University of Chicago, after the earlier work of Munro Edmondson, that the Olmec-Maya Long Count was established 260 years later on a date which coincided with the termination of the Olmec calendar round. Yet this suggests that it was instituted in 550 BC, and not 355 BC as is proposed by several Mayan scholars. See Hall, 'Ancient Olmec and Maya Calculation and Use of Major Eras of Time Based upon the Tropical Year and Planetary Periods', 23rd DDA/HAD Meeting, BAAS, 1992, p.1067

[27] I want to thank Geoff Stray, author of *Beyond 2012,* for checking the accuracy of the 2012 material in this book.

[28] Mackenzie, *Myths of Pre-Columbian America,* p.56.

[29] See Stephens, *Incidents of Travel in Central America, Chiapas and Yucatan,* ii, pp.423–4.

Chapter Seven – Pathway to the Gods

[1] Salazar and Salazar, *The Sacred Valley of the Incas, Myths and Symbols,* p.53.

[2] Urton, *At the Crossroads of the Earth and the Sky,* 1981, pp.56–7.

[3] Salazar and Salazar, p.50.

[4] Ibid.

[5] Ibid., pp.52–3.

[6] In Venezuela, the Warao Indians say that these two celestial crosses are twin turkey-birds, which alternatively fly to the meridian and cry out for the help of Warao children. This reflects the fact that each of these constellations crosses the meridian exactly twelve hours apart. Both are to be found on the Milky Way; however, the Southern Cross is not visible in most parts of the Northern Hemisphere. See Urton, 1981, p.147.

[7] Salazar and Salazar, pp.53–7.

[8] Ibid., pp.57–63

[9] Ibid., pp.64–71.

[10] Ibid., pp.96–9.

[11] Ibid., p.51, cf. Bernabé Cobo, *Historia General de las Indias*, iii, 347, 1653/1956.

[12] Urton, 'Animals and Astronomy in the Quechua Universe', PAPS 125:2 (April 1981), pp.115–6.

[13] Urton, 1981, p.59. See also Urton, 'Animals', pp.110–27, Urton, 'Beasts and Geometry: Some Constellations of the Peruvian Quechuas', *Anthropos* 73 (1978) pp.32–40, and Urton 'Celestial Crosses: The Cruciform in Quechua Astronomy', JLAL 6:1 (1980), pp.87–110.

[14] Sullivan, *The Secrets of the Incas*, p.51.

[15] Ibid.

[16] Ibid., p.55.

[17] For instance, see Catchpole, 'Incan capital looked to heavenly puma', ABC Science Online, 14 September 2004, at www.abc.net.au/science/news/stories/s 1198067; Forgione, 'Il Potere dalle Stelle' *Hera* 59 (December 2004), pp.52–8; Magli, *Misteri e scoperte dell'archeoastronomia*, pp.224–30, and Magli, 'On the astronomical content of the sacred landscape of Cusco in Inka times', *NNJ Architecture and Mathematics* 7:2 (2005). Available also at rxiv.org/abs/physics/0408037

[18] Sullivan, pp.50, 53–4.

[19] Ibid., p.57.

[20] Ibid.

[21] Ibid., p.49.

[22] Ibid., p.367.

[23] Eliade, *Shamanism*, pp.272–3.

[24] Sullivan, pp.58–9.

Part Three: Albion
Chapter Eight – The Winged Serpent

[1] Stukeley, *Abury*, p.34.

[2] Ibid., p.35.

[3] Ibid., p.35.

[4] Ibid., p.18.

[5] Ibid., p.19.

[6] Ibid., pp.62, 92–5.

[7] Ibid., pp.62, 93.

[8] Ibid., p.43.

[9] Burl, *Prehistoric Avebury*, pp.216–7.

[10] Ibid., p.218.

[11] Ibid., p.219.

[12] Ibid., p.218.

[13] Ibid., p.219.

[14] The figure given for the axial orientation of Avebury in Thom, *Megalithic Sites in Britain*, p.100, Table 8.1, is 339.2 degrees. In Thom, Thom and Foord, 'Avebury (1): A New Assessment of the Geometry and Metrology of the Ring', *JHA* 7 (1976), p.191, it is cited as 340.2 degrees.

[15] Stukeley, p.25.

[16] Thom, Thom and Foord, p.191.

[17] Stukeley, p.24.

[18] Gimbutas, *The Language of the Goddess*, pp.185, 265.

[19] Other sites included an 'outlier' at a stone circle in Seascale; another stone row at Ballantrae, Garleffin, in Ayrshire, known as the Grey Stones, as well as further stone circles at Penmaenmawr in the Conway Valley in northwest Wales and Moel ty Ucha in the Berwyn Mountains of northeast Wales Cumbria. See Thom, pp.97–101, Table 8.1; 104–5.

[20] Ibid., p.105.

[21] Burl, p.216.

[22] Skyglobe shows that, based on a light extinction of 1.4 degrees, Deneb would

have been seen to set somewhere between 338.7 and 339 degrees as viewed from Avebury *c.*3000–2500 BC.

[23] Stukeley, p.96.

[24] Hawkins, *Stonehenge Decoded*, and Hawkins, *Beyond Stonehenge.*

[25] Hawkins, *Mindsteps to the Cosmos*, pp.107–110.

[26] Ibid., p.110.

[27] Ibid.

[28] Ibid.

[29] North, *Stonehenge*, p.44 n. 3.

[30] Ibid., pp.94–5, 97.

[31] Ibid., p.80.

[32] Keiller and Piggott, 'The Recent Excavations at Avebury', *Antiquity* 10:40 (1936), p.420 and Fig. 7. Possible 'cup and ring' ornament was also noted on one, or possibly two, other stones examined by them.

[33] Wakefield, *Legendary Landscapes*, p.84.

[34] Keiller and Piggott, p.424.

[35] Ibid., p.420. It is likened by Keiller and Piggott to 'no. 2 of Burkitt's sequence of Irish techniques in IPEK, 1926, 52'.

[36] Gettings, *Dictionary of Demons*, *s.v.* 'Magical calendar', pp.155–6.

Chapter Nine – Goddess of the Swan

[1] Dames, *The Avebury Cycle*, pp.60–63.

[2] Mackenzie, *Ancient Man in Britain*, 1922, p.188.

[3] Hutton, *The Stations of the Sun*, p.135.

[4] Mackenzie, *Scottish Folk-lore and Folk Life*, 1935, p.193.

[5] Graves, *The White Goddess*, p.346.

[6] McCluskey, *Astronomies and Cultures in Early Medieval Europe*, p.65.

[7] Carmichael, *Carmina Gadelica*, i, p.167.

[8] Ibid.

[9] Ibid., i, p.164.

[10] Mac Cana, *Celtic Mythology*, p.93.

[11] MacDonald, 'Musings on Saint Brigit: Mary of the Gael', *Dalriada* 17:1 (An Fheille Bride 2002), p.11.

[12] Ibid.

[13] Carmichael, i, p.169; Mackenzie, 1922, p.187.

[14] Anderson, *The Ancient Secret*, p.118.

[15] Mackenzie, 1935, p.193.

[16] Carmichael, i, p.168.

[17] Macleod, *The Winged Destiny*, p.258. See also Graves, pp.346, & Carmichael, as quoted in Graves, p.361.

[18] Cope, *The Modern Antiquarian*, p.39.

[19] Moore, *The Folk-lore of the Isle of Man*, p.106.

[20] I want to thank my wife Sue for alerting me to this phenomenon, which she became aware of when living in Bredon, Worcestershire.

[21] Hutton, p.137.

[22] Carmichael, i, p.168.

[23] Hutton, p.138.

[24] Mackenzie, 1922, p.188.

[25] Allen, *Star Names: Their Lore and Meaning*, *s.v.* 'Cygnus, the Swan', pp.192–98.

[26] See Williams ab Ithel, *Barddas*, p.liii.

[27] See Ibid., intro.

[28] Matthews, *The Celtic Tradition*, p.51, cf. *Sanas Chormaic* (Cormac's Glossary), trans. John O'Donovan, ed Whitley Stokes, O T Cutter, Calcutta, 1868.

[29] Ibid.

[30] Allen, *s.v.* 'The Galaxy, or Milky Way', pp.475–85.

[31] Hole, *English Folklore*, p.63.

[32] Armstrong, *The Folklore of Birds*, p.48; Mackenzie, 1922, p.190.

[33] Ibid.

[34] De Kay, *Bird Gods*, p.200.

[35] Ibid., p.181.

[36] Ibid., p.201.

[37] Email communication from Eileen Buchanan, dated 20 October 2004. This knowledge was given to her by family members on her mother's side, who were born and raised in Argyll and the Inner Hebrides.

[38] The following account and quotes are taken from Jefferis, 'Ritual Deposition and Feather-Lined Pits in 17th Century Cornwall', revised 2005, ArchaeologyOnline.org at www.archaeologyonline.org/Feather%20Pits%20–%20revised.htm

[39] Ibid.

[40] Carmichael, as quoted in Hutton, p.137.

[41] Hutton, p.137, cf. Carmichael.

Chapter Ten – The Waters of Life

[1] See Hole, *English Custom and Usage*, p.115.

[2] Official records of the Vintners' Company only go back to the beginning of the sixteenth century. However, other sources clearly imply that their involvement in Swan-Upping predates any existing records by hundreds of years. See Crawford, *A History of the Vintners' Company*, pp.268–70.

[3] Some sources state the 'last Monday in July'. See Milbourn, *The Vintners' Company*, p.25.

[4] Blackham, *The Soul of the City: London's Livery Companies*, p.146.

[5] See Ticehurst, *The Mute Swan in England.*

[6] Ibid., pp.93–4, after the mark of John Richers of Swannington, Norfolk, dated 1501; pl. xxi, no. 31, the so-called 'skorge', after the Abbots of Croyland, Leicestershire; 'The Annual Taking Up and Marking of Thames Swans', *Swan Upping: A Brief History* on the Royal Windsor Website at www.thamesweb.co.uk/swans/upping2.html, after the 'Dus de Cleuer', i.e. of Clewer near Windsor in Berkshire, from the second half of the fifteenth century.

[7] Ticehurst, p.123.

[8] See Bayley, *Caer Sidhe: Vol 1 – The Celtic Night Sky*, p.62.

[9] *Swan-Upping: A Brief History*, The Royal Windsor Website, op. cit.

[10] Unwin, 'London Tradesmen and Their Creditors', British History Online, at www.british-history.ac.uk/report.asp?compid=33002

[11] Harben, *A Dictionary of London*, s.v. 'swan', @ www.motco.com/Harben/5214.htm

[12] Milbourn, p.112, cf. Strype's Stow, i, bk. 3, p.i, edition 1720.

[13] Ibid., p.77.

[14] Ibid., p.7.

[15] See the Vintners' Company website at www.vintnershall.co.uk

[16] Milbourn, pp.74, 76–7, 118.

[17] See Crawford, *A History of the Vintners' Company*, pp.263–7.

[18] Milbourn, p.1.

[19] Ibid., p.112; Crawford, p.14.

[20] This now lost temple stood, according to historical writer Michael Harrison, in the vicinity of Sise Lane, since 'Sise' and its earlier variants 'Sancte Cidis', 1358, and 'Seint Sythes lane,' 1401, are almost certainly corruptions of *Isidis*, the genitive case form of the name *Isis* in Latin (the official language of London through until the Saxon conquest around AD 600). See Harrison, *The*

London that was Rome, pp.83, 230.

[21] Other discovered items which confirm the temple's presence in the city include three iron rattles, or *sistra*, and a bronze steelyard weight in the form of the bust of Isis with horns.

[22] The altar was removed from a section of the river-wall in the vicinity of Baynard Street, close to the present site of the Mermaid Theatre. See Marsden, *Roman London*, p.133; Hill, Millett & Blagg, *The Roman Riverside Wall and Monumental Arch in London*, pp.3–6, 195–8.

[23] Marsden, p.50.

[24] Ibid, p.49.

[25] Budge, *The Gods of the Egyptians*, ii, p.374.

[26] Go to the Vinters' Company virtual tour of Vintners' Hall at www.ehouse.co.uk/virtualtours/standard5/8030258.htm

[27] Walsh, 'Medieval English Martinmesse: The Archaeology of a Forgotten Festival', *Folklore* (October 2000).

[28] See 'The Tower', Four History at www.channel4.com/history/microsites/H/history/t-z/tower8.html

[29] Armstrong, *The Folklore of Birds*, p.28 n. 2, 165.

[30] Bayley, *Caer Sidhe: Vol 1 - The Celtic Night Sky*, p.62.

[31] For information of arrival dates of swans and geese into Britain see 'Recording Year: Autumn Migrations', BirdTrack, www.bto.org/birdtrack/recording_year/autumn_migration.htm

[32] De Kay, *Bird Gods*, p.197.

Chapter Eleven – Swan Knights and Swan Maidens

[1] O'Kelly, *Illustrated Guide to Newgrange, p.*65.

[2] Ibid., p.61.

[3] Rolleston, *Myths and Legends of the Celtic Race*, p.121.

[4] See O'Kelly, pp.60–2; Rolleston, pp.121–23, and Squire, *Celtic Myth and Legend*, pp.139–42.

[5] Rolleston, p.122.

[6] 'Sgeul gu Latha: The Coming of Angus and Bride', *Dalriada* 17:1 (An Fheille Bride 2002), pp.27–34.

[7] O'Kelly, p.69.

[8] Armstrong, *The Folklore of Birds*, p.48.

[9] For a full account of Murphy and Moore's 'The Cygnus Enigma', go to *Mythical Ireland* at www.mythicalireland.com/cygnus/

[10] Ibid.

[11] Ibid.

[12] We refer here to Grave # 8 of the Bogebakken cemetery. See Mithen, *After the Ice*, p.181.

[13] Ibid.

[14] Ibid., pp, 181–2.

[15] Grimm, *Teutonic Mythology*, iv, p.1297.

[16] De Kay, *Bird Gods*, p.192.

[17] Kauffmann, *Northern Mythology*, p.56.

[18] Grimm, i, pp.426–7.

[19] Ibid., i, pp.427–8.

[20] Ibid., i, p.428.

[21] De Kay, p.185: 'Icelandic álptir, Norse elptr, elftr, swans, is scarely to be distinguished from Icelandic álfar, albr, elves.'

[22] Ibid., p.186.

[23] Carmichael, *Carmina Gadelica,* ii, *s.v.* '*Eala, eal, ai,* swan.', pp.276–9.

[24] Ibid.

[25] Grimm, i, p.428.

[26] De Kay, p.191.

[27] Grimm, i, p.429.

[28] De Kay, p.181.

[29] Ibid., p.179; Carmichael, ii, *s.v.* '*Eala, eal, ai,* swan.', pp.276–9, cf. Green's *History*.

[30] Grimm, i. p.429.

[31] De Kay, p.192.

[32] North, *Stonehenge*, p.44.

[33] Ibid., p.53 n. 6.

[34] See Bellows, *The Poetic Edda,* ii: 'Lays of the Heroes – Völundarkvitha, 31; p.265 n. 31.

[35] See Becker, 'Frank's Casket', at www.franks-casket.de

[36] Burl, *The Stone Circles of the British Isles*, p.152.

[37] See Collins, *Gateway to Atlantis*, p.352.

[38] Burl, pp.150–1.

[39] Ibid, pp.151–2.

[40] Ibid.

[41] See Ruggles, *Megalithic Astronomy: A New Archaeological and Statistical Study of 300 Western Scottish Sites.*

[42] See Collins, p.352.

[43] Burl, p.153.

[44] Ibid., p.154.

[45] Ibid.

[46] North, p.68.

Part Four: Egypt
Chapter Twelve – The Key to Ascension

[1] It has been suggested that the recently discovered Bosnian pyramids are larger, although so far these have not been fully excavated.

[2] Based on Cole, *The Determination of the Exact Size and Orientation of the Great Pyramid of Giza*, 1925.

[3] Herodotus, *History,* ii, 124.

[4] All dates in Egyptian chronology have been taken from Gardiner, *Egypt of the Pharaohs.*

[5] For instance, Pyramid Texts (henceforth PT) 273–4, 405. All references from the Pyramid Texts derive from Faulkner, *The Ancient Egyptian Pyramid Texts,* unless otherwise stated. With regards to some of the Egyptian words given in this chapter, note that most vowels in ancient Egyptian were not written. Sometimes Egyptologists have been able to reconstruct them, but where vowels remain uncertain, transcriptions either omit them or replace them with 'e' so that the words may be pronounced. Hence the word 'Benben' is actually written ***Bnbn***.

[6] PT 519, 1220; 519, 1216; 520, 1222. See also Faulkner, 'The King and the Star-religion in the Pyramid Texts', JNES 25 (1966), pp.153–7, for further PT references linking the deceased king with the Imperishable Stars.

[7] Belmonte, 'On the Orientations of the Old Kingdom Egyptian Pyramids', JHA 32 (2001), No 26, pp.S1–20. See also Parker, 'Egyptian Astronomy, Astrology, and Calendrical Reckoning,' in Gillispie, *Dictionary of Scientific Biography*, xv, i, 1978, p.718.

[8] PT 519, 1218.

[9] Allen, *Genesis in Egypt*, p.6.

[10] See Von Spaeth, 'Dating the Oldest Egyptian Star Map', IMHMST 42:3 (2000), pp.159–79; Pogo, 'The Astronomical Ceiling-decoration in the Tomb of Senmut, *Isis* 14 (1930), pp.301–25.

[11] Winlock, 'The Egyptian Expedition 1925–1927', BMMA (February 1928), p.56.

[12] Neugebauer and Parker, *Egyptian*

Astronomical Texts: III. Decans, Planets, Constellations and Zodiacs – Text, pp.8–9.

[13] Ibid., pp.189, 194, 196.

[14] Ibid., pp.189–91; Budge, *The God of the Egyptians*, ii, p.312.

[15] Wainwright, 'A Pair of Constellations', *Studies Presented to F L Griffith*, 1932a, pp.375.

[16] PT 463, 876. The Mooring Post does tend to move around a bit in ancient Egyptian art, and so its identity as the pole has been questioned. See Belmonte, p.S5.

[17] Neugebauer and Parker, III, pp.191–2

[18] Stecchini, 'The Dimensions of the Great Pyramid', *A History of Measures: II – Units of Length,* at www.metrum.org/measures/dimensions.htm.

[19] Wainwright, 1932a, p.377; Neugebauer and Parker, III, p.192.

[20] PT 217, 159; 246, 254.

[21] PT 720, 2237.

[22] PT 25, 17; 35, 27; 36, 591, 1613.

[23] Wainwright, 1932a, pp.373–83.

[24] Ibid., p.376 figs. 3–6.

[25] Ibid., p.377.

[26] Ibid.

[27] Ibid., p.377 n. 6.

[28] Neugebauer and Parker, III, p.80.

[29] Wainwright, 1932a, p.380.

[30] Belmonte, S2.

[31] Ibid.

[32] Ibid., p.S1.

[33] See Edwards, *The Pyramids of Egypt*, pp.265–8.

[34] Belmonte, p.S2.

[35] Wainwright, 1932a, p.381.

[36] Ibid.

[37] Ibid., pp.380–1.

[38] Zába, *L'Orientatation Astronomique dans l'Ancienne Égypte*, pp.44–6.

[39] Ibid., pp.47–8, 50–4.

[40] See Stecchini, 'Notes on the Relation of Ancient Measures to the Great Pyramid', in Tompkins, *Secrets of the Great Pyramid*, pp.287–382.

[41] Stecchini, *A History of Measures.*

[42] Ibid.

[43] Ibid.

[44] Spence, 'Ancient Egyptian Chronology and the Astronomical Orientation of the Pyramids', *Nature* 408 (16 November 2000), pp.320–4.

[45] Belmonte, S11–S17.

[46] PT 572, 1474.

[47] PT 478, 980.

[48] Wainwright, 'Letopolis', JEA 18 (1932b), p.168, cf. PT 572, 1474.

[49] Eliade, *Shamanism*, p.487.

[50] Ibid.

[51] Ibid.

[52] Ibid.

[53] Ibid., p.490.

[54] Gen. 28:12.

[55] Eliade, p.492.

[56] Wainwright, 1932b, pp.168, 168 n. 3.

[57] PT 688, 2079.

[58] PT 440, 815.

[59] Budge, *The Book of the Dead*, Pap. Nu, ch, xcviii.

[60] Ibid.

[61] Ibid.

[62] Wainwright, 1932b, p.167.

[63] Wainwright, 1932a, p.382.

[64] Bauval and Gilbert, *The Orion Mystery*, p.206.

[65] Wainwright, 'Iron in Egypt', JEA 18 (1931), p.11; Wainwright, *Sky-religion in Egypt,* 1938, p.13.

[66] Wainwright, 1931, p.14, cf. Plutarch,

De Iside at Oriside, 62, Teubner's edn., *Moralia*, II, 536.

[67] Ibid., p.11.

[68] For instance, PT 570, 1454–1455.

[69] Wainwright, 1931, p.7.

[70] Ibid., p.9.

[71] Ibid., p.6.

[72] Ibid.

[73] Ibid., p.11.

[74] Wainwright, 1932a, p.382.

[75] Ibid., p.378.

Chapter Thirteen – In Search of Sokar

[1] Budge, *The Egyptian Heaven and Hell*, 1906, iii, p.131.

[2] See, for example, Gaballa and Kitchen, 'The Festival of Sokar' *Orientalia* 38 (1969), pp.4, 20; Rundle Clark, *Myth and Symbol in Ancient Egypt*, p.97, where he speaks in terms of 'Sokar of Giza'.

[3] For instance, PT 300, 445.

[4] Petrie, *Gizeh and Rifeh*, pp.2–7.

[5] Gaballa and Kitchen, p.15, after the Palermo Stone.

[6] Weigall, *A History of the Pharaohs*, i, p.110, after Manetho.

[7] See Mortensen, 'Four Jars from the Maadi Culture found in Giza', MDAIK 41 (1985), pp.145–7, and Sanussi and Jones, 'A Site of the Maadi Culture Near the Giza Pyramids', MDAIK 53 (1997), pp.241–53.

[8] Mortensen, p.147.

[9] In all three tools were discovered, two in April 2004 and one in May 2005. These were shown to Dr Jeffrey Spencer of the Department of Ancient Egypt and Sudan at the British Museum on 12 June 2005, who confirmed that they were hand-worked flakes in chert, which if not of Dynastic origin were most probably from the Late Neolithic period.

[10] Hart, *A Dictionary of Egyptian Gods and Goddesses*, *s.v.* 'Sokar', pp.202–3.

[11] For Sokar's involvement in the 'Stretching of the Cord', see Gaballa and Kitchen, p.15. The falcon-headed deity *dwn-'nwy* is connected with the ceremony via the theories presented in Chapter Twelve.

[12] PT 364, 620; 532, 1256.

[13] Gaballa and Kitchen, p.22; Allen, *Genesis in Egypt*, p.41.

[14] PT 669, 1968.

[15] PT 669, 1967–9.

[16] Bauval and Gilbert, *The Orion Mystery*, pp.203–4, after the work of E A Wallis Budge and J P Lauer.

[17] PT 685, 2069.

[18] Van den Broek, *The Myth of the Phoenix*, pp.242–4.

[19] Gaballa and Kitchen, pp.27–8.

[20] Ibid., p.64.

[21] Allen, *Star Names: Their Lore and Meaning*, *s.v.* 'The Galaxy, or Milky Way', pp.475–85.

[22] Allen, *s.v.* 'Eridanus' , pp.215–220.

[23] Hassan, *Excavations at Giza, 1934–5*, vi, I, pp. p.265.

[24] For a full account of the Fourth and Fifth Hours of the *Am-duat* see Budge, i, 1906, pp.62–115.

[25] See Serrano, *Royal Festivals in the Late Predynastic Period and the First Dynasty, p.*92.

[26] Ibid.

[27] Budge, *An Egyptian Hieroglyphic Dictionary*, 1920, ii, *s.v.* 's-ker' and 'seker', p.626b.

[28] Budge, *From Fetish to God in Ancient Egypt*, 1934, p.19, cf. the Pap. Ani, ch. xvii, l, 113.

[29] Ibid., p.19.

[30] Budge, 1906, i, p.93

[31] Ibid.

[32] Ibid, i, p.94.

[33] Gaballa and Kitchen, pp.16, 63.

[34] Breasted, *Ancient Records of Egypt*, ii, p.322.

[35] Reymond, *The Mythical Origin of the Egyptian Temple*, pp.137, 142.

[36] Ibid., p.123.

[37] Ibid., p.34.

[38] Ibid., pp.77, 103.

[39] Ibid., pp.6–7.

[40] Ibid., p.113.

[41] Ibid., p.116.

[42] Ibid., pp.12–3, 55, 106–7, 110, 116, 123–4, 131.

[43] Ibid., pp.87–8, 107, 114, 126

[44] Ibid., p. 110.

[45] Ibid., pp.194, 208.

[46] Ibid., p.29.

[47] Ibid., pp.177, 179.

[48] Ibid., p.263.

[49] Hurry, *Imhotep*, p.17.

[50] Reymond, pp.15, 110.

[51] Ibid., p.68.

[52] Ibid., p.118.

[53] Ibid., pp.69–70, 84–5.

[54] Ibid., p. 108.

[55] Budge, 1920, ii, *s.v.* 'benn', p.217a. Hart, George, *A Dictionary of Egyptian Gods and Goddesses*, 1986, p.57 (entry for 'Benu').

[56] Budge, 1906, i, p.65.

[57] Gaballa and Kitchen, pp.69–70.

[58] Ibid., p.21.

[59] Ibid., p.70.

[60] Reymond, pp.152, 155.

[61] Ibid., pp.181, 200.

[62] Ibid., pp.155–6.

[63] Collins, *Gods of Eden*, p.192.

Chapter Fourteen – The Road to Rostau

[1] See Cox, 'A Sanctuary for Sokar', in Bauval, *The Secret Chamber*, pp.390–6.

[2] No other bright star rose at this same point during the Pyramid Age.

[3] Bauval and Gilbert, *The Orion Mystery*, p.53.

[4] Lehner, *The Complete Pyramids*, pp.106–7.

[5] See, for instance, Legon, 'A Ground Plan at Giza', DE 10 (1988), pp.33–9.; Legon, 'The Giza Ground Plan and Sphinx', DE 14 (1989), pp.53–61.

[6] Breasted, *Ancient Records of Egypt*, ii, p.323.

[7] Goyon, *Le secret des bâtisseurs des grandes pyramides*, pp.165, 174–6.

Chapter Fifteen – The Well of Souls

[1] Wilkinson, *The Complete Gods and Goddesses of Ancient Egypt, s.v.*, 'Gengen-wer', p.213, cf. Pap. Leiden I 350.

[2] Coffin Texts, I, Spell 222, 223; Budge, *The Book of the Dead*, i, ch. liv, lv, lvi, lix, xcv.

[3] Meinertzhagen, *Nicoll's Birds of Egypt*, i, p.64; Houlihan, *The Birds of Ancient Egypt*, pp.50–1.

[4] Coffin Texts, I, Spell 302.

[5] Krupp, 'Astronomers, Pyramids, and Priests', in Krupp, *In Search of Ancient Astronomers*, p.200.

[6] See Conman, 'The Round Zodiac Ceiling of the Temple of Hathor at Dendera', at home.maine.rr.com/imyunnut/den.round.html; Daressy,

'L'Egypt Celeste', BIFAOC 12 (1915), pp.1–34.

[7] Aubourg, 'La date de conception du zodiaque du temple d'Hathor à Dendera', BIFAOC 95 (1995), pp.1–10.

[8] Rolleston, *Mazzorath, or the Constellations.*

[9] Budge, *Gods of the Egyptians*, 1904, ii, p.95.

[10] Ibid., ii, p.374.

[11] Ibid., ii, p.94.

[12] Ibid.

[13] Ibid., ii, p.109.

[14] Ibid., ii, p.108.

[15] See Billing, 'Writing an Image – The Formulation of the Tree Goddess Motif in the Book of the Dead, Ch. 59', SSA 32 (2004), pp.35–50; Buhl, 'The Goddesses of the Egyptian Tree Cult', JNES 6 (1947), pp.80–97.

[16] Budge, 1904, ii. p.108.

[17] Buhl, p.80.

[18] Ibid., p.87.

[19] Pyramid Texts, Utt. 574, 470, and a commentary in Ibid., p.88.

[20] Buhl, p.87.

[21] Ibid., p.91.

[22] Budge, *The Book of the Dead*, 1960, Pap. of Ani, LIX.

[23] Faulkner, *The Ancient Egyptian Coffin Texts,* I, Spell 223.

[24] Allen, *Genesis in Egypt*, p.1.

[25] Ibid., p.3.

[26] Ibid.

[27] Ibid.

[28] Wells, 'The Mythology of Nut and the Birth of Ra', SAK 19 (1992), pp.305–21; Wells, 'Re and the Calendars', 1994, in Spalinger, *Revolutions in Time*, pp.4–5.

[29] For example, Wells cites a lead figurine of a naked woman found at Troy in the nineteenth century by Heinrich Schliemann, and thought to be an 'Asiatic Aphrodite'. It bore a swastika or hooked cross over its genitalia, something 'repeatedly found in all prehistoric sites, and among the ornaments of later date'. See Schuchhardt, *Schliemann's Excavations*, pp.66–7, 67 fig. 60.

[30] Wells, 1994, p.7.

[31] Ibid.

[32] Ibid., p.8.

[33] Ibid., p.20.

[34] Wells, 'Origin of the Hour and the Gates of the Duat', SAK 20 (1993), pp.305–26.

[35] Ibid., p.315.

[36] Belmonte Avilés, 'Some open questions on the Egyptian calendar: an astronomer's view', TdE (2003), pp.7–56.

[37] Wells, 1993, p.314.

[38] Lichtheim, *Ancient Egyptian Literature*, I, 'The Story of Sinuhe', pp.222–35.

[39] Ibid., p.224.

[40] Goedicke, 'The Route of Sinuhe's Flight', *JEA* 43 (1957), pp.77–85; Rabinowitz, *Isle of Fire.*

[41] Malek, Magee and Miles, *Topographical Bibliography of Ancient Egyptian Hieroglyphic Texts, Statues, Reliefs and Paintings*, 2001, available at www.ashmol.ox.ac.uk/gri/s21.html

[42] See Goedicke, op. cit.

[43] Reymond, *The Mythical Origin of the Egyptian Temple*, pp.152, 155.

[44] Ibid., pp.181, 200.

[45] Ibid., pp.155–6.

[46] Collins, *Gods of Eden*, p.192.

Part Five: Origins
Chapter Sixteen – The Swan-Goose of Eternity

1 For information on the geomythical history of Pushkar, see 'Discovery of India: Pushkar Mela' at Mera Bharat Mahan, www.merabharatmahan.org

2 Knappert, *Indian Mythology*, *s.v.* 'Brahma', pp.56–7.

3 Rawson, *The Art of Tantra*, p.202.

4 For instance, Brahma's shrine is found in the north wall of the Nageshwara Shiva Shrine, Dharasuram, near Kumbakonam in Tamil Nadu.

5 Blavatsky, *The Secret Doctrine*, 1889, i, p.20, after Ramayana, Ayodhya Kanda 2–82–10.

6 Zimmer, *Myths and Symbols in Indian Art and Civilization*, p.48.

7 Blavatsky, 'The Hindu Theory of Vibration as the Producer of Sounds, Forms and Colors', AT 5:6 (17 April 2005), pp.1–6.

8 Zimmer, pp.47–50.

9 Encyclopedic Theosophical Glossary, *s.v.* 'Ardhamatra', cf. *Nadabindu-Upanishad*, available at www.theosociety.org/pasadena/etgloss/ard-asr.htm

10 Rawson, p.203 fig. 167.

11 See Sidharth, *The Celestial Key to the Vedas*, pp.64–9.

12 Feuerstein, Kak and Frawley, *In Search of the Cradle of Civilization*, p.139.

13 Witzel, 'Early Sanskritization: Origins and Development of the Kuru State', EJVS 1:4 (December 1995), p.15

14 Ibid., p.15.

15 Skyglobe 3.6 indicated that from Northern India between 3000–2000 BC, Deneb rose at the time of the midwinter solstice at approximately 48 degrees east of north, just three degrees off northeast – the gap closing the further one went back in time until *c.* 4900–4800 BC, when Deneb rose precisely northeast.

16 Witzel, p.16, 16 n. 102.

17 Armstrong, *The Folklore of Birds*, p.44 and pl. 13.

18 The Jatakamala: XXII. The Story of the Holy Swan – SE Quadrant, Upper Register, Reliefs 77 – 80, Buddhism 101, adapted from the 19th century translation by J. S Speyer, at www.borobudur.tv/jataka_022.htm

19 Blavatsky, 1889, i, p.357 fn.

20 See Sidharth, op. cit.

21 Kunte, 'Ancient India's Heritage in Observational Astronomy', VBP 1:1 & 2 (11 April 1994).

22 Personal communication with Dr P K Kunte of Mumbai, India, dated 18 March 2005.

23 Vedamurthy, 'Ancient River', Review of *The River Saraswati – Legend, Myth and Reality*, by Dr S Kalyanaraman, *The Hindu*, 08 January 2002, at hinduonnet.com/thehindu/br/2002/01/08/stories/2002010800120300.htm

24 See, for instance, 'Vedic Saraswati', www.geocities.com/narenp/history/info/river.htm

25 See Feuerstein, Kak and Frawley, for a full account of the Saraswati-Sindhu civilization, and its relationship to both the Rig Veda and the Indus Valley civilization, especially, pp.71, 88–92.

26 Nicholson, 'The Soma Codes: Parts I-III', EJVS 8:3 (27 March 2002), pp.1–92. Available at sers.primushost.com/~india/ejvs/ejvs0803/ejvs0803.pdf

27 Feuerstein, Kak and Frawley, p.132.

28 Rig Veda, I, 164, 20.

29 Feuerstein, Kak and Frawley, p.124.

Chapter Seventeen – The First Astronomers

[1] Schlegel, *Uranographie Chinoise,* 1875, i, 30. However, he does seem to vary the date. For instance, he cites 16,916 years BP (+/- 900 years) on p.36 and 16,000 and 14,600 years BP on p.486.

[2] Flammarion, *Popular Astronomy*, p.536 n. 1.

[3] Schlegel, *Nederlandsch-Chineesch woordenboek,* 1886–1890.

[4] Schelgel, *Thian Ti Hwui: The Hung-League or Heaven-Earth-League,* 1866.

[5] See Staal, *Stars of Jade*, 1984.

[6] Ibid., p.13.

[7] Ibid., p.14.

[8] Ibid., p.36.

[9] Schlegel, 1875, p.207.

[10] Ibid., p.207-8.

[11] Ibid.

[12] Ibid.

[13] For a full argument on how Staal arrived at the date of 15,600 BC for the original construction of Chinese astronomy, see Staal, 1984, pp.5, 13–5, 19, 58–9, 138.

[14] Staal, 1984, pp.100, 103.

[15] Ibid., p.58.

[16] This version of the story comes from Staal, *The New Patterns in the Sky*, 1988, pp.185–6, and Staal, 1984, pp.151–2. Staal gives the names Zhi Nü and Jian Niu in the alternative orthographies Tchi-niu and Kien-niou.

[17] Soothill, *The Hall of Light*, p.114.

[18] Ibid., p.109.

[19] A megalithic structure at Yamazoe in the Yarnabe district of Nara, Honshu Island, Japan, investigated by Teruaki Yanagihara, was found to reflect the Summer Triangle at a date corresponding to *C.* 2000 BC. See Toyokazu, Iwakura Shinden, at www.jomon.or.jp/ewatanabe.html

[20] Staal, 1984, pp.103–4.

[21] Ibid.

[22] Whitehouse, 'Ice Age star map discovered', BBC News, 9 August 2000, at news.bbc.co.uk/1/hi/sci/tech/871930.stm

[23] Rappenglück, 'A Palaeolithic Planetarium Underground – The Cave of Lascaux Pt 1', MD 5:18 (2004), pp.93–119.

Chapter Eighteen – The Point of Creation

[1] I really recommend reading Graham Hancock's book *Supernatural* for a full in-depth study into this fascinating area of study.

[2] Lewis-Williams and Dowson, 'The Signs of All Times', CA 29:2 (April 1988), pp.201–45.

[3] For an excellent article on the growth of the *Psilocybe* group of mushrooms in Europe, see Watling, 'Psilocybe semilanceata – a hallucinogenic mushroom native to Europe', in Hancock, pp.614–7. See also Hancock, op cit, pp.219–27.

[4] Schultes, Hofmann and Rätsch, *Plants of the Gods*, p.55.

[5] See Wasson, 'The Divine Mushroom of Immortality', in Furst, *Flesh of the Gods,* pp.185–200; Munn, 'The Mushrooms of Language', in Harner, *Hallucinogens and Shamanism*, pp.86–122.

[6] Samorini, 'The Oldest Representations of Hallucinogenic Mushrooms in the World', *Integration* 2/3 (1992), pp.69–78.

[7] See Lhote, *The Search for the Tassili Frescoes.*

[8] See Samorini, op cit; Lajoux, *The Rock*

Paintings of Tassili, pp.72–3.

[9] Samorini, op. cit; Lajoux, p.71.

[10] Samorini, op. cit.

[11] Dikov, 'La pétrographie en Sibérie du Nord-Est', *Inter-Nord* 12 (1971). See also Samorini, 'L'Amanita muscaria nella preistoria siberiana Fiume Pegtymel', Samorini Network, www.samorini.net/archeo/tx_arc/arc_peg.html

[12] Rudgley, *The Lost Civilizations of the Stone Age, p.*140.

[13] See Harner, 'The Role of Hallucinogenic Plants in European Witchcraft', in Harner, *Hallucinogens and Shamanism*, pp.125–50.

[14] Kirchner, 'Ein archäologischer Beitrag zur Urgeschichte des Schamanismus', *Anthropos* 47 (1952), pp.271.

[15] Eliade, *Shamanism*, p.504.

[16] Ibid., p.481.

[17] Ibid.

[18] Marshack, *The Roots of Civilization*, pp.369–71.

[19] CNRS stands for Colloques Internationaux du Centre National de la Recherche Scientifique.

[20] Hauptmann, 'The Urfa Region', in Ozdogan and Basgelen, *Neolithic in Turkey*, p.75, fig. 10.

[21] Zick, 'Derälteste Tempel der Welt', *bild der wissenschaft* (August 2000), p.64.

[22] Hauptmann, p.79, fig. 34.

[23] Ibid.

[24] Ibid., p.79, fig. 35.

[25] McKenna, *Food of the Gods*, pp.101, 102 fig. 13, 120.

[26] Ibid., pp.119 fig. 16, 120.

[27] Allegro, *The Sacred Mushroom and the Cross*.

[28] Skeat, *An Etymological Dictionary of the English Language*, *s.v.* 'Cygnet', p.151b.

[29] Allegro, pp.99, 121.

[30] Ibid.

[31] Ibid., p.65, cf. 1 Kings 7:16, etc.

[32] Ibid., p.121.

[33] Rappenglück, 'The Milky Way: Its Concept, function and meaning in ancient cultures', *Astronomy of Ancient Societies*, 2002, English language version, pp.270–276.

[34] Ibid., p.273.

[35] Ibid., p.274.

[36] Ibid., p.272.

[37] Ibid.

[38] Ibid., p.274.

[39] Ibid., after Keller, 1999, pp.179–95.

[40] Ibid., p.272.

[41] Ibid., p.276.

[42] Ibid.

[43] Ibid.

[44] Wasson, 'What Was the Soma of the Aryans?' in Furst, *Flesh of the Gods*, pp.201–213. See also Wasson, *Soma: Divine Mushroom of Immortality*. For criticisms of Wasson identification of Soma as *Amanita muscaria*, see Ott, 'The Post-Wasson History of the Soma Plant', *Eleusis* 1 (1998), pp.9–37 and Flattery and Swartz, *Haoma and Harmaline*.

[45] Another theory is that Soma is in fact the juice of the Syrian rue (*Peganum harmala*), a powerful psychoactive plant and MAO (*Monoamine oxidase*) inhibitor. Extracts of the Syrian rue are known to have been ingested by the Bedouin of Syria, which makes it a good candidate for Soma, especially as this divine ambrosia was venerated also in Iran, ancient Persia, under the name *haoma*. See Ott and also Flattery and Swartz.

[46] See Gooch, *Cities of Dreams*, pp.100–1,

145–6.

[47] Various email communications between Dr Michael Rappenglück and the author during 2005.

Part Six: Cosmos

Chapter Nineteen – The Secret of Life

[1] This account of Jeremy Narby's experiences in the Peruvian Amazon is taken from Narby, *The Cosmic Serpent*; his presentation 'Beyond the Cosmic Serpent' at the Questing Conference/QuestCon05 on 5 November 2005, and personal communication between him and the author in 2005.

[2] See Luna and Amaringo, *Ayahuasca Visions*, Vision 12, pp.70–2; Vision 35, pp.116–8.

[3] Nougier and Robert, *The Cave of Rouffignac*, pl. 17, op. p.102.

[4] Harner, 'The Sound of Rushing Water', in Harner, *Hallucinogens and Shamanism*, pp.16–7.

[5] Strassman, *DMT: The Spirit Molecule*, p.200.

[6] Ibid., p.201.

[7] Sider, *The Fragments of Anaxagoras*, frag. B4a, which talks about seeds of life elsewhere, and of worlds peopled like ours (see pp. 92, 97-8, 102). See also Joseph, *Astrobiology*, pp.55, 58, for another take on Anaxagoras's views on panspermia.

[8] Arrhenius, 'The Propagation of Life in Space', DU 7 (1903), p.481. Reprinted in Goldsmith, *The Quest for Extraterrestrial Life*, pp.32–33.

[9] See Arrhenius, *Worlds in the Making*.

[10] Joseph, p.59.

[11] Ibid.

[12] Ibid.

[13] See, for instance, Hoyle and Wickramasinghe, *Lifecloud*, and Hoyle and Wickramasinghe, *Diseases from Space*.

[14] 'Sugar in Space', 20 June 2000, Science@NASA, available at spacescience.com/headlines/y2000/ast20jun_1.htm

[15] Chalmers, 'Amino acid detected in space', PhysicsWeb, available at physicsweb.org/articles/news/7/8/7

[16] 'Alien life seems yet more likely', NS 188: 2522 (22 October 2005), p.22, cf. *The Astrophysical Journal* 632, p.316.

[17] See Watson, *The Double Helix*.

[18] Rees, 'Nobel Prize genius Crick was high on LSD when he discovered the secret of life', *The Mail on Sunday*, 8 August 2004, pp.44–5.

[19] Ibid.

[20] Crick and Orgel, 'Directed Panspermia', *Icarus* 19 (1973), pp.43–57. Reprinted in Goldsmith, pp.34–7.

[21] 'Francis Crick', obituary, *The Times*, 30 July 2004, pp.68–9.

[22] Crick, *Life Itself*, p.158.

[23] Ibid., p.159.

[24] Hancock, *Supernatural*, pp.475–82.

[25] Davies, 'Do we have to spell it out', NS 183:2459 (7 August 2004), pp.30–1.

[26] Ibid., p.30.

[27] 'Junk DNA', NS 188:2526 (19 November 2005), p.54.

[28] Davies, p.31.

[29] Joseph, p.312.

[30] Huxley, *The Doors of Perception*.

[31] Fosar and Bludorf, *Vernetzte Intelligenz*, 2001.

[32] Ibid., pp.30, 187, 317, 324,

[33] See, for instance, Ibid., pp.11–2, 28–9, 42–7.

[34] Strassman, p.206.

[35] See Southwell, *Secrets and Lies*, p.147; Larson, 'Stoned Scientists' (04 Apr, 2003), CannabisCulture Marijuana Magazine, available at www.cannabisculture.com/articles/2783.html

[36] Ashpole, *The Search for Extra-terrestrial Intelligence*, p.145.

[37] Ibid., pp.145–6.

[38] Mackenzie, *Myths of China and Japan*, p.275.

[39] Drower, *The Mandaeans of Iraq and Iran*, p.199.

[40] Sullivan, *The Secret of the Incas*, p.57.

[41] Ibid.

[42] Ibid., p.49.

[43] Ibid., p.367.

[44] Perry, *The Megalithic Culture in Indonesia*, p.72.

[45] Ibid., p.78.

[46] Ibid., p.80.

[47] Ibid., p.91.

[48] Sagan, *Broca's Brain*, p.77.

[49] Perlman, 'Cave's ancient treasure 77,000-year-old artefacts could mean human culture began in Africa', *San Francisco Chronicle*, 11 January 2002, available at www.sfgate.com/cgi-bin/article.cgi?file=/c/a/2002/01/11/MN151227.DTL

Chapter Twenty – Cosmic Swansong

[1] Examples taken from Thompson, *The History of the Devil*, p.15.

[2] See Clottes, 'Art of the Light and Art of the Depths', in Conkey, *Beyond Art: Pleistocene Image and Symbol, pp.*209–10.

[3] Ibid.

[4] Ibid., pp.207, 210, 214.

[5] Ibid., p.210.

[6] See Devereux, *Stone Age Soundtracks.*

[7] The account is taken from Samorini, 'The Bwiti Religion and the Psychoactive Plant Tabernanthe iboga (Equatorial Africa)', *Integration* 5 (1995), pp.105–114.

[8] Ibid.

[9] Ibid.

[10] Ibid.

[11] Ibid.

[12] Ibid, and see also Samorini, 'The Oldest Representations of Hallucinogenic Mushrooms in the World', *Integration* 2/3 (1992), pp.69–78.

[13] The whole account is from Ovid, *Metamorphoses*, bk. 11, 589–632.

[14] See Ibid.

[15] Lempriere, *A Classical Dictionary, s.v.* 'Somnus', pp.575.

[16] See Collins, 'Gods, Grails and Morphian Contact', available at www.andrewcollins.com/page/articles/Gods,%20Grails%20and%20Morphian%20Contact.htm, for an unorthodox take on the idea of morphian contact.

[17] Ovid, op. cit.

[18] Norbu, *The Crystal and the Way of Light*, pl. 24.

[19] Skeat, *Etymological Dictionary of the English Language, s.v.* 'swan', p.621a.

[20] Ibid., *s.v.* 'song' and 'sonnet', p.581a.

[21] Aesop, *Aesop's Fables*, 284, 303.

[22] *Plato, Phaedo*, 84e-85b.

[23] Batchelor, *The Ainu and their Folk-Lore, p.*450.

[24] Chown, 'Big Bang sounded like a deep hum', 30 October 2003, available at www.newscientist.com/article.ns?id=dn4320

[25] See Cramer, 'The Sound of the Big Bang', 10 November 2003, available at faculty.washington.edu/jcramer/BBSound.html

[26] Thanks go out to Giulio Magli for his suggested editorial changes.

[27] Munzel and Conard, 'Change and Continuity in Subsistence during the Middle and Upper Palaeolithic in the Ach Valley of Swabia (Southwest Germany)', IJO 14 (2004), pp.225–243; Harding, 'After the hunt, Ice Age man chilled out – with a flute', *The Guardian*, 17 December 2004.

[28] Boyle, 'Listening to the Sounds of Science', MSNBC, available at www.msnbc.com/news/372624.asp?cp 1=1

[29] Thanks to Heather Hobden for helping me to track down information regarding these swan pendants. For more on Siberian shamanism and the Palaeolithic cult of the swan visit her site CosmicElk at www.cosmicelk.co.uk

[30] Pettitt, 'Discovery, nature and preliminary thoughts about Britain's first cave art', *Capra* 5, available at www.shef.ac.uk/~capra/5/pettitt.html

[31] Ibid.

[32] Ibid.

[33] Gimbutas, *The Language of the Goddess*, pp.244–5.

[34] Ibid.

[35] Pettitt, op. cit.

[36] Calculated on an elevation of 25 degrees from the proximity of the main ibex engraving, under the assumption that an earthen slope led down into the cave interior, a fact confirmed by Jonathan Hesketh of the Cresswell Crags Visitors Centre. The interior sight of view creates a horizontal window of visibility between 355–0 degrees azimuth.

[37] De Kay, *Bird Gods*, pp.189–90.

[38] See Keeton, 'Avian Orientation and Navigation', ARP 41:1 (March 1979), pp.353–66.

[39] Musser, 'Magnetic Anomalies', SA (August 2000).

Chapter Twenty-One – Children of the Swan

[1] Dar, Lord and Wilkes, 'Nature of the high-energy particles from Cygnus X-3', PR D33:1 (1 January 1986), pp.303; Kolb, 'Searching for Cygnets', in Aubert and Montanet, p.428; Marshak et al, 'Evidence for Muon Production by Particles from Cygnus X-3', PRL 54:19 (13 May 1985), pp.2079–82; Ruddick, 'Model for the Underground Muons Associated with Cygnus X-3' PRL 57: 5 (4 August 1986), p.531.

[2] Dar et al, p.303; Kolb, p.428; Marshak et al, pp.2079–82; Ruddick, p.531.

[3] Cassiday et al, 'Evidence for 10^{18-}eV Neutral Particles from the Direction of Cygnus X-3', PRL 62:4 (23 January 1989), pp.383–6; Sommers and Elbert, 'Implications of the Fly's Eye Evidence for Neutral Particles from Cygnus X-3', ALC 27 (1990), pp.397–402.

[4] Dar et al, p.305; Kolb, p.429.

[5] Marshak et al, p.2079.

[6] Kolb, p.424.

[7] Sadr is currently at declination 40 degree 15 minutes with a right ascension of 20 hours 22 minutes.

[8] See Cramer, 'Children of the Swan', *Analog* (March 1986), available at www.npl.washington.edu/AV/altvw12.html

[9] Dar et al, p.303; Kolb, p.429; Ruddick, p.531.

[10] Dar et al, p.303; Kolb, p.429; Ruddick, p.531.

[11] Kolb, p.429.

[12] Cramer, op cit.

[13] Ibid.

[14] Ruddick, p.533.

[15] Cassiday, p.386.

[16] Dar et al, p.303.

[17] Kolb, p.429.

[18] Ibid., pp.428–31.

[19] Cramer, op. cit.

[20] Maiani, 'Electro Weak Interactions', presentation, EPS Int. Europhysics Con. on High Energy Physics, Bari, Italy, 18–24 July 1985 (November 1985).

[21] Thomsen, 'A disbelief in Cygnets – Cygnus X3', SN 130:6 (9 August 1986), p.89. But see also Ruddick, p.532, who says that only the very largest detectors on the ground could have tracked the decay of airborne muons created by cygnets, and then only if observed horizontally.

[22] Kolb, p.429.

[23] Ibid; Ruddick, p.532.

[24] Muraki et al, 'Search for Ultra High Energy Photons from Cygnus X-3', Proceedings of 2nd Int. Conf. on Grational Microvensis Surveys at Paris, 1995, pp.426–9.

[25] Czapek, Hahn, Krebs and Muller, 'Measurement of the muon flux in the Gotthard underground laboratory', JPGNPP 16:7 (July 1990), pp.1101–1108.

[26] Thomson et al, 'The Observation of Underground Muons from the Direction of Cygnus X-3 During the January 1991 Radio Flare', PRL B 269 (1991), p.220.

[27] Marshak, 'Underground Muons Observed during the April 2000 Flare of Cygnus X-3', ICHEP 2000, abstract available at ichep2000.hep.sci.osaka-u.ac.jp/abs_PA-11.html

[28] Allison et al, 'Cygnus X-3 revisited: 10 years of muon and radio observations', Proceedings of the 26th International Cosmic Ray Conference (ICRC 99), Salt Lake City, Utah, 17–25 Aug 1999.

[29] 'Waiting for Cygnus X-3' Science@N.ASA, available at science.nasa.gov/headlines/y2000/ast25feb_1m.htm

[30] Martí, Paredes and Peracaula, 'Development of a two-sided Relativistic Jet in Cygnus X-3', AA 375 (2001), pp.476–84.

[31] For a review of these theories see Collins, 'In defence of Cygnus X-3 as a Cosmic Accelerator: Response to Criticisms regarding its Production of Neutral Particles with Energies up to PeV', 2006, available as a PDF at www.andrewcollins.com

[32] Ibid.

[33] Mioduszewski et al, 'Radio observations of Cygnus X-3 after the Large Radio Flare in September 2001', www.nrao.edu/~amiodusz/Cygx3head02.pdf

[34] Berezinsky, 'Time delay of the PeV *gamma* ray burst after the October 1985 radio flare of Cygnus X-3' *Nature* 334 (11 August 1988), pp.506–507.

[35] Thomson, 1991, op. cit; Marshak, 2000, op. cit; Allison et al, op. cit.

[36] Email communication between Josep Martí Ribas of the Department of Physics, University of Jaén, Spain, and the author dated 11 January 2006.

[37] Boyd and Smale, 'The Long Term Light Curves of X-ray Binaries Contain Simultaneous Periodic and Random Components', AJ 612 (10 September 2004), pp.1006–17.

[38] Fischer, 'Cygnus X-3: Waiting for the Next Big Bang', *The Cosmic Mirror* 178 (26 February 2000), available at www.astro.uni-bonn.de/~dfischer/mirror/178.html

[39] Dumé, 'Did cosmic rays cause ice ages?' PhysicsWeb, 12 July 2004, physicsweb.org/articles/news/8/7/6

[40] Pennicott, 'Carbon clock could show the wrong time', PhysicsWeb, 10 May 2001, available at physicsweb.org/articles/news/5/5/7

[41] Yiou *et al*, 'Beryllium-10 in the Greenland Ice Core Project ice core at Summit, Greenland', JGR 102 (30 November 1997), No. C12, pp.26,783–26,794.

[42] Taken from LaViolette, *Earth Under Fire*, p.91.

[43] For a good introduction into this subject see LaViolette, 'Evidence for a Global Warming at the Termination I Boundary and its Possible Cosmic Dust Cause', Starburst Foundation, PDF at arxiv.org/ftp/physics/papers/0503/0503158.pdf

[44] Marti et al, 'Possible Hot Spots Excited By The Relativistic Jets Of Cygnus X-3', AA 439 (August 2005), pp.279–285.

[45] Shimada et al, 'Germ cell mutagenesis in medaka fish after exposures to high-energy cosmic ray nuclei: A human model', PNAS 102 (11 April 2005) pp.6063–6067.

[46] See Conant, 'Mining for health', Atlantis Rising, available at healing.about.com/gi/dynamic/offsite.htm?zi=1/XJ&sdn=healing&zu=http%3A%2F%2Fwww.atlantisrising.com%2Fissue4%2Far4mining.html. See also Erickson, 'Radiation and Health: An Overview of Radon Therapy in the United States and Europe', www.radonmine.com/pdf/radonandhealth.pdf

Chapter Twenty-Two – The True God Star

[1] Meinel et al, 'Antiquity's Fingerprints in Ice: A Cosmic Encounter, A Cat's Eye, and Origin of Modern Humans', TAG 05, Sheffield University, 19 December 2005.

[2] Bocquet-Appel and Demars, 'Neanderthal contraction and modern human colonization of Europe', *Antiquity* 74:285 (September 2000), pp.544-52.

[3] See Stringer and Andrews, *The Complete World of Human Evolution.*

[4] Email communication between Aden and Marjorie Meinel and the author dated 4 January 2006.

[5] 1001 parsecs (+/- 259 yrs), after Reed *et al*, 'Hubble Space Telescope Measurements of the Expansion of NGC 6543: Parallax Distance And Nebular Evolution', AJ 118 (November 1999), pp.2430–2441.

[6] Determined through a reassessment of the Yale parallax for Cat's Eye from astrometric telescope measurements. Email communication from Aden and Marjorie Meinel to the author dated 31 December 2005.

[7] Reed et al. op. cit.

[8] See 'Chandra Reveals The X-Ray Glint In The Cat's Eye', 8 January 2001, Chandra Press Room, available at chandra.harvard.edu/press/01_releases/press_010801.html

[9] Ibid.

[10] Email communication from You-Hua Chu to the author dated 9 January 2006.

[11] Email communication from You-Hua Chu to the author dated 8 January 2006.

[12] Email communication from You-Hua Chu to the author dated 9 January 2006.

[13] Guerrero et al, 'The Enigmatic X-ray Point Sources at the Central Stars of NGC 6543 and NGC 7293,' AJL 553 (2001), p.L55; Chu et al, 'Chandra Reveals the X-ray Glint in the Cat's Eye' AJL 553 (2001), p.L69.

[14] Email communication from Robert Gruendl to the author dated 11 January 2006.

[15] Email communication from Robert Gruendl to the author dated 12 January 2006.

[16] As a further note on the subject, Robert Gruendl agrees that distance is not a barrier in terms of high energy *gamma*-rays and/or cosmic rays reaching the Earth. 'The problem is that the total flux which is incident on the Earth from a source will drop as 1/(distance^2). This will be true for even beamed emission or a jet unless the opening angle of the jet is infinitesimally narrow (i.e. the jet when it reaches Earth still spans an area only roughly as wide as the Earth).' Email communication to the author dated 13 January 2006.

[17] Soker, 'The Cat's Eye (NGC 6543)', preliminary report, 2006.

[18] Soker and Bisker, 'Bubbles in Planetary Nebulae and Clusters of Galaxies', *astro-ph*/0601032 (2 January 2006).

[19] Email communication between Noam Soker and the author dated 26 January 2006.

[20] 'It is magnetically active because it rotates fast. It rotates fast because it accreted mass and angular momentum from the primary star, when the primary lost lots of mass on the AGB (Asymptotic Giant Branch). The primary now is small and hot, on its way to becoming a white dwarf.' Email communication between Noam Soker and the author dated 26 January 2006.

[21] Romano Corradi is Senior Support Astronomer at the Isaac Newton Group of Telescopes of the Particle Physics and Astronomy Research Council (PPARC).

[22] Email communication from Romano Corradi to the author dated 24 January 2004. He does, however, not discount the possibility that the companion to the central star might be a neutron star or black hole, maybe one on an extremely lengthy orbit of the central star.

[23] 'We're familiar with the Cygnus region but didn't see any object likely to be producing a jet of cosmic rays', email communication from Aden and Marjorie Meinel to the author dated 23 December 2005.

[24] See, for instance, Meinel, Meinel, Drach-Meinel and Meinel, 'The 250 Ky GRIP archives show the signature of a point source of cosmic rays: an analysis of the data leading to NGC 6543 as being the most probable source', paper presented at the IAU Symposium 234, Planetary Nebulae, Hawaii, April 2006.

[25] Meinel et al, op. cit, and various emails to the author dated December 2005/January 2006.

[26] Email communication from Aden and Marjorie Meinel to the author dated 31 December 2005.

[27] Email communication from Aden and Marjorie Meinel to the author dated 23 December 2005.

[28] The precise length of a lunar year being 354 days, 8 hours and 34 seconds, based on a synodic lunation of 29.530588 days.

[29] See the work of Alexander Marshack, especially *The Roots of Civilization.*

[30] See De Kay, *Bird Gods,* p.198.

[31] Ibid., p.189.

[32] Møller and Mousseau, 'Albinism and Phenotype of Barn Swallows (*Hirunda rustica*) from Chernobyl', *Evolution* 55:10 (2001), pp.2097-2104.

[33] Interview with David Drach-Meinel broadcast on the BBC Radio Five Live programme 'Through The Night' on

22 December 2005. His concluding words (edited very slightly for publication) were as follows:

> We're just trying to talk about some of the scientific results now, but why did it [i.e. the microblazar' particle jet] particularly end up aimed at the Earth? Well, we could say that a higher intelligence was involved in doing this. You could even say that it was the finger of God pointing towards the Earth. There are all sorts of ways you could put it into a faith perspective, and, of course, that is going to be up to a lot of people to make those discussions as to how life does change. Is it simply a matter of chance? Or is there a spiritual side of this? I think it does invite an awful lot of discussion by some very broad minded people of deep faith and deep thinking.

Postscript: April 2006

1 Berry, '2001 replayed', *AN* 20: 3 (March 2006), p. 21.

2 See Dar, 'The Threat to Life from Eta Carinae and Gamma-Ray Bursts' Frascati Physics Series XXIV (2002), pp. 513-23, who explores the potential threat of mass extinctions and global catastrophes caused by jets of GRBs (gamma-ray bursts) and supernovae.

3 Chadha and Cooper, 'Longest gamma-ray burst signals supernova', *AN* 20:4 (April 2006), p. 9.

4 Ibid.

5 Montgomery, *Aquatic Man and African Eve*, available at www.sondela.co.uk/Aqua/Books/AquaApeA4.pdf Montgomery, *Aquatic Man and African Eve – Book Two: African Eve at Home*, available at faculty.mdc.edu/jmcnair/EveA4.pdf

6 See Meinel, Meinel, Drach-Meinel and Meinel, 'The 250 Ky GRIP archives show the signature of a point source of cosmic rays: an analysis of the data leading to NGC 6543 as being the most probable source', paper presented at the IAU Symposium 234, Planetary Nebulae, Hawaii, April 2006.

7 Collins, 'In defence of Cygnus X-3 as a Cosmic Accelerator: Response to Criticisms regarding its Production of Neutral Particles with Energies up to PeV', 2006, available as a PDF at www.andrewcollins.com

Appendix – The Dogon Mystery

1 Hallett, *Pygmy Kitabu*, pp.385–6.

2 James and Thorpe, *Ancient Mysteries*, p.107.

3 Griaule, *Conversations with Ogotemmêli.*

4 Griaule and Dieterlen, 'A Sudanese Sirius System', in Temple, *The Sirius Mystery*, p.327.

5 Griaule and Dieterlen, *The Pale Fox*, 1986, p.504.

6 Griaule and Dieterlen, 'Un Systeme Soudanais de Sirius', *Journal de la Societe des Africanistes* 20 (1950), pp.273–294. Republished as 'A Sudanese Sirius System', in Temple, pp.317–335.

7 Ibid., p.317.

8 Griaule and Dieterlen, pp.550–2.

9 Benest and Duvent, 'Is Sirius a triple star?', AA 299 (1995), pp.621–8.

10 In an article entitled 'Dogon Restudied' (CA 32:2, April 1991, pp.139–67), ecologist Walter E A van Beek – who spent 11 years living with the Dogon at Sanga – argued that since the complex cosmology outlined by Griaule and Dieterlen in *Le renard pâle* had not been confirmed by him or by any other ethnographer or

anthropologist, it must all have been made up by Griaule. He further claimed that the Frenchman spoonfed his informants new ideas concerning astronomy, which would have included knowledge of the existence of Sirius B, the invisible companion of Sirius.

Among those who came forward to contest van Beek's claims and support Griaule and Dieterlen's work was noted Belgian anthropologist Luc de Heusch ('On Griaule on Trial', CA 32:4, August-October 1991, pp.434–7). According to him: 'By refusing to hear the testimony of Griaule's informants, van Beek has robbed the African imagination of its creativity.' (p. 437) Geneviéve Calame-Griaule, Marcel Griaule's daughter and living colleague, also wrote a piece denouncing van Beek's claims against her father ('On the Dogon Restudied', CA 32:5, December 1991, pp.575–7). She said that, 'because he [van Beek] has not found it, none of it existed … In reading his article, one wonders about his research method'. (p. 575) Furthermore, she states, 'van Beek's article contains so many misreadings that it is impossible to correct them in limited space'. (p. 576)

Calame-Griaule was particularly keen to point out that, contrary to what van Beek had suggested, her father was not an astronomer, nor had he been proficient in astronomy on going to Mali in 1931. So he could not, and would not, have fed his informants false information regarding the cosmos, nor revealed to them any knowledge of the existence of Sirius B. (p. 577)

Beyond all this, we find that other anthropologists have accepted and furthered the work of the Griaule-Dieterlen school, including Barbara DeMott, author of *Dogon Masks* (see pp.8–13, 24–5, 32–5) and Teresa Vergani, who has made a study of Dogon cosmological symbolism. ('Ethnomathematics and Symbolic Thought: The Culture of the Dogon', ZDM 99:2 (1998), pp.66–70)

[11] Griaule and Dieterlen, 1986, p.368.

[12] Ibid., pp.257–8.

[13] Ibid., p.461.

[14] Ibid., p.453.

[15] Ibid., p.448.

[16] See, for instance, Coppens, *The Canopus Revelation*, which proposes that *po tolo* might well have been the star Canopus.

[17] Temple, pp.220–5.

[18] Griaule and Dieterlen, 1986, pp.249, 251.

[19] Ibid., p.314.

[20] Ibid. pp.313, 348.

[21] Ibid., pp.313–4.

[22] Ibid., pl. xv (1) p.371.

[23] Ibid., p.345.

[24] For bird-beaked masks see Griaule, *Masques Dogons*, pp.489–90, 493, 503, and for the *kanaga* mask as a representation of Amma, see Griaule and Dieterlen, 1950, p.319.

[25] Griaule and Dieterlen, 1986, pp.136–8, 422, 441.

[26] Ibid., p.129.

[27] Ibid., pp.128, 385.

[28] Ibid., p.499.

[29] Ibid., p.187.

[30] Ibid., pp.187, 345.

[31] Griaule and Dieterlen, 1950, in Temple, p.325.

[32] Griaule and Dieterlen, 1986, pp.345, 347.

[33] Ibid., p.345.

[34] Ibid., p.368.

Index